Lay Counseling is a classic that is now even ~~ever~~ considering the ministry of helping others

Les Parrott, PhD, #1 *New York Ti~~mes~~* of *Saving Your Marriage Before It Starts*

God designed the healing process to be delivered via our relationship with Him, and our relationship with others. When the Body of Christ is trained to unleash the elements of grace and truth with those who struggle, the result is a restored life, marriage, and family. Siang-Yang and Eric have updated this classic work to reflect the latest research. Also, its thoughtful and comprehensive nature will train the lay counselor to do the job, and do it with excellence. An invaluable tool and highly recommended.

John Townsend, PhD, *New York Times* bestselling author, psychologist, leadership expert, and Founder of the Townsend Institute of Leadership and Counseling (drtownsend.com)

The years of seasoned experience are clearly evident as Drs. Tan and Scalise guide us to an understanding and need for lay counseling ministries. Consider this work as the "Everything you always wanted to know about lay counseling and needed to ask" book! It is a must have for any church or ministry when it comes to caring for hurting people.

Linda Mintle, PhD, Chair, Behavioral Health, College of Osteopathic Medicine, Liberty University

Siang-Yang Tan and Eric Scalise have provided simply the best possible resource for equipping lay counselors that you can get. It has everything you need—a history of the movement, biblical models, practical guidance on establishing and conducting lay counseling and caring ministries, discussion of supervision and ethical issues, and even forms you can incorporate. If you are considering lay counseling, this book is absolutely essential.

Everett L. Worthington Jr., PhD, Licensed Psychologist, Professor of Psychology at Virginia Commonwealth University, and coauthor (with Jennifer S. Ripley) of *Couple Therapy: A New Hope-Focused Approach*

Finally, Tan's classic text on Christian lay counseling has been republished! The original book was the best available Christian resource for setting up a lay counseling program—combining submission to biblical authority, a God-centered orientation, a scientist's desire for evidence, and a practitioner's heart—that included many examples of helpful forms for use with such a program. The new edition has all that and more. With the help of an able coauthor, it includes the latest relevant research and Christian resources, along with the clinical and pastoral wisdom that has come with the years since its first publication. This book returns to its place as the definitive mainstream resource on lay counseling for Christians.

Eric L. Johnson, Lawrence and Charlotte Hoover Professor of Pastoral Care, The Southern Baptist Theological Seminary

Having confidence you are equipped is what you will find in these pages. You will be empowered with your God-given gifts.

Gregory Jantz, PhD, Founder of The Center —A Place of Hope

What you hold in your hands represents the most comprehensive, practical, and useful instruction manual in existence on how to minister effectively to those who are hurting. I only wish I had it when I first started a lay counseling program in a large church in 1982! Trained and credentialed both as a minister and as a clinical psychologist, I can attest to the fact that this classic resource is solid both theologically and clinically. My friends Drs. Tan and Scalise are peerless leaders in the field of training lay persons how to become helpful to others in need. Clearly written, well-researched, and eminently applicable, this book is a must-have for any Christian leaders called to help and serve others. I recommend it heartily!

Rev. Jared Pingleton, PsyD, Clinical Psychologist, Vice President of American Association of Christian Counselors

For such a time as this! We need the average believer to become a supernatural encourager to a world that is looking for guidance. From A-to-Z it is all here! Take advantage of it!

Dan Seaborn, President of Winning At Home, Inc. and Chairman of the Marriage & Family Division of AACC

This book is a long overdue and invaluable resource that needs to be in the hands of every pastor and ministry leader. Our churches are filled with hurting people, as well as folks who feel called to help others but who don't know what to do. From a solid biblical foundation, to presenting a practical model, to sharing relevant research, Tan and Scalise give us a much needed step-by-step approach to developing a powerful lay counseling program. This book will encourage you and help you to better "equip the saints to do the work of the ministry."

Dr. Gary Oliver, Executive Director of The Center for Healthy Relationships

For the past forty-five years I have had the opportunity to work in the counseling field, as both a professional and as the Senior Associate Pastor for Dr. David Jeremiah. I passionately believe that lay counselors are gifted individuals who provide life-changing encouragement and hope-saturated change. This book delivers spiritual wisdom, practical insights, and useful tools that equip counselors to love and care for others as God's ambassadors. The combined professional and ministry experience of Drs. Tan and Scalise will inspire readers to engage in ministry-based counseling with personal confidence, practical strategies, and sound biblical integrity.

Dr. Ken Nichols, President of ALIVE Ministries

Scholarly, comprehensive, readable, biblical, practical, ESSENTIAL. Those are six words I'd use in describing this "must have" guide to launching a lay counseling program. Written by two of Christian counseling's premier voices, Tan and Scalise's wisdom and hard work captured here will make your work of launching or strengthening your lay counseling ministry so much easier, clearer, and life-changing.

John Trent, PhD, Gary D. Chapman Chair of Marriage and Family Ministry
and Therapy, Moody Theological Seminary, and President of StrongFamilies.com

Dr. Tan and Dr. Scalise have provided an outstanding resource in this new revised edition that continues to be the golden standard. *Lay Counseling* is the most practically helpful and comprehensive resource to train and equip lay counselors, pastors, and church leaders.

Catherine Hart Weber, PhD, Flourish Center for Wellbeing

Sure to be a standard reference and a classic in the years to come, *Lay Counseling: Equipping Christians for a Helping Ministry* by Siang-Yang Tan and Eric Scalise gives a comprehensive overview and assessment of the development and practice of lay counseling in the church. Completely revised and updated, this book has a solid biblical approach, with extensive research and counseling resources for effectively selecting and training people in helping ministry. Pastors and Christian counselors will find the tools necessary for planning and building a lay counseling program. Highly recommended.

Ian F. Jones, PhD, Professor of Psychology and Counseling;
Chairman, Division of Church & Community Ministries

Lay Counseling: Equipping Christians for a Helping Ministry is one of those books that every pastor and Christian counselor should have. Now it's even better. Siang-Yang Tan and Eric Scalise have teamed up in this new updated version to create a truly dynamic resource. I cannot recommend it more highly.

Mark Laaser, PhD, President and Founder of Faithful
and True, host of The Men of Valor Program

Lay Counseling is a book that needs to be on the shelf of every pastor, counselor, and people-helper. Does it provide us all with the "how-tos" of meeting people in their brokenness? Absolutely it does. But even more than that, there's nobody I would trust more in my own pain than Drs. Tan and Scalise. As you learn from their knowledge and experience penned on these pages, keep in mind that they are written by two men who genuinely personify the empathy Jesus calls us to. That's what makes this book so special.

Joshua Straub, PhD, Marriage and Family
Strategist, LifeWay Christian Resources

Unlike ever before, a profound and heartfelt movement is sweeping Christianity as followers of Christ reach their hands over troubled waters to help follow Christians through their life experiences and problems. Siang-Yang Tan and Eric Scalise, with their many combined decades of biblical wisdom, servanthood, and clinical experience in training lay counselors, provide the most definitive and comprehensive book on lay counseling ever written. Soaked in the heart of Christ and the Scriptures, and seasoned with insights of clinical practice, psychology, and practical "how-to" advice, this book is a foundational "must" for programs and persons pursuing lay counseling.

>**Frederick A. DiBlasio, PhD, LCSW-C,** Professor and Therapist,
>University of Maryland

One of the biggest problems we have to deal with are well-meaning lay counselors with pure dedication and a desire to help someone; but they don't fully understand either the problem or their own limitations. This book is a great tool for lay counselors who want to be the most effective tool possible for transformation.

>**Stephen Arterburn, MEd,** Founder and Chairman of NewLife Ministries

When people suffer emotional pain, they often turn to trusted friends, family, and parishioners for help. These "lay counselors" are often trusted but unprepared to fully address these concerns. This book is a training guide for laypeople in helping hurting people in an effective and appropriate manner.

>**Michael Lyles, MD,** Medical Director, Board Certified Psychiatrist,
>Lyles and Crawford Clinical Consulting

REVISED & UPDATED

Lay
Counseling

EQUIPPING

CHRISTIANS

FOR A

HELPING

MINISTRY

SIANG-YANG TAN
ERIC SCALISE

ZONDERVAN

Lay Counseling, Revised and Updated
Copyright © 1991, 2016 by Siang-Yang Tan and Eric Scalise

This title is also available as a Zondervan ebook.

Requests for information should be addressed to:
Zondervan, 3900 *Sparks Dr. SE, Grand Rapids, Michigan* 49546

Library of Congress Cataloging-in-Publication Data

Names: Tan, Siang-Yang, 1954- author. | Scalise, Eric T., author.
Title: Lay counseling: equipping Christians for a helping ministry / Siang-Yang Tan, Eric Scalise.
Description: Revised and updated edition. | Grand Rapids, Michigan: Zondervan, [2016] | Includes
    bibliographical references and indexes.
Identifiers: LCCN 2016035711 | ISBN 9780310524274 (softcover)
Subjects: LCSH: Peer counseling in the church.
Classification: LCC BV4409.T35 2016 | DDC 253.5—dc23 LC record available at https://lccn.loc
    .gov/2016035711

The information in Chapter 12 is from Dr. Scalise's caregiver training program and is used with permission.

The code information on pages 215-20 is used with the permission of the American Association of Christian Counselors.

Unless otherwise indicated, Scripture quotations are taken from The Holy Bible, New International Version®, NIV®. Copyright © 1973, 1978, 1984, 2011 by Biblica, Inc.® Used by permission of Zondervan. All rights reserved worldwide. www.Zondervan.com. The "NIV" and "New International Version" are trademarks registered in the United States Patent and Trademark Office by Biblica, Inc.®

Scripture quotations marked NASB are taken from the *New American Standard Bible*®. Copyright © 1960, 1962, 1963, 1968, 1971, 1972, 1973, 1975, 1977, 1995 by The Lockman Foundation. Used by permission. (www.Lockman.org)

Any Internet addresses (websites, blogs, etc.) and telephone numbers in this book are offered as a resource. They are not intended in any way to be or imply an endorsement by Zondervan, nor does Zondervan vouch for the content of these sites and numbers for the life of this book.

Cover design: Christopher Tobias / tobiasdesign.com
Cover illustration: © Cloudmagic, Inc.
Interior design: Kait Lamphere

Printed in the United States of America

16 17 18 19 20 21 22 23 24 25 /DHV/ 15 14 13 12 11 10 9 8 7 6 5 4 3 2 1

To Angela
—*Siang-Yang Tan*

To Donna
—*Eric Scalise*

Contents

Foreword

Galatians 6:2 encourages us to "Bear one another's burdens, and so fulfill the law of Christ."

The sun was falling across the sprawling north Georgia Christian College campus on what was one of the most challenging and depressing days of my entire life. I thought that by attending a leadership summit for marriage and relationships, it would lessen the sting from the pain I had been experiencing over the previous few weeks. My hope was that the time away would give me an opportunity to be surrounded by likeminded peers who might take a minute or two and simply pray with me, offer some practical guidance. Sadly, it never happened.

As the evening began to press in, it only reminded me of the personal darkness I was wrestling with at the moment. I began to wonder why God seemed to be silent and why the friends who were around me felt so cold and distant. Have you ever been in that place of lonely despair?

Struggling to find God's wisdom, direction, and strength in the midst of a very difficult decision and challenge in my life, I jumped in the car and just began to drive. I tried calling a mentor-friend from California, but wasn't able to reach him. And then . . . unexpectedly, my cell phone rang.

"Tim, this is Michael. Where are you?"

"Hey Michael. . . . North Atlanta somewhere. I think around Barry College." Tears were welling up in my eyes. He joked a little about me being on his "turf" now and how much he wanted to "school" me the next time we played golf together. The laughter and bantering ... the warmth of a friend ... helped break through the emptiness and breathe some life back into me.

And then, knowing a little of the journey I was on, he simply said, "God told me to call you. I'm leaving work right now, and I am coming to find you." We met, and I cannot begin to describe how profoundly God used him, just when I needed help the most. For the next couple of hours, he listened, shared words of hope, prayed with and inspired me. I felt that regardless of what came my way, he believed in me and would stand by my side, even if all others walked away.

My friend, Michael, is a highly regarded and seasoned Christian psychiatrist.

However, on that night, he was a modern-day "Barnabas," a true son of encouragement. He was God's messenger, and he was doing God's work . . . "burden bearing" . . . a work I believe we are all called to do. It is holy work and a sacred trust that we have been given as counselors and caregivers.

If you could look into the eyes and souls of each person around you right now, and see what moves inside their hearts and minds, you might hear stories of loveless relationships, the pain of a divorce, financial hardship, childhood sexual abuse, a wayward son or daughter, grief and loss, loneliness, abandonment, confusion, battles with addiction, and so much more. The brokenness of today's world is profound. The pace and pressures of life, and the pain and hurt so many experience on a daily basis, can be overwhelming. For some of you reading this right now, I could be describing your own story.

Without a doubt, there is a place and need for competent and professional mental health care. We need godly psychiatrists, psychologists, professional counselors, marriage and family therapists, social workers, and all those who are trained to work with the broken and hurting. I have spent my entire adult life encouraging and educating an army of people helpers to care for others God's way. And I am excited to tell you that He is moving in a powerful way and developing leaders who love Him and are called to serve Him in the helping professions.

Yet, I also believe much of God's amazing life-changing work takes place through faithful and humble men and women who are willing to be available in life's most difficult seasons . . . to listen, pray, practice the ministry of presence, offer support, share a Bible verse or thought, and in many ways, become the eyes and ears, the hands and voice of a loving Savior who seeks to comfort and heal.

I have often shared about my five sisters, who without question, do a lot more care and counseling than I ever have. God often uses ordinary people to be channels for His message of grace, mercy, love, and hope to others. One of my favorite passages of Scripture is found in 2 Corinthians 1:3-4. I believe it is a powerful acknowledgment for soul care ministry in the Bible. Paul said, *"Blessed be the God and Father of our Lord Jesus Christ, the Father of mercies and God of all comfort, who comforts us in all our affliction, so that we may be able to comfort those who are in any affliction, with the comfort with which we ourselves are comforted by God"* (ESV).

I am excited for you to begin this journey with my good friends and colleagues, Dr. Siang-Yang Tan and Dr. Eric Scalise. Together they bring an incredible history of wisdom and experience, as well as deep insight and understanding that will help you become more effective in caring for others, including how to successfully design, implement, and run a dynamic lay counseling ministry. My prayer is that you will learn and incorporate the principles found in this excellent book, and let God do a divine work in your heart and life, so that in turn, you can help champion the cause of Christ in the local church. I am also praying that God will raise up lay counseling and caring ministries all across our land and around the globe. The need is great, and the laborers are few.

Perhaps someday, God will tap you to make that phone call and show up at a restaurant for a Tim Clinton who desperately needs help and support.

Let me close by saying you are in very good hands. In many ways, Dr. Tan reminds me so much of my father. He never misses an opportunity to encourage and strengthen me in the faith. I cannot think of a time when he hasn't prayed over and for me whenever we are together. He is more than one of the most respected Christian psychologists of our day; he is also an ordained senior pastor and passionately believes in the power, presence, and plan of God in our lives. It was a blessing for me to give him the James E. Clinton Award for Excellence in Pastoral Care and Ministry at a recent AACC World Conference—an award in honor of my father who faithfully served the Lord for nearly 60 years as a rural country pastor.

The American Association of Christian Counselors (AACC) has partnered with Dr. Tan and Dr. Scalise for many years as we continue to pursue our own mission of encouraging, educating, and building up the entire community of care. I am excited about what God is going to do in and through your lives and ministries for His kingdom's sake.

Blessings.

—Tim Clinton, EdD
President, American Association of
Christian Counselors (AACC)

Acknowledgments

I would like to thank Eric Scalise for collaborating with me in the writing of this second edition of *Lay Counseling*. He is a special colleague and wonderful friend and brother in Christ. Writing and praying with him have been a real joy.

I also want to thank the many people who, over the past twenty-five years since the first edition of this book was published in 1991, have used it to help them establish lay counseling and caring ministries here in the United States and all over the world, touching many hurting lives with the grace and healing love of God in Jesus Christ by the power of the Holy Spirit.

Special thanks are due to editors Ryan Pazdur, Jim Ruark, and Laura Weller for their support and encouragement in the writing and revision of this book, and to Dr. Tim Clinton for so kindly writing the foreword. Lynn Mori at First Evangelical Church Glendale and Christine Tzeng in the School of Psychology at Fuller Theological Seminary provided helpful administrative assistance to me.

I also want to especially express my deepest appreciation and love for my wife, Angela, and for her love, support, patience, and prayers as I worked on this writing project.

And most of all, I want to thank God for His love, grace, strength, and wisdom. To Him be all the glory!

Siang-Yang Tan, PhD
Pasadena, California

I would like to thank my good friend and colleague Siang-Yang Tan for inviting me to join him on this incredible journey and giving me the opportunity to collaborate with him in coming alongside those who are hurting and broken.

Thank you to editors Ryan Pazdur, Jim Ruark, and Laura Weller for your wisdom and guidance.

Special thanks to Dr. Tim Clinton for your friendship and your kind and gracious words.

I also want to acknowledge the thousands of people God has so graciously allowed me to connect with over the years who have needed care and counsel.

Your stories, your courage, and your unwavering trust in God's faithfulness have both inspired and challenged me in my calling as a Christian counselor. Walking with you through pain, loss, and crises increases my passion for the body of Christ to be a healing community.

To Donna, my amazing partner in life, thank you for your prayers and committed support through every step of the process. I love doing life with you!

Finally, and most importantly, thank You Lord for Your heart of compassion and for the vision You gave for a book like this. You are truly the Wonderful Counselor!

Eric Scalise, PhD
Forest, Virginia

Introduction

"Your problem, Mr. Jones, is that you are a sinner. Give up your drinking and running around, read your Bible, pray more, be in church, and God will resolve all your conflicts."

Is this what we mean by "lay Christian counseling"? The idea of a non-professionally trained person blundering around in the minefields of personality and mental illness may sound hazardous to some. Can we expect the average person without a graduate degree in mental health to be able to meet the needs of those who are depressed, facing addictive issues, or wracked with indecision by complex emotional and psychological problems? According to 2013 National Institute of Mental Health statistics, an estimated 43.8 million American adults (18.5 percent of the national population) could be diagnosed with a mental illness.[1]

The purpose of this new and completely updated second edition of *Lay Counseling: Equipping Christians for a Helping Ministry* is to explore questions like these, provide helpful answers, and bring the lay counseling movement into the twenty-first century. The chapters that follow offer a comprehensive foundation for understanding biblical caregiving. They describe the selection, training, supervision, and evaluation of lay Christian counselors; establish important ethical, legal, and some multicultural principles; and outline how to set up and administer an effective lay counseling service or ministry in a responsible and God-honoring manner. Helpful templates, sample forms, and Christian resources are also provided in the appendices. Additionally, the growing body of literature on both secular and Christian lay counseling is reviewed in chapters 4 and 10 of this book.

WHAT IS LAY COUNSELING?

Counseling has been defined by well-known Christian psychologist Dr. Gary Collins as "a caring relationship in which one person tries to help another deal more effectively with the stresses of life."[2] Collins described *lay* counselors as individuals who may lack the training, education, experience, or credentials to be professional counselors but who nevertheless are actively involved in helping people cope with personal and relational problems.[3] Lay counselors have been referred to as "nonprofessionals" with little or no training in people-helping skills or as "paraprofessionals" with limited expertise.

Interest in lay counseling has grown considerably in recent years, both in the secular world and in Christian circles, including churches and parachurch organizations, and has become a global phenomenon. This movement is due in part to the shortage of professionally trained clinicians, the lack of regulatory infrastructure in many countries, and the resulting need for lay counselors to provide mental health services to the millions who fall between the cracks, especially in churches and other faith-based environments.

A significant aspect of lay counseling is peer counseling (i.e., peers in age, status, and knowledge helping each other), a movement that has spread to elementary and secondary schools, colleges and universities, social agencies, businesses, and churches.[4] In *Christian Peer Counseling: Love in Action*, the authors point out that as far back as 1988, the estimated number of peer counseling programs in elementary and secondary schools across the nation was more than twenty thousand![5] A number of peer counseling associations have also formed, including the California Peer Counseling Association (founded in 1984), the National Peer Helpers Association (formed in 1986), and the International Association of Peer Supporters (founded in 2004), to name a few. Within the Christian community, several organizations also serve the body of Christ in this capacity, including the Christian Association for Psychological Studies (founded in 1956), the Association of Certified Biblical Counselors (formerly known as the National Association of Nouthetic Counselors and founded in 1976), the National Christian Counseling Association (founded in 1981), and the largest and most comprehensive such organization, the American Association of Christian Counselors (founded in 1986).

THE AUTHORS

The original manuscript for this book was written to present an overview of lay counseling, covering both the secular and Christian literature but focusing on a biblical approach, which was developed by Dr. Tan and has been field tested for more than three decades now. Most of his early work was performed in two local churches in Canada (Peoples Church of Montreal, 1976–80, and North Park Community Chapel in London, Ontario, 1980–83), and at the Institute of Christian Counseling, which was set up at Ontario Bible College in Toronto in 1984 for the training of lay or paraprofessional Christian counselors. At present

Dr. Tan continues to conduct lay counselor training in local church and para-church contexts. He has evaluated the effectiveness of such *training*, as well as the effectiveness of the *counseling* done by lay counselors, in collaboration with doctoral students in the Graduate School of Psychology at Fuller Theological Seminary.

Dr. Scalise has also been actively involved in lay counselor training for the past thirty years and has developed ten-, fifteen-, and twenty-week training programs for local churches and ministry organizations. Over two thousand lay counselors have been trained utilizing these materials, both nationally and internationally. Particular attention has been devoted to an authentic Christian perspective on basic helping and crisis intervention skills with a vibrant focus on biblical integration. Together we desire to present a relevant and collaborative effort that will equip and empower thousands to have an impact on the kingdom of God—to reach out to and help the lost and suffering.

THE GOAL: ESTABLISH A LIFELINE

King Solomon understood the power of connection when he wrote, "Two are better than one, because they have a good return for their labor: If either of them falls down, one can help the other up. But pity anyone who falls and has no one to help them up" (Eccl. 4:9–10). The term "on belay" is commonly used among climbers and signifies that a person is now securely tied into a safety system and can therefore proceed with the task of ascending the mountain before them. Crises often feel just like that mountain—looming as a formidable object. The question that often determines the outcome has more to do with how the crisis is managed. Lay caregivers provide the lifeline that assists others in overcoming the obstacles before them.[6]

What is a lifeline? A lifeline enables people to survive a crisis by providing an essential connection. It represents emergency services and care, an anchored line thrown in as a support to someone falling or drowning. A lifeline is a person or process, a source of rescue and support in crises. "The name of the LORD is a fortified tower; the righteous run into it and are safe" (Prov. 18:10). We, as the church universal, must fulfill our mission to be salt and light in the world, and our goal in this book is to help people get closer to God in genuine relationship and to provide support, encouragement, spiritual care, and referral services on a short-term basis during times of significant need.

This updated and revised book contains information that can be used as a practical manual for the establishment of a lay counseling ministry, especially within local churches. It is best utilized, however, in conjunction with other books, materials, and resources, which are cited and recommended in several chapters. We trust and pray that *Lay Counseling* will be a significant help and blessing to all who seek to be channels of Christ's love and truth, and hence to bring His grace and healing to the many who are hurting in this broken world.

CHAPTER 1

The Need for Lay Counseling Ministries

We all live in a fallen world that is tainted by the effects of sin. Despite the psychological sophistication of our modern society, we continue to experience brokenness in our lives. Things are not really getting better. The first crisis counseling intervention took place in the garden of Eden at the fall of humankind, and the relationship between God and humankind was torn asunder. God asked Adam and Eve three questions: "Where are you?" "Who told you that you were naked?" "What is this you have done?" Adam's initial reply was that he was afraid because he was naked, and so he hid himself. Ever since that time, humanity has wrestled with fear and shame over its own nakedness—not in the literal sense, but when we experience failure and rejection. Our natural tendency is to deny, avoid, and cover up. Scott Peck, a psychiatrist and author of the well-known book *The Road Less Traveled*, wrote, "Life is difficult. . . . Life is a series of problems."[1] This is true not only in the secular world, but also within Christian circles, including our churches.

Our congregations and Christian institutions are full of hurting people who are struggling. They need help, but they often find it difficult to open up and share their burdens. They may have no one available to listen and care for them, or their Christian beliefs (or misbeliefs) have brought guilt and shame. Some may feel as if their struggles make them second-class citizens in the kingdom of God. Many of them are afraid of being judged as bad Christians. And they may be wary of seeking help from secular therapists who historically have been antagonistic toward religion and a client's spirituality.

A 2008 survey of over a thousand Protestant pastors revealed that 24 percent spend at least six hours per week in counseling-related activities with parishioners.[2] Christians who acknowledge an omnipotent and compassionate God recognize His divine sovereignty and the mystery of His ways as they face the hardships of life. Many questions invariably follow soon after a tragedy or fiery trial. *"When can I go and meet with God? My tears have been my food day and night, while* people say to me all day long, '*Where* is your God?'" (Ps. 42:2–3, emphasis added). One of the most human of all questions in the midst of the unexplainable, the unwanted, or the unacceptable, is simply, "Why?" "Why me? Why us? Why this? Why now?" The heart cry of the psalmist often echoes in our own anguish, "My God, my God, *why* have you forsaken me? *Why* are you so far from saving me, so far from my cries of anguish?" (Ps. 22:1, emphasis added).

Many believers gain great comfort and solace from the Psalms—transparent glimpses into the life of David and others as they journeyed through life—not always having the answers but ultimately being aware of God's gracious provision in time of need. C. S. Lewis, in his book *The Problem of Pain*, said, "God whispers to us in our pleasures, speaks in our conscience, but shouts in our pain."[3]

Although national trends ebb and flow and can shift with the winds of cultural change, the following statistics are sobering.

- An estimated 15 million *alcoholics* and 10 million *drug addicts* live in the United States. Forty percent of all family problems brought to domestic court are alcohol related. Seventy-five percent of all juvenile delinquents have at least one alcoholic parent. Over 150,000 teens use cocaine, and 500,000 use marijuana once or more per week. In addition, nearly half a million junior and senior high students are weekly binge drinkers. An estimated 10 to 15 million teens need treatment for child abuse each year.[4]

- Between 5 and 10 million people in the United States are addicted to *prescription drugs.*[5]

- Every addict *directly affects at least five other people.* In a 2006 Gallup poll, 41 percent of those polled indicated they had suffered physical, psychological, or social harm as a result of someone else's drinking or drugging (double the level reported in 1974).[6]

- Forty to 80 million Americans suffer from *compulsive overeating*, and 5 to 15 percent will die from the consequences in any given year. Some $20 billion are spent yearly by Americans seeking to lose weight.[7]

- One to 2 percent of adolescent girls (close to 100,000) and 4 to 5 percent of college-age women struggle with *anorexia* and/or *bulimia*.[8]

- There are 2.5 million *pathological gamblers* and another 3 million *compulsive gamblers* in the United States. Gambling is a $500 billion industry. The suicide rate for this population is twenty times higher than the national average. Some 50 million family members are said to be adversely affected.[9]

- There are currently over 300 million *pornographic web pages*, with an estimated 6 to 8 percent of the population diagnosed with some level of sexual addiction. Thirty percent of minors have agreed to meet someone they know only via the Internet, and 14 percent have actually done so.[10]

- No one really knows how many *workaholics* there are, because this addiction has received comparatively little attention thus far. One study indicated that over 10 million adults average 65 to 70 hours of work each week. Several recent studies charge that many of the organizations in which we work and live are like dysfunctional families and force work patterns that promote and encourage workaholism.[11]

- Fifteen million new cases of *sexually transmitted diseases* (chlamydia, gonorrhea, syphilis, HIV/AIDS, etc.) are contracted every year. That translates into about one case every two seconds. Of the top eleven reportable diseases in the United States, five are STDs.[12]

- *Suicide* among those aged fifteen to nineteen has tripled since 1960. Nearly 5,000 teenage suicides take place every year, and for every suicide completed, at least 400 serious attempts fail. Eight percent of high school girls and 5 percent of boys reported making at least one attempt. It is the second leading cause of death among this country's young people. Eighteen percent of the US population will suffer a major depressive episode (12 percent of men and 26 percent of women).[13]

- Over a half million incidents of *domestic violence* occur each year; 92 percent are against women.[14]

- From 45 to 50 percent of all first marriages in this country end in *divorce*, the highest rate in the industrialized world. And 60 to 70 percent of all second marriages end in divorce. The divorce rate has increased nearly every decade since 1860. One million children yearly have parents who are separated or divorced.[15]

- There are nearly 800,000 *adolescent pregnancies* each year (over one per minute). This is the highest rate in any industrialized country in the world. Nearly 30 percent of all teen girls will get pregnant at least once, and two-thirds will not complete high school. One out of every six pregnancies is of a teenager. Nearly 750,000 of those will be aborted. Seventy-nine percent are unmarried, and 80 percent of this group will go on welfare. The annual cost is over $7 billion.[16]

- Approximately one in every four pregnancies will end in *miscarriage* (almost 1 million each year). Approximately 30,000 will be still births.[17]

- Approximately 1.2 million *abortions* are performed every year in the United States, and the reality of post-abortion syndrome is increasingly supported in the research.[18]

- Nearly one in three children now lives in a *single-parent home* (30 percent).

The rate has tripled since 1960. In 1960 5 percent of all births were out of wedlock. By 1991 the figure rose to 30 percent. In 2010 40 percent of all American births and 80 percent of minority births occurred out of wedlock. Eighty-four percent of these homes will have no father and 40 percent will live at or below the poverty level. If current trends continue, the total number of fatherless homes created by unwed childbearing will surpass the number created by divorce.[19]

- Approximately 3 to 4 million *child abuse* reports are filed every year, with an estimated 5 to 6 million children who are actually abused (neglect—65 percent, physical—16 percent, sexual—9 percent, emotional—7 percent), resulting in almost 2,000 deaths. Ninety percent of all abuse is perpetuated by someone the child knows and trusts, and 60 percent involve children under the age of three. Estimated costs annually are over $100 billion for investigation, processing, and treatment.[20]

- Reports of *sexual abuse* have increased from 6,000 in 1976 to well over half a million in 2010. Most specialists agree that the problem is far greater than the cases reported. Over 60 million people experience some form of sexual abuse before they graduate from high school (one out of every three to four girls and one out of every five to six boys). The risk of developing substance abuse problems in this demographic is nearly 400 percent greater.[21]

- About one out of every four children will experience at least one significant *traumatic event* before reaching age sixteen.[22]

- Since 1960 total *crimes* have increased by more than 300 percent (nearly 14 million per year). Ninety percent of Americans will be victims of theft at least once in their lives (87 percent will be victims three or more times). While the population has increased by only 41 percent since 1960, the number of violent crimes has increased by more than 550 percent. Since 1990 alone, more than 250,000 Americans have been murdered, about twice as many who died in Vietnam, Korea, Iraq, and Afghanistan combined. The United States has the highest murder rate of any industrialized country in the world (five times that of all of Europe). There is a greater statistical chance that a person living in Los Angeles will die from a bullet wound than from a car accident.[23]

- The fastest-growing segment of the criminal population is our nation's young people. In the last two decades, the arrest rate for juveniles committing murder increased 93 percent (72 percent for aggravated assault and 24 percent for forcible rape). About 3 million thefts and violent crimes occur on or near a school campus each year (nearly 16,000 incidents per day). Twenty percent of high school students now carry a firearm, knife, razor, club, or some other weapon on a regular basis.[24]

- Eighty to ninety percent of all doctor's visits are *stress related*. Twenty-five percent of all prescriptions written in this country are for psychotropic medications (tranquilizers, antidepressants, anti-anxiety medications, and sleep aids).[25]

Statistics can be overwhelming, and they don't enable us to see how the pains and challenges of life affect individuals. So let's take a closer look at some of these statistics by studying several case studies. While the stories are fictitious and details have been changed, they are based on composites of real-life cases.

Case #1: Ron is a bright, energetic, and deeply committed believer who has been serving in his local church as a lay leader for more than a decade. He is a deacon and also serves as the adviser to the college fellowship in the church. He teaches an adult Sunday school class and often sings in the choir and for special worship services. Ron is highly respected as a mature, spiritual man of God, and he is well liked by his peers, as well as by the pastoral leaders in the church.

At thirty-five, Ron has done well as a professional accountant, having just been made partner of the firm in which he has been working for many years. He is married to a spiritually mature wife who works part-time as a music teacher and is the church choir director. They have three lovely young children. On the surface, Ron and his wife appear to be the perfect couple with an ideal family.

In the past several months, however, Ron has been feeling physically fatigued and emotionally drained. He does not enjoy life as much as he used to and has begun to lose his appetite. He has also been having some difficulty falling asleep, and recent thoughts of wanting to die have concerned him. Deep within, he feels spiritually dry and empty, but he has not been able to tell anyone until he finally spoke to his wife about what he called the "burnout" symptoms he has been experiencing. Ron has realized he has had too many demands placed on him over a long period of time and now feels that he can no longer meet them.

Ron and his wife are both deeply worried about his health and "burnout" symptoms. However, they do not know where to turn for help. He recently tried to talk to a close friend and fellow deacon at church but was told he just needed a vacation and should stop worrying so much. Both Ron and his wife are now reluctant to talk to anybody else in church about how depressed he has really been feeling. Out of frustration and desperation, they eventually make an appointment with a professional therapist recommended by their family physician. However, they do so with mixed feelings and are afraid others in the church may find out Ron is seeing a "shrink."

Case #2: Another situation that often arises in a church context is in the area of marital conflict Take, for example, Jack and Rachel, who have been married five years and have a two-year-old son, Peter. Both of them have been church members for many years and have served in various capacities, including teaching elementary Sunday school and working with the high school youth group.

Since Peter was born two years ago, they have had a very difficult time adjusting to their new status of parenthood, with all its demands, as well as joys. They love Peter very much and were happy to have him, since they had planned to have a child. However, they had not anticipated how much this would change their lives. Peter had been a colicky baby who cried frequently and awoke several times during the night, so that Rachel felt extremely exhausted most of the time, especially in the first year of their son's life. Jack was also affected and often felt tired, though not as exhausted as Rachel. As a result, their communication with each other, as well as their sexual relationship, increasingly suffered. They had significantly less time to spend with one another because most of their time and energy were focused on taking care of Peter's needs.

While Peter is somewhat less demanding now that he is older and able to sleep through more nights, Jack and Rachel have not quite recovered from the stress they have experienced. They find themselves emotionally disconnected, easily irritated and upset with each other, even over small things. They argue frequently and still feel fatigued most of the time. Jack is working full-time as an engineer in a very demanding job, with the ever-threatening possibility of a layoff, and this only makes things worse. Rachel works part-time as a tutor to help out financially. They still do not have much time to spend together and have managed only a couple of date nights. Their intimacy has improved but not to their mutual satisfaction.

Both Jack and Rachel are aware the marriage is rocky and that they are experiencing significant problems. They never expected the birth of a wanted child would involve so much stress and change, yet they still care deeply for each other and do not want their marital relationship to get any worse. Nevertheless, they are not sure who they can talk with about their marital and sexual problems since they feel these are very personal in nature. They fear that people in the church might judge them to be poor Christians if their marital difficulties were to become public.

Jack and Rachel also feel the burden to maintain a good example of victorious Christian living for their youth group. Unfortunately, too much marital conflict and emotional pain have been experienced to pretend nothing is wrong. Their spiritual lives have also been affected adversely so that they no longer pray together on a regular basis. Thinking back on the "good old days" before their son was born, they often wonder angrily why God has allowed all these things to happen. As a couple, Jack and Rachel know they need help and counseling from someone but are hesitant and unsure as to whom they should turn.

Case #3: Paul is a twenty-eight-year-old youth worker on the staff of a parachurch youth organization specializing in outreach to troubled teenagers living in urban ghettos. He has been in full-time ministry with this organization for five years. A gifted and effective youth worker, he has won recognition from local churches, as well as from city officials, for the good work he has done.

Despite all the outward signs of success, Paul struggles inwardly with a profound sense of insecurity and fear of failure. He has done well so far partly because he is driven to succeed by his perfectionism and has worked very hard and long hours. Although he is an excellent public speaker and communicator with adolescents, deep down inside, Paul is still afraid of "blowing it." Because most people have complimented him on his obvious gifts and effectiveness in youth ministry, he has not told anyone about his anxiousness and fears. Paul has often wished he could tell someone his deepest fears and challenges. He grew up under strict and demanding parents who set incredibly high standards of behavior, leaving him to feel inadequate and inferior much of the time despite doing well in whatever endeavors he undertook.

Recently Paul decided to open up with one of his most trusted friends, a colleague in the same parachurch organization. It was difficult, but eventually he succeeded in talking about his feelings. His friend tried to be understanding and eventually told Paul he should not think so negatively. He suggested instead that Paul should pray for the Lord's deliverance from such oppressive thoughts, which he believed were demonic in their source. Paul has prayed for deliverance over the torment with some relief but still feels the need to talk with someone about his inner struggles. He is afraid, however, to be transparent and only be told once more to simply pray for deliverance.

Case #4: Roger is a thirty-eight-year-old husband and father. He has been married for nine years and has two children, ages eight and five. Currently he works as a middle manager for a large engineering firm. The office is located almost an hour away, and the work environment is extremely stressful because of bidding competition and project deadlines. The company has mentioned a possible downsizing of the workforce due to ongoing economic pressures, and middle management is seen as being the most vulnerable. Roger has been with the company for seven years now.

Annette, Roger's wife, also works. She is an office manager for a local pediatrician but may have to leave due to recurring back problems and other health concerns. The possible loss of her income has strained the marriage a bit, especially over the past six months. Roger works late many days and sometimes doesn't get home until after the children have gone to bed. Lately he has appeared to be increasingly irritable, frequently "loses it," and ends up yelling at Annette or the kids.

During his senior year in high school and also while attending college, Roger would drink socially with friends and occasionally get drunk. Annette knew of his drinking when they started dating, but it never seemed to be a problem and she had never actually seen him drunk. Roger's mother was an alcoholic and died four years ago from complications related to her drinking. She was sixty-seven at the time. Her brother (Roger's uncle) has also been in a detox center twice for drinking problems.

One of the reasons Roger was coming home late was because he was stopping at a bar to have a drink with a couple of his coworkers. What started out as a beer or two once a week after work became a six-pack three or four times a week. Drinking on the weekends also became more routine, and he no longer tries to hide it from Annette.

Annette greatly resents the drinking and is becoming increasingly concerned. Her primary way of dealing with the issue is to lecture and moralize the situation. Roger responds with anger, sullenness and, most recently, by leaving the house for hours at a time. He doesn't believe he has a serious problem with alcohol and says he could stop if he really wanted to. Besides, he feels like it "calms him down" after the stress of his workday. He appears aloof and somewhat suspicious of others.

About a month ago, Roger stopped attending church with his family. After a lot of asking and complaining, and even a threat by Annette to separate, Roger has agreed to talk with someone. He says he loves his family but doesn't know "what the big deal" is really all about. He doesn't believe the Bible expressly prohibits drinking altogether.

These examples are just the tip of the iceberg. If you talk to any pastor or church leader today, you'll immediately understand that there is a great need for helping and caring ministries in the church. Christians are human beings with real needs and struggles. Yet as these situations illustrate, many believers with problems do not know where or to whom to turn. Research shows us that when people of faith wrestle with a life crisis, they often first seek out their priest, pastor, or rabbi for counsel and direction. But are these religious leaders ready to help?

Scandals among televangelists, moral failures of pastors, child abuse incidents, and suicides of church members are further real-life examples of how faithful and committed followers of Christ may be hurting in their lives and never receive the help they truly need. Problems like these grow when help is not sought even if available or not received even if given. And often help is not available or forthcoming because too many Christ followers are not sensitive enough to the needs of hurting people, or if they are, they lack the necessary skills and training to minister to those in need. The truth we hope to share in this resource is that we can minister to others in need, but we must first learn to resist the tendency to believe that only mental health professionals can help or counsel effectively.

We receive numerous inquiries from pastors and church leaders around the world about how best to meet people's needs through lay caring and counseling ministries. The good news is that there are leaders in our churches and Christian communities who are moved with compassion when it comes to caring for and ministering to broken lives.

So what sets us apart as Christian counselors? Why should we care about the equipping of lay counselors to minister to those who are hurting in the church? We believe there has been a profound failure among the social sciences to impart moral and spiritual guidance. This is one reason why it is essential for the church to address a significant vacuum within our contemporary society. Just listen to these words from the opening preface of the Humanist Manifesto II (1973), which underscores the widening cultural schism between secular and Christian worldviews:

> As in 1933, humanists still believe that traditional theism, especially faith in a prayer-hearing god, *assumed* to love and care for persons, to hear and understand their prayers and to be able to do something about them, is an *unapproved* and *outmoded* faith. Salvation based on mere affirmation still appears to be *harmful*, diverting people with these *false hopes* of heaven thereafter. Reasonable minds look at *other means* for survival.[26]

As this statement indicates, there has been a shift from the premodern era to the modern, and now to the postmodern era. Philosophical perspectives now embrace pluralism, naturalism, and pantheism, attempting to deconstruct a biblical worldview and create a morally relativistic culture. We cannot ignore this reality, and our Judeo-Christian ethic as counselors calls us to compassionate action. This means taking necessary initiative with competent skill and effort while treating others with respect, and at the same time responding empathically to suffering and injustice.

True Christianity centered in the gospel of Jesus Christ calls us to love and serve one another as deeply as Christ loves us, to reach out and bear one another's burdens, and to be instruments of God's grace and healing. A number of scriptural passages and texts challenge us to live this way, and they form the biblical basis for lay caring ministries, including lay counseling. We will unpack those passages in more detail in the next chapter.

CHAPTER 2

The Biblical Basis for
Lay Counseling

In Matthew 7:24–27 Jesus describes two distinct foundations on which to build one's life—rock and sand—representing those who hear and incorporate the Word of God and those who do not. However, as we see in this passage, the tempest still came against *both houses*. Believers are not immune from the storms of life. There is no guarantee that professing faith in Christ will exempt us from the trials and tribulations that come with life. This includes the trials that can ravage the mind, emotions, and soul. The church needs to stand up and acknowledge that suffering and mental illness are realities, and as Christians, we must learn to step fully into our God-given role as ambassadors of reconciliation and those who help foster healing, restoration, recovery, and transformation.[1]

Over the years, we have conducted many training courses and workshops in local churches on lay Christian counseling. We have also sensed that for many pastors and church leaders, a key question is whether or not lay counseling is a legitimate ministry consideration. Is there biblical support for this orientation? Some wonder if lay counseling is just a means of bringing secular psychology into the church under the guise of "Christian ministry." In more conservative circles of evangelicalism today, there is a deep concern about the "seduction of Christianity" by secular psychology.[2] These are valid concerns that should be addressed before you commit to establishing a lay Christian counseling ministry or training program.

Lay counseling should represent a dynamic process of communication between the helper as a representative of God and the client, who is in need of healing and a restored relationship with the Creator. Yet Christians should not be involved in lay counseling or people-helping just because the world is doing so or because there is a shortage of mental health professionals. The body of Christ should get involved in lay counseling primarily because the Lord, through His Word, the Bible, has called us to be engaged in this ministry to others.

Psychiatrist James Fischer, a student of Sigmund Freud's, was retiring from a fifty-year mental health career when he said the following, illustrating the value of a biblical orientation in counseling:

> If you were to take the sum total of all authoritative articles ever written by the most qualified of psychologists and psychiatrists on the subject of mental hygiene; and if you were to combine them and refine them and cleave out the excess verbiage; and if you were to take the whole of the meat and none of the bones; and if you were to have these unadulterated bits of pure scientific knowledge concisely expressed by the most capable of living poets; you would have an awkward and incomplete summation of the teachings of Christ, particularly the Sermon on the Mount; and it would suffer immeasurably in comparison.[3]

Two categories of scriptural references provide biblical support for a lay counseling ministry. The first category emphasizes the calling of all Christians, including the so-called laity (who are not ordained or professional clergy members), to be involved in ministry or service in general. The second category directs all believers to be involved in ministries to "one another," which can be grouped together under the general umbrella of lay counseling (i.e., people-helping by nonprofessionals and paraprofessionals). We will look at each of these categories in turn.

THE CALL TO MINISTRY IN GENERAL

The Bible teaches that all Christians belong to the universal priesthood of believers (1 Peter 2:5, 9) and are called to minister to each other so that we can all achieve the ultimate goal of maturity in Christ (see Ephesians 4). A growing number of authors have recognized this biblical emphasis and have written on the liberation of the laity, Christian caregiving, lay caregiving, helping laity help others, and training church members in pastoral care.[4] Paul Stevens, teaching elder at Marineview Chapel in Vancouver, British Columbia, in his book *Liberating the Laity*, emphasized that every church has far more work than any one person or pastor can do. He used Ephesians 4:1–16, among other passages, to demonstrate that it is God's will for all the saints to be equipped for ministry or service.[5]

Stevens pointed out that in the Bible, "the laity (Gk. *laikoi*) is the whole people of God—both the clergy and so-called laity. It is a term of honor because the whole people of God in Christ is chosen to be 'a royal priesthood, a holy nation, a people [*laikoi*] belonging to God' (1 Peter 2:9). Christianity arose as an essentially lay movement."[6] Stevens went on to argue for the abolition of the laity, believing that the common Christian believer deserves to be accorded more than second-class status because Jesus Himself honored His people by giving gifts of ministry to all Christians. The laity of the church, just as much as the ordained pastor, has been called to a respectable vocation of serving the Lord and His people. Stevens asserted that the whole *environment*, not just programs, of the church should be designed to equip all Christians or members for such a high calling.

Using Ephesians 4:1–16 as the main scriptural text, Stevens made the following points as biblical foundations for the laity's call to ministry.

1. Unity of Calling

"Vocation or calling . . . is what you do with who you are in Christ. Every believer has been called to be Jesus' disciple and to serve in the kingdom of God. This is the 'one hope' to which we are called (4:4). Fundamentally, then, there is no clergy-laity distinction. All are called by God."[7]

2. Unity of Ministry

Stevens pointed out that though there is one calling (Eph. 4:1), there are many expressions of grace (v. 7) and many gifts for ministry (v. 11). It is because of such diversity, which reflects how essential and needed each of the various ministries is, that the unity of the whole body can be achieved. Each member of the body is therefore indispensable, and unity in ministry results as each part does its work effectively (v. 16). Stevens clarified that the gifts of the Spirit for ministry are not mere functions or activities carried out by the members. "The gifts are *people*, the men and women to whom you are connected in Christ. . . . When Paul speaks of gifts for ministry in verse 11, giving apostles, prophets, evangelists, and pastor-teachers as examples, the emphasis is not on these gifts but on these people. In receiving the grace of Christ, we *become* ministers. We don't *have* a ministry; we *are* one."[8]

3. Unity in Common Life

Stevens emphasized that it is impossible for believers to be in Christ alone or live independently of each other without losing their spiritual health. He pointed out the frequent and innovative ways the word *together* occurs in Paul's epistle to the Ephesians (e.g., see 2:5, 21, 22; 3:6; 4:16). The interdependence of every member in the body of Christ (see also 1 Corinthians 12) reflects the unity in common life of all Christians. Stevens concluded that in Ephesians 4:16, "Paul is saying that every member *in his or her contact with other members* supplies something the body needs. . . . In order to be an equipping environment, therefore, the local church must be structured for relationships."[9]

4. Unity in Purpose

Stevens noted that Ephesians 4:13 and 15 provide the goal of the equipping ministry and the climax of Ephesians 4:1–16—maturity in Christ. Therefore the body of Christ is unified in its common purpose of achieving maturity in Him. The theme of unity—in calling, in ministry, in common life, and in purpose—provides the biblical or theological setting for the heart of equipping. This process involves not just individual members but the whole environment of the local church, such that the whole body together is given clerical status for service or ministry. Ordained pastors should make themselves dispensable by equipping others (all the saints) for ministry or service. However, the Ultimate Equipper is the Lord Jesus Himself, the head of the church, who has given grace and spiritual gifts to His people.

Stevens concluded:

> In short, the equipping ministry of the Lord effectively abolishes what we call the laity by providing for every member to become engaged in ministry. The notion that one person could so embody the charismatic gifts of ministry for the church that he or she might be called *the* minister is an affront to the intention of the Head Equipper. The goal of equipping is not to make people dependent on their leaders, but dependent on the Head. It requires strong leadership in the church to lead people in such a way that they do not become dependent on their human leaders, but are instead released to do the work of ministry themselves.[10]

Christ Himself, as the "head" of the church (Eph. 5:23), is our role model and standard bearer. The prophet Isaiah refers to Him as the "Wonderful Counselor" (Isa. 9:6), and as His body, we are all called to ministry and service. As Stevens put it: "By the grace of God we have been chosen, appointed and anointed, a special people, a holy nation, priests to our God. We are all clergy—priestly ministers."[11]

THE CALL TO LAY COUNSELING AS A SPECIFIC MINISTRY

Assuming you agree that every Christian is called to the work of ministry, you may still wonder if lay *counseling* as a ministry has particular support from the Scriptures. The Bible teaches explicitly that the Lord Jesus came not only to save sinners but also calls us to a radically different lifestyle characterized by agape love. In fact, God has "called us to a holy life—not because of anything we have done but because of his own purpose and grace. This grace was given us in Christ Jesus before the beginning of time" (2 Tim. 1:9). Jesus has given a new commandment to all Christians to love one another as He has loved us (John 13:34–35).

One way to show Christlike love and hence to fulfill the law of Christ is to bear or carry each other's burdens (Gal. 6:2). This directive was given by the apostle Paul to all Christians—and especially to mature, spiritual Christians (v. 1)—to get involved in a burden-bearing or "restoring" ministry to fellow believers who are struggling with sin in their lives. This "restoring" ministry involves counseling in its broad sense of people-helping, but restoring also involves far more. James tells us to confess our sins to each other and to pray for one another so that we may be healed (James 5:16). Confession and prayer are critical components of *Christian* people-helping.

Other passages in the Bible (e.g., Rom. 15:14; Col. 3:16; 1 Thess. 5:14) direct all believers to be involved in admonishing, encouraging, or helping one another. These verses also emphasize that spiritual qualities or qualifications like goodness or caring, knowledge, and wisdom (rather than only having credentials or professional training) are crucial for effective Christian counseling. Such scriptural texts also support the legitimacy of a lay caring and counseling ministry for all believers. However, it should be noted that the Bible also teaches that some Christians may be particularly gifted with appropriate spiritual gifts like exhortation, or *paraklesis* (Rom. 12:8), and are therefore called to spend much of their time and service in lay counseling.

Many years ago, C. Peter Wagner wrote a helpful book titled *Your Spiritual Gifts Can Help Your Church Grow*.[12] In it he defines the spiritual gift of exhortation as "the special ability that God gives to certain members of the body of Christ to minister words of comfort, consolation, encouragement and counsel to other members of the Body in such a way that they feel helped and healed."[13] Wagner went on to say:

> All Christians, of course, have a role of caring for one another. Hebrews 3:13 says, "Exhort one another daily." The lifestyle of Christians in contact with one another should be to counsel and share and encourage at all times. But over and above this, some Christians have a special gift of counseling that should become recognized to the extent that people in the church who are hurting know where to go to find help. When this happens, the Body is in good health. It is a positive growth characteristic.[14]

The proper exercise of spiritual gifts is therefore essential to the healthy growth of a church as a caring community. In our twenty-first-century world, we especially need this caring community. Cultural and technological shifts in society, as well as the rise of individualism and the breakdown of a sense of genuine community and meaningful interpersonal relationships, have led many people to a point of crisis. They need help, and God has established His church as the community best able to address these problems.

Rodger K. Bufford and Robert Buckler proposed a strategy for ministering to mental health needs in the church.[15] They acknowledged that the church's mission has many facets, centering on loving submission to God and ministry to people around us (cf. Matt. 28:18–20; Mark 12:30–31; John 13:34), and noted that meeting personal needs to minimize mental health problems definitely falls within the scope of this mission. They suggested that ministries like lay counseling are important and necessary aspects of the church's mission in the world. They concluded:

> Trained counselors, forming a coordinated multilevel network of care, can extend pastoral counseling care to all members of the church, while relieving the pastoral staff of often unbearable burdens in this area. The use of different echelons of counselors within the local church also recognizes differing abilities and spiritual gifts in the church Body. Those with the gifts of exhortation, helps, and administration are fulfilled as they exercise their gifts, and those to whom they minister are edified through receiving their specialized ministry.[16]

Other authors have noted that there are several biblical words from Scripture that have meanings closely associated with the concept of lay counseling or people-helping. Jay Adams, who pioneered the nouthetic counseling movement in the late 1970s, pointed out that many of the "one another" passages in the New Testament (including those already cited) pertain in some way to lay counseling.[17] Adams asserted that directive or nouthetic counseling (based on a New Testament Greek word *nouthesia*), which involves "change through confrontation out of concern" is the appropriate designation for biblical counseling.[18] Others, like John Carter, have proposed that biblical counseling is more adequately based on *parakaleo* and *paraklesis* rather than only on *noutheteo* or *nouthesia*. *Parakaleo*, or one of its forms, is translated twenty-nine times in the King James Version as "comfort," twenty-seven times as "exhort," fourteen times as "consolation," and forty-three times as "beseech." On the other hand, *noutheteo* and its cognate appear only thirteen times in the New Testament. *Paraklesis* is also listed as a spiritual gift in Romans 12:8.[19] Carter's understanding, that biblical counseling includes not only the nouthetic or directive approach (and the "restoring" ministry referred to earlier), but also comforting, encouraging, and supporting others, is a more holistic way of thinking about the biblical evidence on counseling.

The late Frank Minirth also noted some years ago that there are at least five verbs in the New Testament that are relevant to the ministry of counseling:

parakaleo, noutheteo, paramutheomai, antechomai, and *makrothumeo.*[20] All five of these Greek words appear in 1 Thessalonians 5:14, "And we urge (*parakaleo*) you, brothers and sisters, warn (*noutheteo*) those who are idle and disruptive, encourage (*paramutheomai*) the disheartened, help (*antechomai*) the weak, be patient (*makrothumeo*) with everyone."

We find it helpful to unpack each of these verbs a little further. The first, *parakaleo,* means to strongly exhort, to plead with or beseech. The verb tense comes with a sense of urgency, which is also present in the use of *noutheteo.* With *noutheteo,* however, we are being challenged to admonish others in such a way as if giving instruction. Intentionality is present and is a necessary part of any helping process. The third word, *paramutheomai,* means "to encourage," yet it also challenges us to console and comfort others. The verb tense implies that there is a "proactive seeking out." This is a beautiful picture of the gospel, where Jesus is seen as not simply waiting for those who need restoration to come to Him but is actively seeking out and saving those who are lost (Luke 19:10). The fourth word, *antechomai,* is used in the same manner—to assist those without strength, but to do so through active participation. Lay counseling requires that we must be willing to get our hands dirty. Sinful choices and behaviors rarely come in neat and clean packages. Finally, the word *makrothumeo* requires us to be longsuffering with others. The world too easily discards the wounded sinner. We, however, must faithfully journey on until the Lord releases us from the assignment.

In their book on healing relationships and lay counseling,[21] Stephen Grunlan and Daniel Lambrides reviewed the meanings of these Greek words based on Kittel's *Theological Dictionary of the New Testament.*[22] They concluded that 1 Thessalonians 5:14, where these terms are found in the Scriptures, is addressed to all believers, who are urged, "to be involved in exhorting, encouraging, comforting, and helping—in short, counseling."[23] This verse emphasizes the importance of a flexible and balanced approach to counseling, one that is sensitive to the needs and specific problems of the individual.

In addition to these helpful New Testament passages, we will also need to take into consideration a number of Old Testament passages that are relevant to a biblical approach to effective counseling (e.g., Ex. 18:5–26; 1 Kings 12:9, 28; Ps. 55:13–14; Prov. 12:15; 13:10; 19:20; 20:18). They contain Hebrew words that are often translated as "counsel," with the main connotation of advice in the form of guidance or direction.[24] Many of these passages speak about the nature of our relationships with one another. The Bible tells us that we were created *in* relationship, *through* relationship, and *for* relationship. When God said, "It is not good for the man to be alone" (Gen. 2:18), He was implying that we were formed in such a manner that we require human contact to complement our walk with the

Creator. Our God-given DNA continually seeks to fulfill a need for belonging, connection, fellowship, and community.

So, what do we have at our disposal to meet these needs? What can we offer when our hearts and spirits are passionately stirred by the pain we see in others? The answer, at least in part, lies in the empowering authority of the Bible: "Do your best to present yourself to God as one approved, a worker who does not need to be ashamed and who correctly handles the word of truth. . . . And the Lord's servant must not be quarrelsome but must be kind to everyone, able to teach, not resentful. Opponents must be gently instructed, in the hope that God will grant them repentance leading to a knowledge of the truth" (2 Tim. 2:15, 24–25). Why? Because "all Scripture is God-breathed and is useful for teaching, rebuking, correcting and training in righteousness" (2 Tim. 3:16).

The Greek word for "truth" used in the New Testament is *alethia*, which literally means "nothing hidden." When Jesus described the coming of the Holy Spirit as a Helper, He referred to the third person of the Trinity as the "Spirit of truth" and someone who would guide us into all truth (John 14:17; 15:26; 16:13). Here, the Holy Spirit could be described as *the Spirit who allows nothing to be hidden*, encouraging us as counselors to move beyond the outer appearance and toward the true essence and reality of a given situation. Not only does God look at the heart (1 Sam. 16:7), but He also weighs its motives (Prov. 16:2).

As we can see, there are many scriptural passages that provide a biblical basis for lay ministry in general and lay counseling in particular. Proverbs 11:14 (NASB) says, "Where there is no guidance, the people fall, but in abundance of counselors there is victory." Grace and truth are two covenant values that must be held in equal tension against one another. Grace binds us together, and the truth sets us free. If one value is emphasized over the other, then serious problems often develop and both values may become distorted and diminished.

Balance should be our goal. The Lord has called us to reach out to one another in love, bearing each other's burdens as we help and counsel one another. In so doing, we demonstrate the reality of a genuinely caring and compassionate community that reaches out with the love of Christ to draw more people to Him.

CHAPTER 3

A Biblical Model
for Effective
Lay Counseling

Although psychology as a disciplined study did not originate from Christian sources and historically has had an antibiblical worldview, in its most basic form, psychology is the science of the mind and of human behavior. This broad definition includes the emotions, thinking, identity, personality, and relationships. Neurology, a companion science, involves the study of actual brain functioning. Most conservative theologians would agree that everything in the Bible is true, but not all truth is found in the Bible.

God gave humankind the ability and the intelligence to discover "truths" about the way the world operates, including human beings. The disciplines of the "pure sciences" such as biology, physics, astronomy, chemistry, and mathematics have all led to remarkable discoveries that are not necessarily found in the pages of Scripture. A number of these scientists were agnostic, atheistic, and most certainly humanistic, but their discoveries remain as factual data about the world in which we live. The principles gleaned by their scientific efforts are utilized in multiple ways every day by the Christian community. This includes the operating system of the computer that was used to type this manuscript! The software developers who created these programs were not required to make a profession of faith for their work and research to be useful to us.

Psychology, as a social science, is no different. Theorists like Freud, Carl Jung, Milton Erickson, Alfred Adler, Carl Rogers, and Abraham Maslow were not Christians (in fact, many were hostile to religion in general), but they still discovered a number of true things about the human condition and human behavior. For example, in the study of behavioral dynamics, we know that certain behaviors, if they are positively reinforced, typically lead to an increase of that particular behavior. In other words, if a father gives his child some reward for completing chores in a proficient and timely manner, that child may be motivated to finish his chores. One does not have to be a believer to discover this as a natural reality. Every time a Christian parent gives her child an allowance, she is integrating psychology with her Christianity *whether she understands it or not.*

In other words, just because an unbeliever may have confirmed the existence of a particular "truth" does not imply that the scientific fact is inherently evil or anti-Christian. It is simply an explanation of how one distinct process of human behavior operates, nothing more and nothing less. That is not to say that there is no conflict between the teaching of the unbelieving theorists and what the Bible teaches. The conflict lies in the fact that these theorists did not know how to effectively operationalize these truths into workable models from a biblical framework based on faith.

Maslow, who was a secular personality theorist, made the statement that a person will not attend to a higher human need if a more basic one is being compromised. For instance, the need for belonging in relationships would be considered a higher order need than the physiological needs to satisfy hunger and thirst. Those who are starving to death are more concerned about their next meal than about the quality of their relationships or even a well-crafted Bible study. It is not an issue of godliness or ungodliness; it is a principle of human behavior. Rogers, a humanist, developed a theory called "person-centered therapy" that emphasizes empathy, warmth or respect, and genuineness for other persons as an effective means of helping. Though Rogers was clearly not a Christian, one could argue that these insights can serve as valid components to ministry. Albert Ellis was an avowed atheist, but he discovered that people's thinking patterns flow out of their core belief systems and that this in turn has an impact on emotion and behavior. Again, these findings *confirm* biblical concepts, even though the initial scientific findings were studied and researched by someone who was not supportive of a Christian worldview.

With that in mind, we want to acknowledge that there is a distinct difference between simple psychology and a biblically sound view of counseling and psychology. The Word of God and psychology are not equal voices in the conversation, yet some principles of psychology can be useful. This balanced position recognizes the sovereignty of God's Word over humanity's knowledge but is open to truth that can be gleaned from other sources.

Christian counseling incorporates principles found in the Word of God and *integrates* them with the simple "truths" discovered through the social sciences. Christ-centered helpers who are committed people of faith utilize God's Word as the basis of their caregiving interventions effectively in the healing process. Spiritual disciplines such as prayer, meditation on God's Word, fellowship, fasting, forgiveness, repentance, worship, and the gifts and fruit of the Holy Spirit are available tools to be used in working with others.

Lay counseling is biblically oriented people-helping. It takes a values-based approach, and when it is complemented by Spirit-anointed counselors who understand the valid truths of human psychology, it can become a powerful agent of change in a person's life. It represents the "whole counsel of God" in addressing certain aspects of the human condition.

In his now-classic book *Effective Biblical Counseling*, author and counselor Larry Crabb had a chapter titled "Christianity and Psychology: Enemies or Allies?"[1] When Crabb asked this question, he was drawing attention to one of the key issues surrounding the integration of psychology and Christian theology. Certainly the literature on the topic of integration has continued to grow over the years. Several important books[2] and journal articles[3] have been published. Since this continues to be one of the key issues in Christian counseling today, a few comments about integration are necessary before we unpack a biblical model for effective lay Christian counseling.

FOUR MAIN APPROACHES TO INTEGRATION

In his classic text, Crabb suggested that there are four main models of integration. He offers some colorful and descriptive names and suggests that psychology and Christianity may be viewed as: (a) separate but equal; (b) a tossed salad (equal and mixable); (c) nothing buttery (psychology is irrelevant and unnecessary; only the Scriptures are needed to deal with human problems and needs); and (d) spoiling the Egyptians (using whatever concepts or methods from secular psychology that are consistent with Scripture, hence subjecting them to the authority of Scripture).[4] Crabb's "spoiling the Egyptians" approach is similar to the "Integrates" model of integration,[5] and even though this construct was originally developed several decades ago, it is still a helpful way of understanding and describing the relationship between psychology and Christianity.

Another trend we have found over the years has been the development of an alternative paradigm called the *perspectival model*. In this model, each discipline (theology and psychology) is approached from the perspective of the other and is informed by the other, yet psychology is not seen to fall under the authority of theology.[6] Some have suggested that the term *integration* and its conceptual model should be replaced by the perspectival model,[7] and while we remain aware of the problems and limitations inherent in integrating the interpretation of Scripture with psychology,[8] we still believe that holding to the authority of *Scripture* (not theology as a discipline) is still necessary to engage in *biblical* integration of psychology and Christianity. Several authors have voiced agreement with this view, including Christian psychologist and researcher, Everett Worthington, who has written and critiqued the perspectival model.[9]

A BIBLICAL MODEL FOR EFFECTIVE LAY COUNSELING

As we seek to develop a model for effective lay counseling, the model we propose is based on three of the seminal approaches to Christian counseling that were briefly mentioned in chapter 2. We advocate a blend of insights drawn from Jay Adams's "nouthetic counseling," Gary Collins's "people-helping," and Larry Crabb's "biblical counseling."[10] While these views have seen significant developments over the years, the key insights and methods they advocate remain timely and useful for a lay counseling model. We would also seek to incorporate the views and methods advocated by William Backus and his approach to Christian counseling called "misbelief therapy,"[11] as well as Everett Worthington's practical guide to counseling. Both of these approaches utilize a cognitive-behavioral perspective (i.e., problem feelings are usually due to problem behavior and, more fundamentally, problem thinking).[12]

Our lay counseling model also uses concepts, principles, and techniques from secular approaches that were advocated by Robert Carkhuff,[13] Gerard Egan,[14] and cognitive behavior therapists like Aaron Beck, Albert Ellis, and Donald Meichenbaum.[15] In utilizing these insights, we have sought to find where they are in alignment with scriptural principles and have rejected those that are inconsistent with or directly contradictory to God's Word. This model can best be described as biblically based, comprehensive, and eclectic, with a strong cognitive-behavioral component. It is somewhat similar to H. Norman Wright's work on self-talk, imagery, and prayer in counseling,[16] and it is *one* approach to effective lay counseling from a biblical perspective and, as such, has its strengths and weaknesses. We certainly would not want to suggest that it is the *only* biblical model.

Let's unpack the model a bit further by looking at three key aspects of the model:

1. Basic view of humanity
2. Basic view of counseling
3. Basic principles of effective counseling

BASIC VIEW OF HUMANITY

Much has been written over the years about the *basic psychological and spiritual needs* of human beings. Different lists can be drawn up detailing things like our need for meaning and direction in life and our need for hope or forgiveness.[17] Crabb asserted that human beings basically need a sense of self-worth (not self-worship), which consists of a need for security or love, as well as a need for significance or purpose.[18] Ultimately all such needs can be fully met only through a personal relationship with Jesus Christ.

In developing his list of basic human needs, Crabb preferred to speak of the needs for security and significance with different language. He referred to them as "deep longings in the human heart for relationship and impact,"[19] which only the Lord can quench. Such longings will not be completely satisfied while we live in a fallen world, because full satisfaction of our needs in the Lord can be experienced only in heaven. However, these deep longings can begin to be substantially (not fully) satisfied as we give up our self-protective defenses and admit our need for the Lord and His love and grace.

Ultimately we depend on Christ alone to help us to live life the way He designed it to be lived, and that includes living in the context of a caring community of believers in a local church. Crabb changed some of his terminology because some wrongly assumed that he was teaching a human-centered focus on fulfillment rather than a God-centered focus on obedience. Like Crabb, our model begins with the premise that all people have fundamental needs or longings that God has put within them, which only He can fully meet, and they include longings for relationship or security and for impact or significance.

Our model views humanity's *basic problem* as having to do with sin. Underlying most mental-emotional problems that are nonorganic in nature is the breaking of God's moral laws as revealed in Scripture and the satanic belief that we can handle our own affairs and meet our basic needs or longings without God.[20] However, this model does not assume that *all* emotional suffering or anguish is due to sin (whether personal sin or the sin of others). At times suffering and anguish may be part of God's process of perfecting His children in the image of Christ. We need to remember that Jesus Himself experienced deep distress in the garden of Gethsemane as He struggled with His Father's will to go to the cross and die for a sinful world (Matt. 26:36–39; Mark 14:32–36; Luke 22:40–44). Jesus never sinned (Heb. 4:15), yet He suffered.[21] While more could be said about this, it suggests that we should carefully seek to discern between sin-induced mental-emotional suffering and anguish or deep distress that may be part of obedience to God's will and growing as a Christian.

We also need to keep in mind that there are "mystical" aspects of the spiritual life that we may not fully comprehend, including what St. John of the Cross has described as the "dark night of the soul" (cf. Isa. 50:10). Richard Foster described this experience in his classic book *Celebration of Discipline*:

> The "dark night" . . . is not something bad or destructive. . . . The purpose of the darkness is not to punish or afflict us. It is to set us free. . . . What is involved in entering the dark night of the soul? It may be a sense of dryness, depression, even lostness. It strips us of overdependence on the emotional life. The notion, often heard today, that such experiences can be avoided and that we should live in peace and comfort, joy and celebration, only betrays the fact that much contemporary experience is surface slush. The dark night is one of the ways God brings us to a hush, a stillness, so that He can work an inner transformation of the soul. . . . Recognize the dark night for what it is. Be grateful that God is lovingly drawing you away from every distraction so that you can see Him.[22]

In his book *That Incredible Christian*, A. W. Tozer described a similar experience that he calls "the ministry of the night":

> To do His supreme work of grace within you, He will take away from your heart everything you love most. Everything you trust in will go from you. Piles of ashes will lie where your most precious treasures used to be. . . . Slowly you will discover God's love in your suffering. Your heart will begin to approve the whole thing. You will learn from yourself what all the schools in the world could not teach you—the healing action of faith without supporting pleasure. You will feel and understand the ministry of the night; its power to purify, to detach, to humble, to destroy the fear of death, and what is more important to you at the moment, the fear of life. And you will learn that sometimes pain can do what even joy cannot, such as exposing the vanity of earth's trifles and filling your heart with longing for the peace of heaven.[23]

Christian psychologists need to become acquainted with the processes and the language of the spiritual life to better understand experiences like the dark night of the soul or the ministry of the night so that they do not naively or prematurely attempt to reduce all suffering to painful symptoms. This requires not only psychological assessment skills but spiritual wisdom and discernment. C. S. Lewis, in his book *The Problem of Pain*, wrote, "God whispers to us in our pleasures, speaks in our conscience, but shouts in our pain. It is His megaphone to a deaf world."[24] Sometimes there is no "easy" solution or therapy or healing, but we must simply trust God and His grace to help people grow through deepening and painful spiritual experiences. The best therapy in these situations is to provide understanding, support, and prayer.[25]

Our lay counseling model also asserts that the *ultimate goal* of humanity is to know God and to enjoy Him forever (see the Westminster Shorter Catechism). For a Christian believer, the end goal in life is maturity in Christ and obedience to God's will (cf. Rom. 8:29). This may entail some suffering at times, as we mentioned, but God has promised He will provide sufficient grace (2 Cor. 12:7–9). Although mental-emotional health is a valid and worthwhile goal to seek, it should remain subordinate to our end goal as Christians.

Happiness at all costs or the absence of troubling and painful emotions is not the final goal of life for a Christian believer. This is why we affirm scriptural perspectives on suffering, including the possibility of what C. Stephen Evans called "the blessings of mental anguish."[26] Evans emphasized that "the primary goal of a Christian counselor is not to help people become merely 'normal,' but to help them love God with all their hearts, minds, and souls."[27] As we seek to help hurting people, we need to keep in mind that the elimination of the symptoms of mental-emotional suffering is not always the most valid or appropriate goal of Christian counseling. The *ultimate goal* of Christian counseling should be holiness and not temporal happiness, spiritual health and not just mental-emotional or physical health.[28]

Our lay counseling model assumes a basic cognitive-behavioral perspective. This means that we see problem feelings as *usually* due to problem behaviors (cf. Gen. 4:3–7) and, more fundamentally, as the result of problem thinking (cf. Prov. 23:7; John 8:32). Crabb emphasized that erroneous, unbiblical basic assumptions or beliefs (what Backus has called "misbeliefs") are at the root of nonorganically caused mental-emotional problems.[29] To change problem feelings, a counselor focuses on changing sinful, unbiblical thinking and behaviors. Both insight and behavior change (cf. Eph. 4:22–24) are crucial factors in effective helping.

However, we should not assume that problem feelings are *always* due to problem behavior and problem thinking. Collins has pointed out that we need to focus equally on all three of these—feelings, behavior, and thoughts—and seek a balance. Problem feelings may be due to biological or physical factors at times, even if no specific organic cause can be located, especially with our present limited knowledge regarding such factors.[30] The model we are proposing is open to medical or psychiatric help if necessary. For example, there are two primary types of depression, referred to as either *exogenous* (considered as secondary because it occurs reactively and externally due to psychological, cognitive or environmental factors), or *endogenous* (considered as primary because it occurs autonomously and internally due to biological, genetic, or chemical factors). Clearly there are both physiological causes (e.g., tumors, brain injury, excessive hunger, sleep deprivation, postpartum reactions) and metabolic causes (e.g., chemical imbalances, menopause, diabetes, thyroid dysfunction, substance abuse, electrolyte imbalances, viral infections, premenstrual syndrome) of depression, and an awareness of this necessitates having a holistic approach to caregiving that considers the whole person and his/her needs.

In his discussion of biblical counseling, Crabb emphasized the need to attend to all four major circles or dimensions of a person's experience—the personal, rational, volitional, and emotional areas.[31] Furthermore, as Christian believers, we understand that problem feelings (as well as behaviors and thoughts) may also be the result of demonic activity (demonization), whether demonic attack or oppression, or even demon possession. If so, prayer for deliverance, fasting, and exorcism may be necessary.[32] God's Word encourages us in that "the weapons we fight with are not the weapons of the world. On the contrary, they have divine power to demolish strongholds. We demolish arguments and every pretension that sets itself up against the knowledge of God, and we take captive every thought to make it obedient to Christ" (2 Cor. 10:4–5).

In summary, our lay counseling model takes a biblical approach to human functioning and dysfunction, as well as to counseling, that is mainly cognitive-behavioral in orientation and practice but more comprehensive and broad-based than secular cognitive-behavior therapy.[33] And, as just stated, this model takes a holistic view of persons as physical, mental-emotional, social, and spiritual beings (cf. Luke 2:52). This means that a mental-emotional problem should always be seen in the context of all the areas of a person's life. Adams's concept of total structuring, or looking at a client's problem in relation to all areas of his or her life, is helpful here. Adams advocates investigating and biblically restructuring the major areas of a person's life, even though the person may present only one problem (e.g., depression). The areas to address are (1) church, Bible, prayer, witness; (2) work, school; (3) physical health, exercise, diet, sleep; (4) marriage, sex; (5) finances, budget; (6) family, children, discipline; (7) social activities, friends; (8) other (e.g., reading).[34]

A similar comprehensive and broad-based secular approach to therapy called "multimodal therapy" was developed by the late Arnold Lazarus,[35] a psychologist who did significant clinical work and research in the areas of behavior therapy and cognitive-behavior therapy. Lazarus proposed that human functioning and problems can be conceptualized under seven modalities with the acronym BASIC I.D. (B = Behavior, A = Affect, S = Sensation, I = Imagery, C = Cognition, $I.$ = Interpersonal relationships, $D.$ = Drugs/Biological factors). According to Lazarus,

we are beings who move, feel, sense, imagine, think, and relate to one another. We are biochemical-neurophysiological entities, and our personalities are the products of our ongoing *behavior*, *affective* processes, *sensations*, *i*mages, *c*ognitions, interpersonal relationships, and biological functions. The first letter of each modality forms the acronym BASIC I.B. (if we call the biological modality *D* for "Drugs," we have the more compelling acronym BASIC I.D., but it is important to remember that *D* stands for more than drugs, medication, or pharmacological intervention, but also includes nutrition, hygiene, exercise, and the panoply of medical diagnoses and interventions that affect personality). The BASIC I.D. (or "identity") represents "human personality."

Multimodal therapy involves the comprehensive assessment and treatment of an individual's BASIC I.D. By using this approach, we do not fit clients to the treatment; we fit the therapy to the requirements of the client. The assumption behind this approach is that the BASIC I.D. comprises the entire range of human personality. There is no problem, no feeling, no accomplishment, no dream or fantasy that cannot be subsumed by BASIC I.D.[36]

Lazarus believed in "systematic eclecticism"[37] or technical eclecticism. This means he recommended using whatever counseling techniques that work or have received empirical or research support, while still subscribing to a broad-based social learning, cognitive-behavioral theoretical framework. He uses over three dozen techniques drawn from different schools of psychotherapy or counseling, although many of them are cognitive-behavioral strategies.

Still, while multimodal therapy has much to commend it, as a secular approach it is inadequate and limited, for it ignores the crucial spiritual dimension of human life and experience. We will address some of the specific limitations of secular approaches like multimodal therapy and cognitive-behavior therapy later in this chapter, but at this point we would note that Christian counselors who have adapted Lazarus's BASIC I.D. for use in Christian counseling typically need to add an *S* to make sure that they account for the spiritual dimension of a person's life. The revised acronym would read BASIC I.D.S.

BASIC VIEW OF COUNSELING

Though we have spent a great deal of time talking about counseling to this point in the book, it is necessary at this point to clarify what we mean by the term *counseling* as it is used in this book and how it relates to the lay counseling model we are describing. If you recall, we advocated a definition for counseling proposed by Collins in the introduction as "a caring relationship in which one person tries to help another deal more effectively with the stresses of life."[38]

We would like to expand on that definition a bit at this point. In another of his books, Collins defined counseling as a relationship between two or more persons in which one person (the counselor) seeks to advise, encourage, and/or assist another person or persons (the counselee[s]) to deal more effectively with the problems of life.[39] This type of "counseling" may have a number of goals, including "a changing of the counselee's behavior, attitudes or values; preventing more serious problems from developing; teaching social skills; encouraging expression of emotions; giving support in times of need; instilling insight; guiding as a decision is made; teaching responsibility; stimulating spiritual growth; and helping the counselee to mobilize his inner resources in times of crisis. Unlike psychotherapy, counseling rarely aims to radically alter or remold the personality."[40]

Note that with this definition, Collins differentiates "counseling" from "psychotherapy," although there is an implication that the two terms are on a larger continuum. Others have similarly differentiated between the two terms, pointing out that "there is a continuum from the simplest form of counseling through to the deepest levels of psychotherapy," as Roger Hurding has put it.[41]

Hurding outlined four levels of psychotherapy, following R. H. Cawley's classification: *psychotherapy 1*, which involves the provision of support and encouragement, and hence includes a great deal of what is usually described as counseling; *psychotherapy 2*, which involves the provision of deeper insight into causes of one's personal problems, including the challenging of defenses or psychological masks; *psychotherapy 3*, which refers to dynamic psychotherapy that deals with unconscious processes or phenomena and aims at the remolding of personality, and hence is usually seen as the province of the experienced professional therapist; and *psychotherapy 4*, which refers to behavioral psychotherapy or the application of behavioral therapy techniques to help a client to unlearn "bad habits" or maladaptive behaviors, and to relearn more appropriate and helpful patterns of behavior. Hurding suggested that counseling can be subsumed under psychotherapy 1 and the initial part of psychotherapy 2, while psychotherapy per se should be used to refer to the other levels.[42]

Some other authors, however, disagree with any differentiation between counseling and psychotherapy. Charles Truax and Robert Carkhuff do not differentiate between these two terms and use them interchangeably,[43] as have a number of other contemporary writers of textbooks on counseling and psychotherapy.[44] Our own view and the one assumed in this model is that the terms *counseling* and *psychotherapy* can be used somewhat interchangeably, if we recognize that a continuum does exist. Still, the differences between them are somewhat arbitrary and tend to blur easily.

Another way of defining counseling is by looking at what a counselor does and why people go to counselors for help. Adams listed twenty of the most frequent reasons why people seek help from counselors. They are as follows:

1. Advice in making simple decisions
2. Answers to troublesome questions
3. Depression and guilt
4. Guidance in determining careers
5. Breakdowns
6. Crises
7. Failures
8. Grief
9. Bizarre behavior
10. Anxiety, worry, and fear
11. Other unpleasant feelings
12. Family and marital trouble
13. Help in resolution of conflicts with others
14. Deteriorating interpersonal relationships
15. Drug and alcohol problems
16. Sexual difficulties
17. Perceptual distortions
18. Psychosomatic problems
19. Attempted suicide
20. Difficulties at work/school.[45]

Assuming that these are all common problems that clients face, what are some basic principles of effective counseling from a biblical perspective that lay Christian counselors can use to help their hurting clients?

BASIC PRINCIPLES OF EFFECTIVE COUNSELING

To keep our model clear and simple, we propose fourteen basic principles of effective lay counseling from a biblical perspective.

First, we need to understand that *the Holy Spirit's ministry as counselor or comforter is critical in effective Christian counseling.* Adams was helpful in pointing out that there are always at least three persons involved in every counseling situation: the client, the counselor, and the Holy Spirit.[46] Dependence on the Spirit and His work as counselor is crucial to Christian counseling (cf. John 14:16–17). Marvin Gilbert and Raymond Brock edited two volumes on the Holy Spirit and counseling, emphasizing the need to be aware of and depend on the Holy Spirit's presence, guidance, and ministry during counseling or therapy sessions, as well as in the personal life of the counselor, so that he or she can function as a "Spirit-filled" Christian counselor, fully open to the power and gifts of the Spirit.[47]

Since many Christians are not as aware of the person of the Holy Spirit and how the third member of the triune Godhead (Father, Son, and Holy Spirit) operates in our lives, we would ask you to consider several basic biblical truths about the Holy Spirit. First, note the various ways in which the Holy Spirit comes to us:

- Sent from heaven—1 Peter 1:12
- Without measure—John 3:34
- As a gift—Acts 10:45
- As a helper—John 14:26
- As righteousness, peace, and joy—Romans 14:17
- In power—Acts 1:8
- As truth—1 John 5:6
- As a witness of the resurrection—Acts 5:32

We should also note how the Holy Spirit ministers to people:

- Teaches us all things and brings them to remembrance—John 14:26
- Encourages us—Acts 9:31
- Indwells the believer—Romans 8:11
- Renews us—Titus 3:5
- Gives us life—2 Corinthians 3:6
- Convicts us of sin, righteousness, and judgment—John 16:8
- Guides and discloses—John 16:13
- Bears witness that we are children of God—Romans 8:16
- Searches all things—1 Corinthians 2:10
- Sanctifies us—Romans 15:16
- Helps our weaknesses and intercedes for us—Romans 8:26
- Glorifies Christ—John 16:14

Again and again, the apostle Paul emphasized the work of the Holy Spirit in *forming* the believer in Christ, *conforming* him or her to the will of Christ, and *transforming* the mind of the believer: "Do not conform to the patterns of this world, but be transformed by the renewing of your mind. Then you will be able to test and approve what God's will is—his good, pleasing and perfect will" (Rom. 12:2). Paul further acknowledged the specific presence of the Spirit in sanctification: that which separates Jesus' followers *from* the world's secular beliefs, standards and actions and moves them *into* relationship with God (2 Thess. 2:13).

The work of the Spirit in the believer is "holistic formation": God's forming, conforming, and transforming over the entirety of life's journey, *the whole person in Christ Jesus.* Paul described this progressive development of continuing maturation in Christ: "And we all, who with unveiled faces contemplate the Lord's glory, are being transformed into his image with ever-increasing glory, which comes from the Lord, who is the Spirit" (2 Cor. 3:18). This is the process of growth in holiness called sanctification. This work of the Spirit is not compartmentalized to those areas of life people tend to think of or define as "spiritual," but also consists of encouraging growth and bringing wholeness in *every area of life*: formation in personal faith, in emotional maturity, in social/interpersonal relationships, in vocational call and giftings; in theological and intellectual knowledge; in the ability to adopt practices and habits that encourage health and wellness; and in forming a lifestyle of wise financial and resource stewardship. Together these seven areas form the holistic, integrated nature of the Holy Spirit's gracious work in those who are alive in Jesus Christ.

Second, we believe that *the Bible is the basic guide for dealing with problems in living* (cf. 2 Tim. 3:16–17). God, through Scripture, has provided human beings with the means to deal with problems and to meet their basic needs or longings for meaning, hope, and love.[48] The Christian counselor must have a good grasp of Scripture and theology, and should engage in some study of the Old Testament, New Testament, systematic theology, hermeneutics, apologetics, and Christian ethics. These studies are key foundations for effective lay *Christian* counseling.[49] The Bible is a comprehensive guide to dealing with life's problems, a sufficient guide for relational living, as Crabb puts it.[50]

God's Word speaks meaningfully to every human problem, but only if we study and interpret it carefully in terms of its content, categories, implications, and images, including appropriate extended applications of scriptural truth to complex life situations and problems. In other words, we need to learn not only how to interpret the Scriptures accurately (exegesis and hermeneutics), but also how to apply them practically to life.[51]

Over the years, several authors have attempted to present fundamental doctrines of the Christian faith and how they apply to Christian counseling, emphasizing that good Christian or biblical theology is crucial for good Christian counseling.[52] Our model, however, does not assert that the Bible is an *exhaustive* guide to counseling. We affirm that counselors should make use of truth that is learned via God's general revelation and common grace, truth discovered by non-Christians through research. Thus, while Scripture provides sufficient answers to life's major issues and problems and serves as a comprehensive guide to counseling, it does not cover every detail involved in the counseling process. Our model is open to the use of principles and strategies of counseling derived from psychology or psychiatry that do not contradict the Scriptures.[53] Implicit in all of this is an assumption of the unity of truth, that all truth is God's truth.

With this in mind, we assert that the Bible is our crucial foundation and source for godly wisdom in the counseling process. Jesus said that His sheep would know His voice and would follow Him because the voice of a stranger they would not recognize (John 10:1–5, 27). As caregivers, it is critical that we learn to listen for, recognize, and obey the voice of the Shepherd. As we listen for the, "still small voice" of the Lord, we will learn how to distinguish His wisdom from that of the world. James 3:17 is helpful here in describing the elements of wisdom that "comes from above":

It is first pure:
- Our counsel should not be tainted by worldliness or selfish gain.
- Our counsel should be sound and based on God's Word.

It is peaceable:
- Our counsel should be given with the right attitude.
- Our counsel should not be contentious.

It is gentle:
- Our counsel should be approachable and easily entreated.
- Our counsel should be given with kindness.

It is reasonable:
- Our counsel should be practical and not hyper-spiritual.
- Our counsel should be applicable.

It is full of mercy:
- Our counsel should not be critical or judgmental.
- Our counsel should be compassionate.

It is full of good fruit:
- Our counsel should have a commitment to action.
- Our counsel should have measurable results.

It is unwavering:
- Our counsel should not be circumstantial.
- Our counsel should be based on biblical principles.

It is without hypocrisy:
- Our counsel should reflect the evidence of Christ in our own lives.
- Our counsel should be genuine and transparent.

Third, we must acknowledge that *prayer is an integral part of biblical helping* (cf. James 5:16). At the very least, a Christian counselor should be praying for a client before and in between counseling sessions, and quietly during sessions.

Where appropriate, and especially with Christian clients who are well motivated for help and growth, prayer should also be used with the client during the counseling session. A type of prayer called inner healing or the healing of memories from an emotionally painful past can be particularly helpful in certain cases.[54]

At the same time, we would note that the use of prayer and the Scriptures during counseling sessions requires discernment and sensitivity on the part of the counselor, as well as the consent of the client. This is especially true if the client is not a Christian or if the client is a Christian who is having significant struggles with the Lord and may not be ready to pray yet. There is a time and season for everything (Eccl. 3:1–8)—and it is necessary to find the *proper timing* with regard to the use of prayer and Scripture. Any discussion of spiritual issues or recommendations of spiritual resources in counseling should always be done in a caring and ethical way.[55]

Fourth, remember that *the ultimate goal of counseling is to make disciples or disciplers of clients.* If possible, counselors should seek to fulfill the Great Commission.[56] Crabb says that the basic goal of counseling is to free people to better worship and serve God by helping them toward maturity in Christ.[57] This will necessitate helping clients restore their personal identity in Christ so they can live out an identity-based morality rather than a performance-based morality. Counselors share a message of grace to help people move from a guilt-motivated identity and a life of self-atonement.[58] To do this effectively, a counselor needs to have several character qualities in addition to basic skills and knowledge.

This leads to the fifth principle that underlies our lay counseling model: *the personal qualities of the lay Christian counselor are important for effective counseling.*[59] These include qualities such as the following:

- *Faithfulness:* doing the little things without complaint so more can be entrusted; represents a person who has developed diligence and perseverance. "The things you have heard me say in the presence of many witnesses entrust to reliable people who will also be qualified to teach others" (2 Tim. 2:2).
- *Availability:* understanding that there is a need to be ready in season and out of season with a willingness to accept any assignment given by the Lord. "Then I heard the voice of the Lord, saying, 'Whom shall I send? And who will go for us?' And I said, 'Here am I. Send me!'" (Isa. 6:8).
- *Authenticity:* the capacity to be genuine, appropriately transparent, and vulnerable. "Love must be sincere [without hypocrisy]" (Rom. 12:9).
- *Humility:* the willingness to be broken as a servant for the kingdom's sake; allowing oneself to decrease, so that God may increase. "Take my yoke

upon you and learn from me, for I am gentle and humble in heart, and you will find rest for your souls" (Matt. 11:29).

- *Unconditional love:* caring for others sacrificially in nature and practice, as well as a matter of covenant. "Therefore, as God's chosen people, holy and dearly beloved, clothe yourselves with compassion, kindness, humility, gentleness and patience. Bear with each other and forgive one another if any of you has a grievance against someone. Forgive as the Lord forgave you. And over all these virtues put on love, which binds them all together in perfect unity" (Col. 3:12–14).

Counselors should have a knowledge of God's Word and have wisdom to apply it in practical ways (Rom. 15:14; Col. 3:16), as Adams has emphasized.[60] Some may be especially gifted in people-helping.[61] A lay Christian counselor should be a spiritually mature person (cf. Gal. 6:1–2), who, according to Collins, has self-understanding, understanding of others, acceptance of others, the ability to remain objective, and the ability to get along with people. In addition, he or she should be a real, "born again" believer (John 3:3), God-fearing, honest, willing to refer difficult cases (Ex. 18:21–22), thoroughly familiar with God's Word (2 Tim. 2:15), and a follower of Christ (1 Peter 2:21), who is the "Wonderful Counselor" (Isa. 9:6).[62]

Competent and godly counsel starts with our understanding that becoming equipped is a process. The Lord builds His people like He did the tabernacle, from the inside out. Our part in the process is to allow Him free rein to do whatever foundation work or excavation of the soul is required. We need to be formed, conformed, and transformed into deeper Christlikeness by the Holy Spirit's ministry in our lives.

Sixth, *counselors should recognize that a client's attitudes, motivations, and desire for help are crucial factors for determining whether counseling will be helpful or not.*[63] Some years ago Beverly Gomes-Schwartz reported results from a significant research study called the Vanderbilt Psychotherapy Study.[64] She found that the process dimension that most consistently predicted therapy or counseling outcome was the degree of client involvement in therapy. In her own words, "Patients who were not hostile or mistrustful and who actively contributed to the therapy interaction achieved greater changes than those who were withdrawn, defensive, or otherwise unwilling to engage in the therapy process."[65] Always be aware that there are limits to what you can accomplish with people, especially if they are not interested in changing or are not involved in the process of counseling.

Seventh, *the relationship between the counselor and the client is another significant variable having an impact on the effectiveness of counseling.* Good rapport and communication based on the so-called core conditions for therapeutic change, namely, the *facilitative* conditions of *empathy* (or understanding), *respect* (or caring for someone), and *concreteness* (or being specific), and the *action* conditions of *genuineness* (or being real), *confrontation* (or telling it like it is), and *immediacy* (or what is really going on between the two of you),[66] are important for effective counseling. Ephesians 4:15 seems to sum up this view quite well—speak the *truth* (e.g., covering the conditions of concreteness, immediacy, confrontation, and genuineness) in love (e.g., covering the conditions of respect or warmth, empathy, and genuineness).

That said, we would also agree with Adams that talking alone is not sufficient for dealing with problems. Counseling should lead eventually to definite decisions and actions that are in line with Scripture. For example, *confession*, while essential in dealing with problems involving obvious sins, is often not enough—it should lead to attempts at *reconciliation* and *restitution* where necessary (see Matt. 5:21–26; 18:15–20).[67] *Forgiveness* of others who may have hurt the client is also an important process for the client to work through, with God's grace and help.[68]

Eighth, *effective counseling is a process that unfolds cyclically, from exploration to understanding to action phases.* What do we mean? The views of Carkhuff and Egan are helpful here.[69] We would stress the need to explore and understand adequately the client's problems before undertaking courses of action or giving directives to the client. That process begins by joining the client where he or she is in the given moment—not where the counselor is—and then exploring the presenting issue, determining the right course of action, and finally by taking tangible steps in a new direction.

Jesus was the master of this process, and an excellent illustration of it is His interaction with the woman at the well (John 4:1–42). When Jesus met the woman, she was drawing water, and He joined her in what she was doing by asking for a drink. Culturally we know this Samaritan woman did not have a good reputation in her village because of the time of day she was at the well and the fact that she was alone. Jesus met her in what she was doing and thinking when He described the concept of true worship and living water. As you read the interaction, you can almost see the wheels turning in her head. Again, He shifts the focus of the conversation and this time speaks to matters of the heart when He asks her to bring her husband to Him. By speaking prophetically into this woman's life, He draws her to Himself, and she returns to her village where she is received back into the community because of her testimony that she has met the Messiah. Jesus had several days of fruitful ministry among this community.

Crabb provided an integration of various views on this subject into a comprehensive and biblical model of the counseling process that takes place in seven stages. In *stage one,* the counselor helps the client to identify his or her problem (negative) feelings. Freeing up the emotions is vitally important in lay counseling ministry. The psalmist encourages believers, writing, "Pour out your hearts to him, for God is our refuge" (Ps. 62:8). The process is much like cleaning out an infected wound; it is a sore, sensitive, and painful area that we do not want anyone to touch. However, infections left untreated often spread; so too within the human soul. Infected feelings influence behaviors, thinking, and relationships. Brokenness and woundedness must be cleansed through the agency of the Holy Spirit and in the hands of a capable and trustworthy helper.

In *stage two*, the counselor helps the client to identify his or her problem (negative) behaviors. Recognizing and admitting (or confessing) is a critical first step in the recovery process. A person cannot *extinguish* a problem until he or she can *distinguish* the problem. Breaking the "power of the secret" in a person's life is a liberating experience that then sets a course toward true freedom in Christ. Lamentations 3:40 challenges us: "Let us examine our ways [behavior] and test them, and let us return to the LORD."

In *stage three*, the focus is on identifying the client's problem (wrong) thinking. Such problem thinking often has to do with erroneous, irrational, unrealistic, and eventually unbiblical or sinful assumptions about how to meet the basic needs or longings for security and significance apart from the Lord. Examples of such unbiblical basic assumptions include these: "I will be secure if I have a loving spouse," and "I will be significant if I excel and become the president of the company."

In *stage four*, the counselor attempts to teach or clarify right, biblical thinking (basically "I am secure and significant in Christ and His love for me"), and in *stage five*, to secure a commitment on the part of the client to such biblical thinking in obedience to the Lord and His Word. Renewing the mind transforms us (Rom. 12:2). Imagine trying to weed a garden when it has not rained for weeks on end. The ground is hard, and if we tug, we usually only get the top of the weed, leaving the root firmly entrenched. God is a faithful and loving gardener and He often tries to "weed" in a person's "heart garden." If the heart is hard, the root of the problem remains. God's Word is like a refreshing and cleansing rain (Eph. 5:26); it changes one's thinking on a matter and softens the heart ground. Only then can God remove the weeds (distorted beliefs), root and all.

In *stage six*, the client is encouraged to plan and carry out biblical or right behavior. Exercising the will is possible when a client assumes a measure of personal responsibility over the process. The truth that a lay counselor must fundamentally grasp is that *we* cannot save anyone, change anyone, heal anyone, or restore anyone. We can introduce our clients to the One who is able, and they must make choices at that point.

When Jesus was talking with several of the disciples (Peter, Andrew, James, and John) regarding their occupation as *fishermen*, Jesus used a play on words to describe what they would do in following Him: "I will make you become *fishers of men*" (Mark 1:17 NASB, emphasis added). This can be simply translated: "You catch them and I'll clean them!" Always remember that we "catch" (bring) people into the presence of God, so that He can do the work of cleaning.

Finally, in *stage seven*, the client can identify and enjoy Spirit-controlled feelings of security and significance.[70] When a person's relationship with Christ is healthy, balanced, and based on God's Word, he or she is better able to experience rest and feel secure in that truth, as well as understand that a true sense of value and significance flows out of this relationship.

A ninth principle that underlies our lay counseling model is that *directive or nouthetic counseling is an important part of Christian counseling, but the style or approach used by the counselor should be flexible*. We advocate a lay counseling model that incorporates Adams's nouthetic counseling. The counseling process is guided by several New Testament passages, as well as a number of Old Testament passages relevant to a ministry of effective counseling (e.g., Ex. 18:5–26; 1 Kings 12:9, 28; Ps. 55:13–14; Prov. 12:15; 13:10; 19:20; 20:18). Many of these Old Testament passages contain Hebrew words that are often translated as "counsel" and have meanings associated with advice in the form of guidance or direction.[71] However, we would differ from some of those in the nouthetic counseling model in that we do not believe it is the only valid approach to biblical counseling.

As pointed out earlier, our lay counseling model utilizes many of the insights of Adams and those who have followed him, while also accepting Carter's view that biblical counseling is more adequately based on *parakaleo* and *paraklesis* rather than only on *noutheteo* or *nouthesia*—Greek terms found in the New Testament that are most relevant to counseling from a biblical perspective.[72] Biblical counseling should include not only the nouthetic or directive and confrontational approach, but also utilize other *parakaleo* functions of comforting, encouraging, and supporting at appropriate times.

David Carlson similarly argued from the Scriptures that Jesus' style of relating or helping was flexible in this way. His conversations with people ranged from a prophetic, confrontational style to a more priestly, accepting style, and he had a pastoral style that fell somewhere in between, depending on the need of the person to whom he was ministering. Examples of the prophetic approach to Christian counseling include convicting, confronting, preaching, lecturing, thinking for, talking to, proclaiming the truth, and *disturbing the comfortable*. Examples of the priestly approach to Christian counseling include comforting, confessional, interviewing, listening, thinking with, talking with, affirming truth, and *comforting the disturbed*.[73]

Following this last point, a tenth principle of our lay counseling model is that it *remains flexible with regard to specific techniques or methods to be used in counseling at different stages or phases.* The Scriptures should be the ultimate screening device for accepting or rejecting particular techniques (cf. 1 Thess. 5:21). A number of cognitive-behavioral strategies or other secular techniques may be helpful and can be used by lay Christian counselors with some training and supervision, including the use of self-talk (cognitive restructuring), imagery, relaxation strategies, prayer in counseling (as described by Norman Wright),[74] and misbelief therapy methods (as described by William Backus).[75] In addition, there are several useful secular books on cognitive-behavioral methods that can be used in training lay counselors to help people change, including those by Beck, Cormier, Nurius and Osborn, Craske, and Leahy, and workbooks by Greenberger and Padesky, and Riggenbach.[76]

Again, however, we should carefully limit and qualify our use of cognitive-behavioral methods in Christian counseling, especially when we are training or teaching lay counselors in particular techniques. We suggest the following guidelines for utilizing a biblical approach to cognitive-behavior therapy work with a client:

1. Emphasize the primacy of agape love (1 Corinthians 13) and the need to develop a warm, empathic, and genuine relationship with the client.

2. Deal more adequately with the past, especially unresolved developmental issues or childhood traumas, and use inner healing or healing of memories judiciously and appropriately.

3. Pay special attention to the meaning of spiritual, experiential, and even mystical aspects of life and faith according to God's wisdom as revealed in Scripture and by the Holy Spirit's teaching ministry (John 14:26). Do not overemphasize the rational, thinking dimension, although biblical, propositional truth will still be given its rightful place of importance. The possibility of demonic involvement in some cases will also require serious consideration and appropriate action.

4. Focus on how problems in thought and behavior may often (not always, because of other factors, e.g., organic or biological) underlie problem feelings (Prov. 23:7; Rom. 12:1–2; Eph. 4:22–24; Phil. 4:8). Use biblical truth (John 8:32), not relativistic, empirically oriented values, to restructure thinking and change behavior.

5. Emphasize the Holy Spirit's ministry in bringing about inner healing, as well as cognitive, behavioral, and emotional change. Using prayer and affirmation of God's Word to facilitate dependence on the Lord will produce deep and lasting personality change and will not inadvertently encourage sinful self-sufficiency (cf. Phil. 4:13).

6. Pay more attention to larger contextual factors like familial, societal, religious, and cultural influences, and hence utilize appropriate community resources in therapeutic interventions, including the church as a body of believers and fellow "priests" to one another (1 Cor. 12; 1 Peter 2:5, 9).

7. Use only those techniques that are consistent with biblical truth; do not simplistically use whatever techniques work. This will reaffirm scriptural perspectives on suffering, including the possibility of the "blessings of mental anguish," with the ultimate goal of counseling being holiness or Christlikeness (Rom. 8:29), not necessarily temporal happiness. However, such a goal will include being more open to receiving God's love and grace, and growing thereby to be more Christlike, and overcoming mental anguish due to unbiblical, erroneous beliefs (i.e., misbeliefs).

8. Utilize rigorous outcome research methodology before making definitive statements about the superiority of cognitive-behavior therapy.[77]

An eleventh key principle in our lay counseling model is that *effective counseling requires cultural sensitivity*. Some knowledge of cross-cultural counseling principles and methods, especially those written from a Christian perspective, is helpful and even essential for effective counseling. American society is becoming even more pluralistic and multicultural, and in light of the trends associated with globalization, some awareness of other cultures is needed. The challenge put forth by Collins many years ago is even more pertinent today: "Christian counselors have given very little consideration to cross-cultural counseling, and any approach to biblically based counseling in the future must not neglect this significant area."[78]

Derald Wing Sue and David Sue wrote a well-known secular book on counseling among culturally diverse people, including Asian-Americans, African-Americans, Latinos, and American Indians.[79] Other books and articles on cross-cultural counseling from a biblical perspective have also been published over the last two decades, notably David Hesselgrave's *Counseling Cross-Culturally* and David Augsburger's *Pastoral Counseling across Cultures*.[80] Because this is such a growing area today, we will have more to say about cultural competency in a later chapter.

A twelfth principle for lay counseling is to utilize appropriate *outreach and prevention techniques in lay Christian counseling*. As an extension of the church body, we share in the mission of the church and are called to care for the downtrodden and those in need with the mercy of Jesus. In developing your lay counseling ministry, carefully consider how you can align counseling ministry with the broader ministry of the church and its mission:[81]

- *Going* (evangelism). Go to people with the good news—have a strong commitment to reach out to the hurting and incorporate the gospel message of redemption and transformation.
- *Gathering* (fellowship). Gather people into community—emphasize the critical importance of meaningful relationship for the purpose of personal and spiritual growth, accountability, and connectedness.
- *Giving* (stewardship). Give opportunities for lay counselors to use their God-given gifts to make a difference in the lives of broken people.
- *Growing* (teaching). Grow others into fully devoted followers of Christ—guard the sacred trust that has been given by God in the process of restoration and discipleship, endeavoring to journey alongside those who need care.
- *Glorifying* (worship). Glorify God in all of it—acknowledge that it is God, through the agency of the Holy Spirit, who sets people free, changes broken lives, and is worthy of all honor and praise.

Jeffrey Prater noted that the church has historically provided prevention and community outreach services, and most of the biblically based models for lay Christian counseling have tended to ignore the historical tradition of the church as a caring *community*. Instead, counseling models have tended to focus on individual counseling, namely, that emotional problems are due to *individual* defects or deficits. To correct this imbalance, Prater made six proposals for including lay counselor training in interventions on a broader psychosocial level, so that such training is more integrated with the other outreach ministries of the church:[82]

1. Lay counselors should be trained to assess the role of environmental stressors in the development and maintenance of emotional problems. Examples of such stressors include poverty, unemployment, racism, sexism, and lack of social support, and they may need to be dealt with in counseling.
2. Lay counselors should be trained in the techniques of community outreach and empowerment. They should bring services directly to people where possible and appropriate, rather than merely waiting for people to come and use the services available.
3. Lay counselors should be trained in cultural awareness and sensitivity so that lay counseling services will be appropriate for people besides white, middle-class clients dealing with life problems. Cultural barriers represent a major obstacle to providing mental health services.
4. Lay counselors should be trained to be aware of and make use of

existing support systems and services within churches. Collins, for example, issued this challenge: "We must learn to use worship, study programs, discussion groups, church socials, and other activities—whether religious or not—to help people avoid problems or show them how to cope more effectively with them."[83] Many churches provide informal services to the community, which are not well publicized or known to the public. Examples of such services include pastoral visitation of the sick, provision of transportation to support meetings and other appointments, and friendly visitation of homebound elderly. Lay counselors need to be aware of these informal services and resources so that they can make appropriate referrals of needy people to them.

5. Lay counselors should be trained in how to develop new support systems within the church where needed. Some examples of these systems include small groups for individuals or families, regular breakfast or dinner meetings, Bible studies, and prevention-oriented training seminars on topics like stress management, parenting skills, and conflict resolution.

6. Lay counselors should be trained to communicate more actively and regularly with others, particularly the leaders involved in other outreach ministries of the church, so that a more coordinated and integrated package of ministries would result. Regular meetings could be arranged for the purpose of providing information, mutual encouragement, support, and prayer for one another's ministries.

In the thirteenth principle, we recognize that lay counseling often focuses on crisis events, and therefore *crisis counseling is important.* We live in a broken world, we suffer the sinful choices of others, and we must deal with the consequences of our own unwise or sinful choices. We also face the reality of spiritual warfare and demonic attack. Most crises tend to dissipate within six to eight weeks, though there can be any number of disruptive factors at work. The critical issue is how the crisis is being managed, which often determines the outcome. Managed poorly, the pain, grief, and aftermath can be magnified beyond the pain of the original event. Unresolved issues sometimes result in a person feeling "stuck," creating what is referred to as a *trans-crisis state.*

A helpful place to look as you develop your own lay counseling model is the training program developed by the coauthor of this revised edition of lay counseling, Eric Scalise. In his training program, the ABCs of Crisis Intervention, he details six steps for addressing a crisis situation in counseling:[84]

Step 1. ACHIEVE a Connection with the Other Person

- Instill confidence by demonstrating a strong positive voice and attitude.
- Understand the power of presence in the moment.
- Be calm and in control of yourself.
- Listen! Listen! Listen!
- Encourage the expression of feelings.
- Be empathic as opposed to sympathetic.
- Do not minimize, devalue, or underestimate the situation.
- Begin where the other person is (spiritually, emotionally, cognitively, etc.).
- Accept the person as he or she is (not necessarily the person's choices or behavior).

Step 2. BREAK DOWN the Problem

- Look for the major issue(s) or theme(s).
- Assess how critical the situation or crisis really is in terms of thoughts, feelings, behaviors, experiences, incidents, etc. Be aware of the tendency to deny, minimize, and/or underreport.
- Determine the priorities for effective intervention and/or care, especially any life-threatening or other critical decisions that need to be made—*safety first!*
- Look for those issues that can be attended to easily and quickly.
- Examine what has been tried already.
- Look at new alternatives and directions that can be considered.
- Examine any potential consequences of actions that may be taken.
- Work toward appropriate ownership of the problem or situation.

Step 3. COMMIT to a Plan of Action

- Identify all potential support systems and resources.
- Encourage the formulation of a plan, building on the person's strengths, having two to three initial goals, incorporating specific objectives (smaller steps) to meet those goals, and ensuring that they are attainable, behavioral, and measurable.
- Set time limits to initiate the plan.
- Be firm and supportive in working through resistance.
- Know when you are in over your head.
- Have referral sources available, and be ready to utilize them.
- Contact a supervisor, member of the leadership team, and/or director as appropriate.

Step 4. DOCUMENT the Interaction

- Write down any identifying information.
- Document the important points of what you said, did, or recommended.
- Note any issues or concerns, especially those that may have legal, ethical, or liability-related implications.
- Keep the documentation confidential.

Step 5. EXPLAIN the Plan of Action

- Make sure the person understands exactly what the next step(s) are.
- Consider writing down the plan of action and/or contacts and phone numbers.
- Have the person repeat the plan of action back to you verbally.
- Notify a family member, close friend, pastor, etc. (if appropriate), and explain the plan as appropriate.
- Tell the person that you will follow up, and give him or her the day and time.

Step 6. FOLLOW UP as Soon as Possible

- Contact the person the next day if possible or as agreed upon.
- Verify that the action plan has been implemented/started.

- Provide ongoing support and accountability.
- Assess the ongoing level of isolation and the proactive/consistent commitment to stay connected to available/recommended support systems (both within the church and the community at large).

A final, fourteenth principle underlying an effective lay counseling model is that *lay Christian counselors must be aware of their limited knowledge and skill in helping people with needs and problems.* Lay counselors need to be willing and able to make good referrals in a supportive and sensitive way, steering their clients to other more experienced and better trained counselors or other appropriate professionals (e.g., lawyers, physicians, financial consultants) when necessary. Collins, Grunlan, and Lambrides have developed helpful guidelines regarding when, where, and how to refer a client.[85] William Oglesby has also written a helpful book titled *Referrals in Pastoral Counseling.*[86]

Collins suggested that a referral is necessary when a helper lacks the time, emotional stamina or stability, or the skill or experience to continue the counseling. As a general rule, we should refer whenever we don't seem to be helping someone deal with the problem or grow as a whole person. Even more specifically, it is important to seek outside help for counselees who

- are in legal difficulties;
- have severe financial needs;
- require medical attention;
- are severely depressed or suicidal;
- will require more time than we can give;
- want to shift to another counselor;
- show extremely aggressive behavior;
- make excessive use of drugs or alcohol;
- arouse strong feelings of dislike, sexual stimulation, or threat in the counselor; or
- appear to be severely disturbed.[87]

In this chapter we have attempted to lay out fourteen key principles that should be considered in developing a biblical model for effective lay counseling. Table 1 provides a summary of the main points. In concluding this chapter, we want to emphasize the primacy of agape love (see 1 Corinthians 13) in the process of effective biblical counseling. In a beautiful passage from 1 John, John, often called the "apostle of love," leaves no doubt about God's nature:

"Be*loved*, let us *love* one another, for *love* is from God; and everyone who *love*s is born of God and knows God. The one who does not *love* does not know God, for God is *love*. By this the *love* of God was manifested in us, that God has sent His only begotten Son into the world so that we might live through Him. In this is *love*, not that we *love*d God, but that He *love*d us and sent His Son to be the propitiation for our sins. Be*loved*, if God so *love*d us, we also ought to *love* one another. No one has seen God at any time; if we *love* one another, God abides in us, and His *love* is perfected in us. By this we know that we abide in Him and He in us, because He has given us of His Spirit. We have seen and testify that the Father has sent the Son to be the Savior of the world.

"Whoever confesses that Jesus is the Son of God, God abides in him, and he in God. We have come to know and have believed the *love* which God has for us. God is *love*, and the one who abides in *love* abides in God, and God abides in him. By this, *love* is perfected with us, so that we may have confidence in the day of judgment; because as He is, so also are we in this world. There is no fear in *love*; but perfect *love* casts out fear, because fear involves punishment, and the one who fears is not perfected in *love*. We *love*, because He first *love*d us. If someone says, 'I *love* God,' and hates his brother, he is a liar; for the one who does not *love* his brother whom he has seen, cannot *love* God whom he has not seen. And this commandment we have from Him, that the one who *love*s God should *love* his brother also." (4:7–21 NASB, emphasis added)

When we counsel others in agape love, we show them warmth and develop an empathic and genuine relationship with the client. In Matthew 22:34–40, Jesus distilled the essence of who He is and His divine purpose into just two core statements: first, to love God with all our heart, soul, mind, and strength; and second, to love our neighbors as we do ourselves. His mission statement is "Love God and love people." And that love was manifested to the world in fulfillment of the words of Isaiah (61:1–3). His mission of love, as described by Isaiah, speaks directly to this ministry of lay counseling. As counselors, we "proclaim good news to the poor . . . bind up the brokenhearted . . . proclaim freedom for the captives and release from darkness for the prisoners . . . proclaim the year of the LORD's favor . . . comfort all who mourn . . . bestow . . . the oil of joy . . . and a garment of praise . . . for the display of his splendor."

By emphasizing love, we do not mean to say that techniques are unimportant, simply that they are not the most important factor in effective counseling. In fact, research has shown that *client* variables, then *counselor* variables, and finally, *technique* variables, in that order, are the most important or powerful predictors of counseling or psychotherapy effectiveness and outcomes.[88] From a biblical perspective, however, there are several things we *must* earnestly seek:

- Humility—to approach the one who is hurting
- Discernment—to understand what God is saying and doing
- Wisdom—to know what to do with what God reveals
- Grace—to apply God's solution in the matter
- Power—to push through the resistance of the "evil one"
- Love—to "cover a multitude of sins"

Table 1: Summary of a Biblical Model for Effective Lay Counseling

Basic View of Humanity	Basic View of Counseling	Basic Principles of Effective Lay Counseling
1. Basic psychological and spiritual needs include needs for security (love), significance (meaning/impact), and hope (forgiveness). 2. The basic problem is sin, but not all emotional suffering is due to personal sin.	Somewhat interchangeable with "psychotherapy"	1. The Holy Spirit's ministry as counselor is crucial—depend on Him. 2. The Bible is a foundational and comprehensive (not exhaustive) guide for counseling. 3. Prayer is an integral part of biblical counseling.

Basic View of Humanity	Basic View of Counseling	Basic Principles of Effective Lay Counseling
3. The ultimate goal of humanity is to know and enjoy God and spiritual health.		4. The ultimate goal of counseling is maturity in Christ and fulfilling the Great Commission.
4. Problem feelings are usually due to problem behavior and, more fundamentally, problem thinking—however, biological and demonic factors should also be considered.		5. Personal qualities of the counselor are important, especially spiritual ones.
		6. Client's attitudes, motivations, and desire for help are important.
5. There is a holistic view of persons—with physical, mental/emotional, social, and spiritual dimensions.		7. The relationship between counselor and client is significant.
		8. Effective counseling is a process involving exploration, understanding, and action phases, with a focus on changing problem thinking.
		9. Style or approach in counseling should be flexible.
		10. Specific techniques or methods of counseling should be consistent with Scripture—cognitive-behavioral ones may be especially helpful, with qualifications.
		11. Cultural sensitivity and cross-cultural counseling skills are required.
		12. Outreach and prevention skills in the context of a caring community are important.
		13. Crisis counseling is important.
		14. Awareness of limitations and referral skills are also important.

We end this chapter with a note of appreciation from a former client who was seen in a local church lay counseling service context. Her words, more than anything we can say, capture the primacy of agape love and real caring in effective lay Christian counseling:

So many books
with so many words
yet so hard it is
to say
the things that touch
a human breast
in the passing
of one day.
Like a card
or flower
is a strength'ning hand
like the warming
of the sun
is a list'ning ear, or
the sharing of
a battle
fought, and won . . .
a helper
and a counsellor
when days were hard
and sad . . .
a tender sympathizer
in the sorrow
that I had . . .
a stronger arm to lean upon
a voice
that spoke of God
your heart
so full of hope
I knew He knew the way
I trod . . .
and slowly
an awareness
of the coming

of the morn
for as we spoke
within my soul
a greater hope
was born
until the colours,
red and gold
had filled
the eastern sky. . . .
I mounted up
with eagles' wings
and felt
that I could FLY!
Someone who prayed,
someone who cared
in my life
as the course was run . . .
thank you for being
who you are . . .
a friend,
when I needed one.

CHAPTER 4

The Research Literature on Lay Counseling and the Role of Faith

The literature on lay counseling, as well as the role of faith in counseling, has mushroomed and expanded in recent years in both secular and Christian circles. This chapter reviews some of the literature that is now available,[1] beginning with secular sources and then the existing Christian literature.

SECULAR LITERATURE

Lay counseling has now become a significant aspect of the contemporary mental health scene. As we review the literature, we will begin by looking at some of the reasons why there has been growth in this area and then examine some of the potential problems.

Reasons for Using Lay Counselors

Why has there been sudden growth in developing nonprofessional lay counselors? As we mentioned earlier, there is an acknowledged shortage of mental health professionals to meet the ever-increasing demand for their services. Many articles and books reference a national survey conducted in 1957 in the United States, which found that when people had personal problems and sought help, only about 27 percent of them went to psychiatrists, psychologists, and other professional mental health sources (e.g., specialists or agencies). About 29 percent consulted their family physician, and 42 percent sought help from the clergy.[2] Looking at these data, Gerald Gurin, Joseph Veroff, and Sheila Feld concluded: "These findings underscore the crucial role that non-psychiatric resources—particularly clergymen and physicians—play in the treatment process. They are the major therapeutic agents."[3]

A similar national survey was conducted in 1976, and it also revealed that a significant number of people who sought help for their personal problems consulted lay helpers like the clergy (39 percent) and their family physicians (21 percent). However, this later survey showed that a significantly greater percentage of people—49 percent—were now seeking help from psychiatrists, psychologists, and other professional mental health sources (specialists or agencies).[4] These trends show that in the latter part of the twentieth century, Americans were more willing than ever to consult mental health professionals. Today we are living in what one author has called "the psychological society."[5] Nevertheless, while there has been a sharp rise in the number of people turning to mental health professionals for help, a significant number of people still seek help from nonprofessional or paraprofessional counselors like the clergy and family physicians (as additional and more contemporary research is noted later in this chapter).

A closely related reason in favor of developing a lay counseling model has to do with the phenomenon of "spontaneous remission." This refers to the finding that a good number of patients with emotional disorders seem to recover over a two-year period without any professional treatment at all.[6] Estimates of such spontaneous recovery rates vary from 43 percent to 65 percent of "untreated" patients. However, "spontaneous remission" is a misleading term, since many of such patients obtained counsel, advice, and support from a variety of helping persons, for example, spouses, friends, teachers, physicians, and clergy—"persons untrained in formal psychotherapy, but who practice a kind of natural therapy."[7] Lay counselors such as the clergy and physicians are often sought after by people who have personal problems, and they seem to succeed quite well in helping such people, based on indirect evidence bearing on spontaneous recovery rates.

More direct evidence supporting the effectiveness of lay or paraprofessional counseling is also available from the research literature comparing the effectiveness of lay counseling with that of professional counseling. Earlier reports often quoted in this regard are E. G. Poser's study on group therapy conducted by untrained female college students with schizophrenics,[8] and Robert Carkhuff and Charles Truax's study on lay group counseling involving minimal training.[9] Since that time, additional studies have been conducted. In a widely cited review of forty-two comparative studies published in 1979, J. A. Durlak concluded that paraprofessionals or lay counselors were generally as effective as, and sometimes even better than, professional helpers, especially when the counseling involved more specific target problems presented by college students or adults.[10] However, little information is available on the factors that may account for the effectiveness of such lay counselors, untrained or minimally trained. Some have suggested that "naive enthusiasm"[11] and "flexible attitudes"[12] may be important ones.

Since Durlak's review was published, H. H. Strupp and S. W. Hadley have reported the results of their important Vanderbilt study,[13] which essentially showed that untrained college professors did as well as professionally trained expert therapists in helping neurotic college students. This gives further support to Durlak's findings and conclusion that "professional mental health education, training, and experience do not appear to be necessary prerequisites for an effective helping person."[14] It should be pointed out that more recent reviews of the secular literature have included critiques of Durlak's findings, but the most recent statistical reanalyses of the research evidence from the more reliable studies have supported Durlak's major findings and conclusion.[15]

J. S. Berman and N. C. Norton asked the key question, "Does professional training make a therapist more effective?" Their answer, after further review and statistical reanalysis of the better studies conducted to date comparing the effectiveness of lay counselors with that of professional helpers, is still no.[16] Other acknowledged leaders in the mental health field have expressed similar views based on their own experience and research. For example, after twenty-five years of practicing and researching psychotherapy, Dr. Joseph Matarazzo concluded:

> With the exception of that very small percentage—those, for example, who are severely disturbed by a severe life-crisis, depression or immobilizing anxiety and need the services of a highly trained, licensed psychologist—what I, and the majority of talking psychotherapists, accomplish in psychotherapy cannot be distinguished from what is accomplished between very good friends over coffee every morning in neighborhoods and in countless work settings anywhere.[17]

Similarly, Dr. Jerome Frank has said, "Anyone with a modicum of human warmth, common sense, some sensitivity to human problems, and a desire to help, can benefit many candidates for psychotherapy."[18]

Note that the debate over the research data apparently supporting the effectiveness of lay or paraprofessional counselors and the interpretation of such data is still not settled. In a more recent review of the literature on the effectiveness of psychotherapy or counseling, M. J. Lambert, D. A. Shapiro, and A. E. Bergin summarized the major findings from studies comparing lay or paraprofessional helpers and professional helpers. They drew this cautious conclusion:

> Although the failure of this literature to show unique therapeutic effectiveness for trained professionals is sobering, these studies are flawed in several respects. Many of the studies deal with types of cases that are not typical of those treated in the outcome studies reported in this chapter. Controls, criteria, and follow-up are often not rigorous, and frequently we seem to be observing

improvements in morale of schizophrenics or mildly distressed persons due to attention and support. We are not observing substantial therapeutic effects in the usual kinds of cases. This is not to downgrade the importance of the effects observed but to suggest that they have some limitations. They may not generalize to representative patient populations or less selective groups of paraprofessionals. On the other hand, the studies do suggest that common therapeutic factors are not the sole domain of formal therapy and that they may be useful in many cases or settings. Definitive studies are yet to be done on this matter.[19]

R. P. Lorion and R. D. Felner recently reviewed similar literature and came to this somewhat more optimistic though still cautious conclusion:

The 42 studies in question have been examined with a degree of intensity rarely found in the behavioral sciences. In spite of repeated analyses of their methodological soundness, the reported findings and resulting conclusions are unlikely to be accepted without further debate and question. The issue of concern is too central to be considered closed at this point. If the thrust of this set of reviews is indeed justified, one must, at the very least, consider paraprofessional resources as a legitimate factor in planning mental health services. . . . That they can contribute cannot be discounted. What remains unclear, however, are the conditions under which their contributions can be maximized—the types of interventions and patients for which this resource is most appropriate.[20]

Furthermore, there are two other studies not covered by the reviews cited so far, which appear to support the comparative effectiveness of professional therapists over lay or paraprofessional helpers. In one study, Brigham Young University psychologists Gary Burlingame and Sally Barlow found that group therapy clients led by both professionals and nonprofessionals improved significantly more than clients assigned to a waiting-list control group. At the midpoint of the fifteen-week group therapy series, clients seen by professionals had actually deteriorated, whereas those seen by nonprofessionals had improved significantly. At the end of therapy, there were no significant differences between clients seen by professionals and those seen by nonprofessionals. However, at a six-month follow-up, clients seen by professionals maintained and even built on their gains, whereas those seen by nonprofessionals had gotten worse.[21] The results of this study, therefore, raise some questions about the long-term therapeutic effects of counseling conducted by nonprofessionals and point to the need for more long-term follow-up studies.

In a second study, M. P. Carey and T. G. Burish provided relaxation training to cancer chemotherapy patients, using three delivery techniques: professionally administered, paraprofessionally administered (by a trained volunteer), and audiotaped administered.[22] Professionally administered relaxation training was found to be significantly more effective than paraprofessionally administered and audiotaped administered relaxation training in reducing specific symptoms like physiological arousal and emotional distress. It should be noted, however, as Carey and Burish pointed out, that the hospital setting in which the study was conducted may have been more difficult or troublesome for the paraprofessionals than the professionals, who were also more technically skilled in relaxation training and more clinically experienced in general. Nevertheless, this study did find professionals to be more effective than paraprofessionals or audio recordings in providing relaxation training to cancer chemotherapy patients seen in a hospital setting.

More recently, professionally trained and experienced therapists have been found to do better than paraprofessionals in outpatient settings at having lower numbers of client dropouts.[23] Other results from research favoring professional experience have been reported in a study on manualized treatments with children with conduct disorder and in a study of group cognitive-behavioral therapy for depression at six-month follow-up.[24] David Barlow asserted in 2004 that significant clinical expertise and a strong therapeutic relationship are required to maximize the effectiveness or efficacy of psychological treatments, especially in helping clients with more severe psychopathology, based on findings from some recent research.[25] However, the empirical support for his view is still limited.

Despite the results of these more recent studies that seem to favor professional experience, the majority of outcome studies comparing the effectiveness of professional therapists to lay counselors have found that lay counselors are generally as effective as professional therapists for most common problems experienced by clients, according to more recent reviews[26] and reports or studies.[27] However, the debate over this issue will continue, and much more research is needed before more definitive conclusions can be made about the greater effectiveness of professionally trained and experienced therapists or counselors.

Dr. Bernie Zilbergeld, some years ago, in a significant, but somewhat controversial book, asserted that people would solve most problems better by talking to friends, spouses, relatives, or anyone else who appears to be doing well what the people believe they themselves are doing poorly! He made this assertion, however, only after carefully reviewing numerous research studies and coming to the conclusion that professional psychotherapy or counseling is often of little or no help and at times can even make people worse.[28] His views and conclusions reflect the growing emphasis in the secular literature on the benefits of using lay counselors, as well as the growing disillusionment with professional counseling, since there is still no agreement or consensus concerning its effectiveness despite a significant increase in research studies in recent years.[29]

Several researchers, after reviewing psychotherapy versus placebo studies, have even concluded that for real patients there is no evidence that the benefits of professional counseling or psychotherapy are greater than those of placebo treatment, although the shortcomings of such a review based on statistical reanalyses of the data have been pointed out,[30] and hence not everyone agrees with this conclusion. Other researchers have concluded that the benefits of psychotherapy are now well supported and beyond doubt.[31] Still, many others strongly disagree, pointing out the weaknesses of statistical reanalyses of data on the outcome or effects of psychotherapy, and emphasizing the superiority of behavior therapy over traditional psychotherapy for certain problems like phobic and obsessive-compulsive disorders and some sexual dysfunctions.[32]

At present there is no general agreement regarding the overall effectiveness of psychotherapy or professional counseling, except that many agree that psychotherapy is more effective than no therapy at all. Some authors, like Sol Garfield,[33] have contended that for research studies to yield more meaningful data on the effectiveness of therapeutic interventions more specific and refined questions should be asked. For example: What counseling or therapeutic interventions will be most effective with what clients? What kind of therapist will work best with what interventions and with what clients? Therapeutic interventions or counseling procedures should be tailor-made (individualized), and their effectiveness for specific problems can then be more systematically evaluated.

More recent reviews of the outcome research on the effectiveness or efficacy of psychotherapy, for example, by M. J. Lambert and B. M. Ogles in 2004 and Tan in 2011, have concluded that psychotherapy is at least moderately effective, but it does not help a significant number of people (around 20 percent) and may even be harmful to a small percentage (around 5 to 10 percent). There is also more research evidence for specific empirically supported treatments (ESTs,) and empirically supported therapy relationships (ESRs).[34]

Finally, Dr. Sheldon Korchin listed several other arguments or reasons that have been used to justify the training and use of lay counselors.[35] First, he emphasized the unique abilities of lay indigenous helpers in understanding and working effectively with clients from their own cultures. The assumption behind this argument is that such helpers may be more effective because they understand better, and often share, the cultural values and worldviews of such clients. Second, he mentioned the positive effects on the lay counselor himself or herself of being involved in lay counseling. Such positive effects include the psychological growth and increased competence of the lay counselor. It seems that the lay counselor may benefit as much as the client (if not more) in the lay counseling experience! Reissman has referred to this as the "helper therapy" principle.[36] Korchin argues that nonprofessional or lay counseling serves as an effective means for recruiting lay counselors into professional counseling careers. Several lay counselors may eventually end up pursuing clinical training and becoming professional counselors as a result of their experience doing lay counseling.

Problems with Using Lay Counselors

As mentioned earlier, there are arguments *against* the use of lay counselors as well, and many have noted problems. Korchin has noted several problems related to the use of lay counselors or nonprofessionals in a variety of helping roles.[37] Some problems may be related to lay counseling being a "nonprofessional" role, where role boundaries and limits are sometimes unclear. Lay counselors may try to do more than they are capable of doing or end up confused at times. They wonder whether they should remain "professionally objective" in their helping endeavors, precluding friendships with clients, or if they can be friends with their clients to a greater extent than professional counselors since lay counselors often provide friendship or peer counseling. There may also be problems related to the background and personal qualities of the nonprofessional. The lay counselor may feel insecurity because of lack of experience. Other problems may be related to professional values. Many professional counselors may be unwilling to support more nonprofessional or lay involvement in people-helping because of their own vested interests in and concern for prestige, social status, and income as professionals.

Finally, there may be problems related to program organization, training, and career development. Academic leaders in universities and professional training centers may resist having to train more lay counselors, preferring to concentrate instead on the training and education of professional counselors. Lay counselors may not have secure job opportunities and can face limited career development, finding only transient, temporary roles as nonprofessional helpers. This points to the need to create new teaching or training institutions and job opportunities for lay counselors. In particular, the possibility of negative effects on clients due to lay counseling (perhaps because of factors such as lack of experience and insecurity or unclear role boundaries on the part of the lay counselor) should be of real concern, since research has shown that psychotherapy or counseling provided even by professionals tends to hurt some clients.[38]

Examples, Selection, and Training of Lay Counselors

Korchin has also described a number of nonprofessional programs using lay counselors.[39] They include the use of student volunteers in mental hospitals, mature women as mental health counselors, college students as companion therapists to troubled boys, and indigenous nonprofessionals in dealing with the problems of poverty communities. A well-known prevention program known as the Primary Mental Health Project, conducted by psychologist Emory Cowen and his colleagues in Rochester, New York, has also used lay counselors (housewives as nonprofessional child aides) to work directly with high-risk children in the schools.[40]

In reviewing the selection of lay counselors, Korchin noted there is usually a formal assessment phase, which may involve interviews, psychological tests, and observation, but focuses mainly on personal attributes (e.g., warmth, compassion, general human relations skills, a lack of personal defensiveness, and "positive mental health") rather than intellectual skills, experience, or formal training. In training lay counselors, emphasis has been given to learning both general human-relations skills as well as particular psychological techniques that may be of special relevance to the specific role of the lay counselor.[41] The available literature on selection and training of lay counselors is covered in greater detail in later chapters of this book.

In summary, the secular literature, though somewhat limited over the past several decades, on the whole seems to justify the need for and support the effectiveness of lay counseling in its various forms, even when there are some potential problems or dangers.

CHRISTIAN LITERATURE

Over the past several decades, Christian authors have written numerous publications on lay counseling, especially counseling done within the context of the local church. This may be due to a growing dissatisfaction with and even an outright rejection of secular counseling and psychotherapy.[42] Many Christian authors have affirmed and advocated a scriptural or biblical approach to counseling with a special focus on the spiritual dimension so often neglected by secular approaches. Many of these authors also maintain that biblically based counseling can be conducted by lay Christians (who are not ordained pastors or mental health professionals), especially those who are specially gifted for a counseling ministry[43] or those who at least possess the personal qualities (e.g., goodness, knowledge, and wisdom) and a grasp of the Scriptures, that are seen to be essentials.[44]

Many years ago, psychologist O. Hobart Mowrer, a past president of the American Psychological Association, raised the question "Has evangelical religion sold its birthright for a mess of psychological pottage?"[45] He said:

> For several decades we psychologists looked upon the whole matter of sin and moral accountability as a great incubus and acclaimed our liberation from

it as epoch making. But at length we have discovered that to be free in this sense, that is, to have the excuse of being sick rather than sinful, is to court the danger of also becoming lost. . . . In becoming amoral, ethically neutral and free, we have cut the very roots of our being, lost our deepest sense of selfhood and identity, and with neurotics, themselves, we find ourselves asking: Who am I, what is my deepest destiny, what does living mean?[46]

Today evangelical leaders have begun to reclaim that birthright in a very definite way. Many of them are realizing that Christian or biblically based pastoral and lay counseling are valid, even better alternatives to the mess of psychological pottage. Not all leaders in the evangelical Christian counseling field reject secular clinical psychology and psychiatry completely—however, most, if not all, advocate going beyond the pottage to sound scriptural principles for wholesome living and for dealing with personal problems and the stresses of life.

Books on Biblically Based Approaches to Lay Christian Counseling

Several biblically based approaches to effective lay Christian counseling have been proposed over the past four decades. In the mid-1970s, Dr. Jay Adams advocated nouthetic counseling as a unique scriptural approach, using the Bible as the basic helping manual and emphasizing the need to be directive, to confront the client with the issue of sin.[47] He rejected as unbiblical the prescriptive aspects of secular professional counseling and psychotherapy.

Dr. Gary Collins was also influential in training Christians to become effective lay caregivers through his "people-helping" approach and training program, using what is valid and acceptable from psychology and the behavioral sciences from a biblical perspective, and consulting Scripture as the ultimate authority. He emphasized that effective people-helping requires a warm, empathic, and genuine believer who has good rapport with an open and motivated client. The effective helper focuses on the emotions, thoughts, and behavior of the helpee, using a variety of counseling skills, with the ultimate goal of making disciples and disciplers.[48] Collins wrote a widely used and comprehensive guide to Christian counseling[49] and edited a helpful book on practical approaches to Christian counseling.[50] He also served as general editor for a series of books called Resources for Christian Counseling and wrote the first volume.[51]

Dr. Lawrence Crabb Jr. is another well-known Christian psychologist who proposed a model for effective biblical counseling. His model was based on an integration of psychology and Christianity that gives the Scriptures final authority, and his model has been used by many local churches to train lay Christians.[52]

Essentially Crabb views sinful, unbiblical thinking to be at the root of most problem behaviors and problem feelings (i.e., those that are nonorganically caused). Such thinking involves trying to meet personal needs for security (love) and significance (meaning) apart from one's relationship with Jesus Christ. Crabb proposed three levels of lay counseling ministry for Christians: Level 1 is *counseling by encouragement*, involving all believers; Level 2 is *counseling by exhortation*, involving mature Christians with some basic counseling training; and Level 3 is *counseling by enlightenment*, involving a few gifted Christians with more advanced training in biblical counseling. (See chapter 7 for more on Crabb's three levels of counseling.)

Adams's nouthetic counseling, Collins's people-helping, and Crabb's biblical counseling represent three of the most foundational and influential approaches to Christian counseling. In the decades since they were first proposed, they have undergone some modifications and development, yet they have each had significant impact, especially on lay Christian counseling done in the context of the local church. The finer points of their approaches have been incorporated in the integrated biblical model for effective lay Christian counseling, which we presented in chapter 3.

Other important and more recent books in the area of lay Christian counseling or caregiving include those by Neil Anderson, William Arnold and Margaret Fohl, William Backus, Carol Baldwin, Martin Bobgan and Deidre Bobgan, Duncan Buchanan, Susan Oh Cha, Tim Clinton and Pat Springle, John Drakeford, John Drakeford and Claude King, Timothy Foster, Stephen Grunlan and Daniel Lambrides, Kenneth Haugk, Selwyn Hughes, Robert Kellemen, Karen Lampe, Isaac Lim and Shirley Lim, Stanley Lindquist, Paul Miller, Paul Morris, Evelyn Peterson, Harold Sala, John Sandford and Paula Sandford, Abraham Schmitt and Dorothy Schmitt, Ed Smith, Charles Solomon, Robert Somerville, Melvin Steinbron, Joan Sturkie and Gordon Bear, Siang-Yang Tan, Barbara Varenhorst with Lee Sparks, Richard Walters, Waylon Ward, Edward Welch, Paul Welter, Everett Worthington, and H. Norman Wright.[53] The more general field of "Christian counseling" from an evangelical perspective has also grown, with so many books being published that it is difficult to list all of them.[54]

Journal Articles on Lay Christian Counseling

In addition to the plethora of books now available in the literature on lay Christian counseling, numerous journal articles have been published. They cover a broad range of topics, including literature reviews on lay counseling within the local church; the selection, training, supervision, and evaluation of lay counselors; and lay counseling models and programs.[55] The relevant literature on each of these topics is covered in more detail in later chapters of this book. A special issue of the *Journal of Psychology and Christianity*, the official publication of the Christian Association for Psychological Studies, was devoted to lay Christian counseling.[56] It contains twelve articles covering a number of perspectives, programs, and proposals related to lay Christian counseling, which are briefly described in Tan's guest editorial preceding them. The American Association of Christian Counselors, the world's largest organized group of Christian faith-based caregivers, also publishes a quarterly magazine titled *Christian Counseling Today*. Regular contributors include some of the most well-known and respected leaders in the field.

Research on Lay Christian Counseling

Unfortunately, research regarding the effectiveness of training programs for lay Christian counselors, as well as the counseling provided by such counselors, is limited. Collins, in one of his books, briefly mentioned that the preliminary results of a research project conducted to evaluate the effectiveness of his people-helper training program seem to indicate that it increased both the sensitivity and effectiveness of those who wanted to be people-helpers, but he did not specify the measures used in the project.[57]

Tan also reported preliminary results using a self-report measure of knowledge of counseling and Christian counseling, competence in counseling and Christian counseling, and confidence in one's competence, which showed that lay counseling trainees improved significantly more than a control group of students who took a Bible course at Ontario Bible College.[58] Clearly, more sophisticated measures are needed for evaluating the effectiveness of lay counselor training. In another study, Siang-Yang Tan and Philip Sarff used a more comprehensive set of evaluation measures and administered them before and after a lay Christian counselor training program was conducted in a Chinese evangelical local church context. The results showed that after the training the lay counseling trainees rated themselves to be more knowledgeable and more competent in both counseling and Christian counseling, chose more understanding and less evaluative and supportive response styles, and were rated as being more empathic, respectful, and genuine based on an audiotaped role-play counseling situation. However, no control group was employed in this study.[59] C. A. Schaefer, L. Dodds, and Tan also found positive changes in attitudes toward peer counseling and on several scales on the Personal Orientation Inventory (POI) in a small number of subjects who received growth facilitator training for cross-cultural ministry, but again, no control group was used.[60]

D. M. Boan and T. Owens found peer ratings of lay counselor skill to be useful measures, which are related to client satisfaction, but they did not directly evaluate the effectiveness of their training program, and no control group was used.[61] Paul Welter also used a comprehensive package of evaluation measures to assess the effectiveness of a lay counselor training program for retirement center and nursing home staff and residents. At the end of training, he administered a variety of measures, including an external evaluation of concepts learned, evaluations by the leader and the participants, and evaluation of the trainers, with generally positive findings. However, no comparison or control group was used, and the measures were all administered only at the end of training.[62]

R. Jernigan, Tan, and R. L. Gorsuch, in another study using evaluation measures similar to those employed by Tan and Sarff, included a comparison group of subjects. This group participated in weekly Bible study classes at the same local church as the lay counseling trainees. They found some positive results: when post-training scores were compared to pretraining scores, the lay counseling trainees improved significantly more than the comparison group of Bible study students on self-ratings of knowledge about counseling and Christian counseling, competence in counseling and Christian counseling, and confidence about competence in counseling and Christian counseling, as well as on ratings of genuineness in a video-recorded role play counseling situation, by two independent raters.[63]

A crucial test of the effectiveness of any lay Christian counselor training program must eventually involve the evaluation of the counseling effectiveness of such trained lay counselors in terms of therapeutic outcomes. Evaluation research on the effectiveness of lay Christian counseling per se is even more limited. R. C. Richard and D. A. Flakoll noted that two formal but unpublished studies had been conducted to evaluate the effectiveness of lay counselors providing counseling services through the New Directions Counseling Center.[64] One study by Corcoran investigated client satisfaction and found that on most measures client satisfaction was at least 80 percent.[65] Another study by B. Cuvelier examined counselor satisfaction and also concluded that it was high.[66] However, no control or comparison group was apparently employed, and it is not clear whether the evaluation measures used were adequate and whether they were administered before and after counseling or only at the end of counseling. Harris more recently found that the use of nonpaid, nonprofessional lay helpers in combination with professional pastoral counseling led to a more favorable increase in self-esteem for clients, compared to private professional pastoral counseling only.[67]

Walters reported that lay counselors in a local church context compared favorably with Family Service Association (FSA) professionals on measures of client change and client satisfaction, using mail survey evaluations (FSA questionnaires) sent out to clients six months or more after termination of counseling.[68] His study therefore provides some encouraging but still tentative outcome findings because of methodological flaws obvious in such a retrospective evaluation study, which did not employ control groups.

More recently Y. M. Toh, S. Y. Tan, C. D. Osburn, and D. E. Faber,[69] in an outcome study in 1994 that used pre-and post-counseling assessments with several good outcome measures, found significant positive results in client change with adults who were seen by lay counselors at a local church lay counseling service, but no comparison or control group was employed. In a subsequent controlled outcome study in 1997, Toh and Tan[70] found significantly more improvement in clients randomly assigned to a lay Christian counseling treatment group (n = 22) compared to those randomly assigned to a no-treatment (wait list) control group (n = 24), on all four outcome measures used (target complaints, brief symptom checklist, spiritual well-being scale, and global rating of clients' psychological adjustment). These therapeutic gains were maintained at a one-month follow-up. This is still the only controlled outcome study that has been conducted on the effectiveness of lay Christian counseling provided to adult clients in a local church setting. In a recent review of empirically supported religious and spiritual therapies in 2010, J. N. Hook and colleagues therefore listed lay Christian counseling for general psychological problems as a possibly efficacious treatment, based on the findings of this controlled outcome study.[71]

F. Garzon and K. Tilley, in a 2009[72] review of the empirical evidence for the effectiveness of lay Christian counseling, used the following four major categories of such counseling: (1) active listening approaches (e.g., Kenneth Haugk's Stephen Ministry); (2) cognitive and solution-focused approaches (e.g., early Crabb, Backus, and Tan); (3) inner-healing prayer models (e.g., Francis MacNutt's Christian Healing Ministries; Ed Smith's Theophostic Prayer Ministry); and (4) mixed lay Christian models (e.g., eclectic with an integrated cognitive-behavioral component; Neil Anderson's Freedom in Christ Ministries). They reported some preliminary evidence for the effectiveness of Neil Anderson's Freedom in Christ Ministries and Ed Smith's Theophostic Prayer Ministry, but the lack of controlled outcome studies did not allow for more definitive conclusions.

The only controlled outcome study is still the randomized wait list control group study by Toh and Tan in 1997 already discussed. Garzon and Tilley concluded that more controlled outcome studies are needed to better evaluate the effectiveness of lay Christian counseling. Lay counseling in general has been found to be effective, and often as effective as professional therapy, but lay Christian counseling can only be classified as a possibly efficacious treatment at present, pending further controlled outcome research.

As we noted earlier, controlled outcome studies that compare the effectiveness of lay Christian counseling with no counseling and/or a "placebo" intervention are scarce in the literature. This is not surprising, since good outcome studies evaluating the effectiveness of more *professional* Christian counseling approaches are also limited, although this is a growing research area having a greater focus of attention.[73] Collins has suggested that the ongoing need for Christian counseling research may be due to a lack of time, energy, money, and expertise to do competent evaluative studies.[74] Nevertheless, such studies need to be done, so that the data base supporting lay Christian counselor training programs, as well as lay Christian counseling, can be strengthened. Evaluative research issues are discussed in greater detail in chapter 9 of this book.

THE FAITH FACTOR

While the specific influence and efficacy of lay counseling is still an emerging theme for researchers, the literature on spirituality and the role of faith continues to reveal a great deal of supportive evidence. Spirituality is mysterious but real. It has offered countless millions a place of refuge, solace, comfort, and hope, and a deeper sense of purpose and meaning—especially in times of tragedy or crisis when grief and despair crouch at the doorstep of the soul seeking to rob a person of vitality and life. Although spirituality continues to be an evolving construct among the social sciences, thus far the research literature generally affirms its profound and dynamic impact on mental health and mental health counseling.

In the early days of mental health research, Freud referred to religion as nothing more than a mass neurosis, and that perspective has shaped the overall direction of the mental health sciences. M. McMinn and colleagues reported that psychologists do not assess religious and spiritual issues in most cases and do not therefore include them in treatment plans.[75] Thankfully, this important dimension of the human experience is not being completely ignored.[76] The 2009 standards for graduate-level training from the Council for Accreditation of Counseling and Related Educational Programs (CACREP) actually specify some level of spiritual integration in two of their core curriculum requirements.[77] Religion and spirituality can no longer be simply viewed as an emotional or psychological "crutch," but must be recognized for the potential client strengths they consistently represent in the literature. At its core and within the individual, a person's spiritual orientation often represents the defining value system from which cognition, affect, behavior, and relationship flow.

Defining Spirituality

Spirituality offers a legitimate framework for an individual's value/belief system and from which subsequent behavior is then derived. A recent Internet search using the Google search engine revealed well over 100 million web pages related to the construct. As an emerging theme, spirituality can signify different things to different people due to its multidimensional nature and yet is something that most individuals seem to possess as an important component of their human existence.[78] One might say that it is an inherent aspect of human nature and involves concepts such as wholeness, restoration, hope, comfort, joy, guidance, and belief in the hereafter. G. W. Fairholm referred to spirituality as "the essence of who we are, the intangible, life-giving force in self and all people."[79] In a more practical context, spirituality has been described as a person's multifaceted system of beliefs, morality, values, and knowledge of right and wrong.[80]

Merriam-Webster's Collegiate Dictionary defines the spirit as the "soul of man—the intelligent, immaterial and immortal part of human beings," and simply refers to spirituality as the quality of respecting the spirit. For I. I. Mitroff and E. A. Denton, spirituality is the desire to find ultimate purpose in life and to live accordingly; it is the "basic feeling of being connected with one's complete self, others, and the entire universe."[81] Similar views speak of spirituality as representing the ongoing search for meaning and purpose, an appreciation for the deeper things in life, that which constitutes a person's individual belief system, and an awareness of the presence and divine nature of God.

In theistic terms, spirituality helps define a person's connection and service to God, and in terms of a lived experience, it provides purposeful relationships, a "joyous and compassionate attitude toward oneself and others."[82] As an expression of religious involvement, spirituality can be viewed through the lens of an organized system of beliefs, rituals, and collective traditions.[83] We must also recognize that spirituality is not merely some global, metaphysical, or ethereally vague concept, but it is directly associated with a person's specific theological creeds.

Faith Makes a Difference

Many have asked, "Does faith really matter, especially when treating and resolving complex psychological problems?" The term *pneumatraumatology* was coined to describe an array of trauma-related symptoms that have an impact on a person's sense of spiritual well-being.[84] These include feelings of isolation, inadequacy in the face of overwhelming situations, and no concept of permanence in that which is familiar. Connecting as a human being and offering validation for the experience of pain can provide extraordinary comfort and healing to the distressed spirit.[85] It can also lead to greater empowerment and overall fulfillment[86] and improved coping skills related to chronic illness.[87] A vibrant personal faith encounter has proven to increase resilience, coping, and successful treatment for a variety of conditions, including, chronic pain,[88] poly-substance abuse,[89] and comorbidity among trauma survivors.[90]

A person's religious beliefs and practice often serve as a positive source of interpersonal strength. In one study, when the religious orientation of a therapist was disclosed at the onset of treatment, clients were significantly more likely to have a desire to work with the mental health professional.[91] Some authors indicate that clients want to include spirituality in their treatment, but preferences are not as well understood.[92] According to Duke University researcher Harold Koenig, merely completing a spiritual history with a client (where faith is valued) yields treatment benefits through the process.[93] In one study of patients who were consecutively hospitalized, regular involvement in worship-based activities correlated with lower levels of depression and alcohol abuse.[94] The efficacy of religious practice and spirituality in group therapy outcomes has been demonstrated with substance abuse counseling.[95] Biblically oriented psychotherapy has also proven to be successful in treating different forms of depression, reducing automatic negative thought patterns, and lowering overall pathology levels in a measurable way.[96] In a separate analysis of twenty-four empirical studies, the same conclusions were supported.[97]

The trends are changing, and many mental health professionals are pursuing and not avoiding the integration of spiritual practices in client care as a preferred clinical strategy.[98] This may be because a growing body of research correlates client spirituality with improved health outcomes,[99] as well as the impact on couples therapy.[100] In another thorough review of the quantitative research literature on emotional and mental hygiene, a patient's spiritual orientation was shown to provide helpful coping mechanisms, enhanced pain management, protection against depression, and reduced risks for both substance abuse and suicide.[101]

Numerous community-sample and longitudinal studies have investigated the impact of religious practice on mortality rates. In a large comprehensive meta-analysis, M. E. McCullough and his colleagues reviewed and summarized forty-two study samples that evaluated a total of 126,000 people.[102] They found that religious involvement increased life expectancy by 29 percent. Religious involvement was defined in terms of attendance at services, how personally important participants ranked their faith, and the degree to which participants found strength and/or comfort in their relationship with God. The only other factor in the analysis that remotely approached the efficacy of religious involvement was the lack of obesity. Likewise, within the military community, the Department of Defense's approach to health promotion policies was first evaluated, and then an integrative model (strongly supported via numerous empirical studies) was described that included a greater emphasis on positive spirituality.[103]

Other research studies have focused exclusively on mental health factors. One study of more than four hundred chronic patients confirmed the causal relationship between the participant's faith orientation and his or her symptomatology.[104]

A significant majority (80 percent) utilized some form of religious belief or activity to cope with their symptoms on a daily basis, with 65 percent reporting that their religious practice moderated symptom severity. Nearly half (48 percent) indicated that their faith became even more relevant whenever symptoms worsened, while 30 percent stated that their faith was the most important thing that kept them motivated in treatment. The longer a patient had integrated spiritual coping mechanisms, the lower their symptom levels were in six different categories (obsessive-compulsiveness, interpersonal sensitivity, phobic anxiety, paranoid ideation, psychosis, and total symptomatology).

The most prevalent coping strategies were prayer (59 percent), followed by attending religious services (35 percent), worshiping God (35 percent), meditation (33 percent), reading Scriptures (30 percent), and meeting with a spiritual leader (15 percent). The researchers noted the general unavailability of trained spiritual leaders and suggested that new models of service provision be developed that better linked the professional community with faith-based counselors/clergy members. These results have been confirmed or replicated in numerous studies related to current treatment modalities as well as posttraumatic growth.[105]

When looking specifically at the issue of depression, McCullough and D. Larson examined more than eighty studies conducted over the past one hundred years and found that spiritual/religious factors generally accounted for lower rates and reduced symptomatology. Individuals who placed a high value on their faith and engaged in religious activities were at a significantly reduced rate across all depressive disorders.[106] Meanwhile, those without any religious or faith-based involvement had a 60 percent increased risk of suffering from a major depressive episode. Finally, participation in a faith-based community fostered both hope and caring and was seen as an important preventive measure that helped inoculate people from susceptibility to depression.

Another landmark study discovered a link between religious beliefs and practices (specifically Christian-oriented), rates of depression, and receiving religiously oriented cognitive behavioral therapy.[107] Participants showed reduced symptoms of posttreatment depression, balanced clinical adjustment, and lowered recidivism with this mode of treatment, especially when they were receiving the modality in what was perceived as a framework that was congruent with their beliefs and practices. Another interesting aspect of this particular study involved two randomized groups (those receiving therapy from caregivers who were religiously oriented and those receiving therapy from caregivers who were not religiously oriented), where both sets of participants still showed significant clinical benefits. The researchers noted that even though a religiously oriented therapist was certainly important, the greater value appeared to be the actual content of the treatment regimen (i.e., the specific integration of the tenets of their faith). This supports the notion that Christian-informed therapy (with biblically based content), coupled with pastoral counseling and/or care, demonstrates robust improvement in depression outcomes.

Probably the most negative and destructive aspect of major depression is increased suicide risk. Two national studies, one conducted nearly forty years ago[108] and another more recently,[109] both demonstrated that nonparticipation in religious activities increased suicide risk by almost 400 percent. Koenig and D. Larson reviewed a total of sixty-eight studies that addressed the link between suicide and religion, and found that in fifty-seven of them (84 percent), there were lower rates of suicide among those more actively involved in faith-based activities.[110] Causal determinants that helped promote these results included enhanced self-esteem, improved personal accountability, and an increased awareness of responsibility to God. Statistically similar findings can be found in other studies that take into account an expanded age spectrum.[111] Given the kind of documented results just described in this section from a treatment perspective, there appears to be tangible value for developing a more comprehensive model that integrates the disciplines of psychology and theology.

Understanding and Incorporating a Judeo-Christian Paradigm

Appropriate referrals to chaplains, other clergy members, and faith-based mental health clinicians who are equipped to engage Christian clients within their cultural framework is a valid consideration for expanded and collaborative care.[112] Spiritual practices such as Scripture reading, meditation, and prayer can help foster resilience and recovery from mental illness because they can "function as a reminder for clients of God's concern for the marginalized and disenfranchised members of society and provide hope and optimism about the future."[113] Spirituality gives meaning and purpose to life and can promote client welfare and growth.[114]

Historically the Bible has been a source of comfort, guidance, and spiritual direction for many who are faced with unexpected tragedy, grief, and loss, or when the unexplainable occurs. Since evangelical Christians comprise the largest spiritual minority in the United States (25 percent), there is an identified need for mental health practitioners to understand the cultural narrative and nuances of this segment of the population.[115] A number of indicators confirm that there is a national upward trend of clients seeking to address spiritual issues and concerns in receiving mental health services.[116]

Given the fact that the United States has essentially been a nation at war for over two decades, the extant research overwhelmingly supports the benefits of spiritual integration with treatment for combat stress, traumatic brain injury (TBI), PTSD, and various affective disorders. In fact, the opposite outcome is evidenced when people struggle spiritually. Negative religious coping, especially difficulty in forgiving oneself, has demonstrated increased symptoms of depression and anxiety for veterans suffering from PTSD.[117] In an extensive study conducted with PTSD patients receiving treatment in Department of Veterans Affairs programs—both outpatient (N = 554) and inpatient (N = 831)—the severity of PTSD symptoms was exacerbated by feelings of excessive guilt and weakened religious faith.[118] If veterans who are unable to stay connected to their belief system and faith practices face a greater risk for physiological and psychological distress,[119] then there is a strong incentive to explore the role of spirituality and faith-based interventions when considering a comprehensive health and wellness response.

A key component in the recovery of posttraumatic stress is directly associated with a person's consistent faith alignment.[120] Since the constructs of forgiveness (including self-forgiveness) and the alleviation of guilt are core themes among Christian denominations, clergy and professional caregivers are in a primary position to offer credible help when clients are having difficulty in these areas and to the extent that optimal mental health functioning is compromised. With the research literature clearly supporting the fact that trauma sufferers readily pursue spiritual care,[121] there are a number of meaningful opportunities for mental health professionals and clergy members to collaborate more effectively in this area.[122]

Outside of pastoral counselors and chaplains trained in Clinical Pastoral Education (CPE), few clinicians have received formal training to work effectively with spiritually attuned and motivated clients.[123] This accentuates the existing need to provide competent and culturally relevant resources to counselors, especially when surveys and polling data consistently demonstrate the importance of faith to a majority of Americans. Furthermore, it is critical to respect a client's spiritual autonomy by working within the parameters of their theological worldview.[124] Conversely, spiritual distress can lead to poorer health outcomes.[125] In a review on the use of spiritual interventions among Christian counselors, D. F. Walker, R. L. Gorsuch, and Tan found not only that the most commonly identified factor was the therapist's personal religious beliefs, attitudes, and behavior, but that when congruence existed between client and therapist, the treatment process was enhanced.[126] While many mental health practitioners acknowledge the importance of spiritual values to their clients, the majority of clinicians inadequately assess this domain.[127] Linking clients with church and parachurch resources has proven to be an effective approach.[128] Indeed, "with regard to informed consent, counselors' disclosure about spirituality matters in counseling could enhance a client's informed choice and appropriate counselor referrals."[129]

Spirituality as a Cultural Competency for Educators and Clinicians

CACREP has recognized the deficiency that exists in most graduate academic institutions regarding spiritual competency. Modalities that are utilized may incorporate spiritual autobiographies, role playing, journaling, class presentations, spiritual readings, etc.[130] Yet there remains a lack of effective training protocols and an ongoing general discomfort among counselor trainees and faculty members in addressing and even integrating spirituality within their curriculum and programs.[131] Even though CACREP has mandated in their 2009 standards the need to address spirituality in the core curriculum of counselor education programs, at present neither CACREP nor any other accrediting body specifically addresses spiritually oriented counseling certificate programs.

Research supports the notion that when a client receives care within the confines of his or her basic worldview and foundational value system—of which religious affiliation is a significant marker for most—outcomes are more positive.[132] Koenig's systematic review of nearly 1,600 published health-related studies concludes that the integration of a spiritual paradigm not only demonstrated increased levels of self-esteem, social support, and life satisfaction, but simultaneously reduced levels of anxiety, depression, loneliness, and suicide.[133] The implication is that treatment providers need to think and practice in terms of a bio-psycho-social-spiritual orientation. Based in part on the principles related to attachment theory, it has also been shown that people who report a deeper sense of spirituality demonstrate better stress management, higher self-esteem, and greater interpersonal competence.[134]

These studies indicate that there is a growing need for counselor education programs to more actively incorporate training in spirituality and spiritual interventions from an ethical and spiritual competence perspective.[135] In recent years, there has been a push for counseling practitioners—across disciplines and at all levels—to develop spiritual competencies in the assessment and treatment of mental and emotional disorders.[136] This includes social workers,[137] professional counselors,[138] psychologists,[139] and physicians.[140]

The Joint Commission on Accreditation of Healthcare Organizations (JCAHO), the accrediting body for most hospitals in the United States, now recommends that spiritual assessment be completed with all patients.[141] This discipline is a frequently neglected focus of multicultural training in most academic settings.[142] Research consistently shows that most patients view their faith as a core aspect of life and want to address issues of spirituality in the context of their medical care.[143] However, one study of evangelical Christian clients in need of psychiatric help found that 83 percent of respondents believed therapists did not understand their beliefs and values, resulting in a significant hesitation to initiate services.[144] Perhaps this is why a random sample of more than five hundred members of the American Counseling Association strongly advocated the value of faith-based competency among practitioners.[145]

W. B. Hagedorn and D. Gutierrez examined spiritual competencies developed by one of American Counseling Association's (ACA) divisions, the Association for Spiritual, Ethical, and Religious Values in Counseling (ASERVIC).[146] In reviewing the proceedings at the 2007 ACA national conference in Detroit, Michigan, ASERVIC hosted a panel discussion of educators and clinicians. These individuals were intentionally identified as being nationally recognized for their expertise in teaching and research in the area of spirituality in counseling. Though the efforts of these panel members are to be commended, most counseling students and interns are by and large still unaware of ASERVIC at all.[147] Sadly, there are only a few clearly articulated content and classroom management strategies within secular universities for preparing future counselors in this domain.[148] The following are eight of ASERVIC's competencies that have particular relevance to the discussion:

> *Competency #2.* The professional counselor recognizes that the client's beliefs (or absence of beliefs) about spirituality and/or religion are central to his or her worldview and can influence psychosocial functioning.
>
> *Competency #5.* The professional counselor can identify the limits of his or her understanding of the client's spiritual and/or religious perspective and is acquainted with religious and spiritual resources, including leaders, who can be avenues for consultation and to whom the counselor can refer.
>
> *Competency #6.* The professional counselor can identify limits of her or his understanding of a client's religious or spiritual expression and demonstrate appropriate referral skills and generate possible referral sources.
>
> *Competency #7.* The professional counselor responds to client communications about spirituality and/or religion with acceptance and sensitivity.
>
> *Competency #8.* The professional counselor uses spiritual and/or religious concepts that are consistent with the client's spiritual and/or religious perspectives and that are acceptable to the client.
>
> *Competency #9.* The professional counselor can recognize spiritual and/or religious themes in client communication and is able to address these with the client when they are therapeutically relevant.
>
> *Competency #12.* The professional counselor sets goals with the client that are consistent with the client's spiritual and/or religious perspectives.
>
> *Competency #13.* The professional counselor is able to (a) modify therapeutic techniques to include a client's spiritual and/or religious perspectives,

and (b) utilize spiritual and/or religious practices as techniques when appropriate and acceptable to a client's viewpoint.

As evidenced in the language of these statements—in particular #8 and #12—a client's spiritual and religious values are indeed valid and reasonable determinants for the focus and direction of treatment. The critical alliance counselors must build with their clients is based on an abiding presence of trust. Counselors are expected to utilize appropriate empathy skills and, in doing so, be able to understand the client's perspective, accept differences between themselves and their client's beliefs and values, and also facilitate the personal development of the client's spirituality and growth.[149]

CONCLUDING COMMENTS

Over four decades ago, Thomas Oden, a well-known theologian who has written extensively on the integration of Christian theology and counseling or psychotherapy, issued a strong call for the laicization of counseling and psychotherapy. He affirmed the use of lay therapeutic resources, especially within a religious context, and he critiqued the overprofessionalization, pointing out the limitations of the helping professions.[150] Jay Adams, a little earlier than Oden, also made a similar call to all Christians to be involved in a biblical lay counseling ministry, contending from Scriptures that Christians are competent to counsel.[151] Such calls have not gone unheeded. In fact, they have been prophetic of what has occurred in the last several decades in the field of lay Christian counseling.

A review of both the secular and Christian literature on lay counseling shows clearly that the field has grown tremendously in recent years. Lay counseling has received consistent research support for its effectiveness, although there are still potential problems with using lay counselors, which should be borne in mind. More research needs to be done on lay Christian counseling in particular. Also needed are attempts at evaluating and, if possible, integrating the various approaches to effective lay Christian counseling currently available. Our attempt to do this and to outline a biblical model for effective Christian counseling, as well as lay counseling, was the focus of the previous chapter. However, much work remains to be done, including more sophisticated theological, ethical, and philosophical analyses of current biblical models of Christian counseling. These models need to be tested to determine how *biblical* they are, how *consistent* they are with Christian tradition and theology, and how *effective* they are in helping clients.[152]

CHAPTER 5

Planning and Building
a Dynamic Ministry of
Lay Counseling

Bill is a committed Christian who has served for several years in his church as a Sunday school teacher and chairperson of one of the adult fellowships. After attending a weekend seminar on lay Christian counseling, he saw the great need for a ministry of lay counseling done from a biblical perspective in both local church and parachurch contexts. He also learned the basics of a biblical model for effective lay counseling and people-helping.

Bill returned home from the seminar excited about the possibility of starting a lay counseling ministry in his own local church. He had a real burden for people struggling with personal problems and needs and had done his best to reach out to them in his fellowship group. He had signed up for the seminar because he often felt inadequate in his knowledge and skills, but he also did it out of concern for his pastor, who had been carrying a heavy load of pastoral care and counseling. Bill knew that his pastor would often see twenty to thirty people each week, and he was interested in learning more so that he could help shoulder some of the load of ministry. He hoped to talk with his pastor about building a ministry of lay Christian counseling in their local church, but he wasn't sure what to say or where to start. The seminar schedule was packed tight, and the presenter spent only a few minutes on the practical steps necessary to start a ministry of lay counseling in a local church.

Over the past three decades, we have met hundreds of people who have echoed sentiments similar to Bill's. These were warm and caring individuals who shared a deep desire to reach out and help others in need. More than anything else, they were looking for practical guidance on how to establish a lay helping or counseling ministry in their local churches. That's why we have written this chapter—to provide information for people like Bill to help them realize their vision of building a ministry of lay counseling. The process begins by choosing an appropriate *model* for counseling ministry, one that best fits the needs of your local church.

MODELS FOR A MINISTRY OF LAY CHRISTIAN COUNSELING

To simplify the variety of perspectives and models we have looked at so far, we will present three major models for establishing a ministry of lay Christian counseling: (1) informal-spontaneous, (2) informal-organized, and (3) formal-organized.

1. The Informal-Spontaneous Model

The first model, the informal-spontaneous model, begins with the idea that lay Christian counseling should occur spontaneously and informally in interactions and relationships already present or possible through the existing structures of the church. In other words, the care and counsel are spontaneous, and the setting is informal. Such structures normally include fellowships (e.g., for youth, adults, seniors, singles), Bible study or discipleship groups, outreach or evangelism programs, visitation of church members by pastors or other church leaders, and Sunday school classes, to name a few. Leaders in these ministries may be given some basic training in how to care for or counsel with people, but they do not usually receive regular, ongoing, and close supervision of their caring and counseling ministry. This first model is a common one found in many evangelical churches. It makes use of gifted laypeople and leaders to care and counsel with one another in informal settings and spontaneous ways.

2. The Informal-Organized Model

This model assumes that lay Christian counseling should be an organized and well-supervised ministry, which nevertheless should still occur in informal settings as far as possible. Lay Christian counselors are carefully selected, trained, and supervised, but they are used in a ministry of lay caring and counseling through structures similar to the ones mentioned in the first model, in relatively informal settings compared to a counseling center or a pastor's office. These lay counselors are given systematic training in helping skills and receive regular, ongoing, and relatively close supervision of their counseling ministry, usually by a pastor or director of counseling and care in a particular local church.

An excellent example of the second model is the Stephen Series system of lay caring ministry, founded by Dr. Kenneth Haugk, a pastor and clinical psychologist.[1] The Stephen Series enables a pastor of a local church to use a team of lay "Stephen ministers" to carry out a lay caring ministry to the whole congregation.

These members receive systematic training in lay Christian caregiving and are then used to reach out to or visit with people in and around their congregation who need some level of pastoral care or help. Lay Stephen ministers care and counsel in an organized way, but often in informal settings, including people's homes, nursing homes, and hospitals.

Some of the areas that lay Stephen ministers have been involved in include people who are hospitalized; the terminally ill and their families; those who experience significant grief and loss; people going through separation or divorce; those experiencing an unwanted pregnancy, miscarriage, or stillbirth, as well as their families; people in trouble with the law; parents who have children leaving home for various reasons; military personnel or veterans returning from combat and experiencing reintegration stress; people who are lonely, depressed, or bereaved; new members of the congregation and/or community; those who are shut in or in a nursing home and their families; those who are inactive in church and in need of pastoral visitation; parents and families with disabled children; single parents; people convalescing at home or in an institution; those who have suffered significant financial setbacks or have lost their jobs; people in the process of moving out of town; people going through retirement or forced early retirement; those who are struggling with their faith in God; and persons affected by natural disasters.

While this is not an exhaustive list, it does provide an accurate picture of the comprehensive ministry that lay Stephen ministers (or a similar entity) can have in lay caring and counseling. And while the Stephen Series is meant primarily to train lay Stephen ministers in lay pastoral caregiving, we believe that lay Christian counseling is a part of such caregiving. Other examples of this informal-organized model include inner healing approaches (Elijah House, Shiloh Place, Francis McNutt, Pastoral Care Ministries), as well as mixed models (AACC's Biblical Counseling, Freedom in Christ, Exchanged Lives, The Ancient Paths, Theophostic Ministry).[2]

3. The Formal-Organized Model

This model assumes that lay Christian counseling should not only be an organized and well-supervised ministry but should occur in a formal way, in the context of a lay counseling center or service within the local church as part of its core mission. Such a well-structured and formalized center or service can stand on its own or be a part of a larger counseling center of the church, staffed by professional clinicians and therapists and directed by a licensed mental health professional, whether psychiatrist, psychologist, social worker, counselor, marriage and family therapist, psychiatric nurse, or trained pastoral counselor.

Lay Christian counselors for a formal-organized ministry are therefore carefully selected, trained, and closely supervised on a regular, ongoing basis. Such lay counselors see people or clients in church offices with formal appointments set up. They usually keep specific hours for counseling at the church, whether for a few hours in the afternoon or evening, oftentimes for one particular day per week. They meet regularly for staff meetings, as well as for supervision sessions. Staff meetings are often held monthly, whereas supervision sessions (one-on-one, in dyads, or in small groups) are usually held on a weekly or biweekly basis, with a licensed mental health professional or a trained pastor of lay counseling serving as the supervisor.

In this third model, a high degree of organizational structure is required. A number of variations of this formal-organized model are available, and several churches have already put together very practical and helpful manuals on policies and procedures for implementing such a lay counseling service or center in a local church context.[3]

FIVE STEPS FOR BUILDING A LAY COUNSELING MINISTRY

People like Bill who are interested in building a ministry of lay counseling should consider the following steps as they seek to establish a lay counseling ministry:

Become familiar with the three models for counseling ministry. Assess your congregation and discuss these options thoroughly with your pastor. Would your church be better served by a formal or informal, spontaneous or organized ministry? Or would some combination of models work best? The three models presented above are not mutually exclusive. For example, in a large church of a thousand or more people, all three models could be employed at the same time, resulting in three different levels of caring and helping ministries in the church. After the models are discussed with the pastor or pastoral staff, one or more of the models should be selected as most suitable for the particular church in question. Leadership roles will need to be defined within whatever structure is ultimately chosen.

Garner support for the idea of lay counseling from the pastor, pastoral staff, and church board.[4] The leaders of your church should view such a lay counseling ministry as an extension of pastoral care and counseling and as an essential ministry by the priesthood of all believers (1 Peter 2:5, 9). If you do not have theological and personal support from some or all of the church board and pastoral staff, then it will be difficult, if not impossible, to establish a lay Christian counseling ministry. It is important to have the support of leadership as well as a spiritual covering that can provide ongoing discernment, wisdom, prayer support, and vision for the ministry.

Screen potential lay Christian counselors from the congregation. Using appropriate spiritual and psychological criteria, select the best qualified people for the role of lay counselor. The next chapter spells out these criteria in more detail, as well as a suggested selection process. Initially, the pastor or pastoral staff could recommend people from the congregation who may be good prospects to serve as lay counselors.

Provide a training program for lay counselors. The training program should focus on basic counseling skills within a biblical framework. It should include material mentioned in earlier chapters of this book on the biblical basis for lay counseling and expose people to a biblical model for effective lay counseling. Chapter 7 describes different models of training and gives additional details that go into an effective training program.

Develop programs or ministries where the trained lay counselors can be used. As the program gets under way, the church should continue to provide training and supervision to their lay counselors. The programs you develop will, of course, depend on which model you chose for your ministry in step 1. Every local church is unique, and different churches may choose different models to implement lay caring and counseling ministries. It is important to have a good understanding of the common and felt needs within the congregation so that ministry can be targeted and resources deployed to maximize the effectiveness and impact of helping.

THE CHOICE OF MODELS

The informal-organized model is particularly appropriate for churches that want to be involved in outreach and ministry through lay caring and counseling. It can also be especially suitable to certain ethnic churches, like some Chinese churches whose congregations may still have a strong cultural stigma against seeking help or counseling for personal problems. In such churches, a formal lay counseling center (patterned somewhat after a professional clinic) that uses lay counselors may not be as acceptable for reasons like stigma and the fear of "losing face" for those who are seeking help.

In certain church contexts, the credentials of the counselors are of critical importance, and lay counselors without any professional credentials and/or degrees may not be as respected or accepted. Recognize that both counseling per se, as well as lay or nonprofessional counseling, may not be embraced in certain churches, including some ethnic churches. The informal-organized model for lay caring and counseling ministries can, however, still be used in such churches because it avoids some of the more formal aspects of counseling. The Stephen Series is a good example of the application of this model, having been successfully used in more than twelve thousand congregations from 160 Christian denominations in the United States, Canada, and twenty-four other countries.

Other churches, especially larger ones that have additional resources, personnel, and budget allocations available, may find the formal-organized model most appropriate. A number of churches and congregations have effectively employed this model and established successful lay counseling centers or services, and we give several examples in chapter 10.

TEN GUIDELINES FOR ESTABLISHING A LAY COUNSELING CENTER

How do you implement the formal-organized model in a local church? Trevor Partridge has delineated ten helpful considerations in establishing a professional Christian Counseling Center.[5] Even though most of these principles could apply to any type of lay counseling ministry, we have adapted them here and applied them to the development of a lay counseling center or service.

1. *Determine clear objectives for the counseling service.* Your main objective should be to provide distinctively biblical, Christian counseling services. The counseling center should focus on short-term crisis care and referral, as well as spiritual issues and the use of spiritual resources like prayer and the Scriptures where appropriate. The goal should be to help people grow in holiness or Christlikeness and not simply to bring about temporal happiness. The center may also be a place for outreach and evangelism conducted in a sensitive and balanced way with non-Christian clients who are open and interested in hearing more about the gospel.

2. *Establish the "ethos" or distinctive character and identity of the lay counseling center by giving it an appropriate name.* In a local church context, the counseling ministry often, but not always, will include the name of the particular church. Some churches prefer to call the center by a more general name so it will be perceived as a community counseling service rather than one attending only to the needs of a particular congregation. However, this is not always the case. Think carefully through your goals and the people you hope to reach with this service as you select a name for the center.

3. *Carefully select, train, and supervise the counseling personnel.* The director of the center should be either a licensed mental health professional or a pastor or church leader with some training and experience in counseling who also has

access to a licensed clinician as a consultant. Provide ongoing, regular meetings (weekly, biweekly, or monthly) for further training and supervision of the lay counselors. Weekly meetings typically last an hour; biweekly meetings, two hours; and monthly meetings, from three to four hours. Preferably supervision sessions should be held weekly or biweekly. Some churches also organize special weekend retreats once or twice a year for their lay counselors to facilitate further spiritual growth as well as the development of ongoing counseling knowledge and people-helping skills. Provide good training materials to the lay counselors and develop a small library of journals, articles, books, manuals, audio and video recordings, and Internet resources pertaining to counseling skills, especially from a biblical perspective.

4. *Arrange for suitable facilities for the counseling center.* Lay counselors will need comfortable rooms that offer some level of privacy where they can meet with their clients or counselees. There should be a secure area to maintain client records and other documentation to ensure a high degree of confidentiality. If possible, such facilities should include a reception area and at least two or three counseling rooms. Ideally, you should have one-way observation mirrors and audio and video recording equipment available for training and supervision purposes.

5. *Establish counseling center hours.* Depending on staff and counselor availability, churches have had operating hours during the daytime, evenings, and on weekends, including some capacity to handle emergency situations. The length or duration of counseling sessions should also be determined. Usually appointments should be about an hour for individuals and an hour and a half to two hours for couples, families, or groups.

Some centers may also need to decide whether to have a telephone counseling service or "crisis hotline," and, if so, whether it should be a twenty-four-hour emergency phone-in service. We strongly recommend that you not offer a service like this until there are sufficient numbers of trained lay counselors who can staff the telephones, with adequate supervision and back-up consultation and services by licensed professionals.

Partridge has also suggested that a counseling center will need a "council of reference." This referral network should consist of Christian doctors, psychiatrists, accountants, psychologists, professional counselors, attorneys, and so forth, as well as community and organizational resources such as shelters, food banks, legal aid, group homes, etc. Counselors can then refer clients who need further help to such professionals. It may be helpful to develop a comprehensive resource notebook or kit for each lay counselor with items such as phone numbers, addresses, emails, websites, contact names, and so on, both within the church and the greater local or regional community.

6. *Establish a structure within which the lay counseling center will function.* Appoint a director who has appropriate training or experience. The director will run the center, oversee primary administrative activities, liaison with church leadership, and coordinate the selection, training, and supervision of the lay counselors. The director also usually screens all potential clients either by a telephone interview or an initial intake interview and then assigns them to appropriate lay counselors, depending on the needs or problems presented. On some occasions the director may refer a potential client to a professional clinician because the presenting problem is deemed too complex or severe for a lay counselor to manage.

An alternative approach to having the director screen potential clients is to have the lay counselors themselves conduct the initial intake interview by telephone or in person, but preferably in person. The lay counselors will then report their assessments or findings to the director of the center, who will decide whether to assign the client to a lay counselor or refer the client to a professional. It is also a good idea to establish a church board or committee to oversee the ministry of the center. This committee provides accountability, support, and guidance to the director.

Some churches have a small committee consisting of the pastor and one or two elders or deacons of the church, whereas other churches appoint a larger oversight committee by adding a couple of lay counselors and several professional counselors as well. In relatively small churches, however, it is not uncommon for the director of the center to be directly accountable to the pastor of the church, so that the pastor functions essentially as a one-person "committee." It would be preferable even in such churches to have one or two more members on the committee. Besides appointing a director and establishing a committee, the church should also provide secretarial/administrative support, as well as supplies, furniture, equipment, etc., needed by the center.

7. *Spread the word about the counseling center.* Publicity for the center can be handled in various ways: word of mouth, informational brochures, announcements in the church bulletin or from the pulpit, via email or on the church's website, and advertising in local newspapers. The following are two examples of informational brochures designed for a lay counseling center. The first was developed by Siang-Yang Tan at North Park Community Chapel, a nondenominational, evangelical local church in London, Ontario, Canada, which has about 1,600 members, and the second, by Eric Scalise at Blue Ridge Community Church in Lynchburg, Virginia, which has about 3,000 members. Beyond the name of the center, basic contact information, biographical sketches, times of operation, etc., the brochures contain significant details.

An Introduction

The Counseling Service at North Park Community Chapel

The Counseling Service at North Park Community Chapel exists to meet the spiritual and emotional needs of people in our congregation and in the larger community of London. It functions on a voluntary basis and should not be considered as a professional counseling service. As such, no fees are charged. The service aims to provide

1. friendship and fellowship on a one-to-one basis for those who may need someone to talk to;
2. counseling and supportive help for those who may be facing some life crisis or emotional/spiritual problems;
3. guidance and growth experiences for those who may be searching for practical ways to grow spiritually and mature as a human person; and
4. referrals to professionals or appropriate agencies for those who may seek or need further help.

The Counseling Service operates within a biblical, Christian framework and exists to fulfill the scriptural injunctions to "carry each other's burdens" (Gal. 6:2) and to "love one another" (John 13:34–35). We do care about you and your needs. Call us or speak to us about an appointment. The service is open on Tuesdays and Wednesdays from 7:00 to 10:00 p.m.

Our telephone number is 555-555-5555.

Let us introduce ourselves:

It is important to notice that many of us are not professional counselors, although we all have had some basic training in helping people with their needs or problems. We do care about you as a person and will spend time to talk and help as we are able to do so.

COUNSELING IS BY APPOINTMENT ONLY. To make an appointment, phone the chapel secretary Monday through Friday from 9:00 a.m. to 4:00 p.m. or phone the Counseling Service Tuesday or Wednesday from 7:00 to 10:00 p.m.

Telephone 555-500-5000

Lifeline—A Ministry of Crisis Care and Support

Don't Go through It Alone

In our day-to-day world, the pressures of life are becoming increasingly overwhelming for many of us. As if present struggles aren't enough, unresolved issues from the past can keep us from living fully. The good news is that you don't have to go through it alone.

How to Get Help

To contact a Lifeline caregiver, please call 555-500-5555 x500 and leave a message with your name and phone number. Someone will contact you within 24 hours.

What Lifeline Is

Lifeline is a caregiving ministry of Blue Ridge Community Church. The purpose of this ministry is to provide spiritual care, support, encouragement, and referral services in a safe and confidential manner. Support is typically on a short-term basis during times of significant need or crisis. While in the midst of crisis, a Lifeline caregiver can help bring clarity to the issues involved and define the priorities of care. At the conclusion of the initial care, Lifeline will assist with any needed transition to ongoing support. Lifeline caregivers are trained volunteers under the direction and general supervision of assigned staff members at Blue Ridge Community Church.

What Lifeline Is Not

Regardless of their education, training, licensure, or expertise, Lifeline caregivers do not function in a professional role and do not provide clinically oriented mental health treatment or therapy.

Areas of Caregiving:

Anxiousness/fear	Finances/job stress
Broken relationships	Marital/family conflict
Abuse	Crisis of faith
Death/dying	Loneliness/discouragement
Separation/divorce	Whenever you find yourself
Addiction	in crisis

> "Do not fear, for I have redeemed you; I have summoned you by name; you are mine. When you pass through the waters, I will be with you; and when you pass through the rivers, they will not sweep over you. When you walk through the fire, you will not be burned; the flames will not set you ablaze. For I am the Lord your God, the Holy One of Israel, your Savior . . . you are precious and honored in my sight, and . . . I love you" (Isa. 43:1–4).

When you make announcements inviting people to use the counseling center, they should be made in as nonthreatening a way as possible to reduce the stigma often associated with seeking help from counselors. Emphasize that people who come to the center do not have to experience severe problems before using the services of the center. Present the counseling service as a burden-bearing and lay caring ministry, outlining the diversity and range of its services and stressing that it can meet a variety of needs.

8. *Clarify what specific services the lay counseling center will offer.* The brochure examples we shared describe basic services. To expand on those services, you may consider adding things like a telephone hotline, premarital and marital counseling, parenting and blended family help, various support group resources, and vocational guidance and counseling to the unemployed. Keep in mind that some of these areas of counseling (e.g., vocational counseling and counseling the unemployed) may be more appropriate for a professional Christian counseling center to handle, rather than a lay counseling service, because they can require specialized professional skills like vocational testing and assessment. As an alternative, you might consider arranging special one-day or weekend seminars on particular topics of interest for the benefit of the local community.

Some lay counseling centers use personality or vocational tests as part of the services they offer. When lay counselors utilize these tests, they should be closely supervised by licensed mental health clinicians or by a pastor who has had training and experience with the particular tests involved (e.g., the widely used Taylor-Johnson Temperament Analysis (TJTA), the Myers-Briggs Type indicator, the DISC Personality Test, or the Prepare-Enrich Profile). We recommend that testing should either not be provided at all by lay counselors or that it is provided only minimally and always under careful supervision and guidance. We say this because there are dangers associated with the abuse or misuse of tests, not only by lay counselors, but even by professional clinicians, and the best way to avoid these dangers is not to provide testing services at all, but to utilize qualified, licensed mental health professionals for testing. However, if the director of the center is a licensed professional or someone qualified to conduct testing and interpret the results of the tests given, then he or she may, of course, provide such services through the center. A fee is usually charged for testing services.

Another issue relates to whether notes or files should be kept on clients seen in a lay counseling center. Some churches have chosen not to keep notes or files on clients, instead keeping a record of those who have used the services of the center by recording their names or first names or initials only, their sex and age, and the dates when they were seen. Many centers, confidentially and securely keep very brief notes and files on the clients seen to document the work done by the lay counselors. These records may be of critical importance if follow-up services are provided at a later time and a review of prior care is helpful, or if a malpractice suit is ever filed against the center or a lay counselor.

Potential clients who call in for appointments should also be told of the limits to confidentiality in the counseling situation at the beginning of the intake interview and should sign an informed consent form. A number of states (such as California) now require pastors and pastoral counselors to report incidences of reasonably suspected child or elder abuse (physical or sexual), and to warn appropriate individuals if the client intends to take harmful, dangerous, or criminal action against another human being or against himself or herself. Even though your state may not have similar laws on their books, many lay counseling centers have decided to follow these requirements. The director of the center should be familiar with the specific laws of the state she or he is working in pertaining to the practice of professional mental health services and decide how to apply them to lay counselors, preferably after consulting with an attorney regarding potential liability and risks for litigation. Useful forms for keeping brief notes on clients and for obtaining informed consent for release of information, including limits of confidentiality, etc., can be found in appendix E of this book (which can be reprinted with permission). Client files containing confidential information should be kept under lock and key in a safe and secure location.

9. *Carefully consider the financing for the lay counseling center.* Be sure that the counseling center is included in the annual budget of the church. Staffing needs should be carefully considered as well. A number of churches have succeeded in operating effective lay counseling centers or programs with relatively small budgets using volunteer lay counselors or unpaid staff. Even in these situations, some financial support is still needed for office supplies, books, journals, audio or video equipment, and advertising costs. Some churches ask clients for voluntary donations to help defray expenses. Since you are not offering professional services, it would be wise to avoid asking for donations or charging any fees for lay counseling services, especially to minimize the risk of litigation or malpractice suits.

With regard to possible malpractice suits,[6] churches must also decide whether to obtain liability insurance for the lay counselors and programs offered or, minimally, to have an "emergency fund" for securing legal counsel in the event of a malpractice suit being filed against a lay counselor, staff person, or the center itself. A number of churches with lay counseling centers have attempted to function without any malpractice insurance or emergency fund, but this is highly inadvisable given the litigious nature of society today.

10. *Determine any church affiliation related to the lay counseling center.* While the focus of this chapter has been on establishing a lay counseling center operated by a local church, it is also possible for several local churches in a particular community to collaborate together and establish a center to serve the needs of their respective congregations as well as those of the wider community in which they live. A center like this should direct clients to appropriate churches for further spiritual nurture and growth where necessary.

The ten considerations we have shared here are a helpful starting place for people like Bill. They can begin conversations and discussion as they think through and discuss with their pastors and church leaders to determine if there is interest in setting up a more formal lay counseling center or service. With some adaptation and modification, the models and guidelines we have described and delineated in this chapter can also be applied in parachurch contexts and missionary work where lay caring and counseling ministries are needed. With much prayer, careful planning, and wise decision making, building or establishing a lay counseling ministry can become a reality in many more churches, parachurch organizations, and missions, for the helping and healing of more persons, to the greater glory and honor of God.

CHAPTER 6

Selection of Lay Counselors

"In the next few months, we will be starting a new lay counseling service in our church in order to extend and expand our pastoral care and counseling ministries. As you know, this project has been approved by our church board and pastoral staff. We will be starting a three-month intensive training program for about a dozen lay counselors once they have been selected. If you are interested and feel you have relevant gifts or experience in helping people with their problems and needs, please fill out an application form available at the church office to be considered for selection as a lay counselor. Thank you."

After Pastor Smith made this announcement during a Sunday morning worship service, Bob, a casual member of the church for many years, said to his wife, "I guess it's time for me to get more involved in the church—like you've been nagging me to do for years! I have a stable personality and years of management experience, so I should be able to help quite a few of those poor souls with their problems. I'll get an application form today and fill it in. Pastor Smith will be glad to see me volunteer and happier still to have me as one of the lay counselors!"

Another member of the church, Alice, thought to herself, *I wonder if I should apply to be a lay counselor. I'm not sure if I am qualified, and I don't know what the exact requirements or criteria are, but lots of people pour out their hearts and struggles to me. All I do is listen, try to understand, and pray with them, and apparently it helps, because they usually come back to talk some more with me, and quite a few have told me I've been really helpful. Some even suggested I should consider being a counselor! I guess I should ask Pastor Smith for an application form and discuss this further with him before making up my mind about whether to apply. However, I do want to serve the Lord more in church.*

These fictitious scenarios raise two important questions: (1) What criteria should be used to select lay counselors? and (2) What are the best methods for screening lay counselors?

This chapter attempts to answer these questions.

CRITERIA FOR THE SELECTION
OF LAY COUNSELORS

The careful selection of lay counselors is a crucial step in the development of an effective lay counseling ministry. However, there is less agreement and even less research on what specific criteria should be used to select counselors. Lorraine Hart and Glen King have pointed out, "In spite of the fact that selection is a reasonably well-accepted idea, little concerted research has defined what selection criteria should be."[1] They note that often psychological tests or measures of personality characteristics have been used to select telephone counselors who are paraprofessionals or lay volunteers, including tests like the California Psychological Inventory, Personality Research Form, Omnibus Personality Inventory, Edwards Personal Preference Schedule, Minnesota Multiphasic Personality Inventory, and the Internal-External Locus of Control Scale.[2]

Most of the research that has been conducted on selection criteria for lay counselors has been on the characteristics of volunteers versus those of nonvolunteers. Hart and King, in reviewing the research, concluded that "volunteers have been found to score higher in nurturance, affiliation and empathy . . . to be more idealistic and generous . . . and to be higher in flexibility, achievement via independence, and maturity and sensitivity. These differences do not imply correlation with counseling effectiveness, of course, and there is little research to show that selecting counselors in this way is helpful."[3]

The authors go on to suggest that instead of using personality characteristics to select paraprofessionals, the initial level of their facilitative or helping skills should be considered, since Robert Carkhuff has found that persons with high initial levels of helping skills improved more with training than those with low levels initially.[4] In their own study, however, Hart and King did not find selection based on high levels of initial facilitative or helping skills to be a more potent factor than training, and they concluded that their data provide strong support for the wide range of screening methods that are presently being used in many telephone counseling centers. Nevertheless, they also noted that during training, the experimenter observed that persons who were initially high in facilitative or helping skills were instrumental in producing a better quality of training.[5]

More specifically, progress was limited or slow in a group that consisted only of those functioning at a low level, whereas progress in learning helping skills was much quicker in a group that had several people already functioning at a high level of facilitative skills, who may have served as good models for others in the group. This means that *both* adequate selection (based on high initial levels of helping skills) *and* adequate training probably contribute to the development of effective paraprofessionals or lay counselors.

One well-known procedure for assessing facilitative skills or interpersonal skills is the Group Assessment of Interpersonal Traits (GAIT).[6] Dooley has described it this way:

> The GAIT procedure consists of a series of five-minute discloser-understander dyads followed by evaluations by the participants (peer ratings) or by observers (in person or subsequently from audio or video recordings). Each participant takes each role once. The discloser role entails sharing an authentic present concern about the person's relationships while the understander is asked to show understanding to the discloser. . . . In the GAIT, participants are judged on the Rogerian . . . constructs of Empathy (accurate understanding), Acceptance (warmth or unconditional positive regard), and Openness (emotional honesty or genuineness).[7]

In his study on selecting nonprofessional counselor trainees with the GAIT, Dooley used the following measures to determine which ones would be significantly related to a scale of counseling readiness: pre-GAIT first impression peer ratings, GAIT Empathy, Acceptance, and Openness ratings by peers and by trained audiotape judges, and staff ratings based on written applications submitted by the trainees. After nine months of training, twenty-six trainees were evaluated on the criterion scale of counseling readiness. Pre-GAIT first impression peer ratings and GAIT Empathy, Acceptance, and Openness ratings by peers did not predict counseling readiness. Only the GAIT Empathy rating by trained audiotape judges, as well as the staff ratings, were significantly related to the criterion measure of counseling readiness.[8] This suggests that the GAIT procedure may be somewhat useful for screening lay counselors, but only to a limited degree.

Geraldine Cerling has also reviewed a number of important characteristics for counselors to possess,[9] including this description of an effective helper taken from Gerard Egan's book *The Skilled Helper*:

> First of all committed to his own growth, physical, intellectual, social-emotional, (spiritual) . . . he shows respect for his body through proper exercise and diet. . . . He has adequate basic intelligence, is aware of his own intellectual possibilities, respects the world of ideas. . . . He has good common sense and good social intelligence. . . . He knows that helping is a great deal of work. . . . He is concrete in his expressions, dealing with actual feelings and actual behavior rather than vague formulations or generalities. . . . His speech,

while caring and human, is also lean and to the point. . . . He is an integrator (uses data from the client to help the client understand himself better). . . . He is active, capable of helping his client elaborate actions, programs that lead to constructive behavioral change. . . . He is at home with people. . . . He is not a man who has never known problems, but does not retreat from the problematic in his own life. . . . He is living more effectively than the client, at least in the area the client is having trouble.[10]

This is a formidable list of characteristics, and Egan's book has been widely read and used in many counselor training programs. Cerling also summarized the views of Paul Miller, who wrote a book on peer counseling in the church.[11] According to Miller, four essential characteristics of a counselor are mature attitudes, a capacity for sustained and perceptive listening, skills of tactful intervention, and a deep grasp of human nature. He also described ten essential attitudes and skills for counselors to have: personal warmth, trustworthiness, accurateness in empathy, unconditional positive regard, confidence in counselee's ability to change, inner consistency, growth in personal maturity, appropriate self-disclosure, training in counseling, and a professional stance. Cerling concluded,

> While cited sources showed differences, there appeared to be a consensus that characteristics and qualities enabling a person to be aware of, open to, and available for interaction with other human beings were prized in a helper. Also valued were the individual's capacity and desire for personal growth and development throughout his/her life.[12]

Cerling conducted her own study using a structured questionnaire to survey eighty-one church counseling centers across the United States to determine their criteria for selecting lay counselors. Only twenty-eight (34.6 percent) of the centers used lay counselors, reflecting a general reluctance to utilize lay counselors in such centers. The respondents in her study used two different definitions of "lay" counselors—"lay" as referring to nonprofessional or paraprofessional counselors (as Cerling intended) and "lay" as referring to non-ordained but professional trained counselors (this was not Cerling's intended meaning). The major selection criteria used by the church counseling centers, together with their frequency and percentage, are shown in her table below.[13] In general they reflect the criteria already mentioned earlier by other authors in the counseling field.

Selection Criteria from Cerling's Study

Number	Percentage	
26	17.4	Personal and spiritual maturity [printed response]
24	16.1	Interest in people [printed response]
22	14.8	Willingness to make a commitment to a counseling ministry [printed response]
17	11.4	Graduate level training in a professional field, MA or higher
11	7.4	Commitment to Christ as Savior and Lord [printed response]
8	5.4	Personal Integrity (i.e., dependability, reliability, standing in the community)
7	4.7	Certification by a professional organization, and/or state licensure
5	3.4	Counseling skills (i.e., empathy, acceptance, self-disclosure)
5	3.4	Value commitments (i.e., religious, moral, personal, social)
3	2.0	Ongoing supervision
3	2.0	Personal therapy
3	2.0	Training program within the counseling center
2	1.3	Clinical competence (directly stated; inferred in professional training and certification)
2	1.3	Continued personal growth
2	1.3	Recommendation by pastor and/or faith group
2	1.3	Stable marital relationship
1	0.7	Emotional and psychological stability as determined by MMPI and POI [Personal Orientation Inventory]
1	0.7	Interest in community and parish systems
1	0.7	Interview by executive director
1	0.7	Rich life experience and rewarding personal life
1	0.7	Transportation
1	0.7	Willingness to work for little, if any, financial compensation
1	0.7	Works well in group setting
149	100.1%	

Specific criteria for the selection of lay counselors will differ from church to church and center to center. Minimally we would suggest the following criteria should be used to select lay Christian counselors for a lay counseling ministry:

1. Spiritual maturity. The counselor should be a Spirit-filled, mature Christian and committed Christ follower (cf. Gal. 6:1), who has a good knowledge of Scripture, wisdom in applying Scripture to daily living, and a regular prayer life. The person should be known by those in church leadership, have a healthy response to spiritual and other forms of authority, and have a reputation for being a person of ethical integrity and moral character. Prospective counselors should also have a set length of time in which they have been actively involved in the life of the local congregation (we recommend a minimum of one year).

2. Psychological stability. The counselor should be psychologically stable, not emotionally labile or volatile, but open and vulnerable. He or she should not be suffering from a serious psychological disorder or major marital conflict (if married). If the person has struggled with either a chemical or process/behavioral (e.g., pornography, gambling, eating disorder) addiction, we recommend a minimum of two years of recovery.

3. Love for and interest in people. The counselor should be a warm, caring, and genuine person with a real interest in people and their welfare. This type of ministry is a sacred trust and one that requires a heart of compassion and grace.

4. Spiritual gifts. The counselor should possess appropriate spiritual gifts, such as exhortation. Other examples may include wisdom, knowledge, discerning of spirits, mercy, and healing (see Romans 12 and 1 Corinthians 12).

5. Some life experience. The counselor should have had some life experience, especially within relational contexts and hence not be too young.

6. Previous training or experience in helping people. Academic and formal training or experience would be helpful but not necessary, as this is typically provided within the lay counseling ministry preparation.

7. Age, sex, education, socioeconomic status, and ethnic/cultural background. It would be helpful to have a variety of counselors from different backgrounds, ages, and both men and women.

8. Availability and teachability. The counselor should have the time to be trained (several hours per week during the training cycle), supervised, and involved in a lay counseling ministry. He or she should be responsive, teachable, and open to learning a biblical approach to helping people.

9. Ability to maintain confidentiality. The counselor should be able to understand, respect, and maintain appropriate confidentiality and protect the privacy of clients (according to ministry guidelines).[14]

10. Willingness to submit to any required background checks. The counselor must agree to any required background checks as a matter of standard protocol and to help ensure the church is in compliance with its own risk management policies.

Given these ten selection criteria, what are the best methods to screen potential lay counselors so that only those who possess all or a majority of the criteria are chosen? Looking back at the two people mentioned at the start of this chapter, should both Bob and Shirley be selected? Or should only one of them be chosen? If so, which one? How can we tell?

Methods for the Screening of Lay Counselors

Gary Collins has proposed a helpful process for screening potential lay counselors and applicants to serve in a counseling ministry.[15] *First*, solicit a brief written statement from the potential lay counselor affirming his or her adherence to your church's statement of faith or doctrinal positions, in addition to a testimony of his or her personal salvation and Christian growth experience. It may be helpful to ask for a statement of reasons for wanting to be involved in a lay counseling training program and ministry as well.

Second, require two or three letters of recommendation from different people who know the potential lay counselor or applicant well. Then have the director and another church leader interview the applicant to assess his or her spiritual maturity, stability, and motivation. Do psychological testing of the potential lay counselor (consider using the 16PF [Personality Factor] or the Taylor-Johnson Temperament Analysis [TJTA]). A trained psychologist or other appropriately competent person should interpret the results. Other tests that may be helpful to use include the Minnesota Multiphasic Personality Inventory (MMPI), the Personal Orientation Inventory (POI), and the Myers-Briggs Temperament Type Indicator. Although Collins does not mention the use of measures other than psychological or personality tests, other tests can be helpful for assessing applicants' spiritual qualities (e.g., spiritual well-being, spiritual life and maturity, and spiritual leadership) and spiritual gifts.[16]

Some of these tests include the Shepherd Scale, developed by Rodney Bassett and his colleagues, which is a measure of orthodox Christian belief and adherence to a Christian lifestyle; Craig Ellison's Spiritual Well-Being Scale; Paul Schmidt's Character Assessment Scale, which is a measure of Christian character or maturity; Peter Wagner's Wagner-Revised Houts Questionnaire, which is a spiritual gifts inventory; Dennis Wayman's Spiritual Life Check-Up Questionnaire; and Frank Wichern's Spiritual Leadership Qualities Inventory. A trained psychologist is usually not required to administer these measures of spirituality, which are briefly described below.

1. *The Shepherd Scale.* Developed by Rodney Bassett and his colleagues, this

test is an instrument designed to differentiate Christians from non-Christians, using items based on New Testament texts. It has two components: a thirteen-item *Belief Component* that measures orthodox Christian belief (e.g., "I believe I can have the personal presence of God in my life [John 14:16]," and "I believe that it is possible to have a personal relationship with God through Christ [Rom. 14:22; Eph. 2:14–17; Col. 1:19–20]")[17] and a twenty-five-item *Christian Walk Component* that measures the extent to which a person adheres to a Christian lifestyle (e.g., "I do kind things regardless of who's watching me [Matt. 6:1–6; 25:31–46; Eph. 6:5–9]," and "Status and material possessions are not of primary importance to me [Matt. 6:16–21, 25–33; Luke 12:13–21; 1 Cor. 1:26–31; Phil. 4:10–13].")[18] For each item on the scale, a person is to choose one of the following four possible responses: (1) true, (2) generally true, (3) generally not true, or (4) not true.

2. *The Spiritual Well-Being Scale.* Developed by Craig Ellison and his colleague Raymond Paloutzian, this measure is composed of twenty items, ten of which assess *religious well-being* (e.g., "I don't find much satisfaction in private prayer with God," and "I believe that God loves me and cares for me"), and the other ten of which assess *existential well-being* (e.g., "I don't know who I am, where I came from, or where I'm going," and "I feel that life is a positive experience").[19] A six-point scale is used, ranging from Strongly Agree to Strongly Disagree, for each of the items. Ellison has pointed out that the *Spiritual Well-Being Scale* measures an individual's personal experience or sense of well-being, and this may not be the same as his or her state of spiritual health or spiritual maturity. While a spiritually mature or healthy person would be expected to have a positive sense of spiritual well-being, someone with a positive sense of spiritual well-being may not be spiritually mature (e.g., a young Christian).[20]

3. *The Character Assessment Scale.* Developed by Paul Schmidt, this is a personality test with 225 items assessing a number of morally relevant character traits based on the Bible. It is therefore a measure of Christian character or maturity. An individual taking this assessment has to answer each item as either applicable (true) or nonapplicable (false). The scale has eight research scales for measuring the following character traits, each of which has its corresponding strength and weakness components: (1) *Truth* (with Denial as weakness and Honesty as strength); (2) *Respect* (with Vanity as weakness and Humility as strength); (3) *Concern* (with Envy as weakness and Compassion as strength); (4) *Anger* (with Resentment as weakness and Peacemaking as strength); (5) *Money* (with Greed as weakness and Resourcefulness as strength); (6) *Time/Energy* (with Laziness as weakness and Enthusiasm as strength); (7) *Sexuality* (with Lust as weakness and Sexual Integrity as strength); (8) *Body Health* (with Gluttony as weakness and Physical Fitness as strength).[21]

4. *The Wagner-Revised Houts Questionnaire.* Revised by Peter Wagner, this is an inventory designed to help a person discover his or her spiritual gifts. It consists of 125 items to be answered on a four-point scale as to what extent each item/statement is true of an individual's life (3 = much; 2 = some; 1 = little; and 0 = not at all). A total of twenty-five spiritual gifts are assessed by this measure, with five items for each of the spiritual gifts. For example, the item/statement "I have a desire to speak direct messages from God that edify, exhort, or comfort others" is relevant to the spiritual gift of prophecy.[22] The twenty-five spiritual gifts covered by this questionnaire are prophecy, pastor, teaching, wisdom, knowledge, exhortation, discerning of spirits, giving, helps, mercy, missionary, evangelist, hospitality, faith, leadership, administration, miracles, healing, tongues, interpretation, voluntary poverty, celibacy, intercession, exorcism, and service.[23]

5. *The Spiritual Life Check-Up Questionnaire.* Developed by Dennis Wayman, this test is a measure for determining the present state of a person's spiritual health or spiritual life using a physical check-up analogy. There are six major sections to the questionnaire. Section 1 covers Blood Type, and the key questions are "Are you now a Christian?" and "Have you been baptized?" Section 2 covers Red Blood Cells (oxygen carriers that prevent anemia), with questions on one's devotional life (e.g., "How meaningful is Sunday morning worship to you?" and "How meaningful is private worship to you?") and one's intellectual life (e.g., "Are your doubts and questions being answered?" and "Do you feel you know your Bible and what help you need?" Section 3 covers White Blood Cells (disease fighters for inner spiritual cleansing and renewing) and includes questions like "Do you feel you are a more accepting, forgiving, loving person than you have been?" and "Do you feel you are stronger against temptations (to be impatient, angry, greedy, lustful, etc.)?" Section 4 covers Platelets (blood clotters that stanch the wounds of living in a hurting world), and includes questions like "Have you found someone to help bear the burdens of life?" and "When you fail (or succeed), what happens within you?" Section 5 covers Blood Pressure (hypertension and exercise) and includes questions like "Are you able to turn your finances over to God and tithe, trusting Him to supply?" and "How concerned are you with injustices and other social evils?" The final section, section 6, is on Tired Blood (from imbalanced spiritual diet), and key questions here are "Is your life balanced?" and "Do you feel you have a balance of worship, study, and service to stay in shape?"[24]

6. *The Spiritual Leadership Qualities Inventory.* Developed by Frank Wichern, this test is a measure that assesses a person's attitudes, beliefs, and values pertaining to qualities desired in Christian leaders according to 1 Timothy 3:1–7 and Titus 1:5–9. It contains a total of 222 items measuring the following nineteen qualities of a spiritually mature leader: (1) upright, (2) good reputation, (3) above

reproach, (4) respectable, (5) desire to be an overseer, (6) holy, (7) able to teach, (8) temperate, (9) prudent, (10) able to manage family, (11) husband of one wife, (12) gentle, (13) not quick-tempered, (14) self-controlled, (15) not addicted to wine, (16) not greedy, (17) lover of good, (18) not self-willed, (19) hospitable.[25]

There are other measures of spirituality,[26] but the ones described here are helpful ones to use in the screening of lay counselors.

The methods for screening potential lay counselors proposed by Collins are fairly comprehensive and somewhat stringent. Some churches may decide not to use all of them (e.g., psychological testing may not be easily available in some rural church communities or may be too costly), while other churches may use all these methods and add a couple more of their own.

Finally, be sure to complete any appropriate background checks. These are usually done at the state level and can identify any possible reports, arrests, or convictions related to child/elder abuse, felonies, and nonspeeding vehicular incidents. This should be a mandatory part of the application process.

THE EXAMPLE OF LA CANADA PRESBYTERIAN CHURCH

La Canada Presbyterian Church in Southern California is an example of a local church that has developed a comprehensive and stringent screening process for the selection of lay counselors, consisting of three major phases.[27] In Phase One, all applicants are required to complete a *written questionnaire or application form* with the following nine items (after the name, address, and telephone number(s) of the applicant have been filled in):

1. What do you believe constitutes effective counseling?
2. What does being a Christian mean to you personally?
3. What does it mean to you to counsel others as a Christian?
4. If you have had previous counseling experiences (either as a counselor or counselee) that may be helpful for us to know, please describe them and their significance to you.
5. What (if any) prior training or education have you had that may help you to be a counselor?
6. Prior work experience (list most recent first).
7. Would you please list as references the names, addresses, and phone numbers of two people who would be willing and able to affirm and endorse your participation in this ministry.
8. Why do you want to be a lay counselor?

9. Within the last two years have you experienced (or are you currently experiencing, or expect to experience) any significant life changes, e.g., separation, divorce, death in the family, job change, critical illness, etc.? Please explain.

The written responses of the applicant plus the recommendations of the two references listed on the application form serve as the basis on which applicants are selected for continuation on to Phase Two of the selection process. In Phase Two, selected applicants are interviewed by the church's lay counseling task force of five members, which includes two supervising consultants who are licensed mental health professionals, the lay counseling ministry coordinator/director, and two lay counselors. Each year, whenever possible, a total of sixteen applicants are selected for two group interviews of eight applicants at one time.

The following ten basic questions are asked of the applicants in the group interview process:

1. Please tell us your name and something about your current work situation.
2. What do you understand to be the purpose of the lay counseling ministry?
3. What to you are some of the more important ingredients of effective counseling?
4. What does it mean to you to be a Christian?
5. Admittedly the lay counseling ministry requires a significant commitment of time and effort, perhaps six to ten hours per week. How do you see yourself meeting such a demanding responsibility?
6. Being a La Canada Presbyterian Church lay counselor means more than counseling counselees. It involves being a part of a team of lay counselors who can be at some times intensely earnest and serious while at other times free and frivolous. How might you fit in among such a group?
7. How do you see yourself already or currently involved in the "counseling" of friends or colleagues?
8. How do you think being a lay counselor will meet your needs?
9. How have you felt about this interviewing experience today?
10. Do you have any questions for us?

The interviewers evaluate the answers given by each applicant to each of the ten basic questions, using a scale of 1 to 10 (1 = Unsatisfactory Response: Seemingly without thought; presented uncomfortably; not coincident with the direction of the lay counseling ministry; 5 = Mediocre Response: Somewhat thoughtful; presented somewhat comfortably; practically coincident with the direction of the lay counseling ministry; 10 = Excellent Response: Thoughtful, presented comfortably; coincides with the direction of the lay counseling ministry).

Each interviewer then rates each applicant as to his or her personal sense of the applicant as a counselor on a 1 to 10 scale as follows:

1. Would be psychologically/relationally dangerous.
2. Would probably make most people uneasy.
3. Would probably make many people uneasy.
4. Makes me moderately uneasy.
5. Makes me slightly uneasy.
6. Blah, but not dangerous.
7. Certain others might benefit from this person.
8. I would enjoy time with this person, but don't know if it would be beneficial.
9. I might benefit by seeing this person.
10. I would benefit by seeing this person.

Each interviewer also rates each applicant as to his or her personal sense of the applicant's benefit to the lay counseling ministry on a 1 to 10 scale as follows:

1. Ministry must not have him/her.
2. Ministry would rarely benefit from him/her.
3. Ministry would seldom benefit from him/her.
4. Ministry would infrequently benefit from him/her.
5. Ministry would sporadically benefit from him/her.
6. Ministry would occasionally benefit from him/her.
7. Ministry might benefit a little from him/her.
8. Ministry would probably benefit some from him/her.
9. Ministry would definitely benefit from him/her.
10. Ministry must have him/her.

A final part of the Phase Two interview process is a unique one that involves the eight applicants ranking themselves and each other in terms of their potential of helping or counseling ability. An Applicant Feedback Sheet is used with the following major question: Accurate perception of self and of others is a criterion often used in assessing potential counselor ability. To help us with this process, then, we would like you to consider the following: Imagine someone in need of counseling. Imagine that he or she had somehow been able to observe our interview session here today. Based on our time together, which person of these applicants do you believe the observer would be most likely to select for help? (Please include yourself in the ranking which goes from first to eighth).

A final group of applicants (usually eight to ten) is selected from Phase Two interviews. They go on to Phase Three of the process, the Lay Counseling Initial Intensive Training Program, which usually begins in March and ends in August of each year. Applicants who successfully complete Phase Three training are then selected to become lay counselors for a required minimum time commitment of one year.

CONCLUDING REMARKS

We have described in some detail the methods used by La Canada Presbyterian Church in the selection and screening of lay counselors because they are helpful examples of systematic, comprehensive, rigorous screening methods that can and should be used by local churches wanting to be involved in lay counseling ministries.

However, any thorough screening method can be adapted and modified where necessary without compromising the need to conduct a careful and detailed selection process. Some churches may prefer to conduct personal rather than group interviews of applicants and make the final selection of lay counselors after the interviews rather than after the initial intensive lay counselor training program. Other churches may allow any interested Christian first to sign up for and go through a basic lay counseling skills training program (usually a ten-to-fifteen-week course) and subsequently ask those who have completed the basic training program to apply more formally for possible selection as lay counselors, if they are interested, willing, and able. A selection interview process can then be conducted after applications have been made. Appendices A and B offer a sample application form and reference forms that can be adapted and utilized.

The procedures of selecting and screening lay counselors are not only important and time-consuming, but they can also lead to misunderstanding and disappointment for those applicants who are not selected. Be sure to clearly state the applicant requirements at the outset and explain that not all who apply will necessarily be selected. La Canada Presbyterian Church indicates they are looking for Christians who are regular participants in the life of the church, believe God has gifted them for a counseling ministry, would be willing to participate in a rigorous counselor training program, will comply with ongoing supervision and training, and are able to volunteer six to eight hours a week of involvement in the lay counseling ministry for at least one year. Their lay counseling ministry coordinator also explains in a letter to potential applicants,

We sincerely regret to have to say that not everyone who applies to this Ministry can become a Lay Counselor. We can only select a limited number of participants who we believe will most appropriately meet our current counselor needs. It is our hope and prayer that this selection process will help us discern God's best for you as well as for the lay counseling ministry.

The lay counselors finally selected should be those who possess the kinds of characteristics or criteria described earlier in this chapter, including being spiritually mature and specially gifted by God to engage in a lay counseling ministry that is equivalent to Crabb's Level 3, counseling by enlightenment, requiring some intensive training. Since all Christians are called to counsel or help others at some basic level (e.g., what Crabb has called Level 1, counseling by encouragement), basic training in encouragement or helping skills should be provided to as many interested Christians as possible through different means, such as a Sunday school class or a retreat or workshop on Basic Caring or The Ministry of Encouragement, etc.[28] Periodic sermons from the pulpit on themes of caring for each other or burden bearing are also helpful. We agree with Gary Sweeten's proposal that the church should be viewed as a "therapeutic growth community" in which "the general level of personal and interpersonal functioning" can be raised "by adapting a lay helper training strategy to the whole congregation and then selecting those who are properly talented, skilled, gifted, and called to enter the specific ministry of helping and pastoral care" or lay counseling.[29]

The screening methods described in this chapter are most appropriate for churches interested in starting more organized (whether formal or informal) lay counseling services or ministries. Some churches may prefer to provide basic training in lay pastoral care and counseling skills to all their church leaders who provide such care more informally through small discipleship groups, home fellowships or Bible studies, prayer teams, and visitation programs. Even in such cases, careful selection of church leaders is needed, and some of the screening methods mentioned may still be helpful and appropriate.

We end this chapter by returning to our potential lay counselors, Bob and Alice. Based on the selection criteria discussed in this chapter, it appears that Alice, rather than Bob, would be a better choice for initial selection as a lay counselor. However, the final decision should involve a careful and thorough interview process. Bob may not be selected because he seems to have an arrogant, condescending, and insensitive attitude. Alice has a better chance of being selected because she seems to possess humility and a genuine caring attitude toward people. She likely has spiritual gifts like exhortation and appropriate personality characteristics that have led several people to turn to her repeatedly for help in informal ways. Her spiritual life and maturity (as well as Bob's) should be more thoroughly explored during the interview process, which could include the use of Wayman's Spiritual Life Check-Up Questionnaire.[30]

While the basic selection criteria that we have mentioned should be kept in mind, the criterion of spiritual maturity—including a serious commitment to Jesus Christ as Lord and Savior, and to seeking God and His kingdom first (Matt. 6:33)—should be foundational and essential.

CHAPTER 7

Training of
Lay Counselors

Once a local church or parachurch organization has decided to begin a lay counseling ministry and has selected the lay counselors for that ministry, the crucial task of putting together an adequate and biblically based *training* program remains. There is some evidence, though still inconclusive, that lay counselors are more effective if they have received some training or have had some experience in helping people.[1] In the field of professional counseling and psychotherapy, there has been a recent surge of interest in developing more systematic training programs that focus on improving the actual competency of the trainees in such programs.[2]

The research literature showing that lay counselors are generally as effective as professional counselors in helping people with different types of problems challenges the essence of professional therapist training. However, as Brian Shaw and Keith Dobson, two well-known psychologists and researchers in the area of developing counselor competence, have pointed out, none of the studies reviewed in the research literature reported on the *actual levels* of skillfulness or competency of the professional versus the lay counselors. The question of how counselor competence affects the outcome of the counseling provided is therefore still an open and unanswered one.[3]

Such negligible differences between professional and lay counselors may mean that existing programs of professional training are not particularly effective in producing competent professional counselors who consistently do better counseling than lay counselors. As efforts are made to improve professional training programs in order to raise the levels of competence of professional counselors, a similar diligence is needed to adequately train lay counselors.

What kinds of training programs are best suited for lay counselors? Further research is needed to answer more definitively, but in general, training programs for lay counselors are of much shorter duration, significantly less clinical, and are more focused on a simpler set of helping skills, crisis management, and referral services than professional training programs.

THREE PHASES OF TRAINING

Dr. Gary Collins has suggested dividing training for lay counselors into three phases: pretraining, training, and posttraining.[4]

1. *The Pretraining Phase.* This phase includes selecting training materials, publicizing the training program, selecting participants (open or by invitation only), and possibly conducting an initial course on caring and the discovery of spiritual gifts. Collins suggests his book *The Joy of Caring* or Rick Yohn's *Discover Your Spiritual Gift and Use It* (Tyndale, 1982) for reading and discussion for this basic course.

2. *The Training Phase.* Actual training should provide opportunities for the lay trainees to learn counseling skills by listening to live or video-recorded lectures, reading, observing, engaging in group discussion, and introducing an experiential component (e.g., role plays or use of an "experimental client" or friend, or use of real-life cases in a supervised forum). Most programs include a minimum of forty to fifty hours of training over a period of several months. In this phase of training, the training groups are usually small, with ten to fifteen lay trainees who meet on a regular basis, weekly or biweekly, for two to three hours each time.

Collins suggests that training should include the following: (1) basic biblical knowledge, particularly that which is relevant to people-helping, personal problems, and the person and ministry of the Holy Spirit; (2) knowledge of counseling skills, with opportunity to practice them; (3) understanding of common presenting problems people face (e.g., discouragement, grief and loss, anxiety, excessive stress, or spiritual dryness); (4) awareness of ethics, liability factors, and risk management in counseling; and (5) knowledge of the importance and techniques of referral, as well as community resources. Several good programs incorporating these components are already available for the training of lay Christian counselors, and we will briefly review them later in this chapter.

3. *The Posttraining Phase.* This is a follow-up phase, which should provide further learning opportunities, discussion, and supervision of cases seen by the newly trained lay counselors, and encouragement for them to continue in their new ministry of people-helping.

MODELS OF LAY CHRISTIAN COUNSELOR TRAINING

Several models of lay Christian counselor training have been utilized by churches over the years.[5] In this section, we will review four of the more well-known models along with the respective models developed by each of the authors of this book.

Larry Crabb's Model

Dr. Larry Crabb proposed a model for the training of lay Christian counselors following his biblical counseling approach.[6] He describes three levels of biblical counseling and suggests different training requirements for each level. Level 1 is *counseling by encouragement*, and Crabb believes that every Christian should be trained in Level 1 counseling, which involves learning how to be more sensitive, how to listen, and how to communicate care. With his colleague Dan Allender, he wrote a book called *Encouragement: The Key to Caring*, which is relevant to Level 1 counseling.[7]

Level 2 is *counseling by exhortation*. Crabb suggests thirty-five to forty hours of classroom training for mature believers in Level 2 counseling. Finally, Level 3 is *counseling by enlightenment*, and Crabb recommends that only a few selected Christians in each local church be trained in Level 3 counseling, using a six-month to a year-long training program of weekly classes. He has used his model in training lay Christian counselors through the Institute of Biblical Counseling, which he founded. He is more involved recently in providing spiritual direction training through his organization, which is called New Way Ministries (www. newwayministries.org).

While Crabb's model is a helpful one in delineating different levels of biblical counseling requiring different types and amounts of training, it is not always easy or possible to keep the three levels of counseling so distinct. Level 2 and Level 3 counseling in particular are difficult to keep separate. We therefore suggest that it may be more helpful to train specially selected, mature Christians in effective biblical counseling that actually involves all three levels. Every Christian should have some training in basic listening and caring skills (i.e., Level 1 counseling) as Crabb has recommended. This can be done through the pulpit or preaching ministry of the church and supplemented by Sunday school classes and other special workshops.

Gary Sweeten's Model

Dr. Gary Sweeten, former minister of Christian Growth (nonclergy) at College Hill Presbyterian Church in Cincinnati, Ohio, has also developed a model for the training of lay Christian counselors. His model begins by adapting a lay helper training strategy and applying it to the total congregation of a local church to raise its general level of personal and interpersonal functioning, so that such a church can become a therapeutic growth community. Those who are properly talented, skilled, gifted, and called are then selected to be involved in the specific ministry of helping and pastoral care or lay counseling.[8]

Sweeten's discipleship counseling approach to lay counselor training attempts to integrate psychology, Christian theology, and the power of the Holy Spirit, and makes use of a variety of training materials like books and audio and video recordings. Special training seminars—called Counseling with Power seminars—that cover this approach have been conducted by Sweeten and his colleagues periodically in different parts of the country and even abroad.

The training program has four major components or courses. The first course, Apples of Gold I, is a competency-based interpersonal skills program focused on developing empathy, warmth, and respect in the helper toward the helpee or counselee. The second course, Apples of Gold II, teaches the helper the skills of concreteness, genuineness, self-disclosure, confrontation, and immediate feedback to facilitate speaking the truth in love with accountability. Both these courses are taught sequentially over an eight-week period for two and a half hours each session, with homework assignments given.

The third course, Rational Christian Thinking, integrates principles of rational-emotive therapy with Scripture and seeks to help people in the process of "renewing their minds." It is a six-week course of two and a half hours per session, also with homework assignments. The fourth and final course, Breaking Free from the Past, is the most intense one, requiring some fifty hours of preparation, dealing with past traumas, generational blessings and curses, and personal sins and character defects in the context of self-disclosure and prayer in a supportive small group. Two facilitators lead group members through this process, which also includes some didactic teaching.

Horace Lukens's Model

Dr. Horace Lukens has set forth a model for the training of lay or paraprofessional Christian counselors in which he proposes six sequential levels of training in the curriculum.[9] Level 1, Body Life Skills I, is for all Christians and focuses on basic skills of living in Christian community. It includes skills for entering and building relationships, listening skills, and Carkhuff's core conditions (see the seventh principle in chapter 3). Lukens recommends that specific criteria for defining and measuring such skills be used. Level 2, Theory and Theology, is for Christian leaders and teachers, covering the integration of Christianity and psychology, developmental psychology, and abnormal psychology as specific knowledge areas to which they need to be exposed. Level 3, Personal Awareness, is also for Christian leaders and teachers. In this segment of the training curriculum, the trainees examine their personal needs, issues, and motives as they relate to becoming a counselor/leader. Their gifts and talents, strengths and weaknesses, and temperament or personality characteristics are also explored, with the help of psychological testing.

Level 4, Body Life Skills II, is for lay counselor trainees only. It focuses on further development and refinement of counseling skills for the trainees and includes training in action, sharing, and teaching responses; interviewing skills; problem definition; and the process of counseling. Lukens emphasizes that specific criteria for defining and assessing such skills should be used, and he notes that such criteria needed for evaluating Level 1 and Level 4 Body Life Skills can be found in a book written by William H. Cormier and L. Sherilyn Cormier titled *Interviewing Strategies for Helpers: A Guide to Assessment, Treatment, and Evaluation*. The second edition of this helpful book was titled *Interviewing Strategies for Helpers: Fundamental Skills and Cognitive Behavioral Interventions*, and the eighth edition, titled *Interviewing and Change Strategies for Helpers*, was published in 2016.[10]

Level 5, Practicum, involves counseling supervision for lay counselor trainees who have demonstrated competence in all previous levels of training. Lukens suggests a minimum of forty client hours and ten supervision hours for each trainee. Finally, Level 6, Advanced Training, is for lay counselor trainees who have successfully completed the previous five levels of training and who show an interest in, as well as appropriate talents or gifts for, further advanced training. Areas of such training may include marital and family therapy, vocational evaluation or counseling, financial counseling, and inner healing and deliverance.

Lukens proposes that each level of training be limited to eight or ten weeks in duration. In his training model, he also addresses the development of goals and objectives, counselor selection, skill development, curriculum goals, the scriptural principle of multiplication (i.e., training trainees to become effective trainers), supervision, evaluation of counselor readiness and effectiveness, program evaluation, and the need to establish standard acceptable criteria and levels of training for all paraprofessional Christian counselors.

Kenneth Haugk's Model and the Stephen Series

Dr. Kenneth Haugk founded the Stephen Series of lay caring ministry in 1975. He is a pastor, clinical psychologist, author, and educator, as well as the executive director of Stephen Ministries, a transdenominational, international, nonprofit caring ministry organization based in St. Louis, Missouri. Although Haugk's model applies more generally to a lay caring ministry in the local church context and not to lay counseling per se, much of the lay caring ministry covered by the Stephen Series also involves some level of lay Christian counseling as we have defined it. He developed the Stephen Series with the following steps or components:

1. A congregation should enroll in the Stephen Series by contacting the Stephen Ministries office in St. Louis, Missouri, and by paying a one-time enrollment fee.

2. A congregation should select leaders, such as the pastor, other church staff, and gifted lay leaders to be involved in leadership for the Stephen Series.

3. Selected leaders should attend a twelve-day Leader's Training Course.

4. The congregation should be prepared for the Stephen Series about to be implemented.

5. Lay caregivers should be recruited and selected to be trained as Stephen ministers by the Stephen leaders.

6. Lay caregivers or Stephen ministers should be trained for fifty hours.

7. Stephen leaders should find and prepare those with particular needs to receive care from the trained Stephen ministers.

8. Trained Stephen ministers should be appropriately assigned to people with particular needs that match the gifts and skills of the Stephen ministers.

9. Helping relationships between Stephen ministers and those who are receiving care from them should continue to be supervised on a regular basis. Stephen ministers have to make a two-year commitment to such a lay caring ministry, which includes fifty hours of training, an average of one one-hour visit each week, and meeting for supervision and support twice a month.

The twelve-day Leader's Training Course is an intensive and comprehensive one that covers three main areas: (1) administrative resources, (2) training topics/presentations, and (3) implementing and maintaining Stephen Ministry in the congregation. The training topics/presentations are also the same ones that Stephen leaders will use to provide the fifty hours of training needed by selected Stephen ministers.

The training topics/presentations include the following: what to do during the first helping contact; feelings: yours, mine, and ours; the art of listening; tele-care: the next best thing to being there; effective use of the traditional resources of Christianity; assertiveness: relating gently and firmly; being "professional"; confidentiality; relationship exercise; the "small step" approach; utilizing community resources; when and how to terminate a caring relationship; crisis theory and intervention; stress of hospitalization; ministry to those experiencing grief; ministry to the dying and their family and friends; ministering to depressed persons; ministering to suicidal persons and family and friends; ministering to older persons; ministering to shut-in persons; ministering to those experiencing divorce; ministering to inactive members; childbirth as a family crisis; Jo-Hari window; everything Stephen Ministers wanted to know about caring but were afraid to ask; and supervision: a key to quality Christian care. Available separately is training on ministering to chemically dependent individuals and their families.

In addition to receiving training on the topics listed, Stephen leaders also receive training in implementing and maintaining Stephen Ministry in the congregation. Topics covered include preparing the congregation as a whole for Stephen Ministry; recruiting, selecting, and training Stephen Ministers; commissioning Stephen Ministers; generating and making referrals to Stephen Ministers; supervising Stephen Ministry; and recognizing and affirming the work of Stephen ministers.

Haugk's model and Stephen Series are most applicable to the informal-organized model of lay counseling ministry. The other models of lay Christian counselor training proposed by Crabb, Sweeten, and Lukens contain different levels of training and are applicable to all three models of lay counseling ministry that have been described—the *informal-spontaneous, informal-organized,* and *formal-organized* (see pages 89–91). That said, all of these models, including Collins's delineation of the phases of lay Christian counselor training, are most applicable to the informal-organized and the formal-organized models of lay counseling ministry. Other models of lay Christian counselor training are available, but the ones outlined here are among the most significant and well-known.

EXAMPLES OF LAY CHRISTIAN COUNSELOR TRAINING PROGRAMS

Moving beyond the four key models we have just outlined, we want to point out that there are many *specific programs* available for lay Christian counselor training. Though we don't have space to cover them all, the next section reviews several of the better-known or widely used ones. We have already mentioned Dr. Gary Sweeten's materials for training lay counselors in a local church context. Similarly, the Stephen Series developed by Dr. Kenneth Haugk has already been described. His book *Christian Caregiving: A Way of Life* is a helpful guide for training lay caregivers and is used as a text in the Stephen Series.[11] Dr. Crabb has written a number of helpful books that can be used in a lay counselor training program.[12] He also authored a training manual that was available only through the Institute of Biblical Counseling and its seminars or workshops on biblical counseling.

Dr. Gary Collins is the author of a number of helpful training programs or materials for lay Christian counselors. In 1976 Collins put together the People Helper Pak, a resource containing a text, a growth book, and audiotapes for training lay Christians in basic people-helping skills in twelve sessions.[13] His widely used classic textbook, *Christian Counseling: A Comprehensive Guide,* was first published in 1980 and then expanded, updated, and completely revised in 1988 and again in 2007.[14] He also had a *Christian Counselor's Library* (revised edition) that contained forty audio cassettes, a counselor's manual, counselee worksheets, and a copy of the 1988 revised edition of the textbook, and that was available from the Educational Products Division of Word, Inc. The library or textbook can be used in an extensive program of lay Christian counselor training. Part of the first edition of the library, including the 1980 textbook, was used in a one-year, part-time training course for lay or paraprofessional Christian counselors at the Institute of Christian Counseling, which was set up and directed by Dr. Tan at Ontario Bible College in Toronto in September 1984.

Dr. Jay Adams has authored several books on nouthetic counseling that can be used in a training program for lay nouthetic counselors.[15] He also put together a Competent to Counsel Training Kit. Dr. William Backus has developed a biblical approach to cognitive therapy called misbelief therapy and has written a useful textbook titled *Telling the Truth to Troubled People* for training lay counselors in misbelief therapy.[16] Dr. Charles Solomon originated "spirituotherapy" and has written a couple of books relevant to the training of lay counselors, especially those interested in using his spirituotherapy approach to helping people.[17] This approach is based on the "victorious life" or exchanged-life theology, focusing on the need for a person to appropriate his or her identification with Christ.

William H. ("Skip") Hunt has written a number of training courses for lay Christian counselors, including a relatively well-known one titled "How Can I Help?" This college-level course in personal counseling and evangelism is used to train the ordinary layperson to help friends in crisis. It has also been used by Christian crisis centers across the United States to train staff and volunteers. Hunt is president of Christian Helplines, Inc., a national association of Christian telephone counseling ministries, and can be contacted at PO Box 10855, Tampa, FL 33679, telephone (813) 874-5509.

Robert Kellemen, president of RPM Ministries (Resurrection Power Multipliers), is another author who writes and trains in the field of lay counseling. Kellemen developed the 4E Ministry Training Strategy: Equipping Lay Counselors, Care Givers, and Spiritual Friends.[18] Leaders are trained in four general areas: to *envision* God's ministry, to *enlist* God's ministers for ministry, to *equip* godly ministers for ministry, and to *empower/employ* godly ministers for ministry. A primary orientation to the training model is his advocacy for a congregation to become a church of biblical counseling as opposed to a church with a biblical counseling ministry. Kellemen has also recently released a two-part training series for lay counselors called Gospel-Centered Counseling and Gospel Conversations that expands his earlier model.

The American Association of Christian Counselors (AACC) also produces a significant array of Christian counseling materials and resources (see www. aacc.net). Their primary lay counselor training program consists of two different, comprehensive video-based courses: Caring for People God's Way and Breaking Free. Each course is comprised of thirty fifty-to sixty-minute presentations by leading authors, researchers, and teachers within Christian counseling, and are divided into specific training units that address a wide selection of presenting problems and counseling-related issues. Students may enroll through AACC's Light University.

We mentioned a number of other significant training programs and materials available for lay Christian counselor training in chapter 4.[19] Certain secular books on helping or counseling skills have also been used in lay Christian counselor training programs. They include Lawrence Brammer's *The Helping Relationship*, Robert Carkhuff's *The Art of Helping*, Gerard Egan's *The Skilled Helper*, and William Cormier and Sherilyn Cormier's *Interviewing Strategies for Helpers*.[20]

Also available are some specialized training programs for lay counselors interested in helping ministries with particular populations or groups of people. For example, Dr. Paul Welter developed a specific program for training retirement center and nursing home staff and residents in lay helping and counseling skills. The Board of National Ministries of the American Baptist Churches funded and helped organize this lay counseling program in seven of their retirement centers/nursing homes over a seven-year period, with basically positive evaluations or results.[21] Welter's training program for lay counselors in long-term care settings includes the use of several helpful books he has written.[22]

Emily Osborn developed a fifteen-week training program for lay or paraprofessional family counselors who specialize in helping families with problems or difficulties.[23] Her program was initially conducted at St. Matthew's Episcopal Church in Bellaire, Texas. Several other churches have also begun training their lay counselors in family counseling. For example, at La Canada Presbyterian Church in Southern California, Rev. Chuck Osburn included a special training program on family counseling for their lay counselors, using mainly books by family systems theorists S. Minuchin, V. Satir and M. Baldwin, and G. R. Patterson.[24] It is also important to include training in prevention and outreach services in any lay counselor training program, as Jeffrey Prater has strongly recommended.[25]

TAN LAY CHRISTIAN COUNSELOR
TRAINING PROGRAM

The rest of this chapter will focus on the details of basic training programs we have developed for lay Christian counselors. The first program is one developed by Dr. Tan and is a basic twelve-session training program originally developed in 1981 to train lay Christian counselors at North Park Community Chapel, a local church with over one thousand people in London, Ontario.[26] The training program met biweekly and lasted six months. Each training session was about three hours in duration. The program can be shortened to three months by conducting weekly sessions of three hours each instead of biweekly sessions.

Since the model used in the training program is a biblically based, largely cognitive-behavioral model, the textbook chosen was Dr. Gary Collins's *Christian Counseling: A Comprehensive Guide* (Word, 1988), first published in 1980 but now available in a revised and updated 1988 edition, as well as a 2007 third edition. Other highly recommended or required readings included Jay Adams's *The Christian Counselor's Manual* (Baker, 1973), William Backus and Marie Chapian's *Telling Yourself the Truth* (Bethany House, 1980), Gary Collins's *How to Be a People Helper* (Vision House, 1976), and Lawrence Crabb's *Effective Biblical Counseling* (Zondervan, 1977). Other recommended texts include Everett Worthington's *When Someone Asks for Help: A Practical Guide for Counseling* (InterVarsity, 1982) and Carol Baldwin's *Friendship Counseling: Biblical Foundations for Helping Others* (Zondervan, 1988). These can serve as basic texts for teaching counseling or helping skills to lay Christian counselors. More recent books would also include J. R. Cheydleur's *Called to Counsel* (Tyndale, 1999), E. A. N. Spanotto, H. D. Gingrich, and F. C. Gingrich's *Skills for Effective Counseling: A Faith-Based Integration* (IVP Academic, 2016), and G. Sweeten, D. Ping, and A. Clippard's *Listening for Heaven's Sake* (Teleios, 1993). William Backus's *Telling the Truth to Troubled People* (Bethany House, 1985) is also a very helpful text for training lay counselors from a Christian cognitive-behavioral perspective.

The basic training covered the signs and symptoms of major psychiatric disorders, which was particularly helpful for teaching lay counselors how to appropriately refer counselees to licensed practitioners. The training sessions included lectures, demonstrations of specific counseling skills and techniques (through role plays with the instructor as the counselor), discussion of issues, and role playing in smaller groups (of three or five) with feedback and discussion. We tried to allow sufficient opportunity for each trainee or lay counselor to role-play the counselor as well as the counselee.

Several topics were covered in the original training program and provide a good outline for developing an initial training program:

Session 1: An Integrated, Biblically Based Model for Effective Christian Counseling (see chapters 3 and 4 of this book).

Session 2: Basic Interviewing Skills (e.g., building rapport, listening attentively, watching carefully, handling silence, questioning wisely, responding appropriately, using spiritual resources); Overview of the Counseling Process (exploration, understanding, action phases, and termination).

Session 3: Some Useful Counseling Methods (e.g., homework assignments, relaxation and coping techniques, imagery exercises, including stress-inoculation training, thought-stopping and cognitive restructuring, problem solving, providing information on diet, exercise, and rest, making referrals, bibliotherapy, role-playing strategies and assertiveness or social skills training, Christian meditation, prayer, and inner healing).

These first three sessions covered basic counseling skills and methods within a biblical framework, and such skills and methods were then applied in later sessions to specific problem areas. Required reading for these foundational sessions included Worthington (1982) or Baldwin (1988), Crabb (1977), Backus (1985), and David Seamands's *Healing of Memories* (Wheaton, IL: Victor, 1985). Dr. Tan has also developed a seven-step model for inner healing prayer that is described in S. Y. Tan and J. Ortberg's *Coping with Depression*, rev. ed. (Baker, 2004). Cormier and Cormier (1985 and updated editions) should be consulted by the trainer for helpful descriptions of several useful counseling methods, especially cognitive-behavioral interventions. Another helpful book for the trainer to consult is *Teaching Psychological Skills: Models for Giving Psychology Away* (Brooks/Cole, 1984), edited by Dale Larson.

For the remaining sessions, required readings were assigned for the following topics and chapters from Collins's textbook:

Session 4: Personal Growth of the Counselor and Prevention of Burnout (for sessions 1–4: Collins, 1980, chaps. 1–4; or Collins, 1988, chaps. 1–5; or Collins, 2007, chaps. 1–7).

Session 5: Depression (Collins, 1980, chap. 7; or Collins, 1988, chap. 8; or Collins, 2007, chap. 8).

Session 6: Anger (Collins, 1980, chap. 8; or Collins, 1988, chap. 9; or Collins, 2007, chap. 10).

Session 7: Anxiety (Collins, 1980, chap. 5; or Collins, 1988, chap. 6; or Collins, 2007, chap. 9).

Session 8: Sexuality (Collins, 1980, chaps. 20–22; or Collins, 1988, chaps. 17–19; or Collins, 2007, chaps. 19–21).

Session 9: Marital and Family Problems (Collins, 1980, chaps. 13–15; or Collins, 1988, chaps. 11, 27–30; or Collins, 2007, chaps. 28–32).

Session 10: Spiritual Problems (Collins, 1980, chap. 29; or Collins, 1988, chap. 36; or Collins, 2007, chap. 41).

Session 11: Referrals and Psychiatric Intervention.

Session 12: Using Your Counseling Skills; Setting Up a Counseling Service in a Local Church.

TAN ONE-YEAR, PART-TIME EXPANDED TRAINING PROGRAM FOR LAY CHRISTIAN COUNSELORS

This basic twelve-session training program was later expanded into a more intensive and comprehensive one-year, part-time training orientation. It was first taught in 1984 at the Institute of Christian Counseling of Ontario Bible College in Toronto, with college credit given for three semesters of study and training totaling 108 hours.[27]

The format of the training sessions was similar to the basic training program, with weekly three-hour meetings. There were lectures as well as listening to selected presentations taken from *The Christian Counselor's Library*, edited by Dr. Gary Collins, discussion of issues, and demonstrations of counseling skills or methods through role-playing with the instructor as counselor. At this level of training, a significant portion of time should be spent in practical counseling skills training, implementing role play and discussion with feedback in small groups of three to five trainees, using cases provided or those taken from the counseling ministries of the lay counselors or trainees. Recorded sessions of counseling situations (whether audio or video) should be used as often as possible. Trainees must, of course, obtain the necessary permission from their counselees before presenting and discussing them and their problem situations.

This expanded training program consisted of three major parts, but the original curriculum has since been revised again to utilize more recently published books and to follow Collins's revised 1988 edition, *Christian Counseling: A Comprehensive Guide*. The revised curriculum looks like this:

Part 1:	*Introductory and Personal Issues* (Total time: 12 weeks or 36 hours)
Topics:	A Biblical Model for Effective Counseling; Lay Counseling in the Local Church; Critical Issues in Christian Counseling (including ethical and legal issues and the need for referral); Basic Counseling Skills and Overview of the Counseling Process; Some Useful Counseling Methods; Inner Healing; Personal Growth of the Counselor; Anxiety; Loneliness; Depression; Anger; and Guilt.
Required Reading:	Collins, 1988, chapters 1–10; Worthington, 1982; or Baldwin, 1988.
Recommended Reading:	Jay Adams, *Ready to Restore: The Layman's Guide to Christian Counseling* (Baker, 1981), *The Christian Counselor's Manual* (Baker, 1973), *A Theology of Christian Counseling: More Than Redemption* (Zondervan, 1979); Samuel Southard, *Theology and Therapy: The Wisdom of God in a Context of Friendship* (Word, 1989); Ray Anderson, *Christians Who Counsel: The Vocation of Wholistic Therapy* (Zondervan, 1990); William Backus and Marie Chapian, *Telling Yourself the Truth* (Bethany House, 1980); William Backus, *Telling the Truth to Troubled People* (Bethany House, 1985); Lawrence Crabb, *Effective Biblical Counseling* (Zondervan, 1977), *Understanding People* (Zondervan, 1987), *Inside Out* (NavPress, 1988); and David Seamands, *Healing of Memories* (Victor, 1985).
Part 2:	*Singleness, Marriage, and Developmental Family Issues* (Total time: 12 weeks or 36 hours)
Topics:	Singleness, Choosing a Marriage Partner, Premarital Counseling, Marital Problems, Pregnancy Issues, Family Problems, Divorce and Remarriage, Child Rearing and Parental Guidance, Adolescence, Young Adulthood, Middle Age, and the Later Years.
Required Reading:	Collins, 1988, chaps. 11–15 and 24–30; Norman Wright, *Marital Counseling: A Biblical Behavioral, Cognitive Approach* (Harper & Row, 1981); or Everett Worthington, *Marriage Counseling: A Christian Approach to Counseling Couples* (InterVarsity, 1989); or Deloss Friesen and Ruby Friesen, *Counseling and Marriage* (Word, 1989); and G. A. Rekers, *Counseling Families* (Word, 1988).
Recommended Reading:	Lawrence Crabb, *The Marriage Builder: A Blueprint for Couples and Counselors* (Zondervan, 1982); Keith Olson, *Counseling Teenagers: The Complete Christian Guide to Understanding and Helping Adolescents* (Group, 1984); and Norman Wright, *Premarital Counseling: A Guidebook for the Counselor* (Moody, 1981).

Part 3:	Sex and Interpersonal Issues and Other Issues (Total time: 12 weeks or 36 hours)
Topics:	Interpersonal Relationships, Sex Apart from Marriage, Sex within Marriage, Homosexuality, Violence and Abuse, Inferiority and Self-Esteem, Physical Illness, Grief, Mental Disorders, Alcoholism, Addictions, Financial Counseling, Vocational Counseling, Spiritual Issues, Other Problems, Counseling the Counselor.
Required Reading:	Collins, 1988, chaps. 16–23, 31–38; and William Backus, Telling the Truth to Troubled People (Bethany House, 1985).
Recommended Reading:	William Backus and Marie Chapian, Why Do I Do What I Don't Want to Do? (Bethany House, 1984); Ed Wheat and Gaye Wheat, Intended for Pleasure: Sex Technique and Sexual Fulfillment in Christian Marriage, rev. ed. (Revell, 1981); Clifford and Joyce Penner, The Gift of Sex: A Christian Guide to Sexual Fulfillment (Word, 1981); and John White, Eros Defiled: The Christian and Sexual Sin (InterVarsity, 1977).

The one-year, part-time expanded training program or course for lay or paraprofessional Christian counselors just described can be completed in thirty-six weeks or less than a year if the three parts of the program are conducted sequentially, without a break in between parts. A lay counselor or trainee going through such a program will receive 108 hours of instruction and training on a comprehensive list of topics and problem areas covered in Collins's textbook. However, further training and ongoing supervision will still be needed. The next chapter deals with this important topic and answers the question: How do you supervise lay counselors?

SCALISE LAY CHRISTIAN COUNSELOR TRAINING PROGRAM

The training program developed by Eric Scalise was originally designed in 1986 for a church in Williamsburg, Virginia. Since that time, it has been refined and utilized by more than one hundred different congregations throughout the country with over two thousand lay counselors trained in basic counseling and crisis intervention skills. The current program consists of a fifteen-session course that meets once per week for three hours. Two additional bonus sessions are offered that discuss how to set up and properly run psychoeducational and support group ministries. Trainees are given an extensive handout at the beginning of each session with training notes and bonus materials.

By the end of the course, lay counselors have a comprehensive resource notebook for ongoing reference and review. Attendance is mandatory and all sessions must be completed. If a trainee has to miss a class due to illness or a family emergency, he or she must watch the prerecorded video of the lecture and debrief with the trainer in order to receive credit.

Each session includes lectures and interactive, experiential elements such as role plays, and case management and small group discussion. Trainees are placed in groups of five to seven individuals at the onset of training and remain in their small groups throughout the training period. This enhances relationship-building skills, authentic transparency, and the development of trust, which are all essential to effective lay helping. Current lay counselors, as well as clients (with proper consent) who have benefited from the ministry, share testimonies at each session. And while some training programs attempt to complete all training as a multiple-day or weeklong intensive, we have found that stretching the process over three to four months is beneficial (and recommended) for several reasons. The extended time frame allows for better assimilation of the learning material and practice of core people-helping skills, along with ongoing observation and evaluation of the trainee by ministry leaders to determine their readiness to be deployed.

A key principle is that for God to do something *through* us, he must first do something *in* us. Our specific training goals include the following:

1. Equipping the trainee as a biblical caregiver so that he or she can more fully recognize and help meet the needs of hurting and broken people
2. Providing faith-based and thoroughly biblical training materials, teaching, and exercises that are Christ-centered in their orientation
3. Creating a network of persons who will be trained to assist the church leadership with caregiving needs and in establishing an effective lay caregiving ministry
4. Forming a community of like-minded people who are available to one another for the purpose of support, encouragement, and accountability
5. Giving trainees the opportunity for personal and spiritual growth, insight, and development in the following areas:
   - A better understanding of who they are in Christ and their identity in Him
   - Deeper awareness on the influence of their own family dynamics and life experiences
   - Their spiritual gifts and talents
   - Their strengths and weaknesses
   - Their personal and ministry relationships
   - Their relationship with the Lord

At the conclusion of the training program, lay counselors participate in a follow-up session led by church leadership and the lead trainer(s). The purpose of this session is to orient the lay counselor to specific church policies and protocols, including doctrinal principles. Each trainee is provided with a detailed Community Resource Manual that contains the names, contact information, and a description of various resources, professionals, organizations, services, and agencies within the church, as well as within the broader community. This is useful in their work with clients, as well as for referral purposes. A graduation ceremony is scheduled and trainees who have successfully completed all training requirements are recognized and awarded a certificate of completion (this event can be shared during a regular church service to recognize and honor those who have been called into the lay counseling ministry).

What is the content of the training? Here is an outline of the basic fifteen-week training course and the two bonus sessions:

Session 1—A Biblical Basis for Caregiving
- Mission and Vision: The Goals and Purpose of Lifeline and for the Training Process
- A Biblical Model for Christian Caregiving: Living and Serving in a Broken World
- A Look at Motives and Personal Needs: Potential Pitfalls for the Caregiver
- Character Matters: Qualities of the Christ-Centered Helper
- Called to Care: The Power of Encouragement

Session 2—The Foundation of Relationship
- The Foundation of Relationship: The Power of Perspective
- Decision Making and Problem Solving: The Learning Style Profile
- Becoming Fishers of Men: Connecting with Others
- Disciples and Disciplers: Connecting Others to God
- The Power of Identity: Our Security in Christ

Session 3—Caregiving and the Bible
- Our Worldview: Serving in an Upside-Down Kingdom
- The Holy Spirit and Caregiving: The Priest and the Prophet
- Theological and Psychological Synthesis: Applying Godly Wisdom
- Becoming Partakers of the Divine Nature: Principles of Life and Godliness
- The Caregiver's Role in the Helping Process: An Acts 3 Encounter

Session 4—Effective Listening and Communication Skills
- How Men and Women Communicate: Generalized Tendencies
- Listening as an Art: Essential Skills and Techniques
- Barriers to Effective Communication: How the Process Can Be Hindered
- A Look at Perception: What Happens When We Put God in a Box
- Two-Way Communication: The Role of Trust and Safety

Session 5—The Search for Significance
- Who We Are in Christ: Self-Identity vs. God-Identity
- Addressing the Root Causes: The Fear of Exposure
- The Four False Beliefs: Walking in the Darkness
- The Result of the Fall: Guilt, Shame, Punishment, and Hopelessness
- God's Solutions: Walking in the Light

Session 6—Your Parents and You
- Our Family of Origin: Generational Patterns
- Stages of Development: Bonding and Separateness
- Family Dynamics: Dysfunctional Rules and Roles
- Resetting the Same Scenes: Ego-Defense Mechanisms
- Rewriting the Old Script: Healthy Attachments with God and Others

Session 7—Basic Helping and Crisis Intervention
- The Whole Person Concept: Understanding Needs-Based Care
- Proportional Helping: Balancing Love and Grace with Truth and Action
- Problem Ownership: Bearing One Another's Burdens and Setting Boundaries
- The Nature of Crises: Universal Principles and Coping Mechanisms
- The ABCs of Crisis Intervention: Critical Incident Stress Management

Session 8—Trauma and Abuse
- Trauma and Traumatic Stress: Understanding PTSD
- Complex Trauma: Signs, Symptoms, and Precipitating Factors
- Crossover Trauma: Impersonal and Interpersonal Events
- Mind-Body Connection: The Neurobiology of Stress and Trauma
- Broken Hearts, Broken Spirits: Childhood Sexual Abuse

Session 9—Grief, Loss, and Mood Disorders
- Depression and Anxiety: Signs and Symptoms
- Mood Disorders: Physiology, Guilt, Anger, and Spiritual Factors

- Suicide Risk Management: Using the STOP Protocol
- Loss, Death, and Dying: Understanding the Grief Cycle
- A Theology of Suffering and Hope: Bringing Balance

Session 10—Addictions and Strongholds

- The Addictive Cycle: Stages and Categories of Abuse and Dependence
- Signs, Symptoms, and Strongholds: A Look at Spiritual Bondage
- Prevention and Caregiving: Steps toward Freedom
- Spiritual Warfare: Our Weapons and Our Strategy
- Bulletproof Faith: Putting on the Whole Armor of God

Session 11—Marriage Counseling and Caregiving

- A Biblical View of Marriage: The Excellence of Love and the One Anothers
- Understanding the Love Languages: Words, Time, Service, Gifts, and Touch
- Gold Medal Relationships: Creating a Marriage Two Die For
- The Ten Commandments: Communication, Decision Making, and Conflict Resolution
- Broken and Shattered: Separation, Divorce, and Remarriage

Session 12—Parenting and Blended Families

- The Great Debate: Healthy and Dysfunctional Parenting Styles
- Head to Head: Managing Confrontation and Conflict Resolution
- When "No" Is the Right Answer: Setting Healthy Boundaries
- Strategic and Balanced Discipline: Prevention and Key Factors
- The Father Heart of God: Principles of Discipleship

Session 13—The Process of Change and Healing

- The Road to Recovery: Four Basic Building Blocks
- The Role of Confession: Breaking the Power of the Secret
- Restoration and Transformation: Becoming Vessels of Honor
- Forgiveness and Learning to Let Go: Giving Up Control
- Understanding God as a Father: Our Adoption in Christ

Session 14—Liability, Ethics, and the Law

- Setting Up a Church-Based Caregiving Ministry: Important Considerations
- Next Steps: How and When to Refer
- Caregiving Protocols: Utilizing Resources in the Church and the Community

- Ethics, Liability and the Law: The Hot Issues in Church-Based Caregiving
- Burnout and Compassion Fatigue: Making a Commitment to Balanced Self-Care

Session 15—The Great Commission

- Servanthood: The Highest Calling
- God's Bigger Plan: Rescuing vs. Ministry
- Self, Others, and God: The Ministry of Reconciliation
- Plenipotentiary Leadership: Becoming Ambassadors for Christ
- The Power of a Seed: Viewing Ourselves and Others with the Eyes of Christ

Bonus Session 1—Leading Effective Small Groups (Part 1)

- Church-Based Small Groups: Types and Myths
- Areas of Growth from Small Group Participation
- The Role of the Leader
- Group Values and Goals
- The Initial Stage: Characteristics, Guidelines, and Goals

Bonus Session 2—Leading Effective Small Groups (Part 2)

- The Transition Stage: Characteristics, Guidelines, and Goals
- Effective Facilitator Skills
- Therapeutic Factors and Problem Behaviors
- The Working Stage: Characteristics, Guidelines, and Goals
- The Final Stage: Characteristics, Guidelines, and Goals

CONCLUDING COMMENTS

We have looked at several models of lay Christian counselor training, as well as several examples of available training programs. Ultimately the choice of which model(s) or specific training protocol(s) to use will depend on the following factors: (1) the theoretical counseling preference and theological persuasion of the trainer and the church involved; (2) the model of lay counseling ministry chosen (i.e., whether it will be an informal-spontaneous, informal-organized, or formal-organized model, or some combination of these models); and (3) the specific focus or clientele of the lay counseling ministry (e.g., focusing on individual counseling or marital and family counseling or group counseling or a combination of these; focusing on helping adolescents, adults, or the elderly).

Several good, biblically based training models and programs for lay Christian counselors are now available and can be used to train individuals for a helping ministry. In addition to what we have covered in this chapter, many local churches have developed their own training materials and resources, incorporating the best components from several of the models and programs described in this chapter, and adding other material where necessary.

Regardless of the specific training program you choose, we would encourage you to incorporate the five essential components of a biblically based training program for lay counselors suggested by Dr. Collins at the beginning of this chapter. Further research is also needed to determine what components of a training program are particularly helpful or effective, as well as which specific training model and program is relatively more helpful or effective, or whether most training programs are comparable in effectiveness. The few research or evaluation studies that have been done so far and that were reviewed in chapter 4 have generally yielded favorable results supporting the effectiveness of some of the training programs we have described.[28] More evaluation studies are needed.

Jesus himself initiated his own program of training and discipleship with the original twelve apostles. Dr. Robert Coleman wrote a classic work (originally published in 1963 and revised in 2010)[29] on Jesus' orientation to this transformational and preparatory process—one in which the disciples were being developed to engage a world that needed Christ—titled *The Master Plan of Evangelism*. While the focus of that work is not on lay counseling, Coleman reinforced several of the principles we have discussed in this and previous chapters. He showed that Jesus carefully selected His disciples for the work of ministry; He mentored them, consecrated them and set them apart for the work, and imparted His love to them. He demonstrated the ministry for them and then delegated responsibility to them. Finally, He supervised them and taught them so that they could reproduce what He had done in teaching it to others. Jesus' methods are a wonderful model for any ministry, and they are helpful as we think about training up lay counselors to help and counsel others.

CHAPTER 8

Supervision of Lay Counselors

Lay counselors who have completed a basic training program in lay Christian counseling and begun their lay counseling ministry (after being appropriately screened and selected) will still need ongoing supervision and training. While several resources are available for training lay Christian counselors, the literature on the *supervision* of lay Christian counseling is sparse and limited. In this chapter, we review the secular literature on the clinical supervision of counselors or therapists (whether professional or nonprofessional), as well as the smaller literature on the supervision of Christian counselors, including lay Christian counselors. From this we can glean some practical guidelines to effectively supervise lay Christian counselors, and we will provide a hypothetical verbatim example of how to apply the guidelines in a supervision session.

DEFINITION OF SUPERVISION

Let's start by defining the term *supervision*. When used in the context of counseling or therapy, we are referring to the supervision of clinical work like counseling or therapy. A widely accepted definition of *clinical supervision* is the one proposed by C. Loganbill, E. Hardy, and U. Delworth: "an intensive, interpersonally focused, one-to-one relationship in which one person is designated to facilitate the development of therapeutic competence in the other person."[1] The clinical supervisor is the person responsible for overseeing and guiding the counselor to further develop his or her skills, competence, and effectiveness.

This can be a traditional one-on-one supervision relationship between a more experienced supervisor and a less experienced supervisee or trainee. Yet clinical supervision can also be conducted in several other formats as well, including: dyadic (one supervisor with two supervisees), group (one supervisor with a group of three or more supervisees), and peer (a group of two or more supervisees or peers providing supervision to one another). Because they have limited resources, most lay Christian counseling centers provide supervision in dyadic, group, or peer formats, supplemented when necessary by one-on-one supervision.

Ongoing and regular supervision of lay Christian counselors is essential not only for ethical and legal reasons, but also because there is some evidence from a national survey reported by Wiley that counselors improved most when they received regular face-to-face supervision. In other words, *counseling experience alone did not help counselors improve their ability or competence.*[2] Professional circles typically expect regular supervision at least once a week, usually for at least an hour. A professional trainee in a practicum or internship training may see several counselees each week. Predoctoral interns in doctoral (PhD or PsyD) programs in professional psychology (e.g., clinical or counseling psychology) doing their final year of full-time clinical internship training will often be involved in sixteen or more hours a week of clinical work and usually receive a few hours (e.g., up to five) of clinical supervision a week from different supervisors in individual or group supervision formats.[3]

Lay Christian counselors do not usually see more than a few counselees per week. So we would recommend once-a-week supervision for an hour, whether in individual or group supervision formats. An alternative is to have supervision sessions conducted biweekly or once every two weeks for up to two hours each time, with individual supervision provided on an "as needed" basis.

Supervision should not only be regular, but it should also be effective and helpful. Good supervision involves a balance between *skills training* (the supervisor teaching or modeling more refined and effective counseling skills and methods) and a focus on *process issues or dynamics* (i.e., what is going on internally in the counselor, as well as what is going on interpersonally between the counselor and the counselee). However, you should avoid turning supervision sessions into therapy or counseling sessions for the supervisee (or lay counselor).

A number of helpful books and journals on clinical supervision of counselors or therapists are available, and they are also useful in the supervision of lay counselors. These include books by Ekstein and Wallerstein; Hart; Hess; Kaslow; Robbins; Stoltenberg and Delworth; Estadt, Compton, and Blanchette; and more recently, books by Bernard and Goodyear; Cohen; Falender and Shafranske; and Hess, Hess, and Hess.[4] Important publications on clinical supervision in the secular journals include two special issues of *The Counseling Psychologist* (in 1982 and 1983), and a special series on advances in psychotherapy supervision in *Professional Psychology: Research and Practice* (1987).[5] The special series on training to competence in psychotherapy published in the *Journal of Consulting and Clinical Psychology* (1988) referred to in chapter 7 is also relevant to clinical supervision,[6] as is a significant review chapter on counselor training and supervision by R. K. Russell, A. M. Crimmings, and R. W. Lent in the *Handbook of Counseling Psychology*, edited by S. D. Brown and R. W. Lent.[7] Finally, while the specific literature on supervision of *lay Christian counseling* is sparse, a helpful key article by E. L. Worthington Jr. has been published, as well as articles on clinical supervision from a Christian integration perspective by Tan,[8] and a special issue of the *Journal of Psychology and Christianity* in 2007 on Christian clinical supervision edited by Jamie Aten and Michael Mangis.

PRACTICE MODELS OF SUPERVISION

How is supervision practiced in real life? In his article mentioned above, Worthington briefly describes four main models of supervision:

1. *The Minimum Intervention Model.* In this model of supervision, brief training is provided to lay counselors without any direct supervision of actual counseling done by lay counselors.

2. *The Vertical Supervision Model.* This model, which is advocated by Jay Adams for the training and supervision of nouthetic counselors, typically involves four levels of trainees (supervisees) or lay counselors. The first level of trainees are those who attend classes and receive didactic teaching. The second level of trainees are those who observe more experienced counselors doing actual counseling and then participate in case discussions. The third level of trainees are those who are involved in doing actual counseling, but as junior counselors on a team, and therefore they function as junior cocounselors following the lead of more experienced or senior cocounselors on a team. The fourth level of trainees are those who are sufficiently experienced and trained to function as senior counselors or senior cocounselors for other less experienced or more junior members of a team to observe or cocounsel with. Each team is supervised by a senior staff person.

3. *The Professional Training Model.* In this model, which is patterned after professional training programs and graduate schools, the trainee or lay counselor attends classes and receives didactic instruction, sees counselees in role-play situations or in real life, and often records the counseling sessions. Such counseling sessions are either observed by a supervising professional directly, or else the trainee or lay counselor and supervisor will listen to audio recordings or view video recordings of real-life counseling sessions or of role play.

4. *The Implicit Trust Model.* In this model, the supervisor never directly observes the lay counselor. Rather, the lay counselor verbally reports the counseling session to the supervisor. Unfortunately, such verbal self-reports can be unreliable and possibly misleading, even if unintentionally so.

The practice model of supervision you choose to use with lay counselors will depend on the model for a lay counseling ministry you have chosen. If you are practicing an informal-spontaneous model, then usually the minimal intervention model of supervision (i.e., essentially with no direct supervision) will be predominant, with occasional use of the implicit trust model of supervision (i.e., with some supervision based only on verbal reports provided by the lay counselor).

If an informal-organized model is being practiced, then regular, ongoing supervision of the lay counselors will be provided. However, the actual practice model(s) of supervision used in this context may vary from church to church. A common model of supervision used is still the implicit trust model, based only on verbal reports of the lay counselors. The vertical supervision model, or a variation of it, is also sometimes used in the context of cocounseling. An example of this is when an experienced pastor visits a parishioner together with a lay counselor (or a Stephen's minister), with both individuals providing pastoral care and counseling (i.e., cocounseling) to the parishioner. The experienced pastor will have an opportunity to observe the lay counselor in action in such a cocounseling context and then provide feedback and discussion later on in a supervision session.

The professional training model of supervision, involving the audio or video recording of an actual lay counseling session (or direct observation of such a session through a one-way mirror), is usually not appropriate for an informal-organized model because most of the lay counseling takes place in informal settings like homes, hospitals, and restaurants, where taping is inconvenient or inappropriate. However, we do recommend that supervision include some observation of the lay counselor in action, even in the informal-organized model, and cocounseling is a good way of doing this.

If a formal-organized model is adopted and a lay counseling center is set up, then it is more common to see the professional training model of supervision being used, as well as the vertical supervision model or variations of it (but with cocounseling as its main characteristic). However, some churches have formal and organized lay counseling centers that unfortunately rely on the implicit trust model of supervision and only occasionally cocounseling or the vertical supervision model. We recommend that if the formal-organized model is being practiced, then both the professional training model of supervision and the vertical supervision model be used in the supervision of lay counselors, and not only the implicit trust model.

CONCEPTUAL MODELS OF SUPERVISION: THEORETICAL OR DEVELOPMENTAL

Worthington, in his article, points out that clinical supervision can be conceptualized in two major ways: theoretical or developmental.

The *theoretical model* of conceptualizing supervision is based on the counseling theory or therapeutic orientation of the supervisor. In other words, the supervisor in this model has a clear counseling theory or orientation (e.g., cognitive-behavioral or family systems) that he or she practices within and conducts the supervision accordingly. For example, if the supervisor is a cognitive therapist who believes that dysfunctional and irrational thinking underlies many emotional and psychological problems (e.g., anxiety and some types of depression), he or she will pay particular attention to such thinking in both the supervisee and the counselees and will examine how to restructure or change such thinking. This type of supervisor will also focus more on skills training and helping the supervisee learn specific cognitive therapy techniques (following cognitive or cognitive-behavior therapists like Aaron Beck, Albert Ellis, and Donald Meichenbaum) and will do less on process issues or dynamics involving the feelings of the supervisee and the reciprocal feelings of the supervisee and the counselee in the context of the counseling relationship.

On the other hand, if the supervisor is a psychodynamic or psychoanalytically oriented therapist who believes that unconscious processes and conflicts, often originating from early childhood experiences, are the root causes of many emotional and psychological problems, then he or she will pay more attention to issues like transference (when the counselee unconsciously transfers his or her feelings and attitudes connected to a significant other or parental figure in the past onto the counselor) and countertransference (when the counselor unconsciously transfers his or her feelings and attitudes connected to a significant other or parental figure in the past onto the counselee), which are more process or psychodynamic issues. Such a supervisor will also focus more on teaching therapeutic skills like intensive listening, interpretation of unconscious conflicts and defenses, and dream analysis, consistent with the psychodynamic or the psychoanalytically oriented approach to therapy, which has its roots in Sigmund Freud.

The *developmental model* of conceptualizing supervision cuts across theoretical orientations of supervisors and is based more on the developmental level and needs of the supervisee. This model assumes that the supervisee (or lay counselor) goes through a predictable series of stages of counselor development in the process of supervision, regardless of the counseling theory or therapeutic orientation of the supervisor.

Many views exist regarding the actual stages of counselor development. Worthington has pointed out, however, that some of the most well-known ones are based on the foundational work of R. A. Hogan, who in 1964 proposed four stages of counselor development.[9] Worthington describes Hogan's stages as follows: "The beginning counselor is thought to be insecure and uninsightful; second stage counselors struggle with dependency-autonomy issues; third stage counselors with self-confidence and motivation; fourth stage counselors with personal autonomy and self-assurance."[10] This model has been expanded by C. Stoltenberg[11] and by C. Loganbill, E. Hardy, and U. Delworth,[12] and refined and updated in a textbook on a developmental approach to supervision by Stoltenberg and Delworth.[13]

For stage one counselors, useful supervisory methods include the use of teaching interpretation and support and awareness training, as the trainees seek to imitate the supervisor's style and skills. For stage two counselors who struggle with being overconfident and overwhelmed, helpful supervisory methods include further support and exemplification, as well as ambivalence clarification. For stage three counselors, supervision now includes sharing and exemplification, with professional and personal confrontation taking place in a more collegial way. Finally, stage four counselors are actually considered to be master therapists or counselors, and supervision at this stage is very collegial.

Research findings have tended to support these theories of counselor development,[14] although alternative explanations (e.g., those used in learning theory) for such findings have been proposed by E. L. Holloway, who is more critical of the underlying assumptions and principles of developmental models of supervision.[15] Worthington has noted that the level of development of most lay counselors is at the early stage of counseling in which the counselor's self-preoccupation is a predominant characteristic. He described this level or stage as follows:

> The counselor learns active listening skills and seeks to follow the content and emotion of the client. Because the counselor has doubts about his or her counseling ability, the self-awareness of the counselor intrudes on many of the advanced conceptualization and intervention skills of the counselor. The primary tasks of the paraprofessional counselor, then, would be to learn to apply basic counseling skills without being inhibited by excessive self-focus. Rudimentary conceptualization and intervention skills are used but are rarely the primary focus of the beginning or paraprofessional level counselor.[16]

Worthington also highlights the need for supervisors to develop ways of helping lay counselors manage their anxiety, since increased supervision of lay counselors may lead them to become more self-conscious about their performance in lay counseling. For lay counselors who continue doing the ministry for several years, however, the later stages of counselor development and counseling will be more relevant, and they should be addressed in the supervision of more experienced or advanced lay counselors.

Good supervision will, therefore, involve the use of both theoretical and developmental models of supervision by the supervisor, but with some flexibility and openness in the use of theoretical models (therapeutic orientations or counseling theories) so that rigidity or formula-driven counseling is kept to a minimum. However, the need to teach *specific* counseling skills or competencies to trainees or supervisees has been recently emphasized in the field of professional training and supervision in psychotherapy, where the use of competency-based models of training and supervision has been advocated.[17]

More specific criteria and rating scales are required in such models for determining or assessing the level of competency or skillfulness of the therapist or trainee in terms of his or her interventions.[18] The use of specific treatment manuals for training and supervision in particular types of psychotherapy or counseling is also advocated, for example, cognitive therapy,[19] interpersonal therapy,[20] psychodynamic therapy,[21] experiential therapy,[22] and behavior therapy.[23] The text on therapy supervision edited by A. K. Hess also contains helpful chapters on supervision from different theoretical perspectives.[24]

For lay Christian counseling, more specifically a number of helpful manual-like books for training in specific counseling skills and methods are available. These include cognitive-behavioral oriented books by authors like W. Backus, E. L. Worthington, and H. N. Wright, and books on basic listening and caring skills by authors like C. L. Baldwin and R. P. Walters.[25] If such approaches to lay Christian counseling are used in the training of lay counselors, then their supervision should continue to focus on the refinement of the skills covered in these books.

The development model of supervision should also be applied in the supervision of lay Christian counselors. Supervisors should be aware of the stages of counselor development that most counselors go through in their training and supervision, with particular needs and issues, which are important to address at different stages or levels of counselor development. Stoltenberg and Delworth's text is a helpful one to consult for this purpose. They cover not only the stages of counselor development for the *supervisee* (level one: the beginning of the journey, level two: trial and tribulation, and level three: challenge and growth), but also apply the developmental approach to *supervisors* and their development in supervisory skills.[26]

P. D. Guest and L. E. Beutler have suggested in the professional training literature that supervisors should adjust the way they conduct supervision according to the changing needs of trainees over time. The first therapy or counseling training experience should focus on nonspecific technical skills, with the supervisor being supportive and highly credible. The next step in the professional training experience should address the conceptual difference of various theoretical models for understanding psychological and emotional disorders and change, as trainees grow in confidence in their skills of communication. Specific technical skills may be taught at this stage, with the supervisor functioning more in the role of teacher and authority. The third level of professional training is probably at the predoctoral intern level, and supervision may focus on issues of transference and countertransference as well as the integration of communication and technical skills learned at earlier levels. The supervisor's role at this third level may be one of case review consultant. Finally, at the posttraining or postdoctoral level, the supervisor's role should more appropriately be that of a peer or colleague, and the focus should be on refining technical skills and learning new developments in the field.[27] These helpful guidelines can be adapted and modified for use in the supervision of lay counselors.

THE "IDEAL" SUPERVISOR: CLINICAL, RESEARCH, AND BIBLICAL PERSPECTIVES

In another helpful publication in the professional training literature, M. S. Carifio and A. K. Hess reviewed research and theory directly bearing on behaviors or characteristics that describe the "ideal" or good supervisor. Their review of the published literature suggests that high-functioning supervisors perform with high levels of empathy, respect, genuineness, flexibility, concern, investment, and openness. Good supervisors appear to be knowledgeable, experienced, and concrete in their presentation. They use appropriate teaching, goal-setting, and feedback techniques during their supervisory interactions. Good supervisors also appear to be supportive and noncritical individuals who respect their supervisees and do not attempt to turn the supervisory experience into psychotherapy. While we cannot conclude that there is one correct way of conducting supervision, research in this area has been suggestive of several qualities that can help supervisors do their work in a variety of different settings.[28]

When teaching, a good supervisor can use several techniques to communicate information and knowledge to the supervisee. D. Brannon has provided helpful descriptions of *brainstorming, role play,* and *modeling behavior* (by the supervisor in order to demonstrate particular counseling skills), and *guided reflection.*[29] E. Freeman notes that giving good feedback to a supervisee means giving feedback that is *systematic* (objective, accurate, consistent, and reliable), *timely, clearly understood,* and *reciprocal* (with openness for further discussion and interaction with the supervisee).[30] Finally, A. Rosenblatt and J. Mayer have found that supervisees particularly object to the following four supervisory styles, which good supervisors will typically avoid: *constrictive* (rigidly limiting the supervisee's use of certain techniques in therapy or counseling), *amorphous* (providing unclear guidance or insufficient direction), *unsupportive* (being cold, distanced, uncaring, or even hostile), and *therapeutic* (focusing on the supervisee as a patient or counselee and his or her personality structure and therefore turning supervisory sessions into therapy sessions for the supervisee). The therapeutic style of supervisors was found to be the most objectionable one to supervisees.[31]

From a biblical, Christian perspective, we believe that the "ideal" or good supervisor must also be a spiritually mature person who will focus on the spirituality of the supervisee, taking that into account when discussing the counselees that he or she is seeing. Explicit use of spiritual and faith-based resources like prayer and the Scriptures, as well as discussion of spiritual issues, is encouraged in both supervision and counseling sessions where appropriate and ethical and in dependence on the Holy Spirit. This is especially true within a local church context because many, if not most, of the counselees will be people of faith who want a Christ-centered, biblically based counseling approach. Tan has described this approach as "explicit integration" in psychotherapy or counseling and has provided guidelines for how it can be practiced (even by professional Christian counselors or therapists in a clinically sensitive, ethically responsible, and professionally competent way).[32]

The ultimate goal of Christian therapy or counseling, including the counseling done by lay people, should be to help facilitate the spiritual growth and development of the counselee. Similarly, the essential goal of Christian supervision should be the facilitation of the spiritual growth of the supervisee (as well as of the supervisor). While Christian counseling is not entirely synonymous with Christian discipleship training and spiritual formation, good Christian counseling will involve some level of spiritual direction, what Gary Collins has called "discipleship counseling." And while Christian supervision is not completely identical with Christian discipleship training, good Christian supervision will include some spiritual direction and discipleship training as a crucial component, especially when working with lay counselors. L. E. Lipsker,[33] writing about the professional graduate school training of Christian therapists, and Worthington, writing about the training of lay Christian counselors,[34] have both highlighted the need to focus on biblical integration issues and spirituality in supervision.

Tan has previously written on *intrapersonal integration* (i.e., our own appropriation of faith and our personal integration of psychological and spiritual experience as Christians) and has suggested that it is the most fundamental and foundational category of integration, without which true, biblical integration of psychology and Christianity cannot be substantially achieved in the other categories of integration (i.e., conceptual-theoretical, research, and professional or clinical). Tan points out that the *spirituality* of the person doing integration is a key dimension of intrapersonal integration, and describes several dimensions of true Christian spirituality or greater Christlikeness. Tan unpacks this concept in a way that is helpful for facilitating the development of spirituality in the supervisee or lay counselor and the counselee, as well as the supervisor:

> The term *spirituality* is often used to refer to the disposition or internal condition of people when in such a state as prepares them to recognize and fully appreciate spiritual realities, and such spirituality is ultimately the result of the inworking of the Holy Spirit (1 Cor. 2:14, 15; 3:1, 16). . . . Spirituality, therefore, has many aspects and dimensions to its true, deep meaning.
>
> First, spirituality means *a deep thirst or hunger for God* (Ps. 42:1; Matt. 5:6), what A. W. Tozer has called "the pursuit of God." . . . Such a sincere and Holy Spirit-inspired desire to know God will lead to a growing knowledge of God personally.
>
> Second, spirituality means a *love for God* based on intimate knowledge of God, that leads naturally to *worship and obedience* (Matt. 22:37, 38; Jn. 14:21, 23; cf. Rev. 2:1–7).
>
> Third, spirituality means *being filled with the Holy Spirit and yielding to God's deepening work of grace in our lives and not to the flesh* (Eph. 5:18; Gal. 5:16; Rom. 6:12–13). This will require the consistent use of the following spiritual disciplines of the Christian life as explicated by Foster (1978): the *inward disciplines* of meditation, prayer, fasting, and study; the *outward disciplines* of simplicity, solitude, submission, and service; and the *corporate disciplines* of confession, worship, guidance, and celebration. These disciplines involve *both individual and group life.* . . .
>
> Fourth, spirituality means *acknowledging and using the gifts of the Spirit* for God's purposes and glory (Eph. 4; 1 Cor. 12; Rom. 12; 1 Peter 4) *and manifesting the fruit of the Spirit* (Gal. 5:22–23), which ultimately means *being more Christlike* (Rom. 8:29). . . .
>
> Fifth, spirituality means *developing biblical thinking and a world view that is consistent with God's perspective as revealed in Scriptures* (cf. Rom. 12:2; Phil. 4:8; Col. 3:16a; 2 Tim. 3:16–17). Such thinking will lead, amongst other things, to a balanced ministry to a whole person, to being involved in "Kingdom Business" (Matt. 6:33) in all its breadth and depth. . . .
>
> Sixth, spirituality means *being involved in spiritual warfare requiring the use of supernatural power and resources from God* (cf. 1 Cor. 4:20; Eph. 6:10–18), including the use of prayer and the Scriptures.
>
> Finally, spirituality has *"mystical" aspects*, including what St. John of the Cross described as *"the dark night of the soul."* (cf. Is. 50:10).[35]

Both the counselor and supervisor should encourage the use of the spiritual disciplines (as described by Richard Foster in his book *Celebration of Discipline*) in a gentle, gracious, and nonlegalistic way. The lay counselor needs to model such spirituality for the counselee, just as the supervisor should model it for the supervisee, in dependence on God's grace and the inworking of the Holy Spirit.

OTHER ISSUES IN THE SUPERVISION OF LAY CHRISTIAN COUNSELING

Worthington has pointed out several additional issues that need to be addressed in supervising lay Christian counselors. First is the issue of deciding *who* the supervisor should be. Will the supervisor be an experienced pastor, elder, lay counselor, or professional counselor? How much authority and autonomy will he or she have in the context of church leadership and authority structures? Some authors, such as H. C. Lukens Jr., have proposed that the supervisor should be a licensed mental health professional who is also a Christian.[36]

While we believe it would be ideal or preferable for the supervisor to be a professional counselor or licensed mental health professional, this is not absolutely essential or realistic in every context of a lay counseling ministry. Our recommendation is that the supervisor should minimally be an experienced or better trained pastor or lay leader/counselor, who can then consult with a Christian professional counselor or licensed mental health professional.

In addition, supervisors should intentionally focus on the unique strengths of *lay* or *friendship* counseling, stressing what friends do (and don't do) well, and provide daily and multisituational support during times of crisis for the counselees or clients. Lay counselors need a continual reminder of their limits and should know when and how to make referrals to professionals where appropriate and necessary.

The supervisor should also help lay Christian counselors avoid two common abuses in their ministry. Worthington has called these errors "formula-driven counseling," in which the lay counselor is trained in and uses only a limited set of counseling skills in a rigid way with little sensitivity to the needs and struggles of the counselee, and "Holy Spirit-driven counseling," in which the lay counselor believes the Holy Spirit will provide all the answers, making orderly preparation and forethought unnecessary. The supervisor should teach and model a balanced approach to lay Christian counseling, using a broader range of counseling skills and methods while relying on the Holy Spirit for His guidance and empowerment.

Worthington has also delineated five other issues in the supervision of ongoing lay Christian counseling, including economic and legal issues (e.g., not charging fees for lay counseling and being prepared for possible lawsuits), the need for continuing education of lay counselors (including the provision of reference materials for them), the maintaining or protection of the confidentiality of client information, evaluation of lay counseling (including clearer identification of the goals of the lay counselor for each client or counselee), and utilization of prayer during supervision, which should also be viewed as an opportunity for the supervisor to disciple the lay counselor.[37]

In a 1986 survey of fifteen church-based lay counseling ministries conducted by the Center for Church Renewal of Plano, Texas, six out of the fourteen ministries responding to questions concerning the supervision of lay counselors described their supervision as informal, and eight out of the fourteen as formal. However, whether supervision was formal or informal, only three out of fourteen said that staff actually directly *observed* them at work, although seven out of the fifteen churches did offer some kind of cocounseling.[38] This suggests that lay Christian counseling stands in need of more regular and systematic supervision, as well as better and more effective methods and models of supervision, including observation of actual counseling sessions. This can be done through cocounseling or via a one-way mirror, or indirectly through audio or video recordings of counseling sessions when appropriate. We hope that the methods and models of good supervision we have discussed in this chapter will be beneficial in developing better and more regular supervision of lay Christian counselors, leading to more effective ministry.

As we close, it may be helpful to examine a hypothetical verbatim example that shows how some of the principles for good supervision can be applied in a supervision session. This verbatim involves a one-on-one format with a lay Christian counselor.

One-on-One Supervision: A Verbatim Example

Supervisor (S): Hi, Susan; how are you doing?

Lay Counselor (C): Hi, John. I'm doing okay—a little tired this week, but I'm fine otherwise.

S: Yeah, I understand you have been busy this week with two counselees who are seeing you.

C: That's right. It's the first time since I began as a lay counselor that I've had more than one counselee in any given week! It's great to be able to be used by the Lord to help others who are hurting, but it's hard work!

S: It sure can be! Before we discuss the two counselees and their needs, shall we begin with prayer?

C: Absolutely!

S: Would you like to start, and I'll close in prayer? Then we'll begin our discussion and supervision time.

C: Yes. Dear Lord, thank You for this time with John and for all his help and guidance as I continue to serve You in our lay counseling service here at our church. I pray that Your Holy Spirit will grant us wisdom, discernment, and compassion in our work with my two clients. I also ask for Your loving and healing touch on their lives so that they'll grow spiritually and be made more whole by You. Bless us now I pray, in Jesus' name. Amen.

S: Amen. So, Lord, as Susan has prayed, do guide us both by Your Spirit in knowing how best to aid her in helping these two persons You have given her the opportunity and responsibility of caring for and counseling with. Lead us and bless this supervision time together, to the end that we too may learn from You and from each other and therefore grow, and may the two counselees be further helped and blessed by You as well. In Christ's name we pray. Amen.

C: Amen. Well, it's been an interesting week! Shall I begin with the first counselee, Yvonne?

S: Sure, go ahead.

C: As you already know, Yvonne is a single woman, age thirty-five, whom I have seen now for two sessions. She is struggling with loneliness and depression, mainly over being single when most of her friends are already married. She is a seriously committed Christian who loves the Lord, but she finds it hard to cope with what she calls "being passed by." In the session this past week, she shared a lot more of her deep feelings of loneliness and cried several times. As you suggested, I made an audio recording of this session with her permission, and I understand you've had a chance to listen to parts of it since I gave it to you a couple of days ago.

S: Um-hmm. I did have a chance to listen to some of the tape, but we could spend some of our time today listening to particular segments of it that you or I may be especially interested in. Before we do that or discuss the session further, could you please tell me how you felt about the session yourself?

C: Yeah. It was a somewhat difficult session because she was sharing a lot of her pain, and I felt for her. I remembered, however, what I had learned from our lay counseling training course a few months ago about the need to be empathic and understanding, and not to be too sympathetic or feel so sorry for her that I lose my objectivity in trying to help her. I used the basic listening skills and provided summary reflections of her feelings and thoughts from time to time to convey warmth and empathy and Christian love. I believe I managed to maintain some kind of balance between feeling with her and for her without losing my objectivity, although it was a bit of a struggle with her crying so often.

S: It sure was an emotional session for her and for you too, but I feel you did manage to maintain a healthy objectivity. Your paraphrases and summary reflections in the first part of the session were actually right on, and the counselee opened up even more as a result, as the session progressed. It's hard to "contain" a counselee's pain, and you may have been tempted to rush in to "fix it" quickly, but I'm glad you didn't. You probably remembered too the need to explore and understand or empathize with feelings in good counseling *before* taking any steps of action or intervention with the counselee.

C: Yes, I did, and in that sense, I felt good about what I did.

S: Tell me, what else did you do after exploring and trying to understand and empathize with Yvonne's feelings?

C: Well, later on in the session, following Larry Crabb's model, I asked her what she's been doing in order to identify possible problem behaviors (after exploring and identifying her problem feelings of loneliness, depression, and some anger and resentment). She mentioned staying home a lot and not attending church fellowship meetings as often recently because most of the people in her fellowship are married couples. She's also been eating more junk food, and she feels rotten afterward, although eating food soothes her temporarily from the pain of loneliness and depression. I then asked her what thoughts tend to go through her mind when she's feeling this way, in order to identify possible problem thinking. She was able to note that she would often say the following things to herself when she is alone and feeling lonely and depressed: "I'm not attractive enough for the guys to notice me, and I might as well resign myself to a life of singleness, but I can't take that! It's terrible to be a 'spinster' and not have a husband and kids! I need someone to hold me and love me and take care of me. O God, why have You deprived me of this need? I feel so lonely and depressed, sometimes I wish I were dead! How much longer will I have to experience this pain of being ignored by men and passed by when all my other friends are getting married or are already married. And I am thirty-five! There's no more hope for me, but I can't stand being alone!" She would then cry for a while and beg God in prayer to send her a mate soon.

S: Sounds like Crabb's model helped you to identify some problem behaviors and problem thinking that are associated with her struggles and emotional pain. Good job! You asked some very good questions. What else did you explore regarding her possible problem thinking?

C: I remembered the need to further check out the possibility of suicidal thinking and suicidal risk, since she is depressed. In our first session, she already denied any suicidal intentions, but I felt I needed to pursue this a bit more, so in our last session, I asked her whether she ever felt so down that she wanted to end it all. Her reply was that she sometimes wished she were dead, but she would never end her own life since she believes suicide is sinful and not an option for a Christian. I pushed a bit more and asked if she ever thought of how to end it all even if she did not feel it was the right thing to do. She said only occasionally she would think of taking some pills, but she did not know what to take and how many, and then would block that thought out of her mind. She is not currently taking any medications and did say she tried to avoid pills as much as possible, even aspirin for a headache!

S: So you did check further for suicidal thoughts and suicidal risk. From Yvonne's answers, what is your opinion regarding the suicidal risk for her?

C: I feel there is some risk since she is feeling quite depressed and hopeless about being single, but I don't think the risk is very high at present because she does not have a definite plan and because she has strong Christian beliefs against taking her own life. Also, despite the social isolation she is putting upon herself, she did note that a couple of people from her fellowship do call her and go out with her sometimes for dinner or to a movie, and she feels they do support her with their understanding and prayers. So Yvonne is not completely isolated. Also, she is committed to seeing me weekly for counseling and further support, and she has been able to continue working full-time as a receptionist.

S: Well, you certainly have covered the bases well here, and I really want to commend you for doing a thorough job in exploring the suicidal risk for Yvonne. And I'm glad that you are aware of the need to keep monitoring this, since it can change over time—especially if she isolates herself even more and feels more severely depressed and hopeless. She may then need a referral to a professional therapist or even psychiatrist if antidepressant medication becomes necessary. I also want to reiterate that I'm available, and if you ever have any questions or concerns, or feel that you're getting in over your head, don't hesitate to call me so we can talk things through.

C: Yes, I'm planning to keep on monitoring the suicidal risk from time to time as we counsel together. I'm also aware of the possibility of the need to refer her to a professional therapist or even psychiatrist if her depression worsens. I'll definitely call you if necessary.

S: You also did a good job in helping her to identify her problem thinking. What else happened after that?

C: Yvonne actually was a bit surprised that she was saying all these negative thoughts to herself, but she feels them very deeply when she is depressed and lonely. I took the opportunity to help her see how our thinking can affect our feelings, and I gave her a couple of other examples. She responded quite positively to this. So I decided to assign an A-B-C diary to help her record the activating event (A) triggering off negative thinking or misbeliefs or irrational beliefs (B), leading to particular emotional or behavioral consequences (C), following Albert Ellis and Aaron Beck, which I recalled from the training classes we had. She understood this homework assignment and readily accepted it. I also assigned Backus and Chapian's book *Telling Yourself the Truth* for homework reading as "bibliotherapy," and I loaned her my copy. In retrospect, I feel it might have been better just to assign the A-B-C diary first and discuss it at our next session before assigning Backus and Chapian. I therefore wonder if I overloaded her with homework!

S: That's a good question, and it raises the issue of good timing and pacing in counseling and helping others. I don't necessarily think that you overloaded her, but it would probably have been better to wait till the next session before assigning Backus and Chapian, so you can see further examples of her negative thinking or misbeliefs from her A-B-C diary before intervening further with cognitive restructuring or changing her misbeliefs. Also, it is important when assigning homework readings as bibliotherapy to be more specific about what chapters you would like her to read during the next week, especially since Yvonne is depressed, which may mean she may not be motivated enough to read too much. You want to give her homework assignments that are clear and easy to accomplish, at least initially.

C: Thanks for reminding me of that! I guess I need to be more sensitive to how much she can do at this time since she is depressed and not as motivated or energetic.

S: Yes, that's right. However, overall, you've done a really good job at helping her in this last session. Before we listen to parts of the audio recording, tell me how you ended the session.

C: After assigning the homework, I asked her if she would like us to close in prayer, and she said, "Definitely." So I asked her to pray first, and then I closed in prayer, asking for the Lord's help and healing for her. From her prayer, which we can listen to on the tape, I sensed again a deep pain and longing for God's help, as well as a genuine faith in Him. She definitely has some misbeliefs, however, concerning having to have a husband in order for her life to be happy, etc., which we'll have to deal with in future sessions.

S: Good. Okay, let's listen to parts of the tape now, and then afterward you can tell me about the new counselee who came in to see you for the first time last week.

This hypothetical verbatim example of a supervision session with a lay counselor illustrates how a number of principles and guidelines for good supervision can be applied. They include giving support and encouragement to the lay counselor by a supervisor who is warm, understanding, spiritually mature, and not harshly critical; asking for specific details and using an audio recording (where appropriate) so that the supervisor can provide specific, clear, and helpful feedback to the lay counselor to facilitate effective counseling; teaching and reviewing skills (e.g., how to give homework, assessing suicidal risk and need for referral, briefly reviewing Crabb's model and cognitive restructuring of misbeliefs); focusing a bit on how the lay counselor is feeling (i.e., process or dynamic issues); and using prayer in the supervision session, as well as openly discussing spiritual issues (e.g., Yvonne's use of prayer and her misbeliefs about what she needs for a fulfilling life).

In a dyadic or group supervision context, the same principles and guidelines for good supervision can be applied, except that more time is needed, and other lay counselors should be given opportunities to present their counselees, as well as be provided with feedback and suggestions regarding the counselee being discussed. The confidentiality of the counselee should, however, be safeguarded, and this can be done in a number of ways (e.g., using first names only, getting permission from the counselee to discuss his or her problems in group supervision with the assurance that nothing will be shared *outside* of the supervision group). Confidentiality issues will be discussed in chapter 11, which covers potential pitfalls, as well as legal and ethical issues in lay Christian counseling.

Supervision helps fulfill the critical need for accountability, something counselors at every level (ministerial to professional) must be diligent to pursue. A good principle of ministry is that for whatever arena God has us "giving" to others, we should also be "receiving" from others. Teachers need to be taught, pastors need to be pastored, and counselors need to be counseled. The error among far too many ministry leaders is to view their calling as a strength and therefore without need of ongoing attention. In many ways, an unguarded strength then becomes a double weakness. The enemy of our souls, the evil one, often uses isolation as his number one strategy to defeat and destroy those seeking to walk in a manner worthy of Christ. When we are alone, we are more vulnerable. This holds true for the counselor, as well as for the one seeking counsel.

Peter understood the principle experientially—remember, he was alone when he denied Christ. He was later able to say, "Be alert and of sober mind. Your enemy the devil prowls around like a roaring lion looking for someone to devour" (1 Peter 5:8). Lions instinctively seek out the weak, the injured, the sick, or the alone as their targets. Notice the Scripture above says the enemy pursues some-one—he rarely goes after the *many*, but instead focuses his attention on the *one* who is alone. That person becomes his prey. Endeavor to make accountability and supervision key components of your lay counseling program or ministry.

CHAPTER 9

Evaluation of Lay Counselors

How do we know that a lay Christian counselor training program has been effective in improving the counseling skills (and personal growth) of the lay counselors? And how can we tell that the lay counselors who have been trained are now doing effective counseling with people who need help, producing positive therapeutic effects? These are the two questions that researchers attempt to answer in their evaluation of lay Christian counselors. They want to know how effective is a training program for lay Christian counselors, and how effective is lay Christian counseling itself?

Unfortunately, there has been very little evaluation research conducted to answer such questions. The field of Christian counseling, whether professional or lay, has been far behind in doing solid research to determine the effectiveness of training programs and the different forms of Christian counseling, although the situation has begun to improve in recent years. Several years ago, Dr. Allen Bergin, a noted researcher in evaluating psychotherapy effectiveness, briefly reviewed Roland Fleck and John Carter's book *Psychology and Christianity: Integrative Readings*. His remarks are, by and large, still applicable to the field of Christian counseling: Empirical data are minimal, though research studies are frequently proposed. Indeed, it would be fair to say that most of the field is at the proposal stage—possibly promising but largely untried and untested in professional terms. What is intriguing is that bright, well-trained people are working at it.[1]

Bergin quotes several challenges that should be heeded regarding the claims made about lay Christian counseling, highlighting the need for further study:

Outcome studies in "Christian psychotherapy" also are important—if we are claiming some sort of superiority for "Christian counseling," it's about time we stopped to see if claims are backed up by solid data. . . . We must not allow ourselves to be second-rate professionals. . . . For too long, Christians have copped out on rigorous study and research by claiming all the truth they need to know is contained in the Bible. . . . We are unlikely to arrive at one biblical approach to counseling. . . . The universities do not encourage research into religious experience—variables such as Christian maturity, faith in God, or counseling effectiveness are very hard to investigate empirically. . . . These obstacles have dissuaded many from entering psychological research, but this work must be done if we are to counsel, train, prevent, and theorize effectively.[2]

The research needed will involve the evaluation of lay Christian counselors, and this is something that can not only be done by Christian mental health professional researchers, but also by pastors, church leaders, and other parachurch or missionary organizations. The level of methodological sophistication in the evaluation research will vary from setting to setting, depending on the experience and research training of those conducting the evaluation research. However, we believe that there is an ongoing need for research at all levels, done by leaders who are involved in the training and use of lay counselors in ministry to hurting people. Often, such evaluation research is best conducted in collaboration or consultation with Christian mental health professionals who are well versed and experienced in research. However, in some settings professional researchers may not be available for consultation or collaboration, and the evaluation of lay Christian counselors may need to be done by the leader (e.g., a pastor or church elder or deacon) responsible for the ministry.

In this chapter we will review and describe the major evaluation approaches and the tools available for conducting research, whether it is done by professional researchers or by church leaders involved in the ministry of lay Christian counseling (those who are not academicians or professional researchers). This chapter will also provide some future directions for the evaluation of lay *Christian* counselors. Since the relevant research literature has already been reviewed (see chapter 4), this chapter will focus on the methods and measures used in research in order to better understand how to evaluate lay Christian counselors. Our hope is that many will actually end up *doing* such evaluation in their ministry context.

EVALUATION OF TRAINING PROGRAMS FOR LAY CHRISTIAN COUNSELORS

Before we describe how to evaluate a training program, we would point out that a great deal of evaluation research still remains to be done in *professional* clinical training programs. Some years ago, the American Psychological Association Task Force on the Evaluation of Education, Training, and Service in Psychology made this alarming statement: "There is no evidence that any specific educational or training program or experience is related to professional competence."[3] The Task Force concluded that it is, "important, perhaps imperative, that psychology begin to assemble a body of persuasive evidence bearing on the value of specific educational and training requirements."[4]

Since that time, several helpful publications have appeared that pertain to evaluation and accountability in professional clinical training and to standards and evaluation in the education and training of professional psychologists.[5] These publications are helpful if you are interested in a sophisticated approach to evaluating lay counselors, although the evaluation methods used will need to be adapted and several of the issues discussed will not be relevant to the more narrowly focused evaluation of lay counselors.

There are several good books that can be consulted to gain familiarity with this more academic and technical approach. They comprehensively cover the general research methods applicable to clinical and educational settings.[6] When evaluating lay Christian counselor training programs, the focus of evaluation should primarily be on the *counseling knowledge and skills* acquired by the lay counselors through a particular training program. A secondary focus of evaluation could be on the *personal growth* of the lay counselors, including their *spiritual growth*. More comprehensive analyses of the long-term effects of professional training on counselor behavior and growth have been reported in the secular research literature.[7] For example, Thompson evaluated changes in counselor behavior in three main areas: actual verbal response mode as measured by the Hill Counselor Verbal Response Category System,[8] personal growth as measured by the Personal Orientation Inventory (POI),[9] and general counseling effectiveness as rated by master's level therapists or counselors. Following a similar methodology, several measures can be used to evaluate both the *counseling knowledge and skills* acquired by lay Christian counselors through a specific training program, and their *personal and spiritual growth*.

1. Measures for Evaluation of Counseling Knowledge and Skills

One of the several approaches to evaluating the counseling knowledge and skills gained by lay counselors is to use *self-report measures*, which are usually questionnaires or rating scales that they fill in. Another approach is to use *written responses by the lay counselors to counseling situations* presented to them in written form (or even in audio-or video-recorded form). A third approach is to use *ratings by others (usually trained raters) of the lay counselors' behaviors and skills in a counseling session*, whether simulated (i.e., role play) or actual, and usually audio or video recorded. A fourth approach is to have *peer ratings provided by other lay counselors of a particular lay counselor's skills and effectiveness*. Let's take a closer look at each of these measures in greater detail:

a. *Self-report measures.* One of the most obvious self-reporting measures for assessing the counseling knowledge gained by lay counselors is the use of a *quiz or multiple choice exam/test* covering specific content areas of the training program provided. This would typically be taken by a lay counselor after the completion of the training program. Another self-report measure assesses subjective ratings by the lay counselors of how much they think they know about counseling or Christian counseling, as well as their subjective ratings of how competent or skillful they feel they are in counseling. This assessment is called the Counselor Training Program Questionnaire (CTPQ), and it was developed by Tan as a simple self-report measure for evaluating lay counselor training programs.[10]

There are two versions of this questionnaire. The *pretraining questionnaire* is to be given to lay counselors just before the start of a training program. It contains basic questions about name, age, sex, occupation, education, previous courses in counseling/psychology, and six main items, using 0–100 subjective rating scales, as shown on page 158. The *posttraining questionnaire* is to be given to lay counselors just *after* the training program has been completed. It contains the same six main items but also includes questions about the number of training sessions attended, positive or negative features of the training program, and suggestions for its improvement, if any.

The CTPQ consists of six major items assessing a lay counselor's subjective ratings of his or her *knowledge of counseling, knowledge of Christian counseling, competence* (or skillfulness) *in counseling, confidence* (or certainty) *in competence in counseling, competence* (or skillfulness) *in Christian counseling,* and *confidence* (or certainty) *in competence in Christian counseling.* These same six items are completed by lay counselors just before and just after the training program so that pretraining and posttraining scores can be compared and any significant changes noted. An effective training program should result in significant improvements (i.e., higher scores) on at least four of the six items (i.e., questions 1, 2, 3, and 5), if not on all six items (see CTPQ on next page).

b. *Written responses to counseling situations/scenarios.* The Helping Relationship Inventory is an example of a measure involving written responses by counselors to counseling situations or scenarios.[11] This measure was developed to classify or categorize the response-style preferences of the person (lay counselor) answering the inventory by having her rank, according to what she would most likely say in a particular counseling situation, the five different responses that are listed after each of twenty-five such scenarios involving short client or counselee statements. It has five subscale scores corresponding to the five response styles: Understanding, Probing, Interpretive, Supportive, and Evaluative. Good training programs should lead to a significant increase in preference for Understanding responses by the lay counselors. This inventory is to be given to the lay counselors just before and just after the training program.

Counselor Training Program Questionnaire (CTPQ)

1. How much do you know about **counseling**?

0	10	20	30	40	50	60	70	80	90	100

Nothing at all   Some   A lot

2. How much do you know about **Christian counseling**?

0	10	20	30	40	50	60	70	80	90	100

Nothing at all   Some   A lot

3. How competent do you think you are in **counseling**?

0	10	20	30	40	50	60	70	80	90	100

Not competent at all   Moderately competent   Very competent

4. How confident or certain are you of your competence in **counseling**?

0	10	20	30	40	50	60	70	80	90	100

Not confident at all   Moderately confident   Very confident

5. How competent do you think you are in **Christian counseling**?

0	10	20	30	40	50	60	70	80	90	100

Not competent at all   Moderately competent   Very competent

6. How confident or certain are you of your competence in **Christian counseling**?

0	10	20	30	40	50	60	70	80	90	100

Not confident at all   Moderately confident   Very confident

---

c. *Ratings by others (trained raters) of the lay counselor's behavior and skills in a counseling session.* A common method of utilizing this approach is to have a lay counselor role-play a counseling session just before and just after the training program. However, a real-life counseling situation with an actual client or counselee would also be appropriate (and preferable). The counseling session, whether simulated or real life, is audio or video recorded with permission from the client or counselee if it is a real-life situation. The lay counselor's behavior and counseling skills are rated by two or more trained raters (so that interrater reliability or agreement can be determined) using appropriate rating scales.

One of the most commonly used rating scales is the one developed by Dr. Robert Carkhuff called A Scale for the Measurement of Empathic Understanding, Respect, and Genuineness.[12] It consists of three five-point subscales or dimensions developed to measure core counseling skills of empathy, respect, and genuineness by trained raters. Usually eight-to ten-minute segments of the audio or video recording are rated independently by two or more trained raters who have had previous training and experience in using the Carkhuff scale. The lay counselors are rated before and after the training program so that changes on these three dimensions of core counseling skills can be noted. In a simulated or role-play counseling session, either the same person playing the role of the client or counselee or a different person can be used after the training program, but the presenting problem after the training program should be different from the one used before the training program.

In a study reported by R. Jernigan, S. Y. Tan, and R. L. Gorsuch,[13] the following instructions were given to the lay counselor trainee before video recording a role-play counseling session: "You are a counselor here at the church counseling center. The person whom I will introduce to you has come to the center for help with a personal problem. Do whatever you think may be helpful for this person." The problem presented before the training program involved depression, whereas the one presented after the training program involved fear of failure.

While the Carkhuff scale has been widely used and is still an important one for measuring empathy, respect, and genuineness, it should be noted that the necessary core counseling skills for producing therapeutic change in counselees have been challenged, although there is still considerable support for the positive effect these core conditions have on clients.[14] Furthermore, the Carkhuff scale does not measure other more specific counseling skills—like cognitive-behavioral intervention or problem-solving skills—often taught in lay Christian counselor training programs.

Other rating scales or checklists for assessing a lay counselor's competence or skillfulness in more specific counseling skills are therefore needed to comprehensively evaluate the effectiveness of a particular training program that may teach skills like problem-solving and cognitive-behavioral interventions in addition to basic listening skills. Helpful checklists of these more specific counseling and cognitive-behavioral skills, which can be adapted for use as rating scales, can be found in W. H. Cormier and L. S. Cormier's book *Interviewing Strategies for Helpers: Fundamental Skills and Cognitive-Behavioral Interventions.* Also available is a Cognitive Therapy Scale[15] developed specifically to assess cognitive therapy skills of counselors and therapists trained in Dr. Aaron Beck's approach to counseling and therapy. More specific rating scales for evaluating Christian counseling skills, including the appropriate use of prayer and the Scriptures, are also needed. Audio or video recordings of several counseling sessions (rather than just a single session) are preferable so that ratings of different counseling skills can be better assessed.

d. *Peer ratings of a lay counselor's skills and effectiveness.* In this approach, other lay counselors provide peer ratings, usually using a rating scale or questionnaire of the skills and effectiveness of a particular lay counselor in question, based on their knowledge and observation of this lay counselor in training and supervision sessions. An example of a measure that can be used for this purpose is the one developed by D. M. Boan and T. Owens,[16] who found that the mean scores of such peer ratings of lay counselor skill are related to client satisfaction.

Their revised paraprofessional evaluation form for use as peer ratings of lay counselor skills contains the following instructions:

Please rate your paraprofessional peers on the following items using a scale of 1 to 10. One (1) will indicate a very low score, an almost absence of that quality. Ten (10) will indicate perfection *for a paraprofessional.* A score of 5 indicates the minimally acceptable level, an indication this is not actually a problem, but some improvement is needed. Please try to rate all items, but leave blank any you have not been able to observe. Remember, your impressions count. All ratings are confidential.

The name of the lay counselor or person to be rated is then filled in, with peer ratings by another lay counselor provided in three major areas, each with five items and thus with a total of fifteen items to be rated on the 1–10 point scale.

The first area rated is the *use of supervision,* and it contains the following items: (1) open to feedback from others, (2) uses time effectively, (3) communicates needs clearly, (4) appears able to understand the nature of the problem, (5) puts feedback to good use. The second area is *counseling skills,* with the following items: (6) demonstrates empathic ability, (7) shows nonjudgmental acceptance, (8) able to be appropriately confrontive, (9) communicates precisely and concretely, (10) able to develop rapport with clients. The third and final area is *personal qualities,* with the following items: (11) able to not be defensive, (12) approach to program consistent with training, (13) evokes confidence from others, (14) open to learning, (15) applies faith in a comfortable and appropriate manner.

2. Measures for Evaluation of Personal and Spiritual Growth

Another focus of training programs for lay Christian counselors is to help facilitate the personal and spiritual growth of the lay counselors themselves. Some of the training curriculum may be devoted to topics like personal growth of the counselor, growing in self-awareness, and managing stress and preventing burnout. Several measures can be used to evaluate whether lay counselors have grown personally and spiritually after undergoing a training program in lay Christian counseling.

A widely used psychological measure of personal growth is the Personal Orientation Inventory (POI) developed by E. L. Shostrom to assess self-actualization as defined by Abraham Maslow. A self-actualizing human being is "a person who is more fully functioning and lives a more enriched life than does the average person."[17] The POI consists of 150 forced choice questions or items and takes about thirty minutes to complete. The items are scored twice, first for two basic scales of personal orientation, namely, inner directedness and time competence. The second scoring yields ten subscales that measure the following components of self-actualizing: self-actualized value, existentiality, feeling reactivity, spontaneity, self-regard, self-acceptance, nature of man (constructive), synergy, acceptance of aggression, and capacity for intimate contact.

While this measure has been widely used in both secular and Christian contexts for evaluating the personal growth of counselors as they go through a counselor training program, some serious questions have been raised regarding the relevance and appropriateness of some of the subscales on the POI for Christians. For example, one subscale that many Christian subjects have trouble responding to is the nature of man subscale. In an unpublished preliminary study evaluating the effectiveness of growth facilitator training for cross-cultural ministry with a small group of subjects, C. A. Schaefer, L. Dodds, and S. Y. Tan commented:

> Many participants expressed difficulty with some of the items comprising the nature of man subscale on the POI. Their expressed conflict concerned whether to respond to the items based on their religious belief that persons are corrupted by sin or by their desire to accept persons and view them positively. . . . The conflict regarding this subscale is suggestive of the problems incurred using a secular instrument to evaluate an explicitly Christian program.[18]

Despite these concerns, the POI and other secular instruments for measuring personal growth or change can still be used with some benefit as well as caution in the evaluation of training programs for lay Christian counselors. Other examples of secular measures that have been used or that have potential usefulness include the 16PF, the Myers-Briggs Temperament Type Indicator, and the Taylor-Johnson Temperament Analysis. However, some of the problems with these instruments in a Christian context highlight the need for more explicitly Christian measures of spiritual growth as part of the personal growth of the lay Christian counselor. Regardless of what you choose to use, we highly recommend that you attempt to evaluate the spiritual growth of the lay Christian counselor in some manner as part of the overall evaluation of a training program's effectiveness in influencing personal development or growth.

Several measures are now available for assessing spirituality and spiritual growth, and we have described them in chapter 6. Among such measures, we recommend the following as being of potential usefulness for assessing the spirituality and spiritual growth of the lay Christian counselor: the Spiritual Well-Being Scale developed by C. W. Ellison and R. Paloutzian, the Character Assessment Scale developed by P. F. Schmidt, the Wagner-Revised Houts Questionnaire for discovering spiritual gifts, revised by C. P. Wagner, and the Spiritual Leadership Qualities Inventory developed by F. B. Wichern.[19] In addition to these instruments, another somewhat promising measure of optimal religious functioning and Christian religious maturity that should also be noted is the Religious Status Interview (RSI) developed by Dr. H. Newton Malony. Now available is a self-report version of the RSI called the Religious Status Inventory, with 160 items to be rated on a five-point scale.[20] It has scores on eight major subscales: awareness of God, acceptance of God's grace and steadfast love, being repentant and responsible, knowing God's leadership and direction, involvement in organized religion, experiencing fellowship, being ethical, and affirming openness in faith.

Another measure worth mentioning is the Spiritual Growth Survey developed by F. Smith in an unpublished dissertation submitted to the School of World Mission, Fuller Theological Seminary.[21] It consists of sixty items designed to measure spiritual growth in individuals or groups. It provides scores on the following twelve dimensions: worship, personal devotions, giving, lay ministry, Bible knowledge, missions, fellowship, witnessing, attitude toward religion, distinctive lifestyle, service, and social justice.

Finally, the Age Universal Religious Orientation Scale (I-E Scale) developed by R. L. Gorsuch and G. D. Venable as an adaptation of the Religious Orientation Scale originally put together by G. Allport and J. Ross, should also be noted.[22] It consists of twenty statements to be rated on a five-point scale and provides a ratio of an individual's intrinsic versus extrinsic religious orientation, with intrinsic orientation or motivation being preferable.

As you can see, several scales or measures are available for assessing different dimensions of spirituality or spiritual growth. At least one or two of them (e.g., the Spiritual Well-Being Scale or the I-E Scale, but not both of them since they are highly correlated with each other, and the Religious Status Inventory) should be used to evaluate the personal and spiritual growth of lay Christian counselors undergoing a training program. We would note, however, that measures of spirituality or spiritual growth (e.g., the I-E Scale, the Spiritual Well-Being Scale, or the Spiritual Growth Survey) in Christian lay counselors did not improve significantly after a training program, mainly because the lay counselors or trainees already scored high on these measures before the training programs began.[23] Lay Christian counseling trainees are often specially selected, and spiritual maturity and well-being are usually a significant part of the selection criteria used. Nevertheless, using measures of spirituality in evaluation research may still be helpful since further studies are needed before more definitive conclusions can be made.

As you seek to evaluate a training program, we suggest the following evaluation package as a minimal requirement for evaluation research: the Counselor Training Program Questionnaire (CTPQ), the Helping Relationship Inventory (HRI), and the Spiritual Well-Being Scale (or alternatively, the I-E Scale). These measures are relatively easy to administer and usually will not take more than an hour to complete, although they do have limitations because they are all paper-and-pencil self-report measures. They should be given just before and just after a training program. If possible, the following measures should also be used: the Religious Status Inventory (or RSI), POI or some other psychological measure such as the 16PF, and audio or video recordings of simulated or real-life counseling sessions to be rated by trained raters using the Carkhuff scale and/or other more specific rating scales of lay counselor behavior and skills. In place of the RSI, several other measures of spiritual maturity or spiritual growth described earlier can be used as alternatives. Peer ratings of lay counselor skills can also be helpful.

We admit that this is not an exhaustive list of all possible measures that can be used in conducting evaluation research, but we hope that the measures and approaches we have suggested will help those responsible for conducting lay Christian counselor training programs to do more systematic and consistent evaluations.

A NOTE ON RESEARCH DESIGN FOR EVALUATION OF TRAINING PROGRAMS

In conducting evaluation research, it is important not only to choose the best measures for evaluation but also to use the most appropriate research design for the evaluation study. An example of a somewhat ideal research design (which will probably cost more time, energy, and money, as well as require the expertise of well-trained researchers) is one in which a large enough number of lay counselor trainees (e.g., a total of thirty) is selected and then randomly assigned to two groups (with fifteen in each group). One group will receive the lay counselor training program (usually lasting three to six months), and the other group will be a "waiting-list" control group (who receive no training but wait until the training program is over for the first group) or will serve as a comparison group who receive some other kind of training unrelated to counseling skills (e.g., training in Bible study skills). If enough trainees can be recruited for such a study, it would be even more ideal to use all three groups (i.e., a training group, a "wait-list" group, and a comparison/control group).

Appropriate evaluation measures (e.g., CTPQ, HRI, Spiritual Well-Being Scale, RSI, POI or 16PF, video recording ratings of lay counselor behavior and skills during a simulated or real-life counseling session, and possibly peer ratings of lay counselor skill) should be given to all lay counselor trainees or subjects just before and just after the training program. This example of a somewhat ideal research design will allow you to answer two basic questions: *Did the lay counselor trainees who received the training program improve significantly on the different evaluation measures,* comparing their posttraining scores on such measures to their pretraining scores? Second, and more importantly, *did they improve significantly more than the other group of trainees* who either waited or served as a comparison group who received some other kind of training? If some other kind of training is provided to the second group as a comparison group, it is important to specify what kind of training was provided. The alternative training should not include counseling skills training. However, training in Bible study skills may lead to personal and spiritual growth, so the two groups may not differ significantly on measures of personal and spiritual growth. If the training program is to be judged as effective, however, the groups should differ significantly on measures of counseling knowledge and skills, with the group who received the training program doing better.

What we have just described is one example of a somewhat ideal research design. Many local churches and parachurch or missionary organizations that run lay counselor training programs will not have the time, energy, money, or expertise to conduct such an elaborate study. Our hope is that academic and professional researchers will continue to take up the challenge to conduct evaluation studies similar to the one we have just described. For most others who research lay counselor training programs, it is sufficient if they attempt to do some evaluation of their programs using something like the minimal evaluation package we have suggested, administering it before and after a particular training program.

EVALUATION OF OUTCOME OF LAY CHRISTIAN COUNSELING

The acid test of the effectiveness of any lay Christian counselor training program must involve evaluating the effectiveness of the counseling provided in terms of therapeutic outcomes. A large body of literature exists on the evaluation of psychotherapy outcomes in the field of professional counseling and psychotherapy. It includes earlier books edited by S. L. Garfield and A. E. Bergin; M. J. Lambert, E. R. Christensen and S. S. DeJulio; J. Williams and R. Spitzer; J. H. Harvey and M. M. Parks; and I. E. Waskow and M. B. Parloff, and more recent books edited by M. J. Lambert, and P. E. Nathan and J. M. Gorman, and also two volumes by K. Corcoran and J. Fischer.[24]

Special issues on psychotherapy research also appeared in two important professional journals published by the American Psychological Association—the February 1986 issues of the *American Psychologist* and the *Journal of Consulting and Clinical Psychology*.[25] These significant books and publications provide guidelines and methods for conducting evaluation studies of psychotherapy or counseling outcomes. The guidelines can also be applied to the evaluation of the outcomes of lay Christian counseling with some adaptation or modification where necessary.

At the present time, evaluation research on the effectiveness of lay Christian counseling is even scarcer than the limited research that has been done evaluating lay counselor training programs. The few studies that have been completed evaluating lay Christian counselors have already been reviewed in chapter 4. As in the previous section, we will first review and describe the various approaches and measures that can be used to evaluate the therapeutic outcomes of lay Christian counseling and then suggest a basic or minimal evaluation package of measures (and variations of it) for use in various lay Christian counseling settings. We will end this section with some comments on research design for conducting such outcome evaluation studies.

MEASURES FOR OUTCOME EVALUATION

M. J. Lambert, D. A. Shapiro, and A. E. Bergin wrote a very helpful review chapter some years ago on the effectiveness of psychotherapy and the evaluation of therapeutic outcomes. In order to overcome systematic bias and invalid conclusions as well as to provide a more comprehensive assessment of therapeutic change or effects, they recommend the use of multiple outcome measures from a variety of viewpoints, under the following five categories indicating their source: (1) Patient (Counselee/Client) Self-Report; (2) Trained Outside Observer/Expert Observer

Ratings; (3) Relevant Other Ratings; (4) Therapist (Counselor) Ratings; and (5) Institutional Ratings.[26] Examples of helpful measures in each of these categories will now be briefly listed. Lambert, Shapiro, and Bergin's chapter should be consulted for further details and information.

1. Patient/Client Self-Report

Five main types of measures were listed under this category:

a. *Post-therapy (post-counseling) questionnaires/satisfaction measures* evaluating client-felt improvement, including both global estimates of therapy or counseling-induced improvement, and improvements on specific targets, as well as overall client satisfaction with the counseling or therapy provided.

b. *Symptom checklists,* whether single symptoms/single trait, such as the Beck Depression Inventory or the State-Trait Anxiety Inventory, or multiple symptom checklists like the Hopkins Symptom Checklist or its revision called the Symptom Checklist-90R (SCL-90R).

c. *Self-monitoring* procedures requiring the client to record his or her own thoughts, feelings, and specific behaviors, examples of which include measures of self-talk like the Self-Statement Inventory, the Automatic Thoughts Questionnaire, and the Irrational Beliefs Test.

d. *Personality tests,* including the Minnesota Multiphasic Personality Inventory or MMPI (which unfortunately has serious limitations and appears to be too cumbersome and possibly insensitive for it to be used as a measure of therapeutic change), and the Millon Clinical Multi-Axial Inventory or MCMI.

e. *Measures of self-regulation/self-esteem,* including the Tennessee Self-Concept Scale, Personal Attribute Inventory, Rosenberg Self-Esteem Scale, and the recent Self-Control Schedule, as well as self-monitoring devices like timing devices, mechanical counters, and self-monitoring cards.

2. Expert and Trained Observers

Two main types of expert or trained observer ratings or judgments, using a person or persons external to the therapy as the judge(s), were listed under this category:

a. *Standardized interviews and expert ratings,* including the Social Adjustment Scale, the Denver Community Mental Health Questionnaire, the Global Adjustment Scale, and the Hamilton Rating Scale for Depression.

b. *Behavioral counts,* which include a variety of observational rating forms for particular behaviors and their frequencies, durations, etc., that can be completed by nonprofessional observers. Role Play Tests are one example.

3. Evaluation by Relevant Others

Relevant others can include parents, spouse, siblings, friends, teachers, employer, and other relatives or third parties who are related to the client and can therefore provide outside data to corroborate or verify self-report data on particular behaviors or symptoms. Two main types of measures were mentioned in this category: (a) Measures of Social Adjustment, such as the Katz Adjustment Scale-Relatives Form (KAS-R) and the Personal Adjustment and Role Skills-III (PARS-III); (b) Measures of Sexual Behavior and Marital Satisfaction, such as the Locke-Wallace Marital Adjustment Test and the Sexual Interactional Inventory.

4. Evaluation by the Therapist/Counselor

The counselor can provide ratings of client improvement using measures like target complaints (which require the counselor to list three major target problems the client wants help for and then rate their severity at the beginning and at the termination of counseling—the counselee can also do the same, in which case target complaints become a client self-report measure), Goal Attainment Scaling, Problem-Oriented Record, and the Davis Goal Scaling Form.

5. Assessment through Institutional Means

This method involves the use of data obtained through records kept mainly for the internal use of agencies or organizations like schools, law enforcement agencies, employment offices, hospitals, churches, and community organizations. Examples of such data or measures are recidivism or relapse rates (e.g., rearrest records), hospital readmission rates, and medical utilization records. Such measures or data have obvious limitations; nevertheless, they can also be helpful.

It is difficult, however, to use all five of the major categories of outcome measures just mentioned in the evaluation of psychotherapy or counseling effectiveness, especially in a community setting like a church counseling service or a community mental health center, whose top priority is not research but providing counseling services. Still, some attempt at evaluation of counseling effectiveness can yet be made. Dr. Robert Manthei has described a comprehensive, effective, and simple means of evaluating therapeutic outcome at a community mental health center that can be applied in any treatment or counseling setting by using the following measures: (1) *number of counseling sessions attended* by clients, (2) *type of termination* (mutual counselor and client decision versus unilateral client decision), (3) *three main target complaints* rated by clients as well as counselors, (4) *the eighteen-item General Well-Being Schedule* as a measure of clients' general psychological well-being during the past month, and (5) *the Current Adjustment Rating Scale* as a measure of counselors' ratings of their clients' general well-being before and after therapy or counseling.[27] This helpful package of measures can be adapted and modified for use in a local church lay counseling center functioning within a formal-organized model. We will now describe a modified package, including a number of measures of spirituality or spiritual well-being, as well as a couple of post-counseling questionnaires or surveys.

SUGGESTED MEASURES FOR EVALUATING THE COUNSELING EFFECTIVENESS OF LAY CHRISTIAN COUNSELORS

In addition to documenting the number of counseling sessions attended by clients and the type of termination experienced, the following measures are recommended for use in the evaluation of the counseling effectiveness of lay Christian counselors providing counseling to adult clients, particularly in the context of a formal church lay counseling center:

1. Target Complaints

Three target complaints should be obtained from each client at the beginning of counseling by asking, "What kinds of problems or difficulties are you seeking counseling for? What else? . . . What else?" Clients should then be asked to describe the situations in which each problem or difficulty occurred, and to rate how much the problem or complaint is bothering them, using a thirteen-point box scale with five descriptors (starting with "not at all" at the bottom box, to "a little" at the fourth box, to "pretty much" at the seventh box, to "very much" at the tenth box, and ending with "couldn't be worse" at the thirteenth or top box). Clients are asked to check the appropriate box for each target complaint or problem,[28] at the beginning and at termination of counseling. The same three target complaints noted at the beginning of counseling should be rated at the end of counseling.

2. Symptom Checklist-90R (SCL-90R)

This is a revision of the longer Hopkins Symptom Checklist, with ninety items divided into nine symptom dimensions and three global indices of distress. It is most useful as a global measure of psychological distress or psychopathology.[29]

Clients should be asked to complete this inventory at the beginning and at the end of counseling. An alternative measure to the SCL-90R is the eighteen-item General Well-Being Schedule used by Manthei.[30]

3. Counselor's Global Rating of Client's Psychological Adjustment

At the beginning and termination of counseling, the counselor should make a global rating of the client's psychological adjustment, using a ten-point scale (ranging from one, most extreme maladjustment, to ten, optimal adjustment).[31] An alternative to this global ten-point scale is the current Adjustment Rating Scale used by Manthei, consisting of fourteen items to be rated on nine-point scales by the counselor to evaluate the client's current functioning, satisfactions, and social stimulus value.[32]

4. Measures of Spirituality

The Spiritual Well-Being Scale and the Religious Status Inventory described earlier are recommended as measures of spiritual well-being and spiritual maturity respectively. They should be completed by the client at the beginning and at termination of counseling.

5. Post-counseling Questionnaires/Surveys

Two versions of a post-counseling questionnaire, one to be filled out by the client and the other by the counselor, are recommended. They are adapted from the post-therapy questionnaires used by J. Craig Yagel in a doctoral dissertation submitted to the Graduate School of Psychology at Fuller Theological Seminary.[33] The questionnaires contain items on overall success, overall satisfaction, and overall amount of improvement due to the counseling provided, to be rated on a six-point scale (ranging from 1, extremely poor, to 6, superb). They also include symptom change, personal change, recommending counseling to a close friend with emotional problems, present functioning, current problem-solving ability, and need for further counseling. Five additional items adapted from A.A. Lazarus were included in the client form of the questionnaire to evaluate the client's perception of how helpful, competent, sincere, likable, and interested the counselor was,[34] reflecting the credibility of the counselor and the counseling provided.

The counselor form of the questionnaire also contains two additional items at the end, on the degree of personal integration or psychological health of the client and on the life adjustment or social/vocational functioning of the client, rated for the beginning, as well as the end of counseling. Both forms of the post-counseling questionnaires are reprinted in appendices C and D.

An alternative to these questionnaires is a post-counseling follow-up survey or questionnaire developed by the Family Service Association called the FSA Questionnaire (Form No. 26, Revised).[35] This measure was used by Richard Walters to survey client satisfaction, as well as client change, six months after termination of counseling in a lay counseling program at the First Presbyterian Church in Boulder, Colorado. (The results of the survey have been described in chapter 4.) Walters also found that out of seventeen lay counseling programs surveyed, only two were asking clients to evaluate their programs, both at termination of the lay counseling provided. Follow-up evaluations can also be conducted by using the measures already described earlier and readministering them several months after the termination of counseling. Using only a follow-up survey or questionnaire a few months after the end of counseling without any pre-and post-counseling measures like the ones just described, however, can lead to biased reports, probably in too positive a direction.

We therefore recommend the use of target complaints (rated by the client), the SCL-90R (or a shorter version, the Brief Symptom Inventory, or BSI), the 10-point scale global rating of the client's adjustment (rated by the counselor), the Spiritual Well-Being Scale, the RSI, and the post-counseling questionnaires (both client and counselor forms) in the evaluation of the effectiveness of lay Christian counselors. However, in most local church or parachurch contexts in which lay counseling occurs, this suggested package may still be too ambitious. If so, then we would suggest at the very least, the use of target complaints, the 10-point global rating of client adjustment, the Spiritual Well-Being Scale, and the post-counseling questionnaires (or alternatively, the FSA Questionnaire at termination and/or follow-up). The use of this suggested minimal package of evaluation measures will help to expand the database supporting or refuting the effectiveness of lay Christian counseling ministries, as well as facilitate comparisons of outcomes across different facilities and contexts.

Using a standard package of evaluation measures, however, has a number of obvious drawbacks. First, the package we have suggested may not be specific enough to evaluate effects of other types of counseling like marriage or family counseling, in which case other more relevant measures of marital or family functioning should be used.[36] Second, if specific types of client problems are being seen in the lay counseling center or service, then more specific measures of those problems (e.g., depression or anxiety) should also be used.[37] Finally, the measures we have suggested apply mostly to adult clients. Other measures are needed to evaluate the effectiveness of counseling with younger clients or children.[38]

A NOTE ON RESEARCH DESIGN FOR EVALUATION OF THE EFFECTIVENESS OF LAY CHRISTIAN COUNSELING

Years ago, in 1987, Dr. Gary Collins commented, "I know of no competent research study that investigates the effectiveness of lay counseling among Christians."[39] This comment is no longer true since the 1997 controlled outcome study on lay Christian counseling reported by Y. M. Toh and Tan (mentioned in chapter 4). However, the evaluation of counseling effectiveness is still a very complex endeavor, fraught with methodological issues and difficulties, and therefore controversial. Nevertheless, we would like to make several suggestions to encourage more competent evaluation research on the effectiveness of lay Christian counseling.

First, researchers should use appropriate measures of outcome, such as the ones we have described (including measures of spiritual maturity and spiritual well-being). These measures should be administered at least at pre-and post-counseling, and, if possible, at follow-up a few months or more after the termination of counseling.

Second, as far as possible, clients should be randomly assigned to at least two groups—a group that receives the lay counseling and a control group that receives nothing, but waits (waiting-list, "no-treatment" control group). This approach attempts to answer the question of whether lay counseling is more effective than no counseling. An alternative approach, called the comparative design,[40] involves randomly assigning clients to two types of lay counseling (e.g., nouthetic counseling as developed by Jay Adams versus biblical counseling as developed by Larry Crabb), and comparing the relative effectiveness of the two types of lay counseling without the use of formal control groups, an approach that may be more realistic and ethical to employ in local church lay counseling centers.

While random assignment of clients is ideal, it is often not practical or ethical to place some clients on a waiting list randomly. However, some local church lay counseling centers have a natural waiting list of clients because of the high demand, and this group can then be used as the waiting-list control group, although no random assignment of clients has been done. Statistical procedures can then be employed to determine the comparability of the group of clients receiving lay counseling and the waiting-list control group of clients on a number of measures at pre-counseling. If the two groups do not differ significantly on these measures before counseling or at the start of counseling, then some comparability of the two groups at the beginning of the evaluation study can be assumed.

Third, lay counselors should be given a clearly described manual or protocol to follow, especially if a comparative design is used. For example, those providing nouthetic counseling should be following closely Jay Adams's approach and methods, and those providing biblical counseling should be following closely Larry Crabb's approach and methods. Counseling sessions should be audio or video recorded so that ratings by other objective judges or raters can subsequently be made regarding the extent to which the lay counselors followed the counseling protocol or guidelines to be used in a particular evaluation study.

Finally, evaluation studies should eventually go beyond global studies comparing lay counseling to no counseling, or one type of lay counseling to another type of lay counseling. More specific questions need to be answered, including those having to do with mechanisms of change and particular components or factors of the lay counseling provided that may be more responsible for the outcomes or effects obtained. Different research designs can be employed to answer some of these specific questions, but as Dr. Alan Kazdin, a well-known researcher in this field, has pointed out, the questions that can be addressed by research are astronomical! He made the following comment in reviewing the methodology of psychotherapy outcome research:

> Many basic issues about assessment and design that dictate how to address outcome questions appropriately are also far from resolved. Hence there is no singularly or universally agreed-upon assessment battery or design strategy that could, in any definitive fashion, put to rest particular questions about therapy.[41]

While it will not be possible to conduct a definitive or perfect evaluation study on the outcome of lay counseling, we hope that the suggestions made here will help increase the number of "competent" evaluation or outcome studies in this area. Researchers should also give attention to the ethical issues involved in conducting evaluation research, though space does not permit a detailed discussion of issues like informed consent, confidentiality of records, and the appropriateness of using control groups and random assignment of clients. Many of these have been summarized in a helpful article by Stanley Imber and his colleagues.[42] Such ethical considerations should be addressed *before* starting any evaluation study to ensure that all research is conducted in an ethical manner.

CONCLUDING COMMENTS

As we conclude this chapter, we acknowledge that we have not talked about the approaches and methods for investigating the *process* of therapy or counseling.[43] This is an important area of research, and further studies evaluating the process or actual dimensions and factors of lay Christian counseling that contribute significantly to good outcomes or effects are needed.

Second, the criteria for evaluating the effectiveness of lay Christian counseling should also be widened to include not only measures of client change and client satisfaction, but also the durability and clinical significance (not just statistical significance) of such change, and cost-benefit analyses pertaining to the *efficiency*, and not just the efficacy or effectiveness, of the counseling provided.[44] *Program evaluation* of the effects of the total lay counseling ministry on others in addition to the clients served (for example, on the pastoral staff, church board, congregation, and church life and ministry, as well as the lay counselors themselves) should also be conducted.

Third, funding to financially support better or more competent evaluation studies in the area of lay Christian counseling will be needed. Organizations like the American Association of Christian Counselors, the Christian Association for Psychological Studies International, the California Peer Counseling Association, and the National Peer Helpers Association[45] can be involved in encouraging more evaluation research on lay or peer counseling and possibly making funds available to support such research.

More studies are needed that attempt to evaluate *both* the effectiveness of training programs for lay Christian counselors and the effectiveness of the lay counseling provided by such trained lay Christian counselors. Such studies, while more elaborate and complex, will help to determine what specific lay counselor skills or competencies are related to good outcomes and how well lay Christian counselors can be trained in such skills. A related need is to further determine what selection criteria or measures for lay counselors are significant predictors of good lay counselor training effects, as well as of effective lay counseling.

Finally, we should point out that what has been suggested in this chapter for the evaluation of the effectiveness of lay Christian counseling is most applicable and relevant to the formal-organized model of lay counseling ministry (e.g., in the context of a lay counseling center or service), although some of the measures we have described can also be used with some modification in the context of an informal-organized model of lay counseling ministry. The suggestions that have been made regarding the evaluation of training programs for lay Christian counselors can, however, be applied to both the formal-organized and informal-organized models of lay counseling ministry.

Several years ago, Dr. Joseph Durlak spent some time reviewing the literature comparing the effectiveness of lay and professional counselors, concluding: "Data indicate that paraprofessionals can make an important contribution as helping agents, but the factors accounting for this phenomenon are not understood. . . . It would be a mistake to continue using paraprofessionals without more closely examining their skills, deficiencies, and limitations."[46] His observations remind us that more and better evaluation studies of the skills, deficiencies, and limitations of lay Christian counselors providing lay Christian counseling are needed.

CHAPTER 10

The Local Church, Community Resources, and Lay Counseling

In the previous chapters of this book we looked at various aspects of a Christian approach to lay counseling, including biblical models; research literature; the selection, training, supervision, and evaluation of lay Christian counselors; and building or establishing a ministry of lay counseling.

In this chapter we begin with a look at the findings from a survey of fifteen church-based lay counseling ministries conducted by the Center for Church Renewal in Plano, Texas.[1] Following that, we provide snapshots of lay counseling ministries in local churches, several of which have been described in a book on Christian peer counseling written by Joan Sturkie and Gordon Bear.[2] We also take a look at the lay counseling services set up and directed by one of the authors, Dr. Tan, at Peoples Church of Montreal and North Park Community Chapel in Canada. We conclude by moving beyond the local church to examine lay counseling ministries at parachurch organizations (e.g., Youth for Christ, Young Life, the Navigators), missions, prison ministries, retirement and nursing homes, Christian mental health centers or programs, and other professional community resources.

LAY COUNSELING SURVEY FINDINGS

In 1986 the Center for Church Renewal in Plano, Texas, conducted a survey of fifteen evangelical church-based lay counseling ministries. The churches ranged in size from 450 to 9,000 members and represented a variety of denominational affiliations, geographical locations, and lay counseling models and philosophies.

Five of these churches described themselves as urban, ten of them as suburban, and none as rural. Fourteen churches described themselves as "large" and one of them as "small." Regarding weekly attendance on Sunday mornings, there were five churches with under 1,000 members, seven churches between 1,000 and

2,000, one church between 2,000 and 3,000, one church between 4,000 and 5,000, and one church of 9,000.

The denominational affiliations of the fifteen churches were Assembly of God (1), Bible (1), Christian Church (1), Conservative Baptist (2), Evangelical Presbyterian (1), Independent (1), Missionary Church (1), Presbyterian Church (USA) (5), Reformed Church of America (1), and Southern Baptist (2). One church belonged to both the Conservative and Southern Baptist denominations.

Summarized below are the major findings from the survey under the three main headings provided: (1) lay counselor training, (2) lay counseling, and (3) evaluation.

Lay Counselor Training

a. *Length of Time Programs Had Existed*

The average age of the lay counseling ministries (including the provision of lay counselor training) in these churches was 6.1 years, with a range from 2 to 18 years.

b. *Size*

1. *Number of people who have completed training.* A total of 981 people had been trained as lay counselors by these fifteen churches, with an average of 65 trained people per church, and a range from 1 to 200. The actual number of trained lay counselors produced per year ranged from 3 to 38.

2. *Number of people currently in training.* At the time of the survey, a total of 82 people were still in training (in four of the fifteen churches), with an average of 6 per church.

3. *Number of teachers and trainers.* The average number of trainers was 8, with a range of 2 to 50 (although not all 50 trainers are used in every session in this particular church).

c. *Description of the Training Process*

1. *Classes.* The average number of classes used to train lay counselors was 36, with a range from 6 to 135. Most of the classes met weekly for one-to two-hour sessions. In addition to weekly training sessions, some churches also used weekend retreats, an all-day Saturday seminar, attendance at outside seminars (one day to one week in length), home meetings, and required attendance at a seminary course.

2. *Content.* Out of the thirteen churches that responded to this question, four noted that they were heavily influenced by Larry Crabb's lay counselor training approach, although they described their training as eclectic in content. Two other churches indicated that their training

course content was heavily influenced by the Stephen Series. One church depended completely on Egan's Skilled Helper, and another on Gary Collins's People Helper Pak. The most frequently covered topics (with frequencies of more than 1) in the content of the training course provided were the following (with frequencies given in parentheses): counseling skills (12), training for specific issues (9), crisis counseling (8), marital counseling (8), use of the Bible in counseling (8), theology of man or human nature (7), theology of change (7), how or when to refer (5), relationship of psychology and religion (4), and self-understanding in lay counseling (2). Other topics mentioned only once included authority of Scripture, adult personality inventory, assertion training, assessment/diagnosis, categories of problems, Christian thinking, communication process, confidentiality, depression, feelings, issues of counseling, legal issues, organization, philosophy of counseling, prayer, psychopathology, relating to others, sin, telephone care, and thinking through your faith.

3. *Who teaches?* Eleven churches used staff pastors; ten used trained lay counselors; six used professional counselors from outside; one used a staff counselor; and another used chaplains from outside as trainers or teachers in their training programs.

4. *Use of observation.* Only two churches utilized observation of lay counselors in their training process.

5. *Use of cocounseling.* Seven churches offered some kind of cocounseling, especially in the contexts of premarital counseling and family counseling.

6. *Personal discipleship.* Eight churches described their training as including some component of personal discipleship.

7. *Use of videos.* Eleven churches used videos in their training programs, ranging from Christian presentations on counseling to secular films on various topics.

8. *Seminars.* Fourteen churches included the use of seminars in their training programs (e.g., Larry Crabb's weeklong seminars on biblical counseling, and other local, secular topical seminars).

d. *Length of Lay Counselor Training Program*

The average length or duration of the lay counselor training process or program was about eight months. Eight churches had training programs that lasted six months or less. Four other churches finish their training process in a year or less. Two more churches took two years to complete their training, and one church had an indefinite length.

e. *Selection Process for Lay Counselors*

1. *Is participation in the lay counseling program open to all volunteers, or are those who do lay counseling chosen?* None of the churches had completely open lay counseling programs. Eight churches had open participation in the training part of their programs, but the lay counseling was done only by specially selected lay counselors. The other seven churches limited their training, as well as the lay counseling ministry, to specially selected or chosen lay counselors.

2. *If the lay counselors are chosen, what criteria are involved?* A wide variety of criteria was mentioned for selecting lay counselors. The counselor's character was listed most often, especially traits like teachability, flexibility, strength, and empathy. Second and third on the list were spiritual maturity and commitment to the lay counseling program respectively. Other criteria mentioned included demonstrated informal counseling ability, qualifying personal life experience, and successfully passing a screening interview (required by four churches).

f. *Organizational Structure*

Fourteen churches had a paid staff person who oversaw the lay counseling ministry (but not all of these people actually directed the lay counseling programs per se), and one church used a lay volunteer to oversee the ministry. Eight churches had one paid staff member direct all the lay counselors in the church, whereas in six others, a supervising lay counselor actually directed the other lay counselors, but he or she in turn reported to a paid staff member of the church.

Lay Counseling

g. *Number of Active Lay Counselors*

The average number of lay counselors functioning per church was 16, with a range from 7 to 40.

h. *Time Spent Per Week*

1. *Number of hours of lay counseling per week.* The average number of lay counseling hours per week was 22, with a range from 4 to 50. The majority of the churches surveyed spent a little less than the average of 22.

2. *Number of hours of staff counseling per week.* The average number of hours per week spent by the staff of the churches surveyed in counseling was 34, with a range from 9 to 120. However, the majority of churches spent somewhat less than the average (i.e., about 20 to 30 hours per week).

i. *Types of Counseling Situations in which the Lay Counselors Minister*

The following were the most frequently mentioned types of counseling situations seen by lay counselors (with frequencies of more than once), with the actual frequencies given in parentheses: parenting problems (12), depression (11), marital disputes (11), grief (10), premarital (10), drugs/alcohol abuse (8), self-image (7), anxiety (7), anger (6), child abuse (5), guilt (5), suicide (4), teen pregnancy (4), extramarital affairs (4), vocational (3), relationships (3), adjustment difficulties (3), adolescents (2), shut-ins (2), support counseling (2), family (2), and death (2). The counseling situations, therefore, ranged from relatively light—people calling with basic helping related questions—to more serious situations, such as suicide, substance abuse, and marital problems. There may therefore be very few limits in actual practice as to the ways lay counselors were being used.

j. *Sources of Referrals to the Lay Counselors*

Most of the referrals to the lay counselors came from within the local church body, with church staff, the director of the lay counseling ministry, and church members doing most of the referring. Other Christian organizations outside the church were the next most frequent referral sources. Non-Christian organizations like the police were also mentioned as referral sources. Other referral sources included the lay counselors themselves, recommendations by family members or former clients, recommendations by support groups in the church, or counselees coming forward after a church service for counseling.

k. *Supervision of Lay Counselors*

Fourteen churches responded to questions about the kind of supervision lay counselors received and whether it was formal or informal. Six churches described their supervision as informal, whereas eight others described their supervision as formal. Different forms or structures of supervision were used. For example, four churches held follow-up sessions with church staff for the lay counselors, and three churches noted that staff actually observed the lay counselors at work. One church required written reports from the lay counselors. Other kinds of supervision, each mentioned once, included large group supervision meetings led by church staff, a layered accountability structure among the lay counselors themselves, and meeting with a professional psychologist.

l. *Utilization of Lay Counseling Services*

1. *Are the members of the church using the lay counselors comfortably?* Thirteen churches responded "Yes," but two other churches indicated that their members were uncomfortable with using their lay counselors.

2. *Is there reeducation needed for the church members to be more comfortable?* Eleven churches responded "Yes."

m. *Financial Parameters*

1. *Are there any fees involved?* None of the churches surveyed charged for their lay counseling services, with one exception being a $40 charge for premarital counseling conducted by lay counselors.

2. *Are there any (requested) donations involved?* Only three churches requested donations for their lay counseling services, but no specific amounts of donations were prescribed.

n. *Extrachurch Activity*

What percentage of lay counseling is to nonchurch members? An average of 36 percent of the lay counseling services provided was to nonchurch members, with a range of 0 to 75 percent. The results indicated that the lay counseling ministries surveyed either did one-half or more of their lay counseling outside of the church membership, or did little counseling at all outside of the church membership.

o. *Coordination with Other Ministries*

1. *What are some ways in which the lay counselor's efforts are able to dovetail with the pastoral staff?* The following were some of the answers given: do pastoral care; pinpoint special needs; report visitation needs; lighten pastor's workload; serve as informal leadership core; serve as source of leadership; have women who take "female" counseling from male pastors; take overflow counseling, long-term counseling, or premarital counseling; take/screen walk-ins; take referral cases; take light cases; take prayer requests; do follow-up; provide support groups; and encourage church involvement.

2. *What are some ways in which the lay counselor's efforts are able to dovetail with the professional counseling community?* The following were some of the answers given: take referrals, take those too poor for professionals, give referrals, refer to physicians, pick up spiritual aspects of cases not dealt with by secular counselors, provide support and follow-up. One church, however, did not refer outside the church at all, while another described itself as resistant to the secular counseling community.

p. *Philosophy of Lay Helping*

What theorists most directly influence your counseling model and ministry? Most of the churches described their lay counseling approaches as philosophically eclectic. Ten of them mentioned Reality Therapy as influential in shaping their philosophy of counseling; 7 mentioned Larry Crabb; 3 mentioned Norman Wright; and Jay Adams, Gerard Egan, Gary Collins,

Kenneth Haugk (Stephen Series Ministry), Carl Rogers, and Virginia Satir were each mentioned twice.

Evaluation

q. *Effect on Church Staff*

The effects on the church staff of having a lay counseling ministry were varied and included the following: lightening the staff workload in general; lightening the pastoral workload but increasing the overall staff workload in the form of phone calls and secretarial workload; initially increasing the staff workload but eventually decreasing it; affecting the staff workload minimally; and overall edifying and sensitizing the church staff.

r. *Effect on the Church*

Overall, the effect of a lay counseling ministry on the local church seemed to be positive. The range of responses included the following: prevented problems requiring counseling by education; responded more quickly to needs in the church or responded to previously unmet needs; edified the church body; enhanced the church's overall ministry; made the church a more sensitive and caring one with more listening and financial helping of hurting members; helped the church become more well-rounded; fulfilled the mandate to help the weak; facilitated numerical growth of the church; benefited the family structure, marriages, and communication in general among people in the church; provided a real service to the poor and to those fearful of professional counseling; and had an impact on the church in a diverse but minimal way.

s. *Lessons Learned*

1. *What lessons have you learned that should be repeated in the future; that is, what has worked especially well?* The varied responses included these: keep the training program free of charge; continue to use a two-stage plan of lay counselor training—first level open to everyone, second level only open to some; require a high commitment on the part of the lay counselors; focus on the character and compassion of the lay counselor as more important than just training; work in teams; seek out quality leadership and strong administrative support; form support groups; and use the "excellent" ministry materials and valuable leadership workshops offered by the Stephen Ministry.

2. *What lessons have you learned regarding things that should be avoided in the future?* The different answers to this question included the following things to *avoid:* opening the lay counselor training program to everyone; overloading the lay counselors with too much specialized

information or too heavy academics; following too much a "medical model" of counseling (rather than a "network model"); using a drop-in procedure; using the term *counseling* (which may threaten or frighten off some people); using a paid director to direct referrals (rather than a volunteer), which is a very time-consuming task; having unrealistic expectations for an overly large or quick response to the lay counseling ministry; having lay counselors who think too highly of themselves; letting people counsel or lead support groups without adequate preparation or training; using special training classes (rather than Sunday school classes) because of the greater possibility of legal liability; and advertising that the lay counseling is free, because it may lead to an overwhelming flood of referrals or clients.

3. *What would you do differently if you were starting over?* Some of the various responses included the following: be more careful to choose faithful people to be lay counselors; use a one-way mirror in the training process; use video recording in training the lay counselors; use more experiential training; include more integration of the Bible; limit the training program in the second half to only those who are qualified (many of the churches surveyed were already doing this); pay more attention to training the lay counselors; pay the director of the lay counseling ministry; increase the degree of lay help in a particular lay counseling ministry; and give greater consideration to how to handle potential legal problems.

4. *What do the lay counselors see as benefits of the program?* Among the benefits mentioned were the following: lay counselors felt helped as they helped others; they felt they were performing a genuine and fulfilling ministry; they experienced personal growth in many areas, such as the development of personal communication skills, growth in their marriages, personal revival, discovery of their gifts, and an important step toward a career. Some lay counselors also found the development of positive relationships a significant experience for them, and many benefited from a positive support group experience with other lay counselors. The lay counseling ministry also enabled several people to find their niche in the church by functioning as lay counselors (and thereby closed the church's "back door," so to speak).

5. *Legal considerations.* The possibility of being sued for something a lay counselor has done or said was a fairly common concern among the churches surveyed. Some were considering malpractice insurance, but it is too expensive or prohibitive for most churches. A number of

ways to decrease the risk of being sued were mentioned, including the following: prayer; not charging for the lay counseling services provided; requiring clients to waive the lay counseling ministry's liability; emphasizing biblical counseling; not using terms like counselor and counseling; counseling only church members; providing malpractice insurance for at least the director of the lay counseling ministry, and, if possible, for all the lay counselors; and having an emergency "malpractice suit" fund (to cover court costs until the malpractice suit is thrown out of court, because one church's attorney felt a malpractice law suit would not stick), which is cheaper than buying malpractice insurance. Churches involved in the Stephen Ministry did not feel malpractice insurance was necessary since their lay caring ministry is primarily pastoral in nature.

While the findings of the Lay Counseling Survey just summarized are interesting and helpful, we strongly want to emphasize that they must not be generalized to all lay counseling ministries in local churches. The number of churches surveyed was relatively small, and while some attempt was made to survey evangelical churches representing a variety of denominational affiliations, geographical locations, and lay counseling models and philosophies, the overwhelming majority of the churches were relatively large ones (fourteen of them) in their respective communities. The survey results are limited to a small sample of relatively large evangelical churches in different parts of the United States and should not be generalized to other smaller evangelical churches, to other churches that may not be as evangelical, to parachurch organizations and other contexts of lay counseling ministry, and to other countries. There are also limitations inherent in the use of the survey method of collecting information, including questions regarding how accurate or reliable the answers given may be, since many of them were based on memory or retrospective reports. More surveys and better evaluation of lay Christian counselors are still needed.

EXAMPLES OF LAY COUNSELING MINISTRIES IN LOCAL CHURCHES

It is difficult to estimate how many local churches in the United States and Canada actually have lay counseling ministries. As mentioned in chapter 5, the Stephen Series[3] alone has been successfully used in thousands of congregations throughout the country, in more than 160 denominations, in all fifty states, in seven Canadian provinces, and in twenty-four other countries. A number of churches have been involved in starting a Lay Pastors Ministry, which includes lay pastoral care and counseling. Dr. Melvin J. Steinbron is the founder of the Lay Pastors Ministry, which began in 1978 with a pilot group of five laypeople when he was minister of pastoral care at College Hill Presbyterian Church in Cincinnati, Ohio. At one point, this ministry expanded to at least thirty-six states in the United States, five Canadian provinces, and two foreign countries, fulfilling the biblical injunction to "be shepherds of God's flock" (1 Peter 5:2). Out of this ministry has grown a *network* of churches that have equipped their laypeople to provide pastoral care. Steinbron coordinates this network, conducts training seminars for lay pastors, and publishes materials through his organization: Lay Pastors Ministry, Inc.: Equipping Lay People to Give Pastoral Care (www.laypastors.com).

Several of the better-known local churches with successful lay counseling ministries were briefly described by Joan Sturkie and Gordon Bear in their interesting and helpful book *Christian Peer Counseling: Love in Action.*[4] They give nine examples of local church lay or peer counseling programs under the two major models of lay counseling ministry described earlier: the formal-organized and informal-organized models. The following four churches had successful lay counseling ministries using the formal-organized model:

- Lay Counseling Ministry of La Canada Presbyterian Church (Presbyterian Church, USA), La Canada, California
- Neighbors Who Care—Lay Counseling Ministry of The Neighborhood Church (Assemblies of God), Bellevue, Washington
- Christian Counseling Ministry of The Elmbrook Church (Nondenominational), Waukesha, Wisconsin
- North Heights Lutheran Church Counseling Clinic (Evangelical Lutheran Church in America), Roseville, Minnesota

The following five churches had successful lay counseling ministries using the informal-organized model:

- Lay Shepherding Program of First Baptist Church (American Baptist), Fall River, Massachusetts
- Enrichment Builders Lay Counseling Program, First Baptist Church (Southern Baptist), Jackson, Mississippi
- Peer Ministry of Christ Memorial Lutheran Church (Missouri Synod Lutheran), Affton, Missouri
- Stephen Ministry Program of Union United Methodist Church (United Methodist Church), Irmo, South Carolina

- The Shepherding Ministry of First Congregational Church (United Church of Christ), Hopkinton, Massachusetts

Sturkie and Bear also mentioned the following church, parachurch, or paraprofessional organizations involved in lay counseling training and ministry:

- The Lay Academy of the Episcopal Diocese of California, San Francisco, California
- New Directions Counseling Center (parachurch and paraprofessional organization), Concord, California
- Love Lines, Inc. (parachurch and paraprofessional organization), Minneapolis, Minnesota
- Match-Two (M-2) Prisoner Outreach (paraprofessional organization), Statewide Headquarters, San Quentin, California

In addition to helpful, brief descriptions of these thirteen lay or peer counseling ministries, Sturkie and Bear provide eight true stories from the field, giving a taste of what actually happens in the context of lay or peer counseling ministry. In the final section of their book, the authors reprint fifteen practical and helpful sample forms and program ideas from different lay or peer counseling ministries: (1) Personal Interview Data Form; (2) Program Announcement of a Lay Counseling Ministry; (3) Philosophy of Ministry section from the Manual of the Christian Counseling Ministry of a local church; (4) Trainee Application Form; (5) Donation Policy Declaration; (6) Interest/Availability Statement; (7) Release of Liability Form; (8) Intake Information Form; (9) Job Description (Director); (10) Release of Permission Form; (11) Prayer and Counseling Report Form; (12) Counselee Referral Form; (13) Job Description (Assistant Director); (14) Evaluation (by Supervisor) Form; and (15) Counselor Evaluation Form.

CULTURAL AWARENESS AND COMPETENCY IN LAY COUNSELING

As our society grows increasingly diverse and the people seeking counseling come with multiple, and at times, seemingly incongruent value systems, counselors must learn to integrate and balance both their biblical principles and the need to be culturally relevant while still adhering to the foundation of ethical practice.[5] One exciting development in this regard is the establishment of lay caring and counseling ministries in ethnic churches, including Chinese churches. For example, North York Chinese Baptist Church in Ontario, Canada, completed a training program for lay counselors and started a lay counseling service. Another example is First Evangelical Church Glendale in Glendale, California, a Chinese church with an English-speaking congregation that completed a Stephen Series training program and started a Stephen Ministry of lay caregiving (note that this ministry is not currently in full operation due to other caring ministries provided by the pastoral staff).

We would also take note of the teaching and training ministry of Dr. Peter Chiu—a licensed marriage, family, and child counselor in California who was director of the Department of Counseling and assistant to the General Secretary of Chinese Christian Mission (CCM), which serves Chinese churches worldwide. Several Chinese churches and parachurch organizations in Houston, Vancouver, Singapore, Indonesia, and Taiwan have developed lay counseling programs. In Kowloon, Hong Kong, the Breakthrough Counseling Centre provides counseling training for paraprofessional counselors, seminarians, and church laypeople. Also well-known is the work of the late Selwyn Hughes and his colleagues in England in training lay Christian counselors using a biblical model.

When we look at developments in the African-American church, it is helpful to begin with the observation of Dr. Rose Edgar, who noted that many black churches in the Los Angeles area provide after-school tutoring and family counseling services. She pointed out that one African-American Baptist church in Pasadena had established a counseling center using lay counselors and offering free counseling services, and Second Baptist Church in Los Angeles had a pastor in charge of counseling services who developed and supervised small sharing groups for providing group counseling and support.[6] It is not easy in ethnic congregations like Asian (e.g., Chinese) and African-American churches to establish lay caring and counseling ministries (partly because of the high regard such churches have for their pastors), but it is exciting to see that this is being done successfully in a number of these churches. The need for lay Christian counseling services or ministries in Hispanic churches is also great.[7] Effective counselors will often engage clients through the lens of ethnic diversity while demonstrating respect and cultural competency.

Grief, loss, and suffering are not limited to North America or Western civilization. One can hardly pick up a newspaper today, turn on the television, or go online without hearing about some global tragedy, natural disaster, act of terror, the destructive aftermath of armed conflict, sex trafficking, or other trauma-related stories. The pain is evident and the pain is real, often causing people to yearn for good news, for something positive, something hopeful. The words of the psalmist encourage us: "For God is the King of all the earth. . . . God reigns over the nations" (Ps. 47:7–8) and "The LORD is exalted over all the nations, his glory above the heavens" (Ps. 113:4). Believers, in particular those who are engaged in caregiving ministries and the mental health professions, cannot ignore God's clarion call to "go into all the world" (Mark 16:15)—to be His voice, His eyes and ears, hands and feet, to those who are hurting and suffering from injustice.

The United States has a rich history of compassionate outreach and goodwill, but in a world that continues to shrink due to innovative technologies, instant communication, and complex integrated economies, overtly Westernized counseling strategies may not always be the most optimal approach when it comes to the caregiving paradigm—especially in terms of assessment and treatment protocols, diagnostic categories, certain theoretical constructs, and even the definition of some psychological disorders. Though the core and principled tenets of Christian counseling should always be anchored in God's Word, the methodology and process may require periodic adjustments to remain culturally relevant with a servant-oriented focus.[8] Practitioners should be cognizant of the geographic, ethnic, cultural, and even political nuances that have an impact on the delivery of services and resources.

Today there is a greater global focus on mental health and well-being, including an emphasis on caregiving and counseling. However, the role and recognition of mental health practitioners is significantly different from country to country. While many nations recognize and regulate psychiatrists, and to a lesser extent, psychologists, the disciplines of social work, counseling, marriage and family therapy, and substance abuse intervention do not necessarily have the same distinct titles (at the licensure level) found in the United States. The result has been that churches and Christian organizations everywhere are developing lay counseling and paraprofessional services and training centers to help meet this growing need. Many of the concepts and principles found in this book are easily adaptable and applicable within any culture, and our prayer is that it will be a helpful resource in reaching out to and coming alongside those who need care and counsel.

During the Third Lausanne Congress (Cape Town, South Africa) on World Evangelization in 2010, there was a watershed moment for Christian counseling. The Lausanne Care and Counsel as Mission Interest Group (LCCMIG) met to draft a document that provided a much-needed framework for a growing international counseling effort. The *Cape Town Declaration on Care and Counsel as Mission* (see www.careandcounselasmission.org) outlined the Three-Circle Paradigm of Care and Counsel that focuses on missionary care and support, support for the global church, and care and counsel as mission.[9]

As biblically based counselors and caregivers, each of us has the distinct privilege of faithfully representing Christ in our professional work or lay ministry with others. To accomplish this task effectively, we must employ balance in demonstrating the grace and compassion of a loving Savior, and do so in a culturally sensitive way. One of the messages of Pentecost and the birth of the church is that people were hearing the gospel "each . . . [in] their own language" (Acts 2:6). Likewise, the message we carry as counselors must be relevant for the culture before us and in a "language" that culture can easily comprehend and respond to.

EXAMPLES OF LOCAL CHURCH MODELS

There were two lay counseling centers set up and directed by one of the authors, Dr. Tan, in Canada using the formal-organized model: the first at Peoples Church of Montreal,[10] and the second at North Park Community Chapel in London, Ontario.[11] The lay counseling service at Peoples Church of Montreal was set up in October 1976 with full support and cooperation from the two pastors and church board. This is an evangelical church that had an average Sunday morning worship attendance of between 250 and 300 people. It is located in downtown Montreal, just across from the campus of McGill University, and affiliated with the Associated Gospel Churches.

As an undergraduate student majoring in psychology at McGill University, Tan was involved for a couple of years in a secular, student-run peer counseling group called Interaction McGill. In this group, he was exposed to peer and lay counseling training and services in a secular community outreach context at a major Canadian university, just prior to organizing the lay counseling service at Peoples Church. He had also been involved for several years in leadership in Youth for Christ (YFC) ministries as a volunteer, both in Singapore (which is his country of origin and where he grew up and completed his high school/junior college education) and in Montreal, and therefore had some experience in training volunteer and full-time YFC staff in youth ministry skills, including basic counseling skills.

With this background, and with ongoing reading of the latest developments in biblical, Christian counseling (e.g., books by Adams, Crabb, and Collins), Tan sensed the Lord leading him to set up a lay counseling service at Peoples Church to help lighten the load of pastoral care and counseling for the two pastors (who were already heavily involved in such ministry) and to facilitate the further development of the church body as a caring community.

After obtaining the full support of the pastors and church board, he also received from the pastors recommendations of certain church members or adherents as prospective lay counselors for the service to be established. Those recommended were generally warm and spiritually committed Christians who had a desire to be involved in a ministry of people-helping or lay counseling. Several of them were already performing informal people-helping roles in the church, and a few were serving in different positions of church leadership. An announcement was made in church that people interested in being involved in a lay counseling ministry should contact him or the pastors. Prospective lay counselors were then approached and interviewed briefly, and those deemed appropriate who had the time to commit themselves to such a ministry were selected as lay counselors, with an original group of nine persons.

The initial training for these lay counselors involved a weekend seminar that covered the integrated, biblically based model of effective Christian counseling presented in some detail in chapter 3 of this book, as well as basic counseling skills and methods. Role plays were conducted, with feedback and discussion, sometimes using audiovisual equipment (e.g., video recorders), so that basic counseling skills, such as attentive listening, observing nonverbal cues, handling silence, wise questioning, and appropriate responding, could be taught and learned in a practical way.

The initial, basic training was brief, but subsequent monthly staff meetings, lasting three to four hours each time, included further training sessions on a number of different topics pertaining to lay counseling (e.g., dealing with depression, recognizing signs and symptoms of severe disorders, terminating counseling, and making proper referrals). It took a few months before all the lay counselors were seeing counselees or clients. A small resource library was set up for the lay counselors, consisting of useful books, articles, and audiotape presentations on effective counseling and related topics, mainly from an evangelical, biblical perspective.

Supervision of lay counselors mainly involved case discussions either at staff meetings in a group, or individually between the lay counselor and Tan as director of the service (with permission obtained from counselees or clients). Supervision and training through cocounseling were implemented later. Special training seminars were also periodically scheduled for others, both clergy and laity, who were interested in learning more effective ways of helping people.

The counseling service had five basic functions, four of which have already been mentioned in chapter 5 of this book (as a part of the brochure used at North Park Community Chapel, whose lay counseling service was set up later, patterning it after the one at Peoples Church of Montreal, but with a few significant changes, which are described). The fifth one was a telephone service for those who wanted to call in and talk over the phone during the hours when the service was available. As a nonprofessional, volunteer ministry, the service did not charge any fees or ask for any donations, and it was publicized mainly at Peoples Church, although it did become known to other pastors and churches in the area. The service was open on two weekday evenings each week, from 7:00 to 10:00 p.m. Several lay counselors were available on each of the evenings. Some had appointments made in advance, but usually at least one lay counselor was free to answer the telephone or talk with those who dropped in without an appointment.

Over the four years (1976–80) under Tan's direction, the lay counselors who served in this ministry included two university students, a library assistant, a nurse, an engineer, an office worker, two schoolteachers, a medical intern, and one of the pastors. At the time, Tan was a graduate student in the PhD program in clinical psychology at McGill University and served as director of the service on a voluntary, unpaid basis. A Christian psychiatrist in Montreal served as a consultant and as a professional to whom appropriate referrals could be made. A list of appropriate Christian professionals was compiled for use when other referrals were needed.

Many of the lay counselors informally commented over the years on how they had benefited from their training, supervision sessions, and counseling experience. Many counselees or clients also expressed appreciation for the help given them through the lay counselors and the service. Most of the earlier clients were referrals from the pastors, but referrals from pastors of other churches and self-referrals became more common over the years.

Most of the clients were Christians, although several non-Christians also used the service. No files were kept on clients since the service was a nonprofessional, volunteer ministry, but names of clients were recorded to keep some basic statistics. Over a hundred clients had used the service in four years, with the average number of counseling sessions per client being about eight. The range was one to seventy sessions, but the majority of clients were seen for relatively short-term counseling. A few clients were seen for long-term supportive help.

The lay counseling service at Peoples Church continued to function for a while after Tan left Montreal for a job as a psychologist at University Hospital in London, Ontario. He also taught part-time in the Departments of Psychology, Psychiatry, and Oral Medicine at the University of Western Ontario in London. The majority of trained lay counselors at Peoples Church moved out of Montreal in the early 1980s, so that the service at Peoples Church had to be closed down. It therefore stopped functioning on a formal, organized basis for years now, although one or two of the remaining lay counselors still help informally in lay pastoral care and counseling when the need arises.

While in London, Ontario, Tan set up another lay counseling service similar to the one at Peoples Church, at North Park Community Chapel, which is a non-denominational, evangelical local church with over one thousand members and adherents. In doing so, he made a number of significant changes, however, based on the earlier experience at Peoples Church.

First, before starting the service, a longer and more comprehensive training program was conducted, which lasted for six months. The lay counselors were selected after being recommended by the pastors and interviewed by Tan and the senior pastor, using selection criteria described earlier in this book. Further details of the training program have been given in chapter 7.

Second, a telephone or drop-in service was not provided, so all counseling sessions were by appointment only. This was done for convenience, as well as for safety or security reasons, since a few thefts occurred at Peoples Church when the church side door was left open for people to drop in. At North Park Community Chapel, doors were left locked until the appropriate appointment time, or until a client rang the doorbell.

Third, monthly staff meetings were held, lasting four hours or so for further training and supervision (including role plays), but individual supervision sessions were also arranged between the lay counselors and Tan when necessary, and this was done on a more frequent and regular basis than at Peoples Church.

Fourth, some basic evaluation of the effectiveness of the lay counselor training program was completed using the self-report measure Tan developed (described in the previous chapter). Results were favorable, but no comparison group was used. However, a systematic evaluation of the effectiveness of the lay counseling provided was not conducted.

Fifth, periodic retreats with the lay counselors for further training and support were offered.

Sixth, some counseling appointments were scheduled during the day, since a few of the counselors were homemakers and could meet with those who preferred day appointments to evening ones. Lay counseling was still available two evenings a week.

While no formal outcome or program evaluation was done, many clients expressed deep appreciation for the help they received; the lay counselors commented on how much they had learned and grown through their training and counseling experiences; and the pastors appreciated the service because it helped to lighten their own counseling load while giving opportunities to gifted lay-people in the church to use their spiritual gifts and minister to others. Tan found being involved in such a ministry to be challenging but also deeply rewarding and fulfilling, especially as he saw the Lord touch many broken lives with His healing and grace.

Tan directed the lay counseling service at North Park Community Chapel from 1981 until August 1983, when he moved to Toronto to become director of counseling and to teach at Ontario Bible College and subsequently, in July 1985, to Fuller Theological Seminary in Pasadena, California, where he continues to teach on the faculty of the Graduate School of Psychology.

As recommended in this book, more direct observation of lay counselors, the use of cocounseling, and more systematic and comprehensive evaluation of the effectiveness of training programs, as well as the lay counseling provided by trained lay counselors, and more frequent supervision sessions (biweekly or weekly), could and should be implemented in a lay counseling service like the one at North Park Community Chapel.

Tan has also been involved with several of his doctoral students in clinical psychology at Fuller Theological Seminary in the evaluation of the effectiveness of lay Christian counselor training programs and lay Christian counseling, particularly in the local church context. He has also consulted with several pastors both in the United States and Canada, as well as in Singapore and other Asian countries, who have subsequently used the ideas and guidelines presented in this book to establish lay counselor training programs and lay counseling ministries in their local churches. More formally, he teaches a four-unit elective course at Fuller Theological Seminary titled "Training Lay Counselors in the Church," which has had good enrollments of students from all three Fuller Schools of Theology, Intercultural Studies (formerly World Mission), and Psychology, and hence from different parts of the world. He has also taught that course for Fuller's Extended Education program in Phoenix, Arizona, and anticipates more Bible colleges and seminaries or Christian colleges and universities will offer courses on lay or peer counseling. He has also taught weeklong summer intensive courses focusing on lay pastoral care in the church for the Fuller Korean Doctor of Ministry (KDMin) program in Pasadena, California, with translation provided into Korean. He has presented workshops on lay counseling and setting up a lay counseling ministry at national and international conferences on Christian counseling.

LAY COUNSELING MINISTRIES BEYOND THE LOCAL CHURCH

In this final section, we want to take note of several lay counseling ministries that occur outside the context of the local church. *Parachurch organizations* like Youth for Christ (especially the Youth Guidance Division ministering to troubled youth), Young Life, the Navigators, and Campus Crusade for Christ (now called Cru) have counselor training programs of their own or use available published materials to train their staff members and volunteers, many of whom are not mental health professionals, in counseling skills. For example, Youth for Christ has published a manual for volunteer or associate staff called *The Whole Person Survival Kit*, which can be used to train volunteers involved in either the Campus Life Division, which reaches out to young people in high schools, or the Youth

Guidance Division, specializing in ministry to troubled youth. The manual or kit contains a section titled "The Whole Person Counseling," with the following four chapters: "Counseling Is a Life Well-Lived," "Counseling Is Providing a Relationship," "Counseling Is Exploring for Solutions," and "Counseling Is Having Appointments."[12] Lay counselor training and lay counseling therefore are a crucial part of the ministry of many parachurch organizations.

Prison ministries are another area of outreach that have utilized lay counseling. One organization that specially trains and uses lay volunteer counselors to reach out to prisoners is Match-Two or M-2 Prisoner Outreach, mentioned earlier in this chapter. Although it is a secular organization, many Christians from various churches and denominations have been involved in the M-2 program since it was started in 1971. Its goals are to recruit and train adult volunteers from the community to provide caring relationships for inmates in the California system who are interested in being matched with such volunteer lay helpers. The volunteers agree to visit their assigned inmates at least once a month and also to write letters in between visits. Sturkie and Bear noted that the California Department of Corrections conducted a study some years ago, which showed that M-2 parolees who had twelve or more visits from an M-2 volunteer had an 81 percent better parole success than those parolees who had not participated in the M-2 program.[13]

Another area of expanding lay counseling ministry beyond the local church is in the context of *retirement and nursing homes*. For example, Dr. Paul Welter developed a significant program for the training of retirement center and nursing home staff and residents in helping or counseling skills. This lay counseling program was funded by the Board of National Ministries of the American Baptist Churches for a seven-year period, involving seven of their retirement centers/nursing homes, with a total of 450 staff members and 114 residents trained in helping or counseling skills. Also, a group of trainers was prepared in three of the centers. Most of the completed evaluations of the program were positive, but no control groups were used. Welter has also provided a number of helpful implications or guidelines for lay counselor training in long-term care settings.[14]

Lay counselors or volunteers are also often used in *Christian mental health centers or programs*. For example, years ago at the Psychological Center of the Graduate School of Psychology at Fuller, volunteer helpers or lay counselors were trained and used in a number of outreach programs and services,[15] including the Crime Resistance Involvement Council (CRIC) and Gero-Net. CRIC provided assistance to elderly victims of crime and provided its volunteers who work directly with such victims training in areas such as sympathy skills and crisis intervention strategies.[16] Gero-Net, a component of the Community Assistance

Program for Seniors (CAPS), was a volunteer-based program that offered friendly visitation and some case management services to low-income elderly at risk for institutionalization due to multiple physical and mental health problems. One other example of a program in the Psychological Center that trained and used "lay counselors" is Project IV Family Outreach, which was really a cooperative outreach program with other community agencies, designed to serve children and families, primarily from disadvantaged minorities, who did not otherwise receive help from traditionally structured services. Parents and teachers were the main lay resources trained to implement treatments in the home and at school. The Psychological Center does not exist now at Fuller, but has been replaced with the Fuller Psychological and Family Services on a smaller scale.

Another example of how lay counselors are trained and used in a Christian mental health agency or organization is New Directions Counseling Center, which was a church-related paraprofessional center in the San Francisco Bay Area. It was founded in 1974 to provide low-cost paraprofessional or trained lay counseling services to persons in lower-middle and lower income groups.[17]

One final area of lay counseling ministry beyond the local church is in the context of *missions*. Missionaries need training in interpersonal relationships, cultural adjustment, and coping with stress, as C. B. Johnson and D. R. Penner have pointed out.[18] However, they also need training in lay caring and counseling skills, not only to provide mutual support and help for themselves on the mission field, but also to help or counsel cross-culturally with those they are reaching out and ministering to, usually in Third World countries and places where there is only limited or even no access to professional counseling services. Much more work needs to be done in this area, in developing lay counselor training programs with special cross-cultural counseling skills included, and in developing lay caring and counseling ministries and services on the mission field.[19]

COMMUNITY AND PROFESSIONAL RESOURCES

Beyond the lay counseling and supportive resources that can be provided within a church or ministry organization, additional levels of care are usually available in the broader community. Lay counselors should become familiar with these resources and consider organizing a comprehensive resource manual (with contact information) for the purpose of needed referrals to other professionals. The following are a few of the more common resources that can be found, along with a brief description of each one.

Community Services Board (CSB)—is a point of entry into the state-level, publicly funded system of services for mental health, intellectual disability, and substance abuse. CSBs provide preadmission screening services 24/7, as well as an array of mental health care, often to underserved and indigent citizens.

Home-based services are sometimes referred to as wraparound services and typically attend to the behavioral health needs of minors. Interventions are designed to meet a child's needs from birth to adolescence, including within foster and adoptive home environments. The planning and provision of home-based services require a specific, individualized process that focuses on the strengths and needs of the child and the importance of family support. Several specific clinical interventions are incorporated, such as comprehensive strength-based assessments, mobile crisis services, case management and care coordination, the availability of clinical teams, and individualized support systems, including behavioral specialists. Home-based services are also available to adult citizens with mental illnesses, chemical dependency, intellectual or developmental disabilities, and physical disabilities, as well as those needing assistance with medication management.

Child and adult protective services are part of a state government agency that operates in conjunction with the Department of Social Services in a given community. Their primary role is to investigate known or alleged incidents of neglect and/or abuse (physical, emotional, verbal and/or sexual), provide families with referral to community resources, provide emergency home placement, and work cooperatively with law enforcement agencies and district courts.

Emergency service hotlines include various twenty-four-hour national helplines (secular and Christian). The following are some of the more established help networks: National Suicide Prevention Hotline (800-273-8255), National Drug Abuse Hotline (800-662-4357), Alcohol Hotline (800-331-2900), National Cocaine Hotline (800-COCAINE), Compulsive Gambling Hotline (410-332-0402), Substance Abuse and Mental Health Services Administration (800-662-HELP), National Domestic Violence Hotline (800-799-SAFE), National Sexual Assault/ Rape Hotline (800-656-HOPE), National Child Abuse Hotline (800-252-2873), Elder Abuse Hotline (800-252-8966), National Runaway Switchboard (800-621-4000), Missing Children Hotline (800-USA-KIDS), Crisis Pregnancy (Care Net: 800-395-HELP, Birthright: 800-550-4900), Post-Abortion Crisis Helpline (800-5We-CARE), Christian Adoption (800-BETHANY).

Treatment centers include substance abuse detoxification centers, methadone clinics, and public and private psychiatric hospital programs.

Private practice clinicians are often licensed and regulated at the state level. Each license and certification represents a somewhat unique set of credentials, and lay counselors should have a basic understanding of each one. Here are the most common:

- Licensed Chemical Dependency Counselor (LCDC), Substance Abuse Treatment Professional (SATP), Certified Alcohol and Drug Abuse Counselor (CADAC)—usually has a bachelor or master's degree in chemical dependency counseling; has to successfully pass a state certification or licensure exam; has a thorough understanding of addictive behaviors, detoxification, issues, 12-step work and relapse prevention; and is employed in private and public settings, outpatient clinics, hospitals, and detox centers.

- Licensed Clinical Social Worker (LCSW, CSW, MSW)—has a master's degree in social work or a related behavioral science; typically requires at least two years of supervised postgraduate experience and successful completion of a state licensure exam; often provides family counseling, child placement, individual counseling, psychosocial assessments, case management, employee assistance programs, etc.

- Licensed Marriage and Family Therapist (LMFT)—has a master's degree (MS, MA, MEd) with a specialty in addressing marital, family dynamics and relational difficulties; typically requires at least two years of supervised postgraduate experience and successful completion of a state exam; often employs a "family systems" model of counseling.

- Licensed Professional Counselor (LPC)—has a master's degree (MS, MA, MEd) or a doctoral degree (PhD, EdD); typically requires two thousand to four thousand hours of supervised postgraduate experience and successful completion of a state exam; may specialize in various areas of expertise (e.g., depression and anxiety, eating disorders, play therapy) and counseling models (reality therapy, rational emotive behavior therapy, cognitive-behavioral therapy, etc.).

- Licensed Clinical or Counseling Psychologist (LCP)—has a doctoral degree in clinical psychology (PhD, PsyD, EdD), counseling, or education representing five to six years of graduate study; typically requires a predoctoral internship and successful completion of a state exam; often specializes in diagnostics, research, education, applied counseling, psychotherapy, and personality and intelligence testing.

- Board Certified Psychiatrist (MD)—has a medical degree and is a licensed physician; typically requires four to six years of specialized mental health training beyond completion of medical school; is qualified to dispense psychiatric medications, conduct clinical psychotherapy, have hospital admitting privileges, and supervise mental health treatment in most psychiatric facilities.

In making a choice of referral to an appropriate mental health professional, several questions might be valid considerations:

- What is the individual's Christian, biblical, and theological orientation?
- How compatible is the individual with your denominational distinctives?
- What kind of academic/clinical training did this individual receive, and what degrees were earned?
- What kind of certification or licensure does this individual have?
- What kind of supervision or experience level does the individual have with the specific presenting issue or problem that is being referred?
- What kind of ministry experience does this individual have?
- How does this individual integrate biblical truths into the therapy or treatment process?
- What professional organizations does this individual belong to?
- What days and hours is this individual available for counsel and care?
- What role and level of involvement are expected of you as the referral source?

Once again, discernment and wisdom are needed to plan out the best course of action for those who seek lay counseling services. Sometimes the temptation within faith-based systems is to have an "either/or" mentality—either lay helping or professional/clinical care—either Christ-centered helping or secular resources. The truth is that when someone is hurting, broken, and in crisis, he or she may need a broad array of supportive services. Effective lay counselors and programs must have a comprehensive and holistic commitment to the ministry.

CHAPTER 11

Ethics, Liability, and Pitfalls

A fundamental principle embodied in all mental health ethics codes is "First, do no harm." Christian counselors, clinicians, caregivers, and lay helpers are uniquely positioned to demonstrate the affirmation of life, the upholding of human dignity, the competent service of professionals, and the cultivation of love and respect toward others. Herein lies not only a wonderful opportunity, but also a spiritual responsibility to authentically represent Christ as His ambassadors.

Values are typically incorporated into a person's belief system as wide-ranging preferences for behavior and outcomes. Ethics can be understood as these same values in action. For the clinician and lay counselor alike, they are the practical rules and boundaries that guide professional or ministerial behavior. Regulatory or statutory law can be further distinguished by a set of codified ethics that are deemed so important that civil and criminal penalties have been ascribed to them when these rules are broken. Ethics are far more than a graduate course taken as part of a program of study. They are integrally connected to every facet of a counselor's practice or ministry.

However, some research suggests significant deficiencies regarding ethics preparation that still exist in counselor education programs. This is partly because of poor modeling by supervisors who compromise dual relationship boundaries with their students during the instructional period.[1] Nevertheless, even in secular schools, there is an increased focus on the need for an integrated, morally based philosophy when it comes to ethics training.[2] Most ethical training attempts to address the kinds of problems that licensing and other regulatory boards frequently investigate and render decisions on whenever an alleged violation occurs. This includes theoretical models and decision-making paradigms that focus on issues such as confidentiality, dual relationships, scope of practice, informed consent, duty to warn, and record keeping, to name a few.[3] Yet in a comprehensive review of ethical violations in nearly every state in the country between 2000 and 2007, Scalise discovered that regulatory boards continue to investigate cases and either suspend or revoke practice licenses for these same issues year after year.

Ethical awareness is critical on many different levels. Ongoing supervision and accountability, even between peer-level colleagues, still appears to be the single most determining factor in helping reduce unhealthy isolation and unnecessary risk taking among counselors.[4] A far-reaching qualitative study identified nine specific ethics-related values that help set apart what they referred to as a "master therapist": *relational connection* (the ability to form healthy relationships with clients and colleagues), *autonomy* (acknowledging the right of others to self-determination), *beneficence* (a desire to reduce human suffering and improve the welfare of others), *nonmaleficence* (mindfulness to do no harm), *competence* (committed to the value of being exceptionally skilled), *humility* (an awareness of personal limitations and weaknesses), *professional growth* (the continual seeking of formal and informal learning opportunities), *openness to complexity and ambiguity* (recognizing the uniqueness of people and their presenting problems), and *self-awareness* (attending to emotional needs as well as unfinished personal business).[5]

Every year since 1991, the American Counseling Association has summarized and published the activities of the Ethics Committee. Many similar organizations, including state licensing boards, record and track ethical violations as well as the official rulings that are adjudicated from their investigative processes. More severe disciplinary action can include suspension and license revocation. The counselor may be asked to complete additional coursework or training, enter into personal therapy, or maintain a certain level of clinical supervision before seeking reinstatement. These determinations are often viewed as potentially effective deterrents to practitioners since most founded violations eventually become a matter of public record. Due to the upward trending of ethical misconduct, most states that now require continuing education for mental health practitioners specifically mandate that a certain number of contact hours be devoted to this critical area.

Christian counselors must see people-helping, whether in a ministerial or professional clinical setting, for the high calling that it is and as an absolutely sacred trust. God, like any father, wants to place the lives of His hurting children into safe, competent, and ethical hands. As His ambassadors of reconciliation, we should endeavor at all times to faithfully represent His kingdom and in all things, to be above reproach for, "a trustworthy envoy brings healing" (Prov. 13:17).

In counseling, the three major tenets of ethical practice involve *competence*, *consent*, and *confidentiality*—often referred to as "the three Cs." While they are discussed in further detail later in this chapter, here are brief descriptions to help set the foundation:

Competence
- Signifies integrity
- Is aware of limitations

- Makes truthful and realistic statements regarding the identity, education, training, experience, and credentials of the caregiver, the caregiving process, and expected outcomes
- Avoids dishonest, ignorant, or exaggerated claims
- Is willing to have accountability and an independent review if challenged or requested
- Makes a commitment to keep pace with the latest knowledge and training of Christian caregiving issues, resources, and developments
- Makes needed referrals and only refers to other caregivers who demonstrate an appropriate level of competence themselves
- Seeks out supervision and input when needed or appropriate
- Is aware of personal burnout and when personal problems interfere with the caregiving process
- Seeks out personal help, support, or counseling when needed or appropriate

Consent

- Allows for another person to make an informed and voluntary decision to engage in the caregiving process
- Avoids manipulation and/or coercion of the person seeking care
- Allows the caregiver to accurately disclose the values, likely benefits, time involved, potential risks, and work necessary to achieve agreed upon goals
- Does not allow the person seeking help to consent to negligent or harmful caregiving practices (especially those that involve dual relationships)
- Understands that in the case of an incompetent person (e.g., the severely mentally or emotionally disabled, the organically impaired, those who are actively psychotic, minor children, certain elder persons), consent will be first obtained from a legal representative (e.g., parent, spouse, guardian, attorney)
- Allows for certain exceptions although valid consent may still be sought from a close relative or guardian (e.g., an emergency or life-threatening situation where the person is precluded from making an informed judgment regarding care, the disclosure would unduly alarm the person or reasonably result in refusal to undergo needed care)
- Informs the person seeking help as to the limits of confidentiality

Confidentiality

- Recognizes that every person has a fundamental, moral, and legal right to privacy, to be left alone, and to have a wide range of personal thoughts, opinions, beliefs, and behaviors that are protected from public knowledge

- Recognizes that it is an essential factor in facilitating self-disclosure, the development of trust, and the potential for personal/spiritual growth and change
- Makes a commitment to respect and uphold privacy rights to the fullest extent allowed by law, professional ethics, and the policies and protocols of the organization, ministry, or church
- Initially utilizes the assertion of privileged communication in the face of legal and/or court demands in order to allow for time to discuss the matter with the person seeking help, the leadership of the organization, ministry, or church, and if necessary, with appropriate legal counsel
- Discusses the limitations of confidentiality at the onset of caregiving, including those things that may require disclosure legally, ethically, or as a matter of the organization, ministry, or church's policy and protocol
- Does not directly disclose or utilize confidential information in any supervisory, consultation, teaching, preaching, publishing, public prayer-oriented, or other ancillary activity without the proper authorization and consent of the person seeking help
- Makes every effort to protect and disguise identifying information when presenting in front of groups or in public forums
- Preserves, stores, and transfers any records (handwritten, typed, electronic, etc.) of caregiving activities in such a manner as to protect the person seeking help and his or her privacy rights
- Acknowledges that confidentiality may be limited when human life is imperiled due to suicide, homicide, the significant inability to function, and in cases where the abuse of a child, elder, or dependent person occurs

Throughout this book, we have emphasized that lay caring and counseling ministries are biblically based, significant ministries for the building up of the body of Christ and for reaching out to people who are hurting or who have particular needs. Such ministries do have potential pitfalls and hazards. Lay counselors need to be aware of these dangers and risks to minimize or avoid them so they can conduct their ministries of lay caring and counseling more effectively and in a highly ethical and legal manner that honors and glorifies the Lord.

Legal and ethical issues in pastoral and lay Christian counseling have been "hot" topics in recent years. This is especially the case since the clergy malpractice suit against Grace Community Church in Sun Valley, California, was filed in March 1980 by the parents of twenty-four-year-old Kenneth Nally, who committed suicide by shooting himself on April 1, 1979. The Nallys claimed that the pastors who provided pastoral counseling to their son before his suicide were negligent, and they sued the counseling pastors, the senior pastor, and the church for clergy malpractice. This case received national attention because it was the first case on clergy malpractice ever considered by a US high court, proceeding to the California Supreme Court, which in November 1988 ruled against the Nallys on a five to two vote. The case then went to the US Supreme Court, which in April 1989 refused to review the California Supreme Court decision, thereby letting it stand. These decisions confirmed that pastors and church workers have no legal duty to refer troubled parishioners or church members to licensed psychiatrists.[6]

This ten-year legal battle over clergy malpractice ended with many pastors and lay counselors feeling relieved and vindicated in their pastoral and lay counseling ministries. However, the ethical and legal issues raised by the Nally case require further discussion and clarification, and it is conceivable that another case with more substantial merit could succeed in the courts. With this case in mind, let's take a look at some of the potential problems and legal pitfalls lay counselors can fall into.

POTENTIAL PROBLEMS FOR THE LAY COUNSELOR

Dr. Gary Collins has written a helpful chapter on the counselor and counseling in his textbook *Christian Counseling*, which comprehensively covers the major hazards or potential problems a Christian counselor is likely to encounter. Most of these apply to a lay Christian counselor as well.[7] We will briefly summarize his points here, but the chapter in his book should be consulted for further details. Collins describes eight major areas of potential problems: the counselor's *motivation*, the counselor's *effectiveness*, the counselor's *role*, the counselor's *vulnerability*, the counselor's *sexuality*, the counselor's *ethics*, the counselor's *burnout*, and the counselor's *counselors*.

1. The Counselor's Motivation

Why does a person want to counsel in the first place? Some reasons are legitimate, others less so. Collins lists five possible needs that some counselors may inappropriately try to meet through their counseling ministry: the need for relationships (or intimacy and closeness with people); the need for control (of other people's lives); the need to rescue; the need for information (i.e., curiosity); and the need for personal healing. Wrong or unbalanced motives usually lead to "rescuing" actions versus "ministering" actions. Rescuing is sometimes driven by a need (on the part of the counselor) to feel good, wanted, accepted, or successful. True ministry, on the other hand, fulfills the real presenting need, the purpose of reconciliation, the heartbeat of God, and the Great Commission.

2. The Counselor's Effectiveness

Some people are more gifted for a counseling ministry than others, and an honest evaluation of one's counseling effectiveness or lack thereof is necessary. Some counselors may then realize they are not particularly gifted or good at counseling but can still help or minister to people through avenues other than counseling, such as evangelism, social action, or teaching. The truth however, is that every believer has been given something from God and the purpose of His provision is to better serve others. "Each of you should use whatever gift you have received to serve others, as faithful stewards of God's grace in its various forms" (1 Peter 4:10).

3. The Counselor's Role

Counselors often face role confusion. Based on Dr. Maurice Wagner's suggestions,[8] Collins describes the following nine potential examples of counselor role confusion: visiting instead of counseling; being hasty instead of deliberate; being disrespectful instead of sympathetic; being judgmental instead of unbiased; being directive instead of interpretive; being emotionally overinvolved instead of remaining objective; being impatient instead of realistic; being artificial instead of authentic; and being defensive instead of empathic.

4. The Counselor's Vulnerability

Counselors may experience power struggles, exploitation, and failure in the process of counseling or helping others. Common ways that the counselor's vulnerability can be increased include *manipulation* of the counselor by the client, *transference* on the part of the client when he or she has unresolved developmental issues (i.e., with authority figures), *countertransference* on the part of the counselor when his or her own needs and feelings interfere with the counseling relationship, and *resistance* on the part of the client. Such potential problems are not automatic indicators to stop the caregiving process, but are best dealt with in consultation with a supervisor or colleague.

5. The Counselor's Sexuality

Sexual attraction to clients is real, and there is always the danger of falling into sexual contact and sin. While sexual feelings toward clients are common, Collins suggests the need to exercise self-control through the following means: spiritual protection (especially prayer, meditation on the Scriptures, and dependence on the Holy Spirit), awareness of danger signals (e.g., the counselor spending much time thinking about the client and admiring his or her qualities between sessions, beginning to have sexual fantasies about the client), setting of limits (e.g., regarding length of counseling sessions and telephone contacts), examination of attitudes (by remembering social consequences and implications as well as theological or biblical truth relating to sexual immorality), support-group protection, and an ongoing commitment to maintain transparent accountability and supervisory relationships.

6. The Counselor's Ethics

Ethical problems include issues of confidentiality, dealing with difficult decisions, and conflicts in values.[9] We address this area in greater depth later in this chapter.

7. The Counselor's Burnout

The counselor can be so involved in the ministry of counseling that he or she experiences "burnout." Collins points out that one writer has defined burnout as involving "a progressive loss of idealism, energy, and purpose" for people in the helping professions as a result of their work.[10] Collins suggests several steps to prevent burnout, including having regular periods of prayer and meditation on the Scriptures for spiritual strength; receiving support from a few others; engaging in constant evaluation of the underlying drive to achieve; taking time off; seeking to improve ministry skills, including counseling, conflict management, and assertiveness skills; and encouraging other Christians to be involved in lay caring and burden bearing. Additional information on stress, burnout, and compassion fatigue is offered later in this chapter.

8. The Counselor's Counselors

Every counselor needs to have a counselor or colleague to consult at times. The danger is that such a valid need may go unmet or be neglected (as discussed in the chapter on supervision). Collins emphasizes first of all the counselor's need to depend on the Holy Spirit and on the Lord Jesus, who is Himself the "Wonderful Counselor." He also points out the need for every counselor to have one or two colleagues to consult, share Scripture, and pray with on a regular basis. Counselors need mutual support, because all counseling, including lay counseling, can be draining work, even though it can also be fulfilling. At times counselors may need more formal counseling for their own needs and problems, in which case they should seek professional counseling or therapy, if necessary.

These eight problem areas should be kept in mind by lay counselors, as well as those who train and supervise them, so that such issues can be minimized or avoided. In addition, Dr. Michael Cavanagh, a clinical psychologist and professor at the University of San Francisco, has delineated several destructive myths about helping others—views that many ministers and church workers tend to hold, and which lay counselors should also be careful to avoid. They include the following:

- Love, good intentions, and common sense are all you need (the truth is that what is often needed in counseling is a love that is confronting and challenging and sets limits, along with some counseling knowledge and skills).
- People define their problems accurately (not necessarily true!).
- Most people just need advice and encouragement (some may need much more than this).
- People who seek help really want help (again, not necessarily; some may have other and possibly ulterior motives for seeking help).
- People are reliable eyewitnesses (sometimes they may be, but often they are not).
- You should encourage people to ventilate their feelings (not always, because sometimes ventilation per se may be unhelpful).
- All religious problems have religious solutions (problems are often multifaceted and complex, with multiple causes and possible multiple solutions).

In addition to these common myths about helping, Cavanagh described the following pitfalls that ministers and counselors typically encounter in their attempts to help people: becoming a manager (or director of others' lives), becoming an agent (whom others can exploit), assuming a role other than that of minister or counselor, adhering to one theory, overestimating one's power, yielding to outside pressure, supporting behavior that should not be supported, and dealing with someone already in counseling with another counselor (open communication with the other counselor is then essential).[11]

Both Collins and Cavanagh describe several potential problems and pitfalls, and we would urge every pastor, counselor, and especially lay counselor to be aware of the dangers posed by these beliefs and practices.

LEGAL AND ETHICAL ISSUES RELEVANT TO LAY COUNSELING

Dr. Thomas Needham wrote a helpful chapter in the book *Clergy Malpractice* on helping when the risks are great.[12] He provided good answers to three key questions: What are potentially high-risk situations? Why are the risks increasing? and How can we care carefully? We briefly summarize his main points for the potential benefit of lay counselors.

Needham listed twenty potentially high-risk situations, including direct violations of legal or ethical codes (e.g., sex with a counselee or breach of confidentiality), reflections of poor judgment in counseling situations, examples of going beyond acceptable practices or standards in mental health or pastoral counseling, and situations that increase the risk of harming or embarrassing the counselee. The twenty high-risk situations are as follows:[13]

1. Administration, interpretation, and storing of personality and psychological tests
2. Belief in simple spiritual solutions for complex emotional and psychological problems
3. Belief that all problems are spiritual or physical, with a denial of emotional and psychological dimensions
4. Belief that pastoral and lay counselors need only biblical training to solve such severe problems as neuroses, psychoses, and suicidal intentions
5. Belief that sincerity and good intentions are the major ingredients in pastoral and lay counseling
6. Belief that pastors (and we would add lay counselors) should be all things to all people
7. Counseling psychotic and suicidal individuals
8. Counseling a mentally incompetent patient
9. Advising against medical or psychological treatment
10. Counseling regarding psychiatric medications
11. Denial of the existence or severity of a psychological or psychosomatic disorder
12. Improper care of records
13. Inadequately trained lay and pastoral counselors
14. Failure to give credence to violent intentions or statements
15. Misdiagnosing psychotics as demon-possessed
16. Misrepresenting one's title, position, degree, or abilities (i.e., psychologist, psychotherapy)
17. Poorly supervised lay counselors
18. Recommending divorce
19. Sexual relations with a counselee
20. Violations of confidentiality (by ministerial or secretarial staff)

Additional areas of risk and liability in lay caregiving and counseling include: when matters of competence, consent, and/or confidentiality are overlooked, ignored, or disregarded; when recommending abortion; when the dynamics and protocols surrounding potential dual relationships are overlooked, ignored, or disregarded; when counseling minors, especially when the parents are divorced but have shared legal custody; and when there is a lack of appropriate or timely referrals.

Not all of these high-risk situations are unethical in the sense of breaking ethical codes of mental health or pastoral counselors, or illegal in the sense of breaking the law, although many of them are. However, it would be wise for pastors and lay counselors to avoid these high-risk situations as far as possible, especially those that are obviously unethical or illegal. It should be noted that in some states even the title *counselor* should be used with caution or qualification or even eliminated, depending on the licensing laws of a state governing the use of such titles. Other more clinical terms such as *therapist, therapy, clinician, licensed,* etc., should likewise be avoided altogether. Some lay counseling ministries have therefore used alternative titles, such as *lay caregiver, lay helper,* or *lay minister* in place of *lay counselor* and terms like *lay caregiving, lay helping, lay pastoring,* or *lay shepherding* instead of *lay counseling*.

As to possible reasons for the increasing risks of litigation or being sued in the context of pastoral and lay counseling, Needham mentioned the following: (1) a litigious atmosphere, (2) increased demands for pastoral counseling, (3) new lay ministries, (4) a lag or gap between intention (which may be good and sincere) and ability (to carry out good and sincere intentions), (5) inadequate attitudes toward problems and problem-solving, (6) inadequate training, and (7) inadequate follow-up preaching after a suicide or other crisis situation.

Finally, Dr. Needham provided the following helpful suggestions for minimizing the risks of litigation in answering the question of "How can we care carefully?"

1. Develop a formal counseling policy (which should include determining target needs, assessing resources, determining organizational channels and accountability, establishing selection procedures and training and supervision standards, formulating operational guidelines including policy on the issue of fees or contributions, checking insurance coverage, and developing a feedback loop)
2. Develop adequate selection, training, and supervision
3. Avoid misleading claims
4. Make a thorough evaluation of the problem (by taking a history, using tests where appropriate, determining chronicity and severity of the problem as well as whether it is psychotic, suicidal, or psychosomatic, and evaluating the counselee's resources
5. Learn to benefit from testing (where it is appropriate, and where

adequately trained and qualified persons are available to conduct and interpret the tests used)

6. Determine your level of intervention (e.g., Needham pointed out that level 4 intervention, involving the uncovering of repressed emotions causes the highest risk and should be conducted only by a *skilled* counselor)
7. Make use of consultation and referrals
8. Take advantage of continuing education
9. Guard records and information (i.e., maintain confidentiality)
10. Provide follow-up care

Needham aptly concluded, "The Nally lawsuit . . . has left an indelible concern over the future of pastoral and lay counseling in the local church. I believe we should expand rather than reduce our helping efforts, and this requires that we understand why the risks are increasing. Following the ten suggested guidelines should help churches have an active, effective, and careful caring ministry."[14]

Dr. Walter Becker wrote a concise article dealing specifically with the major legal and ethical considerations relevant to the lay or paraprofessional counselor in the church.[15] He emphasized that trust is the essence of the therapeutic or counseling relationship, and therefore the risk of litigation or being sued by clients increases when trust is decreased or destroyed and clients feel harmed or wronged. There are three main areas in which trust in the counseling relationship should be developed: the *confidentiality* of the relationship, the *competence* of the counselor, and the client's freedom of *choice* (consent).

In the first area of *confidentiality*, Becker recommended that lay or paraprofessional counselors in the church follow the ethical and legal standards of professional counselors in order to maintain the requirements of the state, as well as to hold to the highest standards of ethical conduct. All states now require that professional counselors report incidents of child or elder abuse, or situations involving potential harm to self or violence to others; and more than half have added clergy members and pastoral counselors to that mandate.[16]

Becker, therefore, suggested that lay counselors in the church should follow such requirements to be on the safe side. Many lay counseling centers are already doing this by informing potential clients of such limits to confidentiality and requiring them to sign an informed consent form before beginning the counseling process. Directors of lay Christian counseling centers or even more informal lay counseling ministries need to familiarize themselves with the specific laws of the state in which they are working concerning mandatory reporting and limits to confidentiality in the professional counseling relationship, and then decide whether to follow them for the lay counselors. Even if lay counselors are exempted from following such laws for professional counselors, it may still be wiser for lay counselors to follow them.

Becker also noted that there are limits to confidentiality when counseling with minors, because their parents or legal guardians are responsible for the welfare of minors and therefore some sharing of information and cooperation with the parents or legal guardians is necessary. He further stressed the need to maintain confidentiality in a group counseling context and to carefully store clients' records and guard their security and confidentiality, for example, by keeping them with a licensed professional supervisor.

One other significant issue raised by Becker in the area of confidentiality has to do with *church discipline*. He provided the following guideline:

> Holding a dual relationship of lay counselor and church member active in disciplining a fellow member severely compromises the trust necessary in the counseling relationship. Paraprofessional counselors should not be agents of church discipline. The church counselor needs to be sensitive to the rules of discipline within his or her own denomination, as well as the importance of confession and repentance. Confession to appropriate church leaders should be encouraged so that healing within the church body can occur, but betraying the confidentiality of the therapeutic relationship for the sake of church discipline should be avoided.[17]

While this recommendation may be accepted by many, we are aware that some pastors and church leaders may not choose to follow it—for example, those who use a counseling approach like Adams's nouthetic counseling, in which scriptural direction, including church discipline where necessary and appropriate, is a crucial part of the counseling offered. In this case, we suggest that the counselor inform the potential counselee or client of all the limitations to confidentiality, including matters regarding church discipline, *before* starting lay counseling. Some churches have gotten into serious legal trouble and have been successfully sued (sometimes for millions of dollars) when church membership is discussed and there is no formal, written process regarding church discipline and no signed informed consent stating that congregation members either agree to or accept these policies.

When church discipline is applied to a congregant later in the counseling process, he or she may feel that information shared publicly (e.g., infidelity, addiction, unwanted pregnancy/abortion, homosexuality, etc.) was slanderous, defamed their character, or caused "irreparable emotional harm." This entire topic of church discipline requires great sensitivity and reflection, and we recommend

Dr. Samuel Southard's chapter "Church Discipline: Handle with Care," in the book *Clergy Malpractice* for further reading.[18]

In the second area, *competency*, Becker emphasized that the key is to carefully and adequately select, train, and supervise lay or paraprofessional counselors so that they know and work within the limits of their training and helping ability (including learning how to refer to and work with mental health professionals).

In the third and final area, *choice*, Becker pointed out that freedom of client choice or informed consent means that the counselor should provide sufficient information about his or her qualifications, training, and values, as well as the process, goals, and possible consequences of counseling so that the client can make educated choices. The counselor's views and values should be clearly shared in order for the client to have the ultimate freedom to choose whether to continue with that counselor or to seek help from another counselor.

Becker briefly described the following eight high-risk situations that lay counselors should avoid in order to minimize possible litigation or malpractice suits: charging fees or asking for "donations"; using psychological tests without proper training or supervision; having simplistic beliefs that can lead to superficial treatment, misdiagnosis, and harm; counseling those with severe problems requiring professional intervention; giving advice against medical or psychological treatment; ignoring statements of intent to harm or signs of violent behavior; counseling with a relative or employee; and developing a romantic or sexual relationship with the client.

Becker also provided several helpful suggestions for practice by lay counselors that can help build trust by maintaining confidentiality, facilitating confidence in the lay counselor, and ensuring freedom of choice for the client. Many of his suggestions have already been mentioned earlier in our discussion of Needham's recommendations, and we will therefore not repeat them here. However, one important suggestion that Becker does make is for lay counselors to follow the ethical standards and guidelines of professional counseling organizations like the American Counseling Association, the American Psychological Association, and the American Association of Marriage and Family Therapy.

We would like to point out here that, in our opinion, the application of ethical standards and guidelines of professional counseling and therapy to lay counselors is not such an easy or clear-cut task. Some modification of professional ethical guidelines is needed for lay counselors, especially those who are involved more in peer or friendship counseling, or in lay pastoral care or caregiving, which is broader than therapeutic counseling and where the informal models of lay counseling are more relevant. For example, the ethical guideline found in many professional ethical codes advising against dual relationships that could impair professional judgment or increase the risk of exploitation (for example, counseling with an employee, student, supervisee, close friend, or relative) has often been interpreted as an argument against counseling with *any* friend or even acquaintance. Such an interpretation, of course, cannot be applied to the area of lay counseling involving peer or friendship counseling. We therefore will also discuss the updated and revised *2014 Christian Counseling Code of Ethics* developed by the American Association of Christian Counselors (AACC) and under the direction of Dr. Scalise.[19]

Dr. Worthington has emphasized that supervisors of lay counselors should stress what friends and laypeople do well in counseling, for example, providing excellent emotional support and empathy for people in crisis, giving sound advice prefaced by careful empathic listening and understanding, and providing daily, multisituational support.[20] Such lay or peer counseling often involves counseling with acquaintances or friends, and this is appropriate in the context of nonprofessional lay counseling. However, it is still imperative for the lay counselor involved in such peer or friendship counseling to avoid counseling in situations where his or her objective judgment and helping capacity may be compromised or impaired (e.g., counseling with very close friends, relatives, or employees).

The outcome of the Nally lawsuit made it very clear that pastors, church workers, and lay counselors who are not licensed mental health professionals are not *legally* accountable to meet the stringent ethical codes and community standards for practice of licensed and regulated mental health professionals. However, pastors and lay counselors should still be aware of the high-risk situations reviewed in this chapter and take steps to avoid them.

MALPRACTICE INSURANCE FOR LAY COUNSELORS

In light of the potential for legal liability, we suggest that churches and ministries consider securing malpractice insurance. While such insurance can be expensive, we believe it is essential for churches in today's litigious society, especially those who have lay caregiving and counseling ministries and programs. Some church lay counseling centers have decided not to purchase malpractice insurance, but have chosen to have an emergency fund instead that is used for obtaining legal advice or services in case they are sued for malpractice. Others have chosen to function without malpractice insurance or an emergency fund, but they follow the ethical guidelines and community standards for the practice of professional counseling in order to minimize the risk of litigation.

Each lay counseling center or ministry will have to decide among the different options possible regarding obtaining or not obtaining malpractice insurance. Still, we highly recommend insurance, and there are a number of insurance agencies that now specialize in liability policies for clergy members and churches. Liability workshops for churches and religious or ministry organizations on legal and ethical issues are also readily available today.

According to Dr. Archibald Hart, there are six major types of lawsuits that are typically filed against psychologists and counselors.[21] In his excellent book *Counseling the Depressed*, Hart lists the following: (1) *Breach of contract*, involving a failure on the counselor's part to keep a promise of providing "cure" or effective results. Counselors must, therefore, be careful not to promise "cures." (2) *Physical assault* or physical injury suffered by the client as a result of therapy or counseling. (3) *Sexual assault*, involving unauthorized or unreasonable touching, including having sex with a client. The largest number of lawsuits against psychologists today fall into this category. (4) *Abandonment*, involving failure to continue providing counseling when it is still needed or when counseling has not been properly terminated with clear documentation. (5) *Suicide* of a client, which may result in a lawsuit against the counselor for "failure to protect" or failure to follow the "usual degree of care." (6) *Negligent infliction of emotional distress* (not just *intentional* infliction of emotional distress).

LEGAL STANDARDS
FOR LAY COUNSELORS

Lay counselors functioning under the direction and supervision of a licensed mental health professional (e.g., licensed counselor, psychologist, social worker, psychiatrist) must decide what legal standards to follow. A number of directors of church lay counseling centers who have consulted attorneys on this matter have been told that lay counselors under the supervision and direction of a licensed mental health professional should follow the mandatory reporting laws and limitations to confidentiality that are relevant to that professional's practice. In the case of a director or supervisor who is an ordained minister as well as a licensed mental health professional the mandatory reporting laws pertaining to the licensed mental health professional's practice apparently still take precedence.

It is important, therefore, for churches with licensed mental health professionals directing or supervising their lay counselors to require such lay counselors to adhere to the mandatory reporting laws and limitations to confidentiality that apply to the professionals involved. In the case of a pastor or lay leader who is not a licensed mental health professional directing or supervising lay counselors, such lay counselors are not bound by professional legal requirements, but it is safer to follow them as far as possible. In either case, we recommend that the church consult with a local attorney who can offer clarity and direction on any specific regulations and/or laws in their state.

Several excellent resources are available on the general topic of counseling ethics, including the *Ethical Standards for Christian Counselors* by Dr. James R. Beck and Mr. R. Kent Mathews,[22] the *Code of Ethics for the Christian Association for Psychological Studies* (CAPS) by Dr. Robert R. King Jr.,[23] and of course the *2014 AACC Christian Counseling Code of Ethics*. These proposed ethical codes contain biblical, Christian perspectives and foundations that are important to note.

SUPERVISION OF LAY COUNSELORS

Another issue is that of ethical and legal considerations applied to the *supervision* of lay counselors. This is important, as supervisors are typically held accountable for the counselors they directly supervise. Space does not permit us to go into a detailed discussion of such considerations, but there is a good chapter on ethical and other issues in Cal Stoltenberg and Ursula Delworth's book *Supervising Counselors and Therapists: A Developmental Approach*.[24] Essentially they discuss ethical considerations in terms of competency of the supervisor (who should have received training in supervision skills at the very least, some self-training through reading, consulting, and perhaps attendance at relevant in-service training), dual relationships, and respect for supervisees and the supervisee's ethics (including respect for the supervisor).

Regarding legal considerations, Stoltenberg and Delworth note that the supervisory role carries with it a heavy responsibility. Potential areas of malpractice against the supervisor include situations in which the trainee or supervisee is incapable of providing proper counseling or therapy (even with the supervisor's help), or a counselee consenting to receive counseling without knowing that the counseling will be offered by a trainee. They also discuss the significance of gender and ethnicity issues in the supervision of counselors.

Lay counselors should, of course, obtain permission or written consent from their counselees to share information with their supervisors and possibly other lay counselors in situations involving group supervision. Such information about counselees should be kept confidential by the supervisor or supervisory group involved. Counselees should be told clearly who the supervisor will be, how often supervision will be provided, and who else will be involved in the supervision, including other lay counselors.

DUAL RELATIONSHIPS FOR LAY COUNSELORS

Since church and ministry environments often create the potential for dual relationship scenarios, this topic requires further attention. The most egregious example of "crossing the line" involves sexual misconduct. Counselors who have engaged in some form of sexual or erotic contact with their clients are the number one cause for license suspension, license revocation, and lawsuits. Sadly, sexual misconduct has also penetrated into church-based counseling ministries.

While some differences do exist among different state regulations and the ethical codes of professional associations, there is still broad consistency when it comes to the inappropriateness of intimate, dual, or sexual relationships with *current* clients. Beyond the obvious biblical principles, greater variation in codes is seen with regard to sexual intimacies or dual relationships with *former* clients. Nevertheless, since sexual or romantic relationships are potentially manipulative, practitioners are expected to bear the burden of demonstrating that there has been no exploitation. A client's consent to the initiation of or participation in sexual behavior or involvement with a counselor does not change the nature of the conduct, nor does it lift any regulatory prohibition. Emotionally unhealthy individuals may enter into intimate relationships with a former counselor for inappropriate reasons and with unrealistic expectations.

Regulatory and ethical codes addressing nonintimate dual relationship issues are less obvious and require even more careful examination by the counselor in assessing any potential for harm.[25] The relationship between a counselor and a client (whether current or past) is very unique and by its nature can lead to possible exploitation. While the counseling itself may progress well and be nonharmful, it is the potential for negative outcomes that must be kept in mind. When counselors begin a therapeutic relationship with a client with whom they have another relationship, one of the two relationships is always in jeopardy of being compromised. Clearly, the dynamics and expectations of the relationship will interfere with the critical need for therapeutic objectivity and honesty.

Many counselors live and work in the same communities as their clients, so situations may arise where they come into contact with clients, former clients, and future clients (e.g., in church settings). Assessing potential for harm does become more difficult, but nonetheless, it remains the responsibility of the counselor to examine carefully the "what-ifs." In some cases, it is also important to consider whether there may be potential for harm to other clients or even to the ministry's standing within the community. Since the power differential inherent in the counselor-client relationship makes clients more dependent and more vulnerable, the responsibility clearly lies with the counselor.

The following guidelines may be helpful when facing a dual relationship dilemma: (1) clearly define the nature of the dual relationship from the onset; (2) carefully examine any potential risk of harm to the most vulnerable person(s); (3) anticipate possible consequences, both positive and negative before proceeding; (4) consult both regulations and ethical codes for help and clarification; and (5) diligently seek professional consultation and supervision to process through the issues.

REFERRAL PROTOCOLS FOR LAY COUNSELORS

Knowing when and how to make an appropriate referral during lay counseling is critical, especially as it relates to liability issues and risk management. The following are some referral guidelines that should be considered for inclusion during the training process. A referral should be considered at the following times:

- When the person presents an actual or imminent danger to himself or herself (e.g., severe depression, suicidal intent/behaviors, running away, excessive drug abuse, eating disorders)
- When the person presents an actual or imminent danger to others (e.g., extreme hostility, aggression, violence or threats thereof, perpetration of child or elder abuse)
- When the person has experienced a marked decline in the ability to care for himself or herself and function in day-to-day life, whether at home, school, or in the workplace (e.g., extreme anxiety, panic attacks, severe depression, severe phobias, obsessive-compulsive disorders, uncontrollable and excessive addictive behaviors)
- When the person's excessive alcohol or substance abuse will require detoxification
- When the person's reality testing is severely impaired to the extent that judgment, emotions, memory, and/or orientation are disordered (e.g., delusions, visual/auditory hallucinations, multiple personalities/ dissociation, severe bipolar cycles)
- When the caregiver feels that the problem or situation is beyond his or her abilities, training, experience, competence, availability, or comfort level
- When the person is not responding to short-term support and interventions and may require more in-depth or extensive professional help
- When there is a strong transference or countertransference dynamic that seems at an impasse despite attempts to address the issue
- When the possibility of a dual relationship exists that may negatively affect the caregiving process
- When the person asks for a referral to another caregiver

ETHICS CODES

Both secular and Christian counseling organizations have developed formal codes of counseling ethics. Secular codes include, among others, those of the American Counseling Association (ACA),[26] the American Psychological Association (APA),[27] and the American Association of Marriage and Family Therapy (AAMFT).[28] Faith-based codes include, among others, the Christian Association for Psychological Studies (CAPS),[29] the National Christian Counselor's Association (NCCA),[30] the Association of Certified Biblical Counselors (ACBC),[31] and the American Association of Christian Counselors (AACC).[32] While each of these organizations offers legitimate and well-documented ethical guidelines, we would like to focus on the AACC Christian Counseling Code of Ethics because of its comprehensive nature that addresses both professional and lay counseling services from a biblical standpoint.

The next several pages are reproduced with permission from the AACC and include its introduction sections on A New Code for an Emerging Profession, The Mission of the Code, Uses and Limits of the Code, How the Code is Organized, Biblical and Ethical Foundations, and an outline of the actual Ethical Standards. Our hope is to provide a thorough overview on the subject matter.[33]

A NEW CODE FOR AN EMERGING PROFESSION

The *Code* is a comprehensive, detailed, and integrative synthesis of biblical, ethical, legal, clinical, and systemic information. It was created this way because vaguely worded, content-limited, and overly generalized codes are insufficient for the complexities of the modern, twenty-first-century counseling environment. A more comprehensive and behavior-specific ethical code is needed for Christian counselors, as well as other mental health and ministerial professions, because of:

1. the mounting evidence of unprofessional and incompetent practices among Christian counselors, including increasing complaints of client-parishioner harm;

2. the largely unprotected legal status of Christian counseling, including growing state scrutiny, excessive litigation, and unrelenting legalization of professional ethics; and

3. the vitality and growing maturity of Christian counseling—including its many theories and approaches—indicating the need for an

overarching ethical-legal template to guide the ongoing development of biblical and empirically-sound Christian counseling models.

This *Code*—beyond defining the boundaries of unethical practice—affirmatively educates counselors in the direction of becoming helpers of ethical excellence, capable of more consistently securing the best counseling outcomes. Four streams of influence are evident:

1. the Bible (both Old and New Testaments) and historic orthodox Christian theology;
2. accepted standards of counseling and clinical practice from Christian caregiving and the established mental health disciplines;
3. codes of ethics from other Christian and mental health professions; and
4. current and developing standards derived from mental health and ministry-related law.

The Mission of the Code

The mission of this *Code* is to:

1. help advance the central mission of the AACC—to bring honor to Jesus Christ and promote excellence and unity in Christian counseling;
2. promote the welfare and protect the dignity and fundamental rights of all individuals, families, groups, churches, schools, agencies, ministries, and other organizations with whom Christian counselors work;
3. provide standards of ethical conduct in Christian counseling that are to be advocated and applied by the AACC and the International Board of Christian Care (IBCC), and are respected by other professionals and institutions; and
4. provide an ethical framework from which to work in order to assure the dignity and care of every individual who seeks and receives services.

Uses and Limits of the Code

This *Code* defines biblically based values and universal behavioral standards for ethical Christian counseling. The intent is for it to become a core document by which Christian counselors, clients, and the Church oversee and evaluate Christian counselors and counseling values, goals, process, and effectiveness. Furthermore, the *Code* asserts a Christian counseling standard of care that invites respect and application by the courts, the regulatory bodies of church and state, insurance and managed care groups, other professions, and by society.

Also, this *Code* should be seen as normative, but non-exhaustive. It provides a common definition of awareness, knowledge and practice; however, it does not presume to be a complete picture of Christian counseling nor does it necessarily cover all ethical issues. This *Code* outlines a foundation of preferred values and agreed professional behavior upon which Christian counselors can shape their identity and build their work. It defines principles where practice diversity is acknowledged and encouraged, and also includes limits beyond which practice deviance is not permitted or tolerated.

This *Code* is aspirational throughout the AACC and enforceable in the IBCC. It consists of four major parts—*Introduction and Mission, Biblical-Ethical Foundations, Ethical Standards*, and *Procedural Rules*. From time-to-time, the AACC and the Law and Ethics Committee may draft and offer Guidance Documents to further clarify specific standards of professional and/or biblical conduct. The *Code* also aspires to define, in its Mission and the Biblical-Ethical Foundations statements, the best ideals and goals of Christian counseling. The Ethical Standards and Procedural Rules are the codes of individual practice and organizational behavior that help guide the AACC membership. These statements can be consulted in working out the problems and dilemmas of ethics application and procedural rules interpretation.

Concerning language, the *Code* endeavors to avoid pedantic, legalese, and sexist language, but also avoids a radical inclusivism that de-sexes the name of God. Unless otherwise denoted, the term "client" refers to clients, patients, congregants, parishioners, or helpees. "Counseling" is usually a generic reference to clinical, psychiatric, pastoral, and lay helping.

How the Code Is Organized

A significant formatting change in the Y-2014 *Code* revision is to first define ethical standards that pertain to the entire continuum of counselors and helpers and to then break out specific individual sections that pertain first to licensed practitioners, and then to ministry-based helpers (e.g., pastors, pastoral counselors, chaplains, and lay helpers). This is being done due to ongoing confusion across the continuum and to better follow the logic of the IBCC's credentialing mission and parameters. Additionally, an entirely new section has been added that addresses the ongoing development and use of technology in the helping process.

The *Code* is primarily organized along eight foundational pillars that form the basis for ethical and Christ-centered practice. These *Core Principles* include:

Compassion in Christian counseling—a call to *servanthood*

Competence in Christian counseling—a call to *excellence*

Consent in Christian counseling—a call to *integrity*

Confidentiality in Christian counseling—a call to *trustworthiness*

Cultural Regard in Christian counseling—a call to *dignity*

Case Management in Christian counseling—a call to *soundness*

Collegiality in Christian counseling—a call to *relationship*

Community Presence in Christian counseling—a call to *humility*

Grace for the Task Ahead

This is a dynamic *Code*, one that will anchor the mission of the AACC and retain some elements without change, but one that will also live and grow with the life and growth of the Association and its membership. The *Code* calls for a lifelong commitment to ethical, competent and excellent service, while challenging its adherents to encourage ethical behavior among colleagues, churches, organizations, and communities. The sincere prayer of the AACC leadership team, Executive Board and the Law and Ethics Committee, is that God would give grace to adopt this *Code* professionally, the strength to live it honorably, and the hope to see it as a foundation of common identity and corporate unity.

Biblical-Ethical Foundations of the AACC Ethics Code

1st Foundation: Jesus Christ—and His revelation in the Old and New Testaments of the Bible as the inspired Word of God—is the pre-eminent model for Christian counseling practice, ethics, caregiving activities and the final authority for all matters about which it speaks.

2nd Foundation: Christian counseling maintains a committed, intimate, and dedicated relationship with the worldwide church, and individual counselors with a local body of believers.

3rd Foundation: Christian counseling, at its best, is a Spirit-led process of change, transformation and growth, geared to help others mature in Christ by the skillful synthesis of counselor-assisted spiritual, psychosocial, familial, bio-medical, and environmental interventions.

4th Foundation: Christian counselors are dedicated to Jesus Christ as their "first love," to excellence in client service, to ethical integrity in practice, and to respect for everyone encountered.

5th Foundation: Christian counselors accord the highest respect to biblical revelation regarding the sanctity and defense of human life, the dignity of human personhood, and the sanctity of marriage and family life.

6th Foundation: The biblical and constitutional rights to Religious Freedom, Free Speech, and Free Association, protect Christian counselor public identity, and the explicit incorporation of spiritual practices into all forms of counseling and intervention.

7th Foundation: Christian counselors are mindful of their representation of Christ and His church as Ambassadors of Reconciliation and are dedicated to honor their commitments and obligations in all social and professional relationships.

Note: This statement of "Biblical-Ethical Foundations" is not a Doctrinal Statement, nor is it intended to substitute for one.

Since the actual Code is too lengthy to include in this book, the ethical standards from the table of contents are provided as a matter of orientation.

ETHICAL STANDARDS

ES1–000: A Judeo-Christian Worldview—Practicing through Faith and Values

ES1–100: *Compassion* in Christian Counseling—A Call to *Servanthood*

ES1–200: *Competence* in Christian Counseling—A Call to *Excellence*

ES1–300: *Consent* in Christian Counseling—A Call to *Integrity*

ES1–400: *Confidentiality* in Christian Counseling—A Call to *Trustworthiness*

ES1–500: *Cultural Regard* in Christian Counseling—A Call to *Dignity*

ES1–600: *Case Management* in Christian Counseling—A Call to *Soundness*

ES1–700: *Collegiality* in Christian Counseling—A Call to *Relationship*

ES1–800: *Community Presence* in Christian Counseling—A Call to *Humility*

Use of Technology and Technology-related Applications
ES2–000: Additional Ethical Standards in the Use of Technology

ES2–100: Core Ethical Standards in the Use of Technology

Additional Ethical Standards for Licensed and Professional Christian Counselors
ES3–000: Fees, Client Billing, and Financial Relationships

ES3–100: Third-party Payers and Managed Care Entities

ES3–200: Testing, Assessment, and Clinical Evaluation

Additional Ethical Standards for Pastoral and Lay Christian Counselors
ES4–000: Definitions and Roles of Pastors and Pastoral Counselors

ES4–100: Definitions and Roles of Lay Caregivers and Non-ordained Ministers

Standards for Resolving Ethical-legal Conflicts
ES5–000: Base Standards for Ethical Conflict Resolution

ES5–100: Resolving Conflicts with Employers and Colleagues

ES5–200: Resolving Professional and Organizational Conflicts

ES5–300: Resolving Conflicts with the State and Its Laws

To review and or download an electronic copy of the complete 2014 AACC Christian Counseling Code of Ethics, please go to http://www.aacc.net/about-us/code-of-ethics/.

Some churches and Christian ministries hesitate to develop and engage in caregiving and lay counseling activities and programs because they are anxious about legal exposure and liability. While it would be impossible to eliminate all risk when you feel called to this important ministry arena, the principles and suggestions outlined in this chapter—as well as the rest of the book—offer a solid foundation from which to launch and operate. We must walk by faith but do so with wisdom and discernment, having a commitment to excellence and seeking to honor God in all things. A statement from Dr. Hart offers a poignant closing thought: "The overriding principle . . . is that the counselor must *first* safeguard the well-being of the client. If you follow this principle, there's not much you can do to get yourself in trouble!"[34]

CHAPTER 12

Stress, Burnout, and Self-Care in Lay Counseling

Lay counselors and those who work in the caregiving professions are often thought of as being compassionate people.[1] Indeed, many of us who feel called into the ministry readily identify with the compassion of Christ as He related to those around Him. *Merriam-Webster's Collegiate Dictionary* defines *compassion* as a, "sympathetic consciousness of others' distress, together with a desire to alleviate it." It comes from the Latin word *compat*, which means to "suffer with." Much of the research on this subject underscores the critical importance of the helping relationship, and counselors are frequently in close proximity to the emotional suffering and resulting grief of those they counsel. Herein lies both a potential problem (increased stress and burnout), as well as a wonderful opportunity—to function as God's ambassadors of reconciliation.

The day-to-day issues people bring into the counseling office when seeking guidance and help can be all encompassing. Sometimes the impact and sheer level of pain that confronts us can overwhelm even the most capable and mature counselors. A primary challenge for those who live and function in a caregiving role is the simple reality that self-care is something we tend to focus on when it pertains to our clients and not necessarily to ourselves. The question then becomes not only how do we finish the race God has ordained for us, but how do we finish well? *Stress, burnout, and compassion fatigue are real and can negatively influence counselor ethics and effectiveness, thereby increasing liability risks.*

When people enter into a lay counseling ministry, they probably expect to be successful. Most individuals do not feel passionately called by God to something only to fail. One common distortion is that many of us define success primarily by quantitative measures (e.g., the number of clients we see, positions held, our compensation, how many positive outcomes we have) and not by qualitative measures such as those that make a difference in someone's life by helping him or her become more Christlike. We may face a strong temptation to develop a comparative mind-set. We can create increasingly unrealistic standards that have less to do with trusting God and walking in faith, and more to do with how we compare to the lay counselor or ministry next to us.

Too many counselors and ministry leaders accept very difficult job descriptions, and few other activities have such a broad range of "high expectation" demands. Here is an important principle when it comes to counseling: the individual expectations might be legitimate, but the composite expectations can be consuming and at times destructive. It may feel nice to be affirmed by those we help, but we cannot allow this to become either our primary motivation for service or the source of our identity. Otherwise, in seeking the applause of people, we may allow others to define our calling and purpose.

Paul identified himself to the Corinthians as a "bondservant," but note that it was for "Jesus' sake" (2 Cor. 4:5). In other words, Paul was certainly there to serve the church—yet not primarily for their sakes—but for and to his Lord. If we do not recognize this dynamic, it will catch us off guard and we may accept the false narrative that we are not allowed to fail, hurt, or in essence, be human. The result can be a crisis of faith at both a personal level and within the ministry because we have not learned how to set reasonable boundaries with the people we counsel or we simply choose not to. The truth is that if we become overresponsible for our clients' well-being, we become exhausted and they will never learn or grow. In time we may become desperate for relief and experience burnout.

There are several common outcomes—potentially with ethical consequences—that are frequently set into motion once counselors realize they may not be able to live up to the expectations set by others:

1. *Developing a preoccupation with stress-producing people or situations*. We remain in the intensity of the stress-filled environment and seek after adrenaline-fueled experiences—always moving, always busy, with the appearance of human *doings* rather than human *beings*.

2. *Indulging in escape behaviors* for many of the same reasons our clients do— we are tired of being discouraged, lonely, or in pain, and our chosen path is a way to "self-medicate" via certain substances or behaviors, although usually in an unhealthy manner.

3. *Avoiding intimate relationships with one's spouse or close friends and substituting fantasy for reality*. True relational intimacy requires time and effort, and when we are emotionally and spiritually drained, we are less able to make the necessary investment. Sexual addiction is now a worldwide epidemic. It can be tempting to engage an image on a computer screen because it is easy, there is an immediate emotional/physical reward, and there is little risk of failing or being rejected by that image.

4. *Seeking to control everything and everyone as a means of coping.* Many times control is a survival tool that is embraced rather than a characterological disorder. If we come to believe that we are powerless—perhaps from being hurt through repeated traumatic experiences—we may falsely conclude that if we can simply control our environments and the people in them, we will somehow be safer. Unfortunately, this is rarely the case, as most people do not respond well to excessive control.

5. *Justifying actions by blaming other things and/or other people.* Blame shifting is an attempt, albeit with unintended negative consequences, to avoid responsibility and accountability. If we can make the issue(s) primarily about someone or something else, then we can more easily separate ourselves from the emotional and practical aftermath.

6. *Choosing simply to quit or leave the profession/ministry.* The enemy of our souls would like nothing better than to see us fail and give up. Sadly, the body of Christ too often and too quickly discards its members, and this grieves the Holy Spirit deeply.

So what are the consequences of stress overload? Dr. Hans Selye, a Canadian endocrinologist who is considered the "father" of stress research, began to define the phenomenon during the mid-1930s in terms of what he called the *General Adaptation Syndrome.*[2] The normal pattern is for the body to cycle through a three-step process: alarm, resistance, and exhaustion. He went on to define stress as the "non-specific response of the body to any demand."[3] Think about that statement for a moment. The implication here is that almost any demand placed on the body (including the mind, emotions, and spirit) has the potential to create a stress response.

Stress can have both a psychosocial (within the environment) and a biogenic (within the body) orientation. *Eustress*, which is a normal part of everyday life, is necessary for keeping us alert and active. It enables us to be productive and creative, and assists with decision-making activities. However, a chronically high level of stress becomes *distress* and results in a rapidly downward spiral for day-to-day functioning. The two primary stress hormones that begin this process are adrenaline and cortisol. According to Dr. Archibald Hart:

> The stress cycle starts in the brain. When a stressor is detected as a threat, the amygdala, hypothalamus, and pituitary glands trigger the fight-or-flight stress response. The sympathetic nervous system activates several different physical responses to mobilize for action. The adrenal glands increase the output of adrenaline (also called epinephrine), cortisol and other glucocorticoids, which tightens and contracts the muscles and sharpens the senses. Five main systems

respond to stress and can be compromised by prolonged stress: the cardiovascular system, immune system, nervous system, endocrine or glandular system, and metabolic system. The body also forms free radicals that are associated with degenerative diseases, illnesses, and an acceleration of the aging process.[4]

While the fight-or-flight (and sometimes the *freeze*) response is instinctive, it tends to compromise rational and balanced thinking. This is because adrenaline signals the body to move blood out of the brain and into the major muscle groups where it may be needed more (to prompt swift action and/or reaction). What happens is that the amygdala hijacks the messages from the neocortex (the thinking part of the brain), directs them into the limbic system (the feeling part of the brain), and makes calm responses vastly more difficult—think of road rage when someone cuts you off in traffic after an already demanding day at the office. As you contemplate the myriad of situations, decisions, and stressors most counselors constantly face, is it any wonder that making wise, healthy, and balanced decisions can become a challenge after one's resources (emotionally, cognitively, physically, and spiritually) are pushed to their very limits?

When excessive amounts of adrenaline and cortisol enter the bloodstream, the cumulative effects over time can be harmful. These include: (1) a narrowing of the capillaries and other blood vessels leading into and out of the heart, (2) a decrease in the flexibility and dilation properties of blood vessels and their linings, (3) a decrease in the body's ability to flush harmful (LDL) cholesterol out of its system, (4) an increase in the overall production of blood cholesterol, (5) an increase in the blood's tendency to clot, and (6) increased deposits of plaque on arterial walls. Although the research is still emerging, there is some evidence that increased cortisol levels result in unwanted weight gain and the accumulation of fat cells around one's midsection. This is why a number of dietary and weight-control supplements currently available are designed to reduce these levels (e.g., CortiSlim, CortiStress, Cortistat-PS, Cort-Aid).

According to the American Institute on Stress, 80 to 90 percent of all doctor visits today are stress related.[5] The American Heart Association further states that more than 50 million Americans suffer from high blood pressure, and nearly 60 million suffer from some form of cardiovascular disease, resulting in over a million deaths each year (two out of every five who die—one every thirty-two seconds).[6] Heart disease has been the leading cause of death each year since 1900 and crosses all racial, gender, socioeconomic, and age barriers. Finally, the US Department of Health and Human Services reported that 25 percent of all prescriptions written in the United States are for tranquilizers, sleep aids, antidepressants, and anti-anxiety medication.[7]

We have seen that counselors and ministry leaders are not only susceptible to increased levels of stress, but when stress is combined with a call to love and serve others, the result is what is commonly referred to as *compassion fatigue*. Compassion fatigue can be understood as a comprehensive exhaustion that takes place over time when one is constantly in the "giving" position and as a result, loses his or her ability and motivation to experience joy and satisfaction or to feel and care for others.[8] Counselors, including lay counselors, now join the ranks of other caregivers (e.g., doctors, nurses, social workers, teachers, disaster relief workers, crisis responders) in being among the most vulnerable of groups in this regard. It is sometimes referred to as secondary or vicarious traumatic stress associated with the emotional residue related to the cause of caring. The traumatic event or crisis did not happen to the counselor directly, but he or she was close enough to those on whom it did have an impact, and now its detrimental effects have a causal effect.

We must consider a proactive strategy in addressing the realities of being counselors and caregivers. Before doing so, it is essential that we likewise understand the two primary categories of stress. *First*, there is the stress *of* the ministry. Many would agree that just working and being around people is stressful. *Second*, there is the stress *we bring* into the ministry (e.g., unresolved hurts of our own, patterns of besetting sin, unhealthy relationships, unforgiveness, an insecure leadership style, extreme control needs). Counselors and ministry leaders who have successfully addressed the *second* category of stress (what we bring), will do a much better job in handling the first category.

Here is a potentially difficult but important question we must all ask ourselves from time to time: Is my ministry *causing* the problems in my life, or is my ministry *revealing* the problems in my life? Stress and pressure have a way of squeezing things out of us. The good news is that cause-and-effect dynamics can be improved or resolved and revelation can be used by the Holy Spirit to promote needed adjustments and change. Our role is to have "ears to hear," "eyes to see," and a heart that is willing and open before the Lord.

You might wonder what goes into a good stress prevention or self-care plan. The following are a number of principles you may find helpful in your own journey. Take them and prayerfully develop a personalized approach tailored to your needs and/or situation.[9] Write the plan down and review it at least once every week. Start by being honest with yourself, and be open to what the Holy Spirit is speaking.

1. *Learn how to recognize the stress-producing areas in your life requiring attention, and take ownership of what needs to be done.* Things that remain a secret usually continue to have power over us and may be sources of fear, guilt, and shame. Here is one definition of fear: it is the "darkroom" that develops all our

negatives. Fear is a dark place where negative thoughts, emotions, and behaviors emerge. The only thing that will stop a developing photograph in its tracks is light. This is because light penetrates and darkness does not. Ephesians 5:13 says, "Everything exposed by the light becomes visible—and everything that is illuminated becomes a light."

2. *Learn to depersonalize some of what you do in the ministry, and limit your time around negative people.* Clients frequently bring a host of complaints and problems to counselors where they may not necessarily be encouraged, positive in their outlook, or full of faith in the midst of the pain. This can be draining after a while—remember Jethro's observation of Moses in the wilderness that he was wearing himself out when trying to counsel everyone (Ex. 18). Criticism from a client is a frequent companion of any counselor, but sometimes it is an adult form of crying, whining, or throwing a tantrum. Counselors can become like lightning rods simply because they are in an authority position at the moment by virtue of their title or position. This can be especially true if a person has unresolved issues arising from their family of origin, so it is important to remember that strong negative reactions may not really be about you, your leadership, or your counsel.

3. *Learn not to lose sight of your first love, because "you" are not your ministry.* Before our identities as counselors or ministry leaders and before our identities as husbands, wives, fathers, mothers, or a number of other roles, we are first and foremost the adopted sons and daughters of our heavenly Father. We must not allow the "ministry" to become the "mistress" in our walk with God, because it becomes like chasing the wind and is a formula for discouragement and burnout. Scripture says that Jesus prayed before selecting His apostles, and then "He appointed twelve, so that they would be with Him, and that He might send them out to preach, and to have authority to cast out the demons" (Mark 3:14–15 NASB). It is a blessing and privilege to be given opportunities to preach the gospel, move in the miraculous, and engage in frontline spiritual warfare, but this is not the first reason that God has called or appointed us. It is that we all "might be with Him," our first love.

4. *Learn to rest, because the nature of God has much to do with rest.* Rest, true God-given rest, does not automatically imply inactivity, but trust and dependency. God has so ordained our bodies that about every sixteen hours they need to shut down and be renewed. If you live to a normal life expectancy in this country (around seventy-eight years), you will sleep approximately twenty-five years of that life. Speaker and author Steven Covey told a story about two men who chopped wood side by side all day together. One man stopped every hour and rested, while the other worked straight through the day. When they finished, the man who rested actually chopped more wood. Why—because when he stopped, he also

sharpened his ax. Resting allows us to stay sharp. We sharpen our physical axes, our emotional and relational axes, and especially our spiritual axes. Ecclesiastes 10:10 says, "If the ax is dull and its edge unsharpened, more strength is needed."

5. *Learn to be silent and learn to be still.* What is it about the ministry that often compels us to try and accomplish more than Jesus did? It is hard to imagine anyone busier and more in demand than Christ was during His life on the earth. Yet He clearly understood the value of being alone with the Father. Luke records this for us: "The news about him spread all the more, so that crowds of people came to hear him and to be healed of their sicknesses. But Jesus *often* withdrew to lonely places and prayed" (Luke 5:15–16, emphasis added). The busier we are, the more we need to strategically withdraw, wait on the Lord, and allow the Holy Spirit to renew our strength so that we will soar on wings like eagles, run and not grow weary, walk and not be faint (see Isa. 40:31).

6. *Learn to give your burdens to God each day.* We were not designed to be ministry pack mules. We are sheep. The only burden sheep carry is their wool, and they lose that twice a year. In Matthew 11 Jesus admonished us by saying, "Come to me, all you who are weary and burdened, and I will give you rest. Take my yoke upon you and learn from me, for I am gentle and humble in heart, and you will find rest for your souls. For my yoke is easy and my burden is light" (vv. 28–30).

When a new, young and untrained ox is first brought to the plow, he will often be paired with an older, wiser, and more seasoned animal. A special training yoke is sometimes used. The neck hole for the wise, seasoned old ox fits his neck almost perfectly, but the yoke for the young ox is much larger. The reason—the young ox is not supposed to feel the burden of the load, but only learn what it means to walk alongside the other. It is an easier yoke. Jesus told us His yoke is easy. Nevertheless, it remains a yoke, which means that we cannot simply go anywhere we choose. God does, however, want us to learn to walk alongside Him. If you are constantly feeling the burden of the counseling or ministry yoke, it may mean you are in the lead rather than the Lord.

7. *Learn to triage your daily and life events.* Emergency personnel have been trained to come into a situation, assess the genuine priorities, and begin making decisions regarding the most critical things first. Sometimes it can literally make the difference between life and death. The same is true in counseling. Spiritual triage—discerning what God is doing in the moment, having the wisdom to know how to respond, and being led by the Holy Spirit—is a critical, stress-reducing counseling skill. Not everything that is important is necessarily urgent, and not everything that is urgent is necessarily important. David cried out to God, saying, "Show me your ways, LORD; teach me your paths. Guide me in your truth and teach me, for you are God my Savior, and my hope is in you all day long" (Ps. 25:4–5).

8. *Learn to resolve those things that can be attended to easily and quickly.* Many counselors frequently spend 90 percent of their time, energy, and resources on the 10 percent that they may be able to do very little about. Reversing those numbers could help immensely in how we go about the ministry. Have you ever had a pebble in your shoe? A splinter in your finger? An eyelash in your eye? These are not life-threatening events, but they can be extremely irritating and distracting nonetheless. A simple adjustment (i.e., removing the shoe and shaking it out) can provide immediate relief. Ask God to show you the things in your life that represent pebbles, splinters, and eyelashes—in other words, the "little foxes that ruin the vineyards" (Song 2:15)—and with a little attention, you might experience relief and even freedom. Perhaps it means getting at least one more hour of sleep each night or actually taking a day off and relaxing. It could be any number of minor adjustments having significant payoffs. We only have to be off course on a journey by a little to miss the destination by a lot.

9. *Learn to manage your time by saying no, or your time will control you.* Time does not manage us; it tends to take over. We must be active—and at times determined—in our self-examination and intentional in correction when it comes to this issue. Cemeteries are full of indispensable people. The fact of the matter is that life usually goes on with or without us. If the Lord were to literally call you home today, would someone still counsel with your clients? Write your reports? Finish the project that was started? Visit the hospital? Finalize the budget? The answer is a resounding "Yes." Counselors too often move their spouses, families, and their own self-care out of their schedules when something else comes up and crowds the calendar. We rationalize that we will make it up later, and yet we never seem to have the time.

10. *Maintain a healthy foundation of sleep, diet, and exercise in your daily routine.* Caffeine is the most abused stimulant in the United States and when combined with the adrenaline-fueled lifestyle many of us experience, the impact can have a number of negative consequences. Basically we sleep in ninety-minute cycles. The first sixty minutes or so is when the body repairs itself at the cellular level. The last twenty to thirty minutes of the cycle is when the brain/mind attempts to declutter and restore. This is the rapid eye movement (REM) or dream cycle portion associated with sleep. Most of us need around five sleep cycles per night, and if we are resting properly, the REM sleep should lengthen with each cycle. Caffeine acts like a central nervous system stimulant and has approximately, a seven-hour half-life. This means that seven hours after consuming caffeine, 50 percent of the effect of the stimulant is still having an impact on your body and brain. Studies have shown that 300mg of caffeine (two to four cups of coffee; one to two espressos; a combination of soda, coffee, and chocolate; etc.) can significantly disrupt

the sleep cycle, depending on when it is consumed during the day (as much as 50 percent when the body is trying to restore itself and as much as 70 percent of the REM cycle).

Unfortunately, the effects of sleep loss are accumulative (a "foggy" brain, worsened vision, impaired driving, short-term memory problems, obesity, and even heart disease). A 2005 survey by the National Sleep Foundation concluded that the average person sleeps about 6.9 hours a night, but the body/mind requires closer to eight hours for most people. This means the average person loses almost an entire night's sleep on a weekly basis. We have approximately one week to make up the sleep deficit, and then whatever impact occurs is likely to be present and deteriorating over time.

11. *Learn to delegate to others whenever, wherever, and however it is appropriate.* Some of the most secure counselors are the ones who can let their ministry go and who are comfortable having strong, anointed people around them. Moses heeded his father-in-law's advice (Ex. 18) and surrounded himself with able leaders. Does it really matter if someone else can give a better presentation, teach a better class, write a better article or book, do a better job counseling a client? Hopefully not! Good leaders produce followers. Great leaders produce other leaders. However, the greatest of leaders understand what it means to become a follower again. The important thing is that the kingdom of God is advanced.

12. *Learn the value of authentic relationship, and find one or two key people in your life to be accountable to.* Someone once said, "Accountability is the breakfast of champions, but too many people skip the most important meal of the day." Isolation and the lack of accountability remain a primary strategy that Satan uses to take down any leader—he "prowls around like a roaring lion looking for someone to devour" (1 Peter 5:8). Whenever we are alone (in reality or perception) and cut off from supportive relationships, we are the most vulnerable. We do not necessarily need more "yes men" or "yes women." Most leaders already have their share of them—good people, prayer warriors, faithful and loyal to be sure—but we also need "truth tellers" in our lives. These are individuals who also love us and are safe, whom we can count on to give honest, direct, and transparent feedback. However, we must give these individuals permission and an open invitation to do so. The spiritual landscape is littered with counselors and leaders who have failed to embrace this truth. Look at the foresight of the wisest man who lived. In 1 Kings 4:1–19, we see a wide-ranging list of Solomon's officials (priests, scribes, recorders, military commanders, project managers, governors, and the like). Yet embedded in this list is a priest named Zabud, who is also described as the "king's friend" (v. 5 NASB). Here was Solomon, apparently with the wisdom to have at least one person on his staff who also served in the capacity of *friend*. Who is your

Zabud? If you do not have one, you should be encouraged to find one. Better yet, consider being a Zabud to another counselor.

Christian leadership is a high and sacred calling—to humbly yet transparently represent Christ as His ambassadors to a lost and hurting world. This is the ministry of reconciliation. Paul said it was "as though God were making his appeal *through us*" to implore others to be reconciled to God (2 Cor. 5:20, emphasis added). If we want to "run with perseverance the race marked out for us" (Heb. 12:1), we must be deliberate when it comes to our own self-care. Only then can we put on the compassion of Christ and consistently manifest His grace, truth, and love to all who so desperately need His touch.

However, in bringing this discussion of self-care to a close, we need to have a nuanced, biblical perspective that goes beyond our own efforts at self-care. Tan and Castillo wrote an article on self-care and beyond from a Christian perspective, with the following concluding comments that are most relevant to our discussion:

> We therefore need to go beyond self-care to stewardship of God's resources that involves conserving or preserving, as well as using or spending such resources, depending on the seasons of our lives in the context of God's will for us (see Canning, 2011). We also need to go beyond self-care to embracing sanctified suffering that at times stretch us and knock us off balance so that we may grow to become more Christlike and spiritually mature. . . . Beyond "self"-care—or beyond our abilities to care for ourselves—is God's desire to care for us through friendship with Christ and through friendship with others in Christian community. Beyond self-care is "God-care" for us, and "we-care" or "community-care" in the body of Christ for one another.[10]

Conclusions about
Lay Counseling

Years ago Dr. Rodger Bufford wrote an interesting article on issues and trends in Christian counseling in the *CAPS Bulletin*, which was then the official publication of the Christian Association for Psychological Studies. He covered topics such as the concept of integration (of psychology and Christian faith), Christian approaches to counseling, lay counseling, insularity (of some leaders in the field of Christian counseling), demonology and psychopathology, graduate programs, publications, and ethics. With regard to lay counseling, Bufford said, "The decade of the eighties promises further development in this area."[1]

This prediction came true in the 1980s as lay Christian counseling developed and matured through that decade and on into the '90s, and it has continued to mature over the past several decades. We predict that the movement will continue to grow, especially as further evaluation research investigating the effectiveness of lay Christian counseling and training programs is done. We look forward to the development of more refined, biblically based models of lay caring and counseling ministries; more adequate selection, training, and supervision of lay counselors; deeper appreciation of and greater sensitivity to ethical and legal issues; and heightened awareness of potential pitfalls and ethical/liability dangers inherent in any helping endeavor. Our hope is that many more churches or congregations, parachurch organizations, and mission boards around the world will become involved in a more systematic and organized (but possibly still "informal") ministry of lay caring and counseling because it is biblically based and commanded by our loving Lord. And while lay Christian counseling will continue to grow and develop as a ministry, it is crucial for leaders in this ministry not to elevate it above other significant ministries in the kingdom of God.

We continue to see a need for more biblically based models and approaches to lay Christian counseling. A key element, often missing in many existing models, is the significance of the ministry of the Holy Spirit, including appropriate spiritual gifts and spiritual power in effective lay Christian caring and counseling ministries.

We pointed out in an earlier chapter that spiritual gifts relevant to lay Christian counseling or a helping ministry may include exhortation, wisdom, knowledge, discerning of spirits, mercy, and healing. (Other relevant spiritual gifts may also include prophecy, teaching, faith, miracles, tongues, and intercession.) In this regard, it is interesting to note that the late Dr. Jerome Frank, professor emeritus of psychiatry at Johns Hopkins School of Medicine and an authority in the practice, teaching, and study of psychotherapy, made the following statements years ago:

> Some therapists seem to obtain extraordinary results while the patients of a few do no better, or even fare worse, than if they had received no treatment at all. It would be highly desirable to weed out these "tone-deaf" therapists early in training, thereby preventing harm to patients and sparing the therapists from misery; but unfortunately, adequate screening methods for this purpose do not yet exist. My own hunch, which I mention with some trepidation, is that the most gifted therapists may have telepathic, clairvoyant, or other parapsychological abilities. . . . They may, in addition, possess something . . . that can only be termed "healing power." Any researcher who attempts to study such phenomena risks his reputation as a reliable scientist, so their pursuit can be recommended only to the most intrepid. The rewards, however, might be great.[2]

We recommend that further research be conducted on the role of spiritual gifts like healing, exhortation, wisdom, knowledge, mercy, and discerning of spirits, and the ministry and power of the Holy Spirit in effective Christian counseling, whether lay or professional. Christian mental health professionals and researchers should be bold enough to provide leadership in this endeavor, which we believe can reap great rewards, including the healing of broken lives.

We are not suggesting that counseling knowledge and skills are unnecessary. Yet, as Dr. Frank in a secular context points out, there are frequently important, if not even more crucial, factors that may account for effective and efficient counseling or psychotherapy. They include "healing power," and we know that in a Christian or biblical context the presence and power of the Holy Spirit and spiritual gifts are crucial for effective ministry. Evaluation studies should be conducted to determine whether specially selected lay Christian counselors with such spiritual gifts do better than other lay Christian counselors who may not have such gifts. Comparative outcome studies are also needed to determine whether a Christian counseling approach (whether lay or professional) that explicitly uses appropriate spiritual gifts and relies on the presence and power of the Holy Spirit is more effective than another Christian counseling approach that does not do this explicitly. Such evaluation research should, of course, be conducted with integrity and methodological rigor.

While spiritual gifts and the healing power of the Holy Spirit need more attention and research, it is still important for lay Christian counselors as well as pastors to learn to care and counsel in a systematic and skilled way in order to be effective and truly helpful. As Dr. Wayne Oates pointed out decades ago, those involved in pastoral ministry cannot avoid counseling with people who are hurting. He said, "The choice is not between counseling or not counseling, but between counseling in a disciplined and skilled way and counseling in an undisciplined and unskilled way."[3]

We believe this is true not only for pastors, but for all of us who are committed to ministering to others and to serving the Lord in His kingdom. This revised and updated book has been written to help provide the biblical perspectives and counseling resources needed for learning how to counsel in a disciplined and skilled way, so that Christians, as servants of the Lord Jesus Christ,[4] can be equipped for an effective helping ministry, especially those who may have appropriate spiritual gifts for such a ministry.

As counselors we should view servanthood as the highest of callings, and Scripture has much to say on the subject. Here are a few key verses we encourage you to meditate on (with italics added for emphasis):

- The LORD will rescue his *servants*; no one who takes refuge in him will be condemned. (Ps 34:22)
- "You know that the rulers of the Gentiles lord it over them, and their high officials exercise authority over them. Not so with you. Instead, whoever wants to become great among you must be your *servant*, and whoever wants to be first must be your slave—just as the Son of Man did not come to be *served*, but to *serve*, and to give his life as a ransom for many." (Matt. 20:25–28)
- But now, by dying to what once bound us, we have been released from the law so that we *serve* in the new way of the Spirit, and not in the old way of the written code. (Rom. 7:6)
- What, after all, is Apollos? And what is Paul? Only *servants*. (1 Cor. 3:5)
- This, then, is how you ought to regard us: as *servants* of Christ and as those entrusted with the mysteries God has revealed. (1 Cor. 4:1)
- For what we preach is not ourselves, but Jesus Christ as Lord, and ourselves as your *servants* for Jesus' sake. (2 Cor. 4:5)
- You, my brothers and sisters, were called to be free. But do not use your freedom to indulge the flesh; rather, *serve* one another humbly in love. (Gal. 5:13)
- Whatever you do, work at it with all your heart, as working for the

Lord, not for human masters, since you know that you will receive an inheritance from the Lord as a reward. It is the Lord Christ you are *serving*. (Col. 3:23–24)

- Each of you should use whatever gift you have received to *serve* others, as faithful stewards of God's grace in its various forms. (1 Peter 4:10)
- If anyone speaks, they should do so as one who speaks the very words of God. If anyone *serves*, they should to do so with the strength God provides, so that in all things God may be praised through Jesus Christ. To him be the glory and the power for ever and ever. Amen. (1 Peter 4:11)

Let us end this concluding chapter, as well as this book with the following words from an earlier paper written by Dr. Tan:

> The tremendous development of the field of lay Christian counseling in recent years is encouraging and can result in much help and blessing in ministry to many troubled people to the glory of God, provided such counseling is done in a biblical, Christ-centered way, within appropriate ethical and legal limits, and with the best of selection, training, supervision, and evaluation possible of lay Christian counselors.[5]

OUR CLOSING PRAYER

I pray that out of his glorious riches he may strengthen you with power through his Spirit in your inner being, so that Christ may dwell in your hearts through faith. And I pray that you, being rooted and established in love, may have power, together with all the Lord's holy people, to grasp how wide and long and high and deep is the love of Christ, and to know this love that surpasses knowledge—that you may be filled to the measure of all the fullness of God. (Eph. 3:16–19)

Lay Counselor Application Form

Thank you for your interest in pursuing training and volunteer caregiving with
_____ Lay Counseling Ministry at _____ Church. Please
complete and *print* all information that is requested in a legible manner or mark
N/A if not applicable.

I. DEMOGRAPHIC INFORMATION

Last Name   First Name   Middle Initial

Home Address

City State Zip

Cell Phone   Home Phone

Email Address

Current Status

☐ Single   ☐ Married   ☐ Divorced   ☐ Widowed   ☐ Separated
☐ Engaged

Occupation

Present Employer   Position Title

Address _____

City _____ State _____ Zip _____

Work Phone _____ Supervisor _____

☐ Full-Time   ☐ Part-Time

How long at current job: years _____ months _____

May we contact your current employer for a reference? Yes _____ No _____,
if no please explain:

_____

_____

II. _____ CHURCH INVOLVEMENT

Do you attend?
Sunday Service   ☐ Yes   ☐ No   frequency _____
Sunday School   ☐ Yes   ☐ No   frequency _____
_____ Service ☐ Yes   ☐ No   frequency _____

How are you connected at _____ Church, serving, and/or participating?

_____

_____

_____

III. BACKGROUND INFORMATION

A. Do you speak any language(s) other than English (including sign language)?

   ☐ Yes   ☐ No   If Yes, please list _____

B. Have you ever provided counseling/caregiving on a professional or ministry basis?

   ☐ Yes   ☐ No   If yes, how long _____, where
   _____, and in what capacity?

C. **Populations you have prior experience with (Please check all that apply):**

☐ Children   ☐ Adolescents   ☐ College-Age   ☐ Adults   ☐ Elderly
☐ Couples   ☐ Families

D. **Formal and Informal Education and Training**

List the most recent academic/ministry training programs you have attended.

Year	Academic/Training Institution Degree/ Certification Area of Study	Completed

E. **Areas of Counseling/Ministry Experience**

Based on education, training, and ministry or clinical experience, *please check all that apply:*

☐ ADD/ADHD	☐ Addictions	☐ Adoption Issues
☐ Alcoholism	☐ Anger Management	☐ Anxiety
☐ Bipolar Disorder	☐ Career Counseling	☐ Child Abuse
☐ Chronic Pain	☐ Coaching	☐ Codependency
☐ Compassion Fatigue	☐ Conflict Resolution	☐ Crisis Intervention
☐ Cutting/Self-Injury	☐ Dementia/Alzheimer's	☐ Depression
☐ Developmental Disorders	☐ Dissociation	☐ Divorce Recovery
☐ Domestic Violence	☐ Eating Disorders	☐ Financial Issues
☐ Gender Identity Issues	☐ Grief and Loss	☐ Infidelity
☐ Learning Disabilities	☐ Marital Conflict	☐ Mediation
☐ Men's Issues	☐ Missionary Issues	☐ Obsessive/Compulsives
☐ Occult/Cults	☐ Parenting Issues	☐ Pastors/Ministers
☐ Personality Disorders	☐ Phobias	☐ Physical Disabilities

☐ Post-abortion Syndrome ☐ Posttraumatic Stress ☐ Pregnancy Issues
☐ Premarital ☐ Psychological Assessment ☐ Rape Recovery
☐ Sexual Abuse ☐ Sexual Addiction ☐ Sexual Dysfunction
☐ Singles ☐ Spiritual Warfare ☐ Stress and Burnout
☐ Suicide ☐ Women's Issues
☐ Other (please specify) _____

F. Availability

☐ Daytime   ☐ Evenings   ☐ Weekends

Are you available a minimum of 2–3 hours per week for _____ ministry?
☐ Yes   ☐ No

IV. SPIRITUAL ORIENTATION AND PRACTICE

Whether we are devoted believers or still seeking to understand God, we all have a spiritual story. Please take a few moments to briefly describe your spiritual beliefs and feelings on the following questions. Attach more pages if necessary. Please note that during the interview process you will have additional opportunity to discuss your spiritual journey and relationship with God.

A. Who is Jesus Christ?

_____
_____
_____

B. How does a person become a Christian?

_____
_____
_____

C. Describe your beliefs about the Bible.

_____
_____
_____

D. Describe your beliefs about the Holy Spirit.

_____

_____

_____

E. How would you incorporate God's Word and spiritual practices and disciplines in your caregiving activities (e.g., prayer, Scripture reading, fasting, meditation, worship, solitude)?

_____

_____

_____

V. PERSONAL REFERENCES

Please use the attached reference forms to provide three references. Completed forms should be placed in an envelope, sealed, and signed across the back flap by the person giving the reference. Attach the three envelopes to this application form. A minimum of two references should be from _____ Church, and all should meet the following criteria:

- Be at least 21 years of age.
- Has preferably known you for at least one year.
- Is not related to you.
- Has a definite knowledge of your character.

VI. ATTESTATION

The following statements require your attestation (affirming each one to be true to the best of your knowledge). Please be sure to respond to each section that directly pertains to you. A Yes or No response will not necessarily disqualify you from training or ministry opportunities.

Christian Personal Testimony

The foundation to all ministry and identity as a volunteer Christian lay counselor/caregiver, is a living, vibrant, and personal relationship with Jesus Christ. Please respond to the following items by checking the appropriate box:

I have read the _____ Church Doctrinal and Mission Statement and hereby attest that I am in full agreement with their tenets.

☐ Yes   ☐ No   ☐ Unsure (please explain) _____

_____

_____

A. I attest that I am a true believer in Jesus Christ; that I have accepted His atoning work of salvation on the cross for the forgiveness of my sins; that I have personally accepted Him as my Savior and Lord; and that as a result of my confession, I have been born again by His Holy Spirit to a new life in Christ.

☐ Yes   ☐ No   ☐ Unsure (please explain) _____

_____

_____

B. Have you ever been charged with or convicted of any misdemeanor or felony other than minor moving violations in a vehicle?

☐ Yes   ☐ No

If Yes, please explain briefly here and then *attach a separate paper* (no more than two pages) to describe in detail the case and its disposition.

_____

_____

_____

I affirm and attest by my signature below that I have answered all the questions in the _____ application truthfully and with full disclosure, and I have attached all requested supporting documentation.

_____
Applicant Signature   Date

Lay Counselor Application Reference Forms

Name of Applicant (please print clearly): _____

The above named applicant is applying for volunteer ministry with _____ at _____ Church. _____ is a network of lay Christian caregivers who are capable and trained, and with a strong and authentic Christian foundation to their ministerial service. The purpose of _____ is to identify and assist the hurting, as well as recognize Christ followers who can offer the highest quality of care to those they serve. As a *personal reference*, we are asking you to provide us your assessment of this applicant's qualifications.

Name of Reference: _____

Title: _____

Organization/Church (if applicable): _____

Address: _____

_____
(Street)   (City)   (State)   (Zip)

Phone: Work: ( ) _____ Home: ( ) _____ Cell: ( ) _____

Email: _____

How long and in what capacity have you known the applicant?

Years _____ Months _____

_____

_____

Please rate the applicant on the following characteristics using the descriptions provided below. Please check only one box for each characteristic.

	Exceptional	Above Average	Average	Below Average	Unsure
1. Demonstrates a positive and authentic relationship with Jesus Christ.					
2. Reflects a commitment to ongoing growth in his/her personal and spiritual life.					
3. Demonstrates kindness and compassion, and takes initiative in showing care to others.					
4. Has a willingness to address his/her own mistakes and accepts accountability to others.					
5. Has a reputation for being a person of ethical integrity, moral character, and spiritual maturity.					
6. Demonstrates the ability to effectively guide and direct others when in a position of leadership.					
7. Has effective relational/"people" skills and is able to set appropriate boundaries.					

I recommend _____ (check one):

___ Highly ___ Moderately ___ With Reservation

Signature: _____ **Date:** _____

If you would like to add any additional comments, feel free to write on the back of this page or attach a separate letter. Please put the completed reference form (and other comments) in a *sealed envelope* with your *signature across the back flap* and return to the applicant. Thank you for your participation.

APPENDIX C

Post-counseling
Questionnaire—Client Form

Your name: _____

The following ratings give you an opportunity to give us an honest appraisal of your counseling experience. We are interested in your perceptions regarding the results of your counseling. Please be open and honest in your assessment, as this is the only way we can improve our services. Thank you, once again, for your cooperation and assistance with the questionnaire.

The first three items should be rated on the following 6-point scale:

1	2	3	4	5	6
Extremely Poor	Poor	Adequate	Good	Very Good	Superb

_____ 1. How would you rate the overall success of your counseling?
_____ 2. How would you rate your overall satisfaction with the results of your counseling?
_____ 3. How would you rate the overall amount of improvement that has occurred as a result of your counseling?

Please answer the following questions by marking *one* option for each question. (Circle the answer that best applies.)

4. To what extent have your complaints or symptoms that brought you to counseling changed as a result of the counseling provided?

(1) Completely disappeared   (2) Very greatly improved
(3) Considerably improved   (4) Somewhat improved
(5) Not at all   (6) Got worse

5. How much do you feel you have changed as a result of the counseling provided?

   (1) A great deal   (2) A fair amount   (3) Somewhat
   (4) Very little   (5) Not at all

6. How strongly would you recommend counseling with your counselor to a close friend with emotional problems?

   (1) Strongly recommend   (2) Mildly recommend
   (3) Recommend but with reservations (4) Would not recommend
   (5) Advise against

7. On the whole, how do you feel you are getting along now?

   (1) Extremely well   (2) Very well   (3) Fairly well
   (4) Neither well nor poorly (5) Fairly poorly (6) Very poorly
   (7) Extremely poorly

8. How well do you feel you are dealing with any unresolved or new problems now?

   (1) Very adequately   (2) Fairly adequately
   (3) Neither adequately nor inadequately (4) Somewhat inadequately
   (5) Very inadequately

9. How much in need of further counseling do you feel now?

   (1) No need at all   (2) Slight need   (3) Could use more
   (4) Considerable need (5) Very great need

10. How helpful do you feel your counselor was to you?

   (1) Completely helpful   (2) Very helpful   (3) Pretty helpful
   (4) Somewhat helpful   (5) Slightly helpful (6) Not at all helpful

11. How competent do you feel your counselor was?

   (1) Completely competent (2) Very competent (3) Pretty competent
   (4) Somewhat competent   (5) Slightly competent
   (6) Not at all competent

12. How sincere do you feel your counselor was?

(1) Completely sincere   (2) Very sincere   (3) Pretty sincere

(4) Somewhat sincere   (5) Slightly sincere   (6) Not at all sincere

13. How likable do you feel your counselor was?

(1) Completely likable   (2) Very likable   (3) Pretty likable

(4) Somewhat likable   (5) Slightly likable   (6) Not at all likable

14. How interested do you feel your counselor was?

(1) Completely interested   (2) Very interested   (3) Pretty interested

(4) Somewhat interested   (5) Slightly interested   (6) Not at all interested

Your counselor: _____

Date: _____

APPENDIX D

Post-counseling Questionnaire— Counselor Form

Your name: _____

Client's name: _____

In filling out the following items, please feel free to use the full range of possible answers. If the outcome of the counseling has been excellent, indicate so. In the same manner, a poor or mediocre counseling outcome should also be rated as such. The first three items should be rated on the following six-point scale:

1	2	3	4	5	6
Extremely Poor	Poor	Adequate	Good	Very Good	Superb

_____ 1. How would you rate the overall success of the counseling provided?

_____ 2. How would you rate the client's overall satisfaction with the results of his/her counseling?

_____ 3. How would you rate the overall amount of improvement the client has experienced as a result of the counseling provided?

Please answer the following questions by marking *one* option for each question. (Circle the answer that best applies.)

4. To what extent have the client's complaints or symptoms that brought him/ her to counseling changed as a result of the counseling provided?

    (1) Completely disappeared   (2) Very greatly improved
    (3) Considerably improved   (4) Somewhat improved
    (5) Not at all   (6) Got worse

5. How much do you feel the client has changed as a result of the counseling provided?

   (1) A great deal   (2) A fair amount   (3) Somewhat
   (4) Very little   (5) Not at all

6. On the whole, how do you feel the client is getting along now?

   (1) Extremely well   (2) Very well   (3) Fairly well
   (4) Neither well nor poorly (5) Fairly poorly
   (6) Very poorly   (7) Extremely poorly

7. How well do you feel the client is dealing with any unresolved or new problems now?

   (1) Very adequately   (2) Fairly adequately
   (3) Neither adequately nor inadequately   (4) Somewhat inadequately
   (5) Very inadequately

8. How much in need of further counseling do you feel the client is?

   (1) No need at all   (2) Slight need   (3) Could use more
   (4) Considerable need (5) Very great need

Finally, please give two ratings for each of the following items. The first (Beginning) is for your sense of where the client stood at the beginning of counseling. The second (End) is for his/her standing at termination.

9. The degree of personal integration or psychological health of the client:

1	2	3	4	5	6	7	8	9
Highly Disorganized			Optimally Integrated			Defensively Organized		

   Beginning _____   End _____

10. The life adjustment or social/vocational functioning of the client:

1	2	3	4	5	6	7	8	9
Low								High

    Beginning _____   End _____

APPENDIX E

Sample Lay Counseling Forms

SAMPLE FORM 1.
CARE RECEIVER WELCOME LETTER

Care Receiver Welcome Letter
ABC Lay Counseling Ministry
Address and Phone Number

Dear Care Receiver,

We are grateful you have contacted _____ Lay Counseling Ministry, and we look forward to helping you navigate through this crisis in your life. You will soon be contacted by the caregiver who has been prayerfully assigned to help support and work with you. We continually seek God's guidance in which caregivers to match with those who contact _____ for help. Your caregiver will schedule a first meeting with you on a day and time that is convenient for both of you.

We know God can use even this difficult time to help you grow spiritually and draw you closer to Him. This is very important to your recovery and healing, and your caregiver's desire is to guide you forward in that direction. However, the journey is often not an easy one and will require commitment on your part. So we thought it would be helpful to let you know a little more about what to expect from caregiving, including your role in the process.

1. Your caregiver may give you homework assignments to complete between your scheduled meetings. The completion of any homework assignments is vital to your recovery and healing and shows your investment in the process.
2. Your caregiver will schedule meeting times with you and make the appropriate reservations for a room at the church building or [location]. We ask that you keep all scheduled appointments, and if you are not able to attend, call your caregiver in advance to reschedule. Please respect

your caregiver's time that he/she has committed to you. Caregivers are volunteers who devote themselves to you and to this ministry.

3. If your caregiver feels that you are not following through with your part of the helping process, he or she may discontinue the caregiving. Our desire is to see caregiving through to a mutually agreed closure, but if you are not committed to the process, we may have to conclude the caregiving and make an appropriate referral.

We are confident that you can find healing, especially as you and your caregiver invite Christ into your time together. Our ministry team will continue to lift you up in our prayers.

> With warm regards and God's blessings,
> Signature

SAMPLE FORM 2.
INTAKE AND PERSONAL HISTORY FORM

Personal History
ABC Lay Counseling Ministry
Address and Phone Number

Name of Client: _____

Date of Birth: _____

I. PRESENTING PROBLEM(S)

A. Describe the reason(s) you are seeking lay counseling.

_____

_____

_____

B. What do you think your family/spouse or significant other feels is the reason lay counseling may be needed?

_____

_____

_____

C. Have you had any previous treatment and/or counseling? If so, where? When? With whom? How long? Is there any history of suicidal thoughts or gestures?

_____

_____

_____

D. Do you have any medical conditions for which you are taking medication or being treated? (List medications/attending physicians.)

_____

_____

II. FAMILY HISTORY AND ENVIRONMENT (INCLUDING STEPFAMILIES)

A. Who do you currently live with? For how long? Describe these relationships if any.

_____

_____

_____

_____

B. Describe your relationship with your family of origin (the family you grew up with). Were either of your parents divorced? If so, how old were you at the time? What is/was the home environment like (e.g., calm, chaotic, abusive, etc.)?

_____

_____

_____

_____

C. How are/were disagreements resolved in your family of origin? How is/was anger or aggression displayed? Who handles(ed) discipline? What form of discipline is/was utilized?

_____

_____

_____

_____

_____

D. What is the significant psychiatric, substance abuse, or medical history of your family of origin?

_____

_____

_____

_____

Parents/Siblings (Name)	Sex M/F	Age	Marital Status	How Related to Client	Where Living	Education Level	Occupation

Spouse/ Significant Other(s)	Children by Spouse(s)	Age	Sex M/F	Marital Status	Where Living	Education Level	Occupation

III. DEVELOPMENT AND CHILDHOOD HISTORY

A. **Pregnancy/Birth.** Describe any problems or abnormal conditions during this period.

_____

_____

_____

_____

B. **Infancy through Elementary School.** Describe any developmental problems during this period (e.g., speech, walking, enuresis, etc.).

_____

_____

_____

_____

Describe any health problems, hospitalizations, or treatment during this period.

_____

_____

_____

_____

Did you have any of the normal childhood diseases? Were there any complications?

_____

_____

_____

_____

Describe any major/traumatic events or disruptions in the family during this period.

_____

_____

_____

_____

C. **Middle Years (Jr. High through High School).** Describe major physical, relational, and/or emotional problems or hospitalizations/treatments during this period (including abuse).

_____

_____

_____

_____

Describe any major/traumatic events or disruptions in the family during this period.

_____

_____

_____

_____

D. **Young Adulthood to Present.** Describe any major physical, emotional, and/or relational problems or life events that were traumatic or disruptive during this period (including abuse).

_____

_____

_____

_____

IV. DRUG AND ALCOHOL HISTORY

Have you used alcohol?   _____ Yes   _____ No

If Yes, describe your usage (i.e., type, amount, frequency, and for how long).

_____

_____

_____

Have you ever used illicit drugs?   _____ Yes   _____ No

If Yes, describe your usage (i.e., drugs used, amount, frequency, and for how long).

_____

_____

_____

Have you abused prescriptions/over-the-counter drugs? ____ Yes ____ No

Describe your usage (i.e., prescriptions/medications used, amount, frequency, and for how long).

_____

_____

_____

What methods of use were most common (i.e., oral, injection, inhalation, etc.)?

_____

_____

_____

How did ethnic origin, age, gender or sexual orientation interact with any drug/alcohol use?

_____

_____

What were the daily activity patterns that tended to support the drug/alcohol use?

_____

_____

_____

V. EDUCATION HISTORY

What is the highest level of education you completed? _____

What are/were your feelings about school, classes, and peer relationships?

_____

_____

_____

_____

Did you have any learning-related problems, learning-disabled classes, or traumatic events/stressors?

_____

_____

_____

_____

VI. PEER, SOCIAL, AND LEISURE HISTORY

Do you have close/intimate friendships? __ None __ 1–5 __ 6–10 __ 10+

How often do you talk or spend time with your friends? Are they supportive?

_____

_____

Describe the history of your friendships, church groups, social/cultural groups, gangs, etc.

_____

_____

Are/were these relationships healthy, or do/did they contribute to the problems you have experienced?

_____

_____

What types of social, recreational, or hobby-related activities do you participate in?

_____

_____

_____

Do/did any of the above activities/interests contribute or relate to problems you have?

_____

_____

VII. MARITAL/SIGNIFICANT OTHER AND SEXUAL HISTORY

Marital status: _____

If married, spouse's name: _____

Dates of marriage: _____

Previously married? _____   Spouse's name: _____

Dates of marriage: _____

Have you been married more than twice? _____   How many times? _____

If not married, are you currently in a serious relationship?   _____ Yes   _____ No

If Yes, with whom? _____   For how long? _____

What is your sexual orientation?_____

Do you use birth control?   _____ Yes   _____ No

Are you currently sexually active?   _____ Yes   _____ No

If Yes, with more than one partner?   _____ Yes   _____ No

What are your attitudes/beliefs about sexuality? What impact does this have in your life?

_____

_____

If married or in a serious relationship, describe your relationship with your spouse or significant other (i.e., emotional, sexual, social, conflicts, level of communication, spirituality, etc.).

_____

_____

_____

_____

VIII. RELIGIOUS AND SPIRITUAL INFLUENCE

Do you identify with a religion and/or spiritual group/church/community? Please describe.

_____

_____

_____

_____

What is your perception of God?

_____

_____

_____

_____

Describe any involvement with cults or the occult (including astrology, séances, tarot cards, palm reading, fantasy games, etc.).

_____

_____

_____

_____

Describe your religious upbringing (i.e., church membership. attendance, youth groups, etc.).

_____

_____

_____

_____

Describe any specific religious/spiritual values and beliefs you or your family adhere to.

_____

_____

_____

_____

How did all the above influences affect your feelings of self-identity and need for approval?

_____

_____

_____

_____

How do/did the above values contribute, if any, to you current situation or problems?

_____

_____

_____

_____

IX. EMPLOYMENT HISTORY

Currently employed? _____ Yes _____ No   How long? _____
Place of employment: _____
Duties/responsibilities: _____

_____

Describe any other relevant employment history.

_____

_____

_____

How long unemployed (if applicable)? _____

Describe your activities during the period of unemployment.

_____

_____

Describe your job motivation/satisfaction.

_____

_____

_____

Describe any job-related stressors or factors.

_____

_____

_____

Describe your relationship with your supervisor(s) and coworkers.

_____

_____

_____

What are your current vocational pursuits or aspirations?

_____

_____

_____

Describe any financial stressors or factors. How do you manage your finances, budget, etc.?

_____

_____

_____

_____

X. MILITARY HISTORY

Have you ever served in the armed forces? _____ Yes _____ No

What branch? _____ How long did you serve? _____

Highest rank achieved: _____

Dates of service: _____

Type of discharge:_____

XI. LEGAL HISTORY

Any charges pending? ____ Yes ____ No

If Yes, nature of charges: _____

Next court date: _____ Where? _____

Currently on parole or probation? _____

Name of probation/parole officer? _____

Describe any legal involvement (past or present) including with Child or Adult Protective Services.

_____

_____

_____

XII. STRENGTHS AND WEAKNESSES

Describe what you perceive to be your strengths and assets.

_____

_____

_____

Describe what you perceive to be your weaknesses or problem areas.

_____

_____

_____

XIII. GOALS AND EXPECTATIONS FOR LAY COUNSELING

What problem(s) do you want to focus on during lay counseling?

_____

_____

_____

_____

In what areas of your life do you feel like you want to see or need improvement?

_____

_____

_____

_____

What are your expectations regarding lay counseling and the outcome?

_____

_____

_____

What expectations do your family members/significant other(s) have for lay counseling?

_____

_____

_____

_____

_____

Client Signature   Date
_____

Parent/Guardian Signature   Date

SAMPLE FORM 3.
INFORMED CONSENT AND CARE AGREEMENT FORM

Consent and Care Agreement Form
ABC Lay Counseling Ministry
Address and Phone Number

THE NATURE AND PURPOSE OF THE ABC LAY COUNSELING MINISTRY

ABC is a caregiving ministry of _____ Church. The purpose of this ministry is to provide spiritual care, support, encouragement, and referral services in a safe and confidential manner. Support is typically on a short-term basis during times of significant need or crisis. While in the midst of crisis, an ABC caregiver can help bring clarity to the issues involved and define the priorities of care. At the conclusion of initial care, ABC will assist with any needed transition of ongoing support. ABC caregivers are trained volunteers under the direction and general supervision of assigned staff members at _____ Church. Regardless of their education, training, licensure or expertise, ABC caregivers do not function in a professional role and do not provide clinically oriented mental health treatment or therapy.

CONFIDENTIALITY POLICY

All communications, records, and contacts with ABC caregivers will be held in strict confidence. Information may be released in accordance with the laws of [state] only when:

1. the care seeker and/or guardian (if care seeker is under 18 years of age) signs a written release of information indicating informed consent to such release; or
2. the care seeker expresses serious intent to harm himself/herself or someone else; or
3. there is evidence or reasonable suspicion of abuse against a minor child, elder person 65 years or older or a dependent adult; or
4. there is evidence demonstrating a gross distortion of reality or the ability to function in normal daily routines; or
5. the ABC caregiver feels that counsel, assistance, and/or supervision may be required from the ABC leadership team.

If any of the conditions exist in 2, 3, or 4 above, the ABC caregiver may additionally seek out counsel, assistance, and direction from the pastors and elders of _____ Church. In all such cases, information is still held in strict confidence other than the personnel identified in this policy.

CONTACT INFORMATION

Please indicate the phone number(s) and/or email address(es) at which we have your consent to contact you:

Phone Number   Email Address

_____

_____

SERVICE AGREEMENT

I/we, the undersigned care seeker(s) or guardian(s), have read, discussed as needed, and fully understand this *Consent and Care Agreement Form* and acknowledge that by signing below, I/we do agree with all consent and authorization statements that are given and confirm consent and authorization for use and/or disclosure of the confidential information described herein with the people and/or organizations named in this *Consent and Care Agreement Form*.

_____
Care Seeker Name (Please Print)   Date

Care Seeker Signature — Date

Guardian, If Client Is a Minor (Print) — Date

Guardian's Signature — Date

SAMPLE FORM 4.
SESSION AND COMMUNICATION NOTES

ABC Lay Counseling Session and Communication Notes

Date you met/spoke with care receiver: _____

Give a brief summary of the time together/conversation:

_____
_____
_____
_____
_____

Describe any significant concerns/issues that surfaced (i.e., medical, suicide, abuse, legal, violent behavior, etc.):

_____
_____
_____
_____

Describe any specific action steps you took based on the time together:

_____
_____
_____
_____

Date for next session, or indicate if this was the final caregiving session:

_____

Signature of Caregiver — Date

SAMPLE FORM 5.
AFTERCARE PLAN

Aftercare Plan
ABC Lay Counseling Ministry
Address and Phone Number

Name of Care Receiver:

LIVING ARRANGEMENTS OF CARE RECEIVER

Recommendations:_____
_____
_____

MEDICATION FOLLOW-UP

Recommendations:_____
_____

Name of Physician: _____
Address: _____
Phone Number: _____

MEDICAL/PHYSICAL FOLLOW-UP

Recommendations:_____
_____
_____

Name of Physician: _____
Address: _____
Phone Number: _____

PSYCHOTHERAPY/COUNSELING FOLLOW-UP

Recommendations:_____

_____

_____

Name of Therapist:_____

Address: _____

Phone Number: _____

SUPPORT GROUP FOLLOW-UP

Recommendations:_____

_____

Contact Information: _____

_____

VOCATIONAL/EDUCATIONAL FOLLOW-UP

Recommendations:_____

_____

Contact Information: _____

_____

SPIRITUAL/PASTORAL RESOURCES AND FOLLOW-UP

Recommendations:_____

_____

Contact Information: _____

_____

OTHER (E.G., REHAB, LEGAL, FINANCIAL, ETC.)

Recommendations: _____

_____

_____

Contact Information: _____

_____

Miscellaneous Instructions/Recommendations: _____

_____

_____

REFERRALS FOR ALTERNATIVE CARE

Please check if applicable: ☐

Whether due to my own request, the unavailability of certain therapeutic services/
clinical expertise, incompatibility with my lay counselor, a conflict in values and
beliefs, or any other stated reason, I am being given the following three referrals and their contact information for alternative care. I understand that it is my
responsibility to follow up and make the initial contact with another counselor.

1. _____

2. _____

3. _____

Reason for referral request: _____

ATTESTATION AND SIGNATURE

The above aftercare plan and/or any referral(s) for follow-up have been thoroughly
explained to me. I understand the recommendations, including any potential limitations, and have had the opportunity to discuss any questions or concerns I have
with my lay counselor. I also understand that I have the right to refuse any and all
recommendations for aftercare and follow-up.

Please check one of the following:

☐   I am terminating lay counseling *against the advice* of my lay counselor.

☐   I am terminating lay counseling *with the approval* of my lay counselor.

Care Receiver Signature   Date

Parent/Guardian Signature (if Minor)   Date

Lay Counselor   Date

SAMPLE FORM 6.
CONSENT FOR RELEASE OF INFORMATION FORM

Consent for Release of Information
ABC Lay Counseling Ministry
Address and Phone Number

I, _____, do hereby consent and authorize *ABC Lay Counseling* to:

☐ *Release all records* of my (or my dependent's) lay counseling or other work done by ABC Lay Counseling *to the following* or *discuss* my (or my dependent's) counseling or other work done by ABC Lay Counseling *with the following*:

1. _____

    (Name of Person or Organization)

    _____

    (Except for the Following Information)

2. _____

    (Name of Person or Organization)

    _____

    (Except for the Following Information)

☐ This consent is valid and is to be acted on regarding the records of:

(Name of Care Receiver)

☐ This consent will terminate *without* express written revocation by the care receiver (or guardian in the case of a minor) on the following date:

_____ or when: _____

I understand that I have no obligation whatsoever to disclose the requested information and that I may revoke this consent at any time by informing any of the noted individuals or organizations. I also waive, on behalf of myself (or dependent minor) and any persons who may have interest in this matter, all provisions of law relating to the disclosure of confidential information and release ABC Lay Counseling from all legal responsibility or liability that may arise from this authorization.

_____   _____   _____   _____
Client Name (Please Print)   Date   Client Signature   Date

_____   _____   _____   _____
Guardian If Client Under 18 (Please Print)   Date   Guardian Signature   Date

_____   _____
ABC Lay Counseling Representative   Date

Notes

INTRODUCTION

1. "Any Mental Illness (AMI) among U.S. Adults," National Institute of Mental Health, www.nimh .nih.gov/health/statistics/prevalence/any-mental-illness-ami-among-adults.shtml.et.
2. G. R. Collins, *Innovative Approaches to Counseling* (Waco, TX: Word, 1986), 73.
3. Ibid., 74.
4. G. R. Collins, "Lay Counseling within the Local Church," *Leadership* 1 (1980): 78–86; S. Y. Tan, "Lay Counseling: The Local Church," *CAPS Bulletin* 7, no. 1 (1981): 15–20.
5. J. Sturkie and G. R. Bear, *Christian Peer Counseling: Love in Action* (Dallas: Word, 1989), 18.
6. S. Y. Tan and E. T. Scalise, "On Belay: The Role of the Church in Lay Helping Ministry," *Christian Counseling Today* 21, no. 2 (2015): 46–50.

CHAPTER 1

1. M. Scott Peck, *The Road Less Traveled* (New York: Touchstone, 1978), 15.
2. M. Kellyon, "LifeWay Research Finds Pastors' Long Workhours Can Come at the Expense of People Ministry," January 5, 2010, www.lifeway.com/Article/LifeWay-Research-finds-pastors-long-work -hours-can-come-at-the-expense-of-people-ministry.
3. C. S. Lewis, *The Problem of Pain* (1940; repr., San Francisco: HarperSanFrancisco, 2001), 91.
4. U.S. Dept. of Health and Human Services (https://www.usa.gov/federal-agencies/u-s-department -of-health-and-human-services); National Center for Health Statistics (http://www.cdc.gov/nchs).
5. Ibid.
6. Gallup (http://www.gallup.com/poll/24256/families-drug-alcholo-abusers-pay-emotional-toll.aspx).
7. U.S. Dept. of Health and Human Services (https://www.usa.gov/federal-agencies/u-s-department-of -health-and-human-services); Centers for Disease Control & Prevention (http://www.cdc.gov/nchs).
8. Ibid.
9. U.S. Dept. of Health and Human Services (https://www.usa.gov/federal-agencies/u-s-department -of-health-and-human-services).
10. Ibid.
11. U.S. Dept. of Labor Statistics (https://www.bls.gov); U.S. Dept. of Health and Human Services (https://www.usa.gov/federal-agencies/u-s-department-of-health-and-human-services).
12. U.S. Dept. of Health and Human Services (https://www.usa.gov/federal-agencies/u-s-department-of -health-and-human-services); Centers for Disease Control & Prevention (http://www.cdc.gov/nchs).
13. U.S. Dept. of Health and Human Services (https://www.usa.gov/federal-agencies/u-s-department-of -health-and-human-services); National Center for Health Statistics (http://www.cdc.gov/nchs).
14. U.S. Dept. of Justice (https://www.justice.gov/); U.S. Dept. of Health and Human Services (https:// www.usa.gov/federal-agencies/u-s-department-of-health-and-human-services).

15. National Center for Health Statistics (http://www.cdc.gov/nchs).

16. U.S. Dept. of Health and Human Services (https://www.usa.gov/federal-agencies/u-s-department-of
-health-and-human-services); National Center for Health Statistics (http://www.cdc.gov/nchs).

17. U.S. Dept. of Health and Human Services (https://www.usa.gov/federal-agencies/u-s-department-of
-health-and-human-services); National Center for Health Statistics (http://www.cdc.gov/nchs).

18. U.S. Dept. of Health and Human Services (https://www.usa.gov/federal-agencies/u-s-department-of
-health-and-human-services); National Center for Health Statistics (http://www.cdc.gov/nchs).

19. U.S. Dept. of Health and Human Services (https://www.usa.gov/federal-agencies/u-s-department-of
-health-and-human-services); National Center for Health Statistics (http://www.cdc.gov/nchs).

20. U.S. Dept. of Health and Human Services (https://www.usa.gov/federal-agencies/u-s-department-of
-health-and-human-services); National Center for Health Statistics (http://www.cdc.gov/nchs); U.S.
Dept. of Justice (https://www.justice.gov/).

21. U.S. Dept. of Health and Human Services (https://www.usa.gov/federal-agencies/u-s-department-of
-health-and-human-services); National Center for Health Statistics (http://www.cdc.gov/nchs); U.S.
Dept. of Justice (https://www.justice.gov/).

22. National Center for Health Statistics (http://www.cdc.gov/nchs).

23. U.S. Dept. of Justice (https://www.justice.gov/).

24. U.S. Dept. of Justice (https://www.justice.gov/).

25. The American Institute of Stress (https://www.stress.org/).

26. Human Manifesto II, emphasis added (http://americanhumanist.org/humanism/
humanist_manifesto_ii).

CHAPTER 2

1. E. T. Scalise, "From the E-Team," *Christian Counseling Today* 21, no. 2 (2015): 4.

2. See. D. Hunt and T. A. McMahon, *The Seduction of Christianity* (Eugene, OR: Harvest House,
1985); D. Hunt, *Beyond Seduction* (Eugene, OR: Harvest House, 1986). See also M. Bobgan and
D. Bobgan, *Psychoheresy: The Psychological Seduction of Christianity* (Santa Barbara, CA: Eastgate,
1987). For examples of responses to Hunt and McMahon's views, see E. Paulk, *That the World
May Know* (Atlanta: K-Dimension, 1987), as well as R. Wise, "Speaking Out: Welcome to the
Inquisition," *Christianity Today*, May 16, 1986, 10; T. C. Muck, "Open Season," *Christianity
Today*, November 21, 1986, 16–17; W. C. Lantz, "Book Reviews—The Seduction of Christianity,"
Journal of Psychology and Christianity 5, no. 1 (1986): 55–58; and K. L. Williams, "Seduction of the
Innocents (Featured Book Review)," *Journal of Psychology and Theology* 15 (1987): 168–70.

3. James Fischer, *A Few Buttons Missing* (Philadelphia: J. B. Lippincott, 1951), 273.

4. See, e.g., D. Detwiler-Zapp and W. C. Dixon, *Lay Caregiving* (Philadelphia: Fortress, 1982); R. E.
Grantham, *Lay Shepherding: A Guide for Visiting the Sick, the Aged, the Troubled, and the Bereaved*
(Valley Forge, PA: Judson, 1980); K. C. Haugk, *Christian Caregiving—A Way of Life* (Minneapolis:
Augsburg, 1984); S. J. Menking, *Helping Laity Help Others* (Philadelphia: Westminster, 1984); A.
Schmitt and D. Schmitt, *When a Congregation Cares* (Scottdale, PA: Herald, 1984); S. Southard,
Comprehensive Pastoral Care (Valley Forge, PA: Judson, 1975); S. Southard, *Training Church Members
for Pastoral Care* (Valley Forge, PA: Judson, 1982); R. P. Stevens, *Liberating the Laity* (Downers Grove,
IL.: InterVarsity, 1985); H. W. Stone, *The Caring Church* (San Francisco: Harper & Row, 1983).

5. Stevens, *Liberating the Laity*, 26–42.

6. Ibid., 21.

7. Ibid., 29.

8. Ibid., 30, emphasis in the original.

9. Ibid., 31–32.

10. Ibid., 36–37.

11. Ibid., 41.
12. C. Peter Wagner, *Your Spiritual Gifts Can Help Your Church Grow* (Ventura, CA: Regal, 1979). See also rev. ed. (1994).
13. Ibid., 154.
14. Ibid.
15. R. K. Bufford and R. E. Buckler, "Counseling in the Church: A Proposed Strategy for Ministering to Mental Health Needs in the Church," *Journal of Psychology and Christianity* 6, no. 2 (1987): 21–29.
16. Ibid., 28.
17. See Jay Adams, *Ready to Restore: The Layman's Guide to Christian Counseling* (Grand Rapids: Baker, 1981), 4.
18. Ibid., 9.
19. J. Carter, "Adams' Theory of Nouthetic Counseling," *Journal of Psychology and Theology* 3 (1975): 143–55.
20. F. B. Minirth, *Christian Psychiatry* (Old Tappan, NJ: Revell, 1977), 37.
21. S. Grunlan and D. Lambrides, *Healing Relationships: A Christian's Manual for Lay Counseling* (Camp Hill, PA: Christian Publications, 1984).
22. G. Kittel, ed., *Theological Dictionary of the New Testament*, 10 vols. (Grand Rapids: Eerdmans, 1967).
23. Grunlan and Lambrides, *Healing Relationships*, 25.
24. Ibid., 21–23; see also H. N. Wright, *Training Christians to Counsel: A Resource Curriculum Manual* (Eugene, OR: Harvest House, 1977), 22.

CHAPTER 3

1. L. J. Crabb Jr., *Effective Biblical Counseling* (Grand Rapids: Zondervan, 1977), 31.
2. See, e.g., J. D. Carter and B. Narramore, *The Integration of Psychology and Theology: An Introduction* (Grand Rapids: Zondervan, 1979); G. R. Collins, *The Rebuilding of Psychology: An Integration of Psychology and Christianity* (Wheaton, IL.: Tyndale, 1977); G. R. Collins and H. N. Malony, *Psychology and Theology: Prospects for Integration* (Nashville: Abingdon, 1981); M. P. Cosgrove, *Psychology Gone Awry* (Grand Rapids: Zondervan, 1979); L. J. Crabb Jr., *Effective Biblical Counseling* (Grand Rapids: Zondervan, 1977); W. J. Donaldson, ed., *Research in Mental Health and Religious Behavior* (Atlanta: Psychological Studies Institute, 1976); J. H. Ellens, *God's Grace and Human Health* (Nashville: Abingdon, 1982); C. S. Evans, *Preserving the Person: A Look at the Human Sciences* (Downers Grove, IL.: InterVarsity, 1977); C. S. Evans, *Wisdom and Humanness in Psychology* (Grand Rapids: Baker, 1989). Also K. E. Farnsworth, *Wholehearted Integration: Harmonizing Psychology and Christianity through Word and Deed* (Grand Rapids: Baker, 1985); J. R. Fleck and J. D. Carter, eds., *Psychology and Christianity: Integrative Readings* (Nashville: Abingdon, 1981); M. A. Jeeves, *Psychology and Christianity: The View Both Ways* (Leicester, England: InterVarsity, 1976); S. J. Jones, ed., *Psychology and the Christian Faith* (Grand Rapids: Baker, 1986); W. K. Kilpatrick, *Psychological Seduction* (Nashville: Thomas Nelson, 1983); R. L. Koteskey, *Psychology from a Christian Perspective* (Nashville: Abingdon, 1980); H. N. Malony, ed., *Wholeness and Holiness: Readings in the Psychology/Theology of Mental Health* (Grand Rapids: Baker, 1983); J. M. McDonaugh, *Christian Psychology* (New York: Crossroad, 1982); P. D. Meier, F. B. Minirth, and F. B. Wichem, *Introduction to Psychology and Counseling: Christian Perspectives and Applications* (Grand Rapids: Baker, 1982); D. G. Myers, *The Human Puzzle: Psychological Research and Christian Belief* (New York: Harper & Row, 1978); M. S. Peck, *The Road Less Traveled: A New Psychology of Love, Traditional Values, and Spiritual Growth* (New York: Simon & Schuster, 1978); H. Vande Kemp, *Psychology and Theology in Western Thought, 1672–1965: A Historical and Annotated Bibliography*, in collaboration with H. N. Malony (Milwood, NY: Kraus International, 1984); M. S. Van Leeuwen, *The Person in Psychology: A Contemporary Christian Approach* (Grand Rapids: Eerdmans, 1985); M. S. Van Leeuwen, *The Sorcerer's Apprentice: A Christian Looks at the Changing Face of Psychology* (Downers Grove, IL:

InterVarsity, 1982); P. C. Vitz, *Psychology as Religion: The Cult of Self-Worship* (Grand Rapids: Eerdmans, 1977). More recently, see also D. W. Appleby and G. Ohlschlager, eds., *Transformative Encounters: The Intervention of God in Christian Counseling and Pastoral Care* (Downers Grove, IL: IVP Academic, 2013); J. R. Beck and B. Demarest, *The Human Person in Theology and Psychology: A Biblical Anthropology for the Twenty-First Century* (Grand Rapids: Kregel, 2015); T. Clinton, and G. Ohlschlager, eds., *Competent Christian Counseling*, vol. 1 (Colorado Springs: Waterbrook, 2002); T. Clinton, A. Hart, and G. Ohlschlager, eds., *Caring for People God's Way* (Nashville: Thomas Nelson, 2005); J. H. Coe, and T. W. Hall, *Psychology in the Spirit: Contours of a Transformational Psychology* (Downers Grove, IL: IVP Academic, 2010); G. R. Collins, *Christian Counseling: A Comprehensive Guide*, 3rd ed. (Nashville: Thomas Nelson, 2007); A. Dueck, and K. Reimer, *A Peaceable Psychology: Christian Therapy in a World of Many Cultures* (Grand Rapids: Brazos, 2009); D. N. Entwistle, *Integrative Approaches to Psychology and Christianity*, 2nd ed., (Eugene, OR: Wipf and Stock, 2010); K. S. Flanagan, and S. E. Hall, eds., *Christianity and Developmental Psychopathology: Foundations and Approaches* (Downers Grove, IL: IVP Academic, 2014); S. P. Greggo, and T. A. Sisemore, eds., *Counseling and Christianity: Five Approaches* (Downers Grove, IL: IVP Academic, 2012); R. Hawkins, and Tim Clinton, *The New Christian Counselor* (Eugene, OR: Harvest House, 2015); V. T. Holeman, *Theology for Better Counseling* (Downers Grove, IL: IVP Academic, 2012); E. L. Johnson, *Foundations for Soul Care: A Christian Psychology Proposal* (Downers Grove, IL: IVP Academic, 2007); E. L. Johnson, ed., *Psychology and Christianity: Five Views* (Downers Grove, IL: IVP Academic, 2010); I. F. Jones, *The Counsel of Heaven on Earth: Foundations for Biblical Christian Counseling* (Nashville: B&H, 2006); S. L. Jones, and R. E. Butman, *Modern Psychotherapies: A Comprehensive Christian Approach*, 2nd ed. (Downers Grove, IL: IVP Academic, 2011); M. R. McMinn, *Sin and Grace in Christian Counseling: An Integrative Paradigm* (Downers Grove, IL: IVP Academic, 2008); M. R. McMinn, *Psychology, Theology, and Spirituality in Christian Counseling* (Wheaton, IL: Tyndale, 1996); M. R. McMinn, and T. R. Phillips, eds., *Care for the Soul: Exploring the Intersection of Psychology and Theology* (Downers Grove, IL: InterVarsity, 2001); P. Moes, and D. J. Tellinghuisen, *Exploring Psychology and Christian Faith: An Introductory Guide* (Grand Rapids: Baker Academic, 2014); G. W. Moon, and D. Benner, *Spiritual Direction and the Care of Souls* (Downers Grove, IL: InterVarsity, 2004); G. L. Moriarty, ed., *Integrating Faith and Psychology: Twelve Psychologists Tell Their Stories* (Downers Grove, IL: InterVarsity, 2010); S. Muse, *When Hearts Become Flame* (Rollingsford, NH: Orthodox Research Institute, 2011); D. Powlison, *Seeing with New Eyes: Counseling and the Human Condition through the Lens of Scripture* (Phillipsburg, NJ: P&R, 2003); J. Pugh, *Christian Formation Counseling: The Work of the Spirit in the Human Race* (Mustang, OK: Tate, 2008); J. S. Ripley, and E. L. Worthington Jr., *Couple Therapy: A New Hope-Focused Approach* (Downers Grove, IL: IVP Academic, 2014); A. M. Sabates, *Social Psychology in Christian Perspective* (Downers Grove, IL: IVP Academic, 2012); F. L. Schults, and S. J. Sandage, *Transforming Spirituality: Integrating Theology and Psychology* (Grand Rapids: Baker Academic, 2006); D. H. Stevenson, B. E. Eck, and P. C. Hill, eds., *Psychology and Christianity Integration: Seminal Works That Shaped the Movement* (Batavia, IL: Christian Association for Psychological Studies, 2007); S. Y. Tan, *Counseling and Psychotherapy: A Christian Perspective* (Grand Rapids: Baker Academic, 2011); E. L. Worthington Jr., *Forgiving and Reconciling* (Downers Grove, IL: InterVarsity, 2003); E. L. Worthington Jr., *Coming to Peace with Psychology: What Christians Can Learn from Psychological Science* (Downers Grove, IL: IVP Academic, 2010); E. L. Worthington Jr., E. L. Johnson, J. N. Hook, and J. D. Aten, eds., *Evidence-Based Practices for Christian Counseling and Psychotherapy* (Downers Grove, IL: IVP Academic, 2013); M. A. Yarhouse, R. E. Butman, and B. W. McRay, *Modern Psychopathologies: A Comprehensive Christian Approach* (Downers Grove, IL: IVP Academic, 2005); M. A. Yarhouse, and J. N. Sells, *Family Therapies: A Comprehensive Christian Appraisal* (Downers Grove, IL: IVP Academic, 2008); M. A. Yarhouse, and E. S. N. Tan, *Sexuality and Sex Therapy: A Comprehensive Christian Appraisal* (Downers Grove, IL: IVP Academic, 2014).

3. See, e.g., numerous articles published in the following sources: *Journal of the American Scientific Affiliation; Journal of Psychology and Christianity* (formerly *CAPS Bulletin*); *Journal of Psychology and Theology; Christian Counseling Today; Christian Counseling Newsletter.*

4. Crabb, *Effective Biblical Counseling*, 31–56.

5. Carter and Narramore, *Integration of Psychology and Theology*, 103–15.

6. See, e.g., Ellens, *God's Grace and Human Health;* and Farnsworth, *Wholehearted Integration.*

7. Ellens, *God's Grace and Human Health*, 99.

8. For a discussion of these issues, see L. J. Crabb Jr., "Biblical Authority and Christian Psychology," *Journal of Psychology and Theology* 9 (1981): 305–11, and the following responses: G. Breshears and R. E. Larzelere, "The Authority of Scripture and the Unity of Revelation: A Response to Crabb," *Journal of Psychology and Theology* 9 (1981): 312–17; J. H. Ellens, "Biblical Authority and Christian Psychology II," *Journal of Psychology and Theology* 9 (1981): 318–25; J. D. Guy, "Affirming Diversity in the Task of Integration: A Response to 'Biblical Authority and Christian Psychology,'" *Journal of Psychology and Theology* 10 (1982): 35–39.

9. E. L. Worthington Jr., "Grace Theology" (featured review of J. H. Ellens, *God's Grace and Human Health*, Nashville: Abingdon, 1982), *Journal of Psychology and Theology* 12 (1984): 137–38.

10. See S. Y. Tan, "Lay Counseling: The Local Church," *CAPS Bulletin* 7, no. 1 (1981): 15–20, for an earlier and briefer description of the model.

11. W. Backus, *Telling the Truth to Troubled People* (Minneapolis: Bethany House, 1985); also see W. Backus and M. Chapian, *Telling Yourself the Truth* (Minneapolis: Bethany House, 1980); W. Backus and M. Chapian, *Why Do I Do What I Don't Want to Do?* (Minneapolis: Bethany House, 1984); and W. Backus, *Telling Each Other the Truth* (Minneapolis: Bethany House, 1985).

12. E. L. Worthington Jr., *When Someone Asks for Help: A Practical Guide for Counseling* (Downers Grove, IL.: InterVarsity, 1982).

13. R. R. Carkhuff, *Helping and Human Relations*, vols. 1 and 2 (New York: Holt, Rinehart and Winston, 1969); R. R. Carkhuff, *The Development of Human Resources* (New York: Holt, Rinehart and Winston, 1971); R. R. Carkhuff, *The Art of Helping* (Amherst, MA.: Human Resources Development, 1972).

14. G. Egan, *The Skilled Helper: A Systematic Approach to Effective Helping*, 3rd ed. (Monterey, CA.: Brooks/Cole, 1986).

15. See W. H. Cormier and L. S. Cormier, *Interviewing Strategies for Helpers: Fundamental Skills and Cognitive Behavioral Interventions*, 2nd ed. (Monterey, CA.: Brooks/Cole, 1985), for a good description of the major cognitive-behavioral approaches and interventions, including Aaron Beck's cognitive therapy, Albert Ellis's rational-emotive therapy, and Donald Meichenbaum's stress-inoculation training and cognitive-behavior modification. See also S. Y. Tan, "Cognitive-Behavior Therapy: A Biblical Approach and Critique," *Journal of Psychology and Theology* 15 (1987): 103–12, for a biblical or Christian perspective on cognitive-behavior therapy, and F. Craigie and S. Y. Tan, "Changing Resistant Assumptions in Christian Cognitive-Behavioral Therapy," *Journal of Psychology and Theology* 17 (1989): 93–100. More recently, see S. Y. Tan, "Use of Prayer and Scripture in Cognitive-Behavioral Therapy," *Journal of Psychology and Christianity* 26 (2007): 101–11; and S. Y. Tan, "Addressing Religion and Spirituality from a Cognitive Behavioral Perspective," in K. Pargament, A. Mahoney, and E. Shafranske, eds., *APA Handbooks in Psychology: APA Handbook of Psychology, Religion, and Spirituality*, vol. 2 (Washington, DC: American Psychological Association, 2013), 169–87.

16. H. Norman Wright, *Self-Talk, Imagery, and Prayer in Counseling* (Waco, TX.: Word, 1986).

17. See J. E. Adams, *The Christian Counselor's Manual* (Grand Rapids: Baker, 1973).

18. See Crabb, *Effective Biblical Counseling.*

19. L. J. Crabb Jr., *Understanding People: Deep Longings for Relationship* (Grand Rapids: Zondervan, 1987), 15. See also W. Kirwan, *Biblical Concepts for Christian Counseling* (Grand Rapids: Baker, 1984), 73–115, for a description of the following similar, genuine needs of human beings since

Adam fell into sin and the loss of personal identity that occurred as a consequence—the need to belong, the need for self-esteem, and the need for control.

20. See J. E. Adams, *Competent to Counsel* (Grand Rapids: Baker, 1970), and Crabb, *Effective Biblical Counseling.* There have also been a number of publications in the secular literature dealing with how moral and spiritual decay may underlie many mental-emotional problems. See, e.g., K. Menninger, *Whatever Became of Sin?* (New York: Hawthorne, 1973), and G. Wood, *The Myth of Neurosis* (New York: Harper & Row, 1986). See also A. E. Bergin, "Psychotherapy and Religious Values," *Journal of Consulting and Clinical Psychology* 48 (1980): 95–105.

21. See V. Grounds, *Emotional Problems and the Gospel* (Grand Rapids: Zondervan, 1976), 31–41, for an insightful discussion of the possibility of such anguish or deep distress experienced by Jesus as being equivalent to the emotion of anxiety or fear, and particularly the fear of death.

22. R. Foster, *Celebration of Discipline* (New York: Harper & Row, 1978), 89–91.

23. A. W. Tozer, *That Incredible Christian* (Beaverlodge, AB: Horizon House, 1977), 122, 124.

24. C. S. Lewis, *The Problem of Pain* (1940; repr., San Francisco: HarperSanFrancisco, 2001), 91.

25. S. Y. Tan, "Intrapersonal Integration: The Servant's Spirituality," *Journal of Psychology and Christianity* 6, no. 1 (1987): 34–39, p. 37. See also P. R. Welter, *Counseling and the Search for Meaning* (Waco, TX.: Word, 1987).

26. C. S. Evans, "The Blessings of Mental Anguish," *Christianity Today,* January 1986, 26–29.

27. Ibid., 29.

28. See Grounds, *Emotional Problems and the Gospel,* 105–11.

29. See Crabb, *Effective Biblical Counseling.*

30. See G. R. Collins, *How to Be a People Helper* (Santa Ana, CA.: Vision House, 1976).

31. Crabb, *Understanding People.*

32. See R. K. Bufford, *Counseling and the Demonic* (Waco, TX.: Word, 1988); K. Koch, *Christian Counseling and Occultism* (Grand Rapids: Kregel, 1972); and J. Wimber with K. Springer, *Power Healing* (New York: Harper & Row, 1987), 97–125, 230–35. See also M. I. Bubeck, *The Adversary: The Christian versus Demonic Activity* (Chicago: Moody, 1975), and *Overcoming the Adversary* (Chicago: Moody, 1984); C. F. Dickason, *Demon Possession and the Christian: A New Perspective* (Chicago: Moody, 1987); J. W. Montgomery, ed., *Demon Possession* (Minneapolis: Bethany Fellowship, 1973), and M. Shuster, *Power Pathology Paradox: The Dynamics of Evil and Good* (Grand Rapids: Zondervan, 1987).

33. See Tan, "Cognitive-Behavior Therapy: A Biblical Approach and Critique."

34. Adams, *Christian Counselor's Manual,* 409–12.

35. See A. A. Lazarus, ed., *Multimodal Behavior Therapy* (New York: Springer, 1976); A. A. Lazarus, *The Practice of Multimodal Therapy* (New York: McGraw-Hill, 1981); A. A. Lazarus, ed., *Casebook of Multimodal Therapy* (New York: Guilford, 1985).

36. Lazarus, *Practice of Multimodal Therapy,* 13–14.

37. Ibid., 4.

38. G. R. Collins, *Innovative Approaches to Counseling* (Waco, TX.: Word, 1986), 73.

39. G. R. Collins, *Effective Counseling* (Carol Stream, IL.: Creation House, 1972), 13.

40. Ibid., 13–14.

41. R. F. Hurding, *The Tree of Healing: Psychological and Biblical Foundations for Counseling and Pastoral Care* (Grand Rapids: Zondervan, 1988), 22.

42. Ibid., 24–25.

43. C. Truax and R. Carkhuff, *Toward Effective Counseling and Psychotherapy* (Chicago: Aldine, 1967).

44. See, e.g., G. Corey, *Theory and Practice of Counseling and Psychotherapy,* 3rd ed. (Monterey, CA.: Brooks/Cole, 1986); and A. Ivey and L. Simek-Downing, *Counseling and Psychotherapy: Skills, Theories, and Practice* (Englewood Cliffs, NJ: Prentice Hall, 1980).

45. Adams, *Christian Counselor's Manual,* 277–78.

46. Ibid., 4–8.

47. M. G. Gilbert and R. T. Brock, eds., *The Holy Spirit and Counseling: Theology and Theory* (Peabody, MA.: Hendrickson, 1985); and *The Holy Spirit and Counseling: Principles and Practice* (Peabody, MA: Hendrickson, 1988). See also John White, *When the Spirit Comes with Power* (Downers Grove, IL.: InterVarsity, 1988); and J. P. Ozawa, "Power Counseling: Gifts of the Holy Spirit and Counseling," and "Prayer and Deliverance in the Healing of Chronic Disorders: Hope for the Hopeless," papers presented at the International Congress on Christian Counseling, November 1988, in Atlanta, Georgia, and more recently, S. Y. Tan, "Holy Spirit: Role in Counseling," in D. G. Benner and P. Hill, eds., *Baker Encyclopedia of Psychology and Counseling*, 2nd ed. (Grand Rapids: Baker Academic, 1999), 568–69, and S. Y Tan, *Counseling and Psychotherapy: A Christian Perspective* (Grand Rapids: Baker Academic, 2011), 363–67.

48. See Adams, *Christian Counselor's Manual*; and Crabb, *Effective Biblical Counseling*.

49. See G. R. Collins and L. M. Tournquist, "Training Christian People Helpers: Observations on Counselor Education," *Journal of Psychology and Theology* 9 (1981): 69–80.

50. Crabb, *Understanding People*.

51. Ibid. See also J. E. Adams, *What to Do on Thursday: A Layman's Guide to the Practical Use of the Scriptures* (Grand Rapids: Baker, 1982); J. E. Adams, *The Use of the Scriptures in Counseling* (Grand Rapids: Baker, 1975); and W. O. Ward, *The Bible in Counseling* (Chicago: Moody, 1977). For two good books on basic principles of biblical interpretation, see G. D. Fee and D. Stuart, *How to Read the Bible for All Its Worth* (Grand Rapids: Zondervan, 1982), and H. A. Virkler, *Hermeneutics: Principles and Processes of Biblical Interpretation* (Grand Rapids: Baker, 1981).

52. See, e.g., J. E. Adams, *A Theology of Christian Counseling (More Than Redemption)* (Grand Rapids: Zondervan, 1979); D. Capps, *Biblical Approaches to Pastoral Counseling* (Philadelphia: Westminster, 1981); Crabb, *Understanding People*; W. Hulme, *Counseling and Theology* (Philadelphia: Fortress, 1967); Kirwan, *Biblical Concepts for Christian Counseling*; S. B. Narramore, *No Condemnation* (Grand Rapids: Zondervan, 1984); S. Southard, *Theology and Therapy: The Wisdom of God in a Context of Friendship* (Dallas: Word, 1989); and R. S. Anderson, *Christians Who Counsel: The Vocation of Wholistic Therapy* (Grand Rapids: Zondervan, 1990).

53. For a helpful and well-written book on such principles and strategies, see W. R. Miller and K. A. Jackson, *Practical Psychology for Pastors* (Englewood Cliffs, NJ: Prentice Hall, 1985). See also E. Kennedy, *On Becoming a Counselor: A Basic Guide for Non-Professional Counselors* (New York: Seabury, 1977).

54. See Wright, *Self-Talk, Imagery, and Prayer*; and D. Seamands, *Healing of Memories* (Wheaton, IL.: Victor, 1985).

55. See A. A. Nelson and W. P. Wilson, "The Ethics of Sharing Religious Faith in Psychotherapy," *Journal of Psychology and Theology* 12 (1984): 15–23.

56. Collins, *How to Be a People Helper*.

57. Crabb, *Effective Biblical Counseling*.

58. See J. D. Carter, "Toward a Biblical Model of Counseling," *Journal of Psychology and Theology* 8 (1980): 45–52; Narramore, *No Condemnation*; and D. C. Needham, *Birthright: Christian, Do You Know Who You Are?* (Portland, OR.: Multnomah, 1979).

59. Collins, *How to Be a People Helper*.

60. Adams, *Christian Counselor's Manual*.

61. P. D. Morris, *Love Therapy* (Wheaton, IL.: Tyndale, 1974).

62. Collins, *Effective Counseling*, 17–20.

63. Collins, *How to Be a People Helper*.

64. H. H. Strupp and S. W. Hadley, "Specific vs. Non-specific Factors in Psychotherapy: A Controlled Study of Outcome," *Archives of General Psychiatry* 36 (1979): 1125–36.

65. B. Gomes-Schwartz, "Effective Ingredients in Psychotherapy: Prediction of Outcome from Process Variables," *Journal of Consulting and Clinical Psychology* 46 (1978): 1023–35, p. 1032.

66. Carkhuff, *Development of Human Resources*, 170–71.

67. Adams, *Christian Counselor's Manual*.

68. See L. Smedes, *Forgive and Forget: Healing the Hurts We Don't Deserve* (New York: Pocket Books, 1984); and R. P. Walters, *Forgive and Be Free: Healing the Wounds of Past and Present* (Grand Rapids: Zondervan, 1983).

69. See Carkhuff, *Helping and Human Relations*; Carkhuff, *Development of Human Resources*; and Egan, *Skilled Helper*.

70. See Crabb, *Effective Biblical Counseling*; and L. J. Crabb Jr., "Biblical Counseling: A Basic View," *CAPS Bulletin* 4 (1978): 1–6. See also Crabb, *Understanding People*, and Kirwan, *Biblical Concepts for Christian Counseling*, for further insights into how to understand and help people at deeper levels, including unconscious processes.

71. H. N. Wright, *Training Christians to Counsel: A Resource Curriculum Manual* (Eugene, OR.: Harvest House, 1977), 22.

72. J. Carter, "Adams' Theory of Nouthetic Counseling," *Journal of Psychology and Theology* 3 (1975): 143–55.

73. See D. E. Carlson, "Jesus' Style of Relating: The Search for a Biblical View of Counseling," *Journal of Psychology and Theology* 4 (1976): 181–92.

74. Wright, *Self-Talk, Imagery, and Prayer*.

75. Backus, *Telling the Truth to Troubled People*. See also M. R. McMinn, *Cognitive Therapy Techniques in Christian Counseling* (Dallas: Word, 2008).

76. J. Beck, *Cognitive Behavior Therapy: Basics and Beyond*, 2nd ed. (New York: Guilford, 2011); S. Cormier, P. S. Nurius, and C. Osborn, *Interviewing and Change Strategies for Helpers: Fundamental Skills and Cognitive Behavioral Interventions*, 6th ed. (Belmont, CA: Brooks/Cole, 2009); M. G. Craske, *Cognitive-Behavioral Therapy* (Washington, DC: American Psychological Association, 2010); R. L. Leahy, *Cognitive Therapy Techniques: A Practitioner's Guide* (New York: Guilford, 2003). See also D. Greenberger and C. A. Padesky, *Mind over Mood*, 2nd ed. (New York: Guilford, 2015); and J. Riggenbach, *The CBT Toolbox* (Eau Claire, WI: Premier, 2012).

77. Tan, "Cognitive-Behavior Therapy," 108–9.

78. G. R. Collins, ed., *Helping People Grow: Practical Approaches to Christian Counseling* (Santa Ana, CA: Vision House, 1980), 342.

79. D. W. Sue and D. Sue, *Counseling the Culturally Diverse: Theory and Practice*, 7th ed. (Hoboken, NJ: Wiley, 2016). See also L. Comas-Dias and E. E. H. Griffith, eds., *Clinical Guidelines in Cross-Cultural Mental Health* (New York: Wiley, 1988), and M. McGoldrick, J. Giordano, and N. Garcia-Preto, eds., *Ethnicity and Family Therapy*, 3rd ed. (New York: Guilford, 2005).

80. D. Hesselgrave, *Counseling Cross-Culturally* (Grand Rapids: Baker, 1984); D. Augsburger, *Pastoral Counseling across Cultures* (Philadelphia: Westminster, 1986). See also C. R. Ridley, "Cross-Cultural Counseling in Theological Context," *Journal of Psychology and Theology* 14 (1986): 288–97; J. M. Uomoto, "Delivering Mental Health Services to Ethnic Minorities: Ethical Considerations," *Journal of Psychology and Theology* 14 (1986): 15–21; S. Y. Tan, "Psychopathology and Culture: The Asian-American Context," *Journal of Psychology and Christianity* 8, no. 2 (1989): 69–80; and S. Y. Tan, "Cultural Issues in Spirit-Filled Psychotherapy," *Journal of Psychology and Christianity* 18 (1999): 164–76; and S. Y. Tan and N. J. Dong, "Psychotherapy with Members of Asian American Churches and Spiritual Traditions," in P. S. Richards and A. E. Bergin, eds., *Handbook of Psychotherapy and Religious Diversity*, 2nd ed. (Washington, DC: American Psychological Association, 2014), 423–50.

81. S. Y. Tan and E. T. Scalise, "On Belay: The Role of the Church in Lay Helping Ministry," *Christian Counseling Today* 21, no. 2 (2015): 46–50. See also E. T. Scalise, *Lifeline Training Manual* (Lynchburg, VA: Blue Ridge Community Church, 2015).

82. J. S. Prater, "Training Christian Lay Counselors in Techniques of Prevention and Outreach," *Journal of Psychology and Christianity* 6, no. 2 (1987): 30–34.

83. G. R. Collins, "Psychology Is Not a Panacea but . . ." *Christianity Today*, November 16, 1979, 22–25, p. 25.

84. Scalise, *Lifeline Training Manual*.

85. See Collins, *How to Be a People Helper*, 108–15; and S. Grunlan and D. Lambrides, *Healing Relationships* (Camp Hill, PA: Christian Publications, 1984), 14.

86. W. B. Oglesby Jr., *Referrals in Pastoral Counseling*, rev. ed. (Nashville: Abingdon, 1978).

87. Collins, *How to Be a People Helper*, 113.

88. See A. E. Bergin and M. J. Lambert, "The Evaluation of Therapeutic Outcomes," in S. L. Garfield and A. E. Bergin, eds., *Handbook of Psychotherapy and Behavior Change*, 2nd ed. (New York: Wiley, 1978), 139–89.

CHAPTER 4

1. This chapter serves as an updated version of the literature review provided in S. Y. Tan, "Lay Counseling: The Local Church," *CAPS Bulletin* 7, no. 1 (1981): 15–20, and in S. Y. Tan, "Lay Christian Counseling: Present Status and Future Directions," invited paper presented at the International Congress on Christian Counseling, Lay Counseling Track, November 1988, in Atlanta, Georgia, and more recently in S. Y. Tan, "Lay Christian Counseling for General Psychological Problems," in E. L. Worthington Jr., E. L. Johnson, J. N. Hook, and J. D. Aten, eds., *Evidence-Based Practices for Christian Counseling and Psychotherapy* (Downers Grove, IL: IVP Academic, 2013), 40–58.

2. See Joint Commission on Mental Illness and Health, *Action for Mental Health* (New York: Science Editions, 1961).

3. G. Gurin, J. Veroff, and S. Feld, *Americans View Their Mental Health* (New York: Basic Books, 1960), 341.

4. See J. Veroff, R. A. Kulka, and E. Douvan, *Mental Health in America: Patterns of Help-Seeking from 1957 to 1976* (New York: Basic Books, 1981). See also R. Swindle, K. Heller, B. Pescosolido, and S. Kilkuzawa, "Responses to Nervous Breakdowns in America Over a 40-Year Period: Mental Health Policy Implications," *American Psychologist* 55 (2000): 740–49. They reported, "Between 1957 and 1996, participants increased their use of informal supports, decreased their use of physicians, and increased their use of nonmedical mental health professionals" (p. 740).

5. M. L. Gross, *The Psychological Society* (New York: Random House, 1978).

6. See A. E. Bergin and M. J. Lambert, "The Evaluation of Therapeutic Outcomes," in S. L. Garfield and A. E. Bergin, eds., *Handbook of Psychotherapy and Behavior Change*, 2nd ed. (New York: Wiley, 1978), 139–89.

7. Ibid., 150.

8. E. G. Poser, "The Effect of Therapists' Training on Group Therapeutic Outcome," *Journal of Consulting Psychology* 30 (1966): 283–89.

9. R. R. Carkhuff and C. B. Truax, "Lay Mental Health Counseling: The Effects of Lay Group Counseling," *Journal of Consulting Psychology* 29 (1965): 426–31.

10. J. A. Durlak, "Comparative Effectiveness of Paraprofessional and Professional Helpers," *Psychological Bulletin* 86 (1979): 80–92.

11. See Poser, "Effect of Therapists' Training."

12. See M. J. Rioch, "Changing Concepts in the Training of Psychotherapists," *Journal of Consulting Psychology* 30 (1966): 290–92.

13. H. H. Strupp and S. W. Hadley, "Specific vs. Nonspecific Factors in Psychotherapy: A Controlled Study of Outcome," *Archives of General Psychiatry* 36 (1979): 1125–36.

14. Durlak, "Comparative Effectiveness of Paraprofessional and Professional Helpers," 80.

15. See, e.g., N. T. Nietzel and S. G. Fisher, "Effectiveness of Professional and Paraprofessional Helpers: A Comment on Durlak," *Psychological Bulletin* 89 (1981): 555–65; J. A. Durlak, "Evaluating Comparative Studies of Paraprofessional and Professional Helpers: A Reply to Nietzel and Fisher," *Psychological Bulletin* 89 (1981): 566–69; A. Hattie, C. F. Sharpley, and H. J. Rogers, "Comparative

Effectiveness of Professional and Paraprofessional Helpers," *Psychological Bulletin* 95 (1984): 534–41; J. S. Berman and N. C. Norton, "Does Professional Training Make a Therapist More Effective?" *Psychological Bulletin* 98 (1985): 401–7. For other reviews of the research literature with similar conclusions, see R. P. Lorion and J. Cahill, "Paraprofessional Effectiveness in Mental Health: Issues and Outcomes," *Paraprofessional Journal* 1, no. 1 (1980): 12–38; and D. M. Stein and M. J. Lambert, "On the Relationship between Therapist Experiences and Psychotherapy Outcome," *Clinical Psychology Review* 4 (1984): 1–16.

16. See Berman and Norton, "Does Professional Training Make a Therapist More Effective?" 407.

17. J. Matarazzo, "Comment on Licensing," *A.P.A. Monitor* 10 (September–October 1979): 36.

18. J. D. Frank, *Persuasion and Healing*, 2nd ed. (New York: Schocken, 1974), 167.

19. See M. J. Lambert, D. A. Shapiro, and A. E. Bergin, "The Effectiveness of Psychotherapy," in S. L. Garfield and A. E. Bergin, eds., *Handbook of Psychotherapy and Behavior Change*, 3rd ed. (New York: Wiley, 1986), 157–211, p. 175.

20. See R. P. Lorion and R. D. Felner, "Research on Mental Health Interventions with the Disadvantaged," in S. L. Garfield and A. E. Bergin, eds., *Handbook of Psychotherapy and Behavior Change*, 3rd ed. (New York: Wiley, 1986), 739–75, p. 763.

21. See S. Bergin, "Therapy: Beyond 'Warm Fuzziness,'" *Psychology Today*, April 1988, 14.

22. See M. P. Carey and T. G. Burish, "Providing Relaxation Training to Cancer Chemotherapy Patients: A Comparison of Three Delivery Techniques," *Journal of Consulting and Clinical Psychology* 55 (1987): 732–37.

23. See D. M. Stein and M. J. Lambert, "Graduate Training in Psychotherapy: Are Therapy Outcomes Enhanced?" *Journal of Consulting and Clinical Psychology* 63 (1995): 182–96.

24. See P. C. Kendall et al., "Cognitive-Behavioral Treatment of Conduct-Disordered Children," *Cognitive Therapy and Research* 14 (1990): 279–97; and J. I. Bright, K. D. Baker, and R. A. Neimeyer, "Professional and Paraprofessional Group Treatments for Depression: A Comparison of Cognitive-Behavioral and Mutual Support Interventions," *Journal of Consulting and Clinical Psychology* 67 (1999): 491–501.

25. See D. Barlow, "Psychological Treatments," *American Psychologist* 59 (2004): 869–78.

26. See D. C. Atkins and A. Christensen, "Is Professional Training Worth the Bother? A Review of the Impact of Psychotherapy Training on Client Outcome," *Australian Psychologist* 36 (2001): 122–31; L. Bickman, "Practice Makes Perfect and Other Myths about Mental Health Services," *American Psychologist* 54 (1999): 965–78; A. Christensen and N. Jacobson, "Who (or What) Can Do Psychotherapy: The Status and Challenge of Nonprofessional Therapies," *Psychological Science* 6 (1994): 8–14; Tan, *Counseling and Psychotherapy*, 399–400; S. Y. Tan, "Lay Christian Counseling for General Psychological Problems," in E. L. Worthington Jr., E. L. Johnson, J. N. Hook, and J. D. Aten, eds., *Evidence-Based Practices for Christian Counseling and Psychotherapy* (Downers Grove: IL: IVP Academic, 2013), 40–58; and S. Y. Tan, "Lay Helping: The Whole Church in Soul-Care Ministry," in T. Clinton and G. Ohlschlager, eds., *Competent Christian Counseling* (Colorado Springs: WaterBrook, 2002), 424–26, 759–62.

27. See B. S. Ali, M. H. Rahbar, S. Naeem, and A. Gul, "The Effectiveness of Counseling on Anxiety and Depression by Minimally Trained Counselors: A Randomized Controlled Trial," *American Journal of Psychotherapy* 57 (2003): 324–36; F. Neuner et al., "Treatment of Posttraumatic Stress Disorder by Trained Lay Counselors in an African Refugee Settlement: A Randomized Controlled Trial," *Journal of Consulting and Clinical Psychology* 76 (2008): 686–94; S. Dewing et al., "Lay Counselors' Ability to Deliver Counseling for Behavior Change," *Journal of Consulting and Psychology* 87 (2014): 19–29.

28. B. Zilbergeld, *The Shrinking of America: Myths of Psychological Change* (Boston: Little, Brown, 1983).

29. See S. L. Garfield, "Effectiveness of Psychotherapy: The Perennial Controversy," *Professional Psychology: Research and Practice* 14 (1983): 35–43.

30. See L. Prioleau, M. Murdock, and N. Brody, "An Analysis of Psychotherapy versus Placebo Studies," *Behavioral and Brain Sciences* 6 (1983): 275–310; and a "Continuing Commentary" on this article published in *Behavioral and Brain Sciences* 7 (1984): 756–62. See also *Journal of Consulting and Clinical Psychology* 51 (1983): 3–74 (special section: "Meta-Analysis and Psychotherapy"); J. S. Searles, "A Methodological and Empirical Critique of Psychotherapy Outcome Meta-Analysis," *Behavior Research and Therapy* 23 (1985): 453–63; and D. A. Shapiro, "Recent Applications of Meta-Analysis in Clinical Research," *Clinical Psychology Review* 5 (1985): 13–34.

31. See M. L. Smith, G. V. Glass, and T. I. Miller, *The Benefits of Psychotherapy* (Baltimore: Johns Hopkins University Press, 1980).

32. See S. J. Rachman and G. T. Wilson, *The Effects of Psychological Therapy*, 2nd enl. ed. (New York: Pergamon, 1980).

33. S. L. Garfield, *Psychotherapy: An Eclectic Approach* (New York: Wiley, 1980).

34. See M. J. Lambert and B. M. Ogles, "The Efficacy and Effectiveness of Psychotherapy," in M. J. Lambert, ed., Bergin and Garfield's *Handbook of Psychotherapy and Behavior Change*, 5th ed. (New York: Wiley, 2001), 139–93; see also M. J. Lambert, "The Efficacy and Effectiveness of Psychotherapy," in M. J. Lambert, ed., Bergin and Garfield's *Handbook of Psychotherapy and Behavior Change*, 6th ed. (New York: Wiley, 2013), 169–218; S. Y. Tan, *Counseling and Psychotherapy: A Christian Perspective* (Grand Rapids: Baker Academic, 2011), 389–400.

35. See S. J. Korchin, *Modern Clinical Psychology* (New York: Basic Books, 1976), 519–21.

36. F. Reissman, "The 'Helper Therapy' Principle," *Social Work* 10 (1965): 27–32.

37. Korchin, *Modern Clinical Psychology*, 530–33.

38. See, e.g., A. E. Bergin and M. J. Lambert, "The Evaluation of Therapeutic Outcomes," in D. Mays and C. M. Franks, eds., *Negative Outcome in Psychotherapy and What to Do about It* (New York: Springer, 1985); H. H. Strupp, S. W. Hadley, and B. Gomes-Schwartz, *Psychotherapy for Better or for Worse: An Analysis of the Problem of Negative Effects* (New York: Jason Aaronson, 1977).

39. Korchin, *Modern Clinical Psychology*, 523–28. See also introduction, n. 6.

40. See E. L. Cowen, M. A. Trost, D. A. Dorr, R. P. Lorion, L. D. Izzo, and R. V. Isaacson, *New Ways in School Mental Health: Early Detection and Prevention of School Maladaptation* (New York: Human Sciences, 1975).

41. Korchin, *Modern Clinical Psychology*, 528–29; for two well-known models or programs for training lay counselors, see R. R. Carkhuff, *Helping and Human Relations*, vols. 1 and 2 (New York: Holt, Rinehart and Winston, 1969); G. Egan, *The Skilled Helper*, 3rd ed. (Monterey, CA.: Brooks/Cole, 1986).

42. See, e.g., Adams, *Competent to Counsel*; M. Bobgan and D. Bobgan, *The Psychological Way/The Spiritual Way* (Minneapolis: Bethany House, 1979); *How to Counsel from Scripture* (Chicago: Moody, 1985).

43. See P. D. Morris, *Love Therapy* (Wheaton, IL: Tyndale House, 1974).

44. J. E. Adams, *The Christian Counselor's Manual* (Grand Rapids: Baker, 1973).

45. O. H. Mowrer, *The Crisis in Psychiatry and Religion* (Princeton, NJ: D. Van Nostrand, 1961), 60.

46. O. H. Mower, "Sin, the Lesser of Two Evils," *American Psychologist* 15 (1960), 301–4.

47. Adams, *Competent to Counsel and Christian Counselor's Manual*. See also J. E. Adams, *Ready to Restore* (Grand Rapids: Baker, 1981). More recently, Adams's nouthetic counseling approach has been refined and updated in books on biblical counseling, such as: L. Cozzi, *The Love of God in Biblical Counseling* (Bloomington, IN: WestBow Press, 2016); H. Eyrich and W. Hines, *Caring for the Heart: A Model for Christian Counseling* (Ross-shire, UK: Christian Focus Publications, 2002) B. Kellemen, and K. Carson, eds., *Biblical Counseling and the Church* (Grand Rapids: Zondervan, 2015); B. Kellemen, and J. Forrey, eds., *Scripture and Counseling* (Grand Rapids: Zondervan, 2014); R. W. Kellemen, *Equipping Counselors for Your Church* (Phillipsburg, NJ: P&R, 2011); R. W. Kellemen, *Gospel-Centered Counseling: How Christ Changes Lives* (Grand Rapids: Zondervan, 2014); R. W. Kellemen, *Gospel Conversations: How to Care Like Christ* (Grand Rapids: Zondervan, 2015);

H. Lambert, *The Biblical Counseling Movement after Adams* (Wheaton, IL: Crossway, 2012); H. Lambert, *A Theology of Biblical Counseling: The Doctrinal Foundations of Counseling Ministry* (Grand Rapids: Zondervan, 2016); J. MacDonald, B. Kellemen, and S. Viars, eds., *Christ-Centered Biblical Counseling: Changing Lives with God's Changeless Truth* (Eugene, OR: Harvest House, 2013); D. Powlison, *Seeing with New Eyes: Counseling and the Human Condition through the Lens of Scripture* (Phillipsburg, NJ: P&R, 2003); D. Powlison, *The Biblical Counseling Movement: History and Context* (Greensboro, NC: New Growth, 2010).

48. G. R. Collins, *How to Be a People Helper* (Santa Ana, CA: Vision House, 1976), and G. R. Collins, *People Helper Growthbook* (Santa Ana, CA: Vision House, 1976).

49. G. R. Collins, *Christian Counseling: A Comprehensive Guide* (Waco, TX: Word, 1980). A revised edition was published in 1988, and a third edition in 2007.

50. G. R. Collins, ed., *Helping People Grow: Practical Approaches to Christian Counseling* (Santa Ana, CA.: Vision House, 1980).

51. Collins, *Innovative Approaches to Counseling* (Waco, TX.: Word, 1986).

52. L. J. Crabb Jr., *Basic Principles of Biblical Counseling* (Grand Rapids: Zondervan, 1975), and L. J. Crabb Jr., *Effective Biblical Counseling* (Grand Rapids: Zondervan, 1977). See also L. J. Crabb Jr. and D. B. Allender, *Encouragement: The Key to Caring* (Grand Rapids: Zondervan, 1984); L. J. Crabb Jr., *Understanding People: Deep Longings for Relationship* (Grand Rapids: Zondervan, 1987), and L. J. Crabb Jr., *Inside Out* (Colorado Springs: NavPress, 1988).

53. N. T. Anderson, *Discipleship Counseling: The Complete Guide to Helping Others Walk in Freedom and Grow in Christ* (Ventura, CA: Regal, 2003); W. V. Arnold and M. A. Fohl, *Christians and the Art of Caring* (Philadelphia: Westminster, 1988); W. Backus, *Telling the Truth to Troubled People* (Minneapolis: Bethany House, 1985); C. L. Baldwin, *Friendship Counseling: Biblical Foundations for Helping Others* (Grand Rapids: Zondervan, 1988); M. Bobgan and D. Bobgan, *How to Counsel from Scripture* (Chicago: Moody, 1985); D. Buchanan, *The Counseling of Jesus* (Downers Grove, IL: InterVarsity, 1985); S. O. Cha, *Developing Restorative Connections: A Workbook for Lay Counselors and Community Builders* (San Bernardino, CA: Life Note Press, 2014); T. Clinton and P. Springle, *Coffee Cup Counseling* (Forest, VA: AACC Press, 2015); J. W. Drakeford, *People to People Therapy* (New York: Harper & Row, 1978); J. W. Drakeford and Claude V. King, *Wise Counsel: Skills for Lay Counseling* (Nashville: Sunday School Board of the Southern Baptist Convention, 1988); T. Foster, *Called to Counsel* (Nashville: Oliver Nelson, 1986); S. Grunlan and D. Lambrides, *Healing Relationships* (Camp Hill, PA: Christian Publications, 1984); K. C. Haugk, *Christian Caregiving* (Minneapolis: Augsburg, 1984); S. Hughes, *A Friend in Need* (Eastbourne, England: Kingsway, 1982); R. W. Kellemen, *Equipping Counselors in Your Church* (Phillipsburg, NJ: P&R, 2011); K. Lampe, *The Caring Congregation: How to Become One and Why It Matters* (Nashville: Abingdon Press, 2011); K. Lampe, *The Caring Congregation: Training Manual and Resource Guide* (Nashville: Abingdon Press, 2014); I. Lim and S. Lim, *Comfort My People: Christian Counseling—A Lay Challenge* (Singapore: Methodist Book Room, 1988). Also S. E. Lindquist, *Action Helping Skills* (Fresno, CA: Link-Care Foundation, 1976); P. M. Miller, *Peer Counseling in the Church* (Scottdale, PA: Herald, 1978); Morris, *Love Therapy*; E. Peterson, *Who Cares? A Handbook of Christian Counseling* (Wilton, CN: Morehouse-Barlow, 1980); H. Sala, *Coffee Cup Counseling: How to Be Ready When Friends Ask for Help* (Nashville: Thomas Nelson, 1989); J. Sandford and P. Sandford, *The Transformation of the Inner Man* (Tulsa: Victory House, 1982); A. Schmitt and D. Schmitt, *When a Congregation Cares* (Scottdale, PA: Herald, 1984); E. M. Smith, *Healing Life's Deepest Hurts* (Ann Arbor, MI: Vine, 2002), and E. M. Smith, *Theophostic Prayer Ministry: Basic Training Seminar Manual* (Campbellsville, KY: New Creation, 2007); C. R. Solomon, *Counseling with the Mind of Christ* (Old Tappan, NJ: Revell, 1977); R. B. Somerville, *Help for Hotliners: A Manual for Christian Telephone Crisis Counselors* (Phillipsburg, NJ: Presbyterian and Reformed, 1978); M. J. Steinbron, *Can the Pastor Do It Alone? A Model for Preparing Lay People for Lay Pastoring* (Ventura,

CA: Regal, 1987). Also J. Sturkie and G. R. Bear, *Christian Peer Counseling: Love in Action* (Waco, TX: Word, 1989); S. Y. Tan, *Lay Counseling: Equipping Christians for a Helping Ministry* (Grand Rapids: Zondervan, 1991); B. B. Varenhorst with L. Sparks, *Training Teenagers for Peer Ministry* (Loveland, CO: Group, 1988); R. P. Walters, *The Amity Book: Exercises in Friendship Skills* (Grand Rapids: Christian Helpers, 1983); W. O. Ward, *The Bible in Counseling* (Chicago: Moody, 1977); E. T. Welch, *Side by Side: Walking with Others in Wisdom and Love* (Wheaton, IL: Crossway, 2015); P. Welter, *How to Help a Friend* (Wheaton, IL: Tyndale, 1978); P. Welter, *Connecting with a Friend: Eighteen Proven Counseling Skills to Help You Help Others* (Wheaton, IL: Tyndale, 1985); E. L. Worthington Jr., *When Someone Asks for Help: A Practical Guide for Counseling* (Downers Grove, IL: InterVarsity, 1982); E. L. Worthington Jr., *How to Help the Hurting: When Friends Face Problems with Self-Esteem, Self-Control, Fear, Depression, Loneliness* (Downers Grove, IL: InterVarsity, 1985); H. N. Wright, *Training Christians to Counsel* (Eugene, OR: Harvest House, 1977).

54. See, e.g., volumes in the *Resources for Christian Counseling* series (Dallas: Word), G. R. Collins, gen. ed.; and G. R. Collins, *Helping People Grow*. Also, for a comprehensive review and critique of both secular and Christian counseling approaches, see R. F. Hurding, *The Tree of Healing: Psychological and Biblical Foundations for Counseling and Pastoral Care* (Grand Rapids: Zondervan, 1988), published in Great Britain as *Roots and Shoots: A Guide to Counseling and Psychotherapy*; and S. Y. Tan, *Counseling and Psychotherapy: A Christian Perspective* (Grand Rapids: Baker Academic, 2011).See also S. P. Greggo and T. A. Sisemore, eds., *Counseling and Christianity: Five Approaches* (Downers Grove, IL: IVP Academic, 2012), and R. Hawkins and T. Clinton, *The New Christian Counselor* (Eugene, OR: Harvest House Publishers, 2015).

55. See, e.g., W. W. Becker, "A Delivery System within the Church: The Professional Consultant and the Laity," *CAPS Bulletin* 7, no. 4 (1981): 15–18; D. M. Boan and T. Owens, "Peer Ratings of Lay Counselor Skill as Related to Client Satisfaction," *Journal of Psychology and Christianity* 4, no. 1 (1985): 79–81; G. L. Cerling, "Selection of Lay Counselors for a Church Counseling Center," *Journal of Psychology and Christianity* 2, no. 3 (1983): 67–72; G. R. Collins, "Lay Counseling within the Local Church," *Leadership* 1 (1980): 78–86; J. Harris, "Nonprofessionals as Effective Helpers for Pastoral Counselors," *Journal of Pastoral Care* 39, no. 2 (1985): 165–72; H. C. Lukens Jr., "Training Paraprofessional Christian Counselors: A Survey Conducted," *Journal of Psychology and Christianity* 2, no. 1 (1983): 51–61; H. C. Lukens Jr., "Training of Paraprofessional Christian Counselors: A Model Proposed," *Journal of Psychology and Christianity* 2, no. 3 (1983): 61–66. Also E. B. Osborn, "Training Paraprofessional Family Therapists in a Christian Setting," *Journal of Psychology and Christianity* 2, no. 2 (1983): 56–61; R. C. Richard and D. A. Flakoll, "Christian Counseling Centers: Two Effective Models," *CAPS Bulletin* 7, no. 4 (1981): 12–15; R. C. Richard and D. A. Flakoll, "Integration in Action: The Use of Lay Counselors," *Theology News and Notes* 21, no. 4 (1975): 14–16. Also S. Y. Tan, "Lay Counseling: The Local Church," *CAPS Bulletin* 7, no. 1 (1981): 15–20; S. Y. Tan, "Training Paraprofessional Christian Counselors," *Journal of Pastoral Care* 40, no. 4 (1986): 296–304; S. Y. Tan, "Training Lay Christian Counselors: A Basic Program and Some Preliminary Data," *Journal of Psychology and Christianity* 6, no. 2 (1987): 57–61; S. Y. Tan, "Care and Counseling in the 'New Church Movement,'" *Theology, News and Notes* 33, no. 4 (1986): 9–11, 21; S. Y. Tan, "Lay Counseling (An Interview)," *Christian Journal of Psychology and Counseling* 4, no. 2 (1989): 1–5; S. Y. Tan, "Lay Christian Counseling: The Next Decade," *Journal of Psychology and Christianity* 9, no. 3 (1990): 59–65; S. Y. Tan, "Religious Values and Interventions in Lay Christian Counseling," *Journal of Psychology and Christianity* 10, no. 2 (1991): 173–82; More recently, see F. Garzon and K. Tilley, "Do Lay Christian Counseling Approaches Work? What We Currently Know," *Journal of Psychology and Christianity* 28 (2009): 130–40; F. Garzon, E. L. Worthington Jr., S. Y. Tan, and R. K. Worthington, "Lay Christian Counseling and Client Expectations for Integration in Therapy," *Journal of Psychology and Christianity* 28 (2009): 113–20; Y. M. Toh, S. Y. Tan, C. D. Osburn, and D. E. Faber, "The Evaluation of a Church-Based Lay Counseling Program:

Some Preliminary Data," *Journal of Psychology and Christianity* 13 (1994): 270–75; Y. M. Toh and S. Y. Tan, "The Effectiveness of Church-Based Lay Counselors: A Controlled Outcome Study," *Journal of Psychology and Christianity* 16 (1997): 260–67.

56. *Journal of Psychology and Christianity* 6, no. 2 (1987): 1–84, on "Lay Christian Counseling," S. Y. Tan, guest ed.

57. Collins, *People Helper Growthbook*, 7.

58. Tan, "Training Paraprofessional Christian Counselors," and Tan, "Training Lay Christian Counselors: A Basic Program and Some Preliminary Data."

59. See S. Y. Tan and P. Sarff, "Comprehensive Evaluation of a Lay Counselor Training Program in a Local Church," invited paper presented at the International Congress on Christian Counseling, Lay Counseling Track, November 1988, in Atlanta, Georgia.

60. See C. A. Schaefer, L. Dodds, and S. Y. Tan, "Changes in Attitudes toward Peer Counseling and Personal Orientation Measured during Growth Facilitator Training for Cross-Cultural Ministry," unpublished manuscript, 1988.

61. Boan and Owens, "Peer Ratings of Lay Counselor Skill."

62. P. R. Welter, "Training Retirement Center and Nursing Home Staff and Residents in Helping and Counseling Skills," *Journal of Psychology and Christianity* 6, no. 2 (1987): 45–56.

63. R. Jernigan, S. Y. Tan, and R. L. Gorsuch, "The Effectiveness of a Local Church Lay Christian Counselor Training Program: A Controlled Study," paper presented at the International Congress on Christian Counseling, Lay Counseling Track, November 1988, in Atlanta, Georgia.

64. Richard and Flakoll, "Christian Counseling Centers: Two Effective Models," 14.

65. J. Corcoran, "Effectiveness of Paraprofessional Counselors at a Community Counseling Center: The Client's Perspective," unpublished manuscript, 1979.

66. B. Cuvelier, "A Needs Assessment and Evaluation Plan of Lay Counselors for New Directions Counseling Center," unpublished manuscript, 1980.

67. J. Harris, "Non-professionals as Effective Helpers for Pastoral Counselors," *Journal of Pastoral Care* 39, no. 2 (1985): 165–72.

68. R. P. Walters, "A Survey of Client Satisfaction in a Lay Counseling Program," *Journal of Psychology and Christianity* 6, no. 2 (1987): 62–69.

69. Toh, Tan, Osburn, and Faber, "Evaluation of a Church-Based Lay Counseling Program."

70. Toh and Tan, "Effectiveness of Church-Based Lay Counselors."

71. J. N. Hook, E. L. Worthington Jr., D. E. Davis, D. J. Jennings II, A. L. Gartner, and J. P. Hook, "Empirically Supported Religious and Spiritual Therapies," *Journal of Clinical Psychology* 66 (2010): 46–72.

72. Garzon and Tilley, "Do Lay Christian Counseling Approaches Work? What We Currently Know."

73. See E. L. Worthington Jr., "Religious Counseling: A Review of Published Empirical Research," *Journal of Counseling and Development* 64 (1986): 421–31, and note 7.

74. Collins, *Innovative Approaches to Counseling* (Waco, TX: Word, 1986), 178.

75. M. McMinn, W. Hathaway, S. Woods, and K. Snow, "What American Psychological Association Leaders Have to Say about Psychology of Religion and Spirituality," *Psychology of Religion and Spirituality* 1 (2009): 3–13.

76. M. K. Briggs, and D. Rayle, "Incorporating Spirituality into Care Counseling Courses: Ideas for Classroom Application," *Counseling and Values* 50 (2005): 63–75; J. S. Young, M. Wiggins-Frame, and C. S. Cashwell, "Spirituality and Counselor Competence: A National Survey of American Counseling Association Members," *Journal of Counseling and Development* 85 (2007): 47–53.

77. R. A. Dobmeier, and S. M. Reiner, "Spirituality in Counselor Education Curriculum: A National Survey of Student Perceptions," *Counseling and Values* 57 (2012): 47–65.

78. M. L. O'Reilly, "Spirituality in Mental Health Clients," *Journal of Psychosocial Nursing and Mental Health Services* 42 (2004): 44–53.

79. G. W. Fairholm, *Capturing the Heart of Leadership: Spirituality and Community in the New American Workplace* (Westport, CN: Praeger, 1997).

80. Ibid; T. Gall, C. Charbonneau, N. H. Clarke, K. Grant, A. Joseph, and L. Shouldice, "Understanding the Nature and Role of Spirituality in Relation to Coping and Health: A Conceptual Framework," *Canadian Psychology* 46 (2005): 88–104.

81. I. I. Mitroff, and E. A. Denton, *A Spiritual Guide of Corporate America: A Hard Look at Spirituality, Religion, and Values in the Workplace* (San Francisco: Jossey-Bass, 1999).

82. M. Lerner, *Spirit Matters: Global Healing and the Wisdom of the Soul* (Charlottesville, VA: Hampton Roads, 2000).

83. D. A. Helminiak, "Treating Spiritual Issues in Secular Psychotherapy," *Counseling and Values* 45 (2011): 163–89.

84. D. R. Bidwell, "Developing an Adequate 'Pneumatraumatology': Understanding the Spiritual Impacts of Traumatic Injury," *Journal of Pastoral Care and Counseling* 56 (2002): 135–43.

85. O'Reilly, "Spirituality in Mental Health Clients," 37.

86. L. M. Nichols, and B. Hunt, "The Significance of Spirituality for Individuals with Chronic Illness: Implications for Mental Health Counseling," *Journal of Mental Health Counseling* 33 (2011): 51–66.

87. A. Narayanasamy, "Spiritual Coping Mechanisms in Chronic Illness: A Qualitative Study," *Journal of Clinical Nursing* 12 (2004): 116–17.

88. N. F. Glover-Graf, I. Marini, J. Baker, and T. Buck, "Religious and Spiritual Beliefs and Practices of Persons with Chronic Pain," *Rehabilitation Counseling Bulletin* 51 (2007): 21–33.

89. A. Heinz, D. H. Epstein, and K. L. Preston, "Spiritual/Religious Experiences and In-Treatment Outcome in an Inner-City Program for Heroin and Cocaine Dependence," *Journal of Psychoactive Drugs* 39 (2007): 41–49.

90. R. D. Fallot, "Spirituality and Religion in Psychiatric Rehabilitation and Recovery from Mental Illness," *International Review of Psychiatry* 13 (2007): 110–16.

91. C. Gregory, "The Effect of Psychologist's Disclosure of Personal Religious Background on Prospective Clients," *Mental Health, Religion & Culture* 11 (2008): 369–73.

92. R. Saenz, and M. Waldo, "Client's Preferences Regarding Prayer during Counseling," *Psychology of Religion and Spirituality* 5 (2013): 325–34.

93. H. G. Koenig, "Religion, Spirituality and Medicine: Application to Spiritual Practice," *Journal of the American Medical Association* 284 (2000): 1708.

94. M. Baetz, D. B. Larson, G. Marcoux, R. Bowen, and R. Griffin, "Canadian Psychiatric Inpatient Religious Commitment: An Association with Mental Health," *Canadian Journal of Psychiatry* 47 (2002): 159–65.

95. C. A. Lietz, and D. R. Hodge, "Incorporating Spirituality into Substance Abuse Counseling: Examining the Perspectives of Service Recipients and Providers," *Journal of Social Research* 39 (2013): 498–510.

96. W. B. Johnson, R. Devries, C. R. Ridley, D. Pettorini, and D. R. Peterson, "The Comparative Efficacy of Christian and Secular Rational-Emotive Therapy with Christian Clients," *Journal of Psychology and Theology* 22 (1994): 130–40.

97. P. S. Mueller, D. J. Plevak, and T. A. Rummans, "Religious Involvement, Spirituality and Medicine: Implications for Clinical Practice," *Mayo Clinic Proceedings* 76 (2001): 1225–35.

98. S. Kliewer, "Allowing Spirituality into the Healing Process," *Journal of Family Practice* 53 (2004): 22–31.

99. W. R. Miller, C. E. Thoresen, "Spirituality, Religion, and Health: An Emerging Research Field," *American Psychologist* 58 (2003): 24–35.

100. J. S. Ripley, E. L. Worthington, E. B. Davis, C. Leon, J. W. Berry, A. Smith, and T. Sierra, "Efficacy of Religion-Accommodative Strategic Hope-Focused Theory Applied to Couples Therapy," *Couple and Family Psychology: Research and Practice* 3 (2014): 83–98.

101. D. B. Larson, and S. S. Larson, "Spirituality's Potential Relevance to Physical and Emotional Health: A Brief Review of Quantitative Research," *Journal of Psychology and Theology* 31 (2003): 37–51.

102. M. E. McCullough, W. T. Hoyt, D. B. Larson, H. G. Koenig, and C. E. Thoresen, "Religious Involvement and Mortality: A Meta-analytic Review," *Health Psychology* 19 (2000): 211–22.

103. M. W. Parker, "Soldier and Family Wellness across the Life Course: A Developmental Model of Successful Aging, Spirituality, and Health Promotion, Part I," *Military Medicine* 166 (2001A): 485–90.

104. L. Tepper, S. A. Rogers, E. M. Coleman, and H. N. Malony, "The Prevalence of Religious Coping among Persons with Persistent Mental Illness," *Psychiatric Services* 52 (2001): 660–65.

105. M. Baetz, D. B. Larson, G. Marcoux, R. Bowen, and R. Griffin, "Canadian Psychiatric Inpatient Religious Commitment: An Association with Mental Health"; G. Fitchett, L. A. Burton, and A. B. Sivan, "The Religious Needs and Resources of Psychiatric Inpatients," *Journal of Nervous and Mental Disease* 185 (1997): 320–26; K. S. Kendler, C. O. Gardner, and C. A. Prescott, "Religion, Psychopathology, and Substance Use and Abuse: A Multimeasure, Genetic-Epidemiologic Study," *American Journal of Psychiatry* 154 (1997): 322–29; A. Shaw, S. Joseph, and P. A. Linley, "Religion, Spirituality, and Posttraumatic Growth: A Systematic Review," *Mental Health, Religion & Culture* 8 (2005): 1–11.

106. M. E. McCullough, and D. B. Larson, "Religion and Depression: A Review of the Literature," *Twin Research* 2 (1999): 126–36.

107. R. L. Propst, R. Ostrom, P. Watkins, T. Dean, and D. Masburn, "Comparative Efficacy of Religious and Nonreligious Cognitive-Behavioral Therapy for the Treatment of Clinical Depression in Religious Individuals," *Journal of Consulting and Clinical Psychology* 60 (1992): 94–103.

108. G. W. Comstock, and K. B. Partridge, "Church Attendance and Health," *Journal of Chronic Disease* 25 (1972): 665–72.

109. P. A. Nisbet, P. R. Duberstein, C. Yeates, and L. Seidlitz, "The Effects of Participation in Religious Activities on Suicide versus Natural Deaths in Adults 50 and Older," *Journal of Nervous and Mental Disease* 188 (2000): 543–46.

110. H. G. Koenig, M. McCullough, and D. Larson, *Handbook of Religion and Health* (New York: Oxford University Press, 2001).

111. Larson and Larson, "Spirituality's Potential Relevance to Physical and Emotional Health"; D. Rasic, S. Belik, B. Elias, L. Katz, and J. Sareen, "Spirituality, Religion and Suicidal Behavior in a Nationally Representative Sample," *Journal of Affective Disorders* 114 (2001): 32–40.

112. Larson and Larson, "Spirituality's Potential Relevance to Physical and Emotional Health."

113. D. R. Hodge, "Spirituality and People with Mental Illness: Developing Spiritual Competency in Assessment and Intervention," *Families in Society* 85 (2004): 38.

114. R. L. Steen, D. Engels, and W. T. Thweatt, "Ethical Aspects of Spirituality in Counseling," *Counseling and Values* 50 (2006): 108–11.

115. D. R. Hodge, "Developing Cultural Competency with Evangelical Christians," *Families in Society* 85 (2004): 251–62.

116. J. Q. Morrison, S. M. Clutter, E. M. Pritchett, and A. Demmitt, "Perceptions of Clients and Counseling Professionals Regarding Spirituality in Counseling," *Counseling and Values* 53 (2009): 183–94; E. M. Rose, J. S. Westefeld, and T. N. Ansley, "Spiritual Issues in Counseling: Clients' Beliefs and Preferences," *Journal of Counseling Psychology* 48 (2001): 61–71.

117. C. V. Witvliet, K. A. Phipps, M. E. Feldman, and J. C. Beckham, "Posttraumatic Mental and Physical Health Correlates of Forgiveness and Religious Coping in Military Veterans," *Journal of Traumatic Stress* 17 (2005): 269–73.

118. A. Fontana and R. Rosenheck, "The Role of Meaning in the Pursuit of Treatment for Posttraumatic Stress Disorder," *Journal of Traumatic Stress* 18 (2005): 133–36.

119. A. J. Weaver, H. G. Koenig, and F. M. Ochberg, "Posttraumatic Stress, Mental Health Professionals, and the Clergy: A Need for Collaboration, Training, and Research," *Journal of Traumatic Stress* 9 (2006): 847–56.

120. D. S. Charney, "In Session with Dennis S. Charney, MD: Resilience to Stress," *Primary Psychiatry* 13 (2006): 39–41; Y. Y. Chen, and H. G. Koenig, "Traumatic Stress and Religion:

Is There a Relationship? A Review of Empirical Findings," *Journal of Religion and Health* 45 (2006): 371–81.

121. A. Fontana, and R. Rosenheck, "Trauma, Change in Strength of Religious Faith, and Mental Health Service among Veterans Treated for PTSD," *Journal of Nervous and Mental Disease* 192 (2004): 579–84.

122. J. A. Sigmund, "Spirituality and Trauma: The Role of Clergy in the Treatment of Posttraumatic Stress Disorder," *Journal of Religion and Health* 42 (2003): 221–29; A. J. Weaver, H. G. Koenig, and F. M. Ochberg, "Posttraumatic Stress, Mental Health Professionals, and the Clergy: A Need for Collaboration, Training, and Research."

123. M. T. Burke, H. Hackney, P. Hudson, J. Miranti, G. A. Watts, and L. Epp, "Spirituality, Religion, and CACREP Curriculum Standards," *Journal of Counseling & Development* 77 (1999): 252–57; D. L. Schulte, T. A. Skinner, and C. D. Claiborn, "Religious and Spiritual Issues in Counseling Psychology Training," *The Counseling Psychologist* 30 (2002): 118–34.

124. W. B. Johnson, C. R. Ridley, and S. L. Nielsen, "Religiously Sensitive Rational Emotive Behavior Therapy: Elegant Solutions and Ethical Risks," *Professional Psychology: Research and Practice* 31 (2000): 14–20.

125. K. L. Pargament, H. G. Koenig, N. Tarakeshwar, and J. Hahn, "Religious Struggle as a Predictor of Mortality among Medically Ill Elderly Patients: A Two-Year Longitudinal Study," *Archives of Internal Medicine* 57 (2001): 1881–85.

126. D. F. Walker, R. L. Gorsuch, and S. Y. Tan, "Therapists' Use of Religious and Spiritual Interventions in Christian Counseling: A Preliminary Report," *Counseling and Values* 49 (2005): 107–19.

127. W. L. Hathaway, S. Y. Scott, and S. A. Garver, "Assessing Religious/Spiritual Functioning: A Neglected Domain in Clinical Practice?" *Professional Psychology: Research and Practice* 35 (2004): 97.

128. J. Shifrin, "The Faith Community as a Support for People with Mental Illness," in R. D. Fallot, ed., *Spirituality and Religion in Recovery from Mental Illness* (San Francisco: Jossey-Bass, 1998), 69–81.

129. R. L. Steen, D. Engels, and W. T. Thweatt, "Ethical Aspects of Spirituality in Counseling," *Counseling and Values* 50 (2006): 109.

130. Dobmeier and Reiner, "Spirituality in Counselor Education Curriculum," *Counseling and Values* 57 (2012): 47–65.

131. W. B. Hagedorn, and D. Gutierrez, "Integration versus Segregation: Applications of the Spiritual Competencies in Counselor Education Programs," *Counseling and Values* 54 (2009): 32–47.

132. R. D. Fallot, "Spirituality and Religion in Psychiatric Rehabilitation and Recovery from Mental Illness," *International Review of Psychiatry* 13 (2001): 110–16; S. M. Hage, A. Hopson, M. Siegel, G. Payton, and E. Defanti, "Multicultural Training in Spirituality: An Interdisciplinary Review," *Counseling and Values* 50 (2006): 217–34; D. R. Hodge, "Spiritually Modified Cognitive Therapy: A Review of the Literature," *Social Work* 51 (2006): 157–66; Koenig, McCullough, and Larson, *Handbook of Religion and Health*; D. B. Larson, and S. S. Larson, "Spirituality's Potential Relevance to Physical and Emotional Health: A Brief Review of Quantitative Research."

133. Koenig, McCullough, and Larson, *Handbook of Religion and Health*.

134. P. C. Hill, and K. I. Pargament, "Advances in the Conceptualization and Measurement of Religion and Spirituality: Implications for Physical and Mental Health Research," *American Psychologist* 58 (2003): 64–74.

135. M. K. Briggs and D. Rayle, "Incorporating Spirituality into Care Counseling Courses: Ideas for Classroom Application," *Counseling and Values* 50 (2005): 63–75; Walker, Gorsuch, and Tan, "Therapists' Use of Religious and Spiritual Interventions in Christian Counseling"; C. R. Hall, W. A. Dixon, and E. D. Mauzey, "Spirituality and Religion: Implications for Counselors," *Journal of Counseling and Development* 82 (2004): 504–7; W. A. Grams, T. S. Carlson, and C. R. McGeorge, "Integrating Spirituality into Family Therapy Training: An Exploration of Faculty Members' Beliefs," *Contemporary Family Therapy* 29 (2007): 147–61.

136. Hodge, "Developing Cultural Competency with Evangelical Christians."

137. P. Gilligan, and S. Furness, "The Role of Religion and Spirituality in Social Work Practice: Views and Experiences of Social Work Students," *British Journal of Social Work* 36 (2006): 617–37.

138. Young, Wiggins-Frame, and Cashwell, "Spirituality and Counselor Competence."

139. S. M. Hage, A. Hopson, M. Siegel, G. Payton, and F. Defanti, "Multicultural Training in Spirituality: An Interdisciplinary Review," *Counseling and Values* 50 (2006): 217–34.

140. Kliewer, "Allowing Spirituality into the Healing Process."

141. Joint Commission on Accreditation of Healthcare Organizations, "Spiritual Assessment." Standards—Frequently Asked Questions, accessed April 5, 2010, www.jacho.org/standard/pharmfaq_mpfrm.html.

142. Hage, Hopson, Siegel, Payton, and Defanti, "Multicultural Training in Spirituality: An Interdisciplinary Review."

143. Kliewer, "Allowing Spirituality into the Healing Process."

144. L. D. Furman, D. Perry, and T. Goldale, "Interaction of Evangelical Christians and Social Workers in the Rural Environment," *Human Services in the Rural Environment* 19 (1996): 5–8.

145. Young, Wiggins-Frame, and Cashwell, "Spirituality and Counselor Competence."

146. Hagedorn and Gutierrez, "Integration versus Segregation: Applications of the Spiritual Competencies in Counselor Education Programs."

147. Dobmeier and Reiner, "Spirituality in Counselor Education Curriculum."

148. B. M. Shaw, H. Bayne, and S. Lorelle, "A Constructivist Perspective for Integrating Spirituality into Counselor Training," *Counselor Education and Supervision* 51 (2012): 270–80.

149. G. Corey, M. Corey, and P. Callanan, *Issues & Ethics in the Helping Professions*, 8th ed. (Pacific Grove, CA: Brooks/Cole, 2011).

150. T. C. Oden, N. C. Warren, K. B. Mulholland, C. R. Schoonhoven, C. H. Kraft, and W. Walker, *After Therapy What? Lay Therapeutic Resources in Religious Perspective* (Springfield, IL: Charles C. Thomas, 1974).

151. J. E. Adams, *Competent to Counsel* (Grand Rapids: Baker, 1970).

152. For an incisive theological, philosophical, and ethical analysis and critique of several secular modern psychologies, with relevance to Christian counseling approaches as well, see D. S. Browning, *Religious Thought and the Modern Psychologies* (Philadelphia: Fortress, 1987). See also Hurding, *The Tree of Healing*, and Tan, *Counseling and Psychotherapy*.

CHAPTER 5

1. For further information about the Stephen Series, contact: Stephen Ministries, 8016 Dale, St. Louis, MO 63117 (Tel. 314–645–5511). See also K. C. Haugk, *Christian Caregiving* (Minneapolis: Augsburg, 1984).

2. F. Garzon, E. L. Worthington, S. Y. Tan, and R. K. Worthington, "Lay Christian Counseling and Client Expectations for Integration in Therapy."

3. For copies of helpful manuals on policies and procedures, write to the following two churches that have set up formal lay counseling centers: Lay Counseling Center, Arcadia Presbyterian Church, 121 Alice Street, Arcadia, CA 91006; and Counseling Resource Center of First Presbyterian Church, 1820 15th Street, Boulder, CO 80302. There will be a charge for the manuals.

4. See G. R. Collins, "Lay Counseling within the Local Church," *Leadership* 1 (1980): 78–86, in which several of the steps mentioned in this chapter were first suggested.

5. Trevor J. Partridge, "Ten Considerations in Establishing a Christian Counselling Centre," *The Christian Counselor's Journal* 4, no. 4 (1983): 31–33. For more information on the establishment of professional counseling centers, see John C. Carr, John E. Hinkle, and David M. Moss III, eds., *The Organization and Administration of Pastoral Counseling Centers* (Nashville: Abingdon, 1981); and H. Wahking, "A Church-Related Professional Counseling Service," *Journal of Psychology and Christianity* 3, no. 3 (1984): 58–64. See also T. J. Sandbeck and H. N. Malony, "The Church Counseling Center: A Modern Expression of an Ancient Profession," *CAPS Bulletin* 7, no. 4 (1981):

9–12; and R. C. Richard and D. A. Flakoll, "Christian Counseling Centers: Two Effective Models," *CAPS Bulletin* 7, no. 4 (1981): 12–15.

6. For a helpful book on the subject of malpractice as related to the church and clergy, see H. Newton Malony, Thomas L. Needham, and Samuel Southard, *Clergy Malpractice* (Philadelphia: Westminster, 1986). See also R. K. Sanders, ed., *Christian Counseling Ethics: A Handbook for Psychologists, Therapists and Pastors*, 2nd ed. (Downers Grove, IL: IVP Academic, 2013); and J. L. Sandy, *Church Lay Counseling Risk Management Guidebook* (Fort Wayne, IN: Brotherhood Mutual Insurance Company, 2009).

CHAPTER 6

1. See L. E. Hart and G. D. King, "Selection versus Training in the Development of Paraprofessionals," *Journal of Counseling Psychology* 26 (1979): 235–41, p. 236.

2. See I. N. Sandler, "Characteristics of Women Working as Child Aides in a School-Based Preventive Mental Health Program," *Journal of Consulting and Clinical Psychology* 39 (1972): 56–61.

3. See Hart and King, "Selection versus Training," 236.

4. R. R. Carkhuff, *Helping and Human Relations: A Primer for Lay and Professional Helpers* (vols. 1, 2) (New York: Holt, Rinehart and Winston, 1969).

5. See Hart and King, "Selection versus Training," 239.

6. See G. Goodman, *Companionship Therapy: Studies in Structured Intimacy* (San Francisco: Jossey-Bass, 1972).

7. D. Dooley, "Selecting Nonprofessional Counselor Trainees with the Group Assessment of Interpersonal Traits (GAIT)," *American Journal of Community Psychology* 3 (1975): 371–83, p. 372.

8. Ibid., 371, 379–80.

9. G. L. Cerling, "Selection of Lay Counselors for a Church Counseling Center," *Journal of Psychology and Christianity* 2, no. 3 (1983): 67–72.

10. Ibid., 68. See also G. Egan, *The Skilled Helper* (Monterey, CA: Brooks/Cole, 1975), 22–24.

11. Ibid., 69. See also P. Miller, *Peer Counseling in the Church* (Scottdale, PA: Herald, 1978).

12. Ibid., 69.

13. Ibid., 71; reprinted by permission.

14. S. Y. Tan, "Care and Counseling in the 'New Church Movement,'" *Theology, News and Notes* 33, no. 4 (1986): 9–11, 21, p. 11.

15. See G. R. Collins, "Lay Counseling within the Local Church," *Leadership* 1 (1980): 81.

16. See R. L. Bassett, R. D. Sadler, E. E. Kobishen, D. M. Skiff, I. J. Merrill, B. J. Atwater, and P. W. Livermore, "The Shepherd Scale: Separating the Sheep from the Goats," *Journal of Psychology and Theology* 9 (1981): 335–51; C. W. Ellison, "Spiritual Well-Being: Conceptualization and Measurement," *Journal of Psychology and Theology* 11 (1983): 330–40; P. F. Schmidt, *Manual for Use of the Character Assessment Scale*, 2nd ed. (Shelbyville, KY: Institute for Character Development, 1983); C. Peter Wagner, *Wagner-Modified Houts Questionnaire for Discovering Your Spiritual Gifts* (Pasadena, CA: Fuller Evangelistic Association, 1989); D. L. Wayman, "A Spiritual Life Check-Up," *Leadership* 4, no. 4 (1983): 88–92; F. B. Wichern, *Spiritual Leadership Qualities Inventory* (Richardson, TX: Believer Renewal Resources, 1980), and *The Spiritual Leadership Qualities Inventory Instruction Manual* (Richardson, TX: Believer Renewal Ministries, 1980), with *Scoring Sheets* and *Scoring Key*; and J. S. Townsend II and F. B. Wichern, "The Development of the Spiritual Leadership Qualities Inventory," *Journal of Psychology and Theology* 12 (1984): 305–13.

17. See Bassett et al., "The Shepherd Scale," 349.

18. Ibid., 350.

19. See Ellison, "Spiritual Well-Being," 340.

20. Ibid., 332.

21. See Schmidt, *Manual for Use of the Character Assessment Scale*; and J. H. Elzerman and M. J.

Boivin, "The Assessment of Christian Maturity, Personality, and Psychopathology among College Students," *Journal of Psychology and Christianity* 6, no. 3 (1987): 50–64, esp. 53–54.

22. See Wagner, *Wagner-Modified Houts Questionnaire*, 3, 13.

23. Ibid., 14–17.

24. See Wayman, "Spiritual Life Check-Up," 90–92.

25. See Wichern, *Spiritual Leadership Qualities Inventory Instruction Manual*, 2–4, and app. D, 14ff.

26. For other examples of measures of different dimensions of spirituality, see R. E. Butman, "The Assessment of Spiritual and Psychological Well-Being," paper presented at the National Convention of the Christian Association for Psychological Studies (CAPS), April 1987, in Memphis, Tennessee (available from the author, who is a faculty member of the Psychology Department of Wheaton College, Wheaton, IL 60187), as well as R. E. Butman, "The Assessment of Religious Development: Some Possible Options," *Journal of Psychology and Christianity* 9, no. 2 (1990): 14–26; and D. E. Smith, "The Christian Life Assessment Scales: Christian Self-Perception," *Journal of Psychology and Christianity* 5, no. 3 (1986): 46–61. See also: P. C. Hill and R. W. Hood Jr., eds., *Measures of Religiosity* (Birmingham: Religious Education, 1999).

27. See *La Canada Presbyterian Church Lay Counseling Ministry Information Packet*, available from Chuck Osburn, DMin, Lay Counseling Ministry Coordinator, La Canada Presbyterian Church, 626 Foothill Boulevard, La Canada, CA 91011.

28. Some useful books for this purpose of equipping all the saints for the basic ministry of caring or encouraging one another include G. R. Collins, *The Joy of Caring* (Waco, TX: Word, 1980): L. J. Crabb Jr., and D. Allender, *Encouragement: The Key to Caring* (Grand Rapids: Zondervan, 1984); K. C. Haugk, *Christian Caregiving* (Minneapolis: Augsburg, 1984); M. Slater, *Stretcher Bearers* (Ventura, CA: Regal, 1985).

29. G. R. Sweeten, "Lay Helpers and the Caring Community," *Journal of Psychology and Christianity* 6, no. 2 (1987): 14–20, p. 14.

30. See Wayman, "Spiritual Life Check-Up."

CHAPTER 7

1. See A. Hattie, C. F. Sharpley, and H. J. Rogers, "Comparative Effectiveness of Professional and Paraprofessional Helpers," *Psychological Bulletin* 95 (1984): 534–41, who concluded that paraprofessionals or lay counselors show greater therapeutic effectiveness the longer their training or the more experienced they are. However, see also J. S. Berman and Norton, "Does Professional Training Make a Therapist More Effective?" *Psychological Bulletin* 98 (1985): 401–7, who found that extensive preparation (training) or prior experience with the counseling task or frequent supervision by a professional were factors that could not account for the lack of difference in therapeutic effectiveness between professionals and paraprofessionals or lay counselors. Further clarification of the role of training and supervision, as well as experience, on the therapeutic effectiveness of lay counselors is therefore needed. See also A. M. Graziano and J. N. Katz, "Training Paraprofessionals," in A. S. Bellack, M. Hersen, and A. E. Kazdin, eds., *International Handbook of Behavior Modification and Therapy* (New York: Plenum, 1982), 207–29.

2. Series on "Training to Competence in Psychotherapy," *Journal of Consulting and Clinical Psychology* 56 (1988): 651–709.

3. See F. B. Shaw and K. S. Dobson, "Competency Judgments in the Training and Evaluation of Psychotherapists,"

4. G. R. Collins, "Lay Counseling within the Local Church," *Leadership* 1 (1980): 78–86.

5. See S. Y. Tan, "Lay Christian Counseling: Present Status and Future Directions," invited paper presented at the International Congress on Christian Counseling, Lay Counseling Track, November 1988, in Atlanta, Georgia.

6. See L. J. Crabb Jr., "Biblical Counseling" in G. R. Collins, *Helping People Grow* (Santa Ana, CA: Vision House, 1980), 165–85; and L. J. Crabb Jr., *Effective Biblical Counseling* (Grand Rapids: Zondervan, 1977).

7. L. J. Crabb Jr., and D. Allender, *Encouragement: The Key to Caring* (Grand Rapids: Zondervan, 1984).

8. G. R. Sweeten, "Lay Helpers and the Caring Community," *Journal of Psychology and Christianity* 6, no. 2 (1987): 14–20. Dr. Sweeten's training materials can be obtained by contacting Equipping Ministries International, P.O. Box 62837, Cincinnati, OH 45262–0837 (Tel. 800-364-4769).

9. H. C. Lukens, "Training of Paraprofessional Christian Counselors: A Model Proposed," *Journal of Psychology and Christianity* 2, no. 3 (1983): 61–66. He proposed this model after conducting a survey of Christian counseling and training programs, and finding that only eight out of seventy-seven programs provided training at the lay or paraprofessional level, with the length of training clustering between five months and two years. Few areas of consistency were found with regard to the nature and goals of training, the selection of lay counselors, the skills and knowledge taught, the length of training, the qualifications of the supervisors, the nature or type of supervision, and the criteria used for evaluating quality of training. See Lukens, "Training Paraprofessional Christian Counselors: A Survey Conducted," *Journal of Psychology and Christianity* 2, no. 1 (1983): 51–61.

10. William H. Cormier and L. Sherilyn Cormier, *Interviewing Strategies for Helpers: A Guide to Assessment, Treatment, and Evaluation* (Monterey, CA: Brooks/Cole, 1979), *and Interviewing Strategies for Helpers: Fundamental Skills and Cognitive Behavioral Interventions* (Monterey, CA: Brooks/Cole, 1985). See also S. Cormier, P. S. Nurius, and C. J. Osborn, *Interviewing and Change Strategies for Helpers*, 8th ed. (Belmont, CA: Brooks/Cole, 2016). For a Christian faith-based approach to counseling skills training, see E. A. N. Spanotto, H. D. Gingrich, and F. C. Gingrich's *Skills for Effective Counseling: A Faith-Based Approach* (Downers Grove, IL: IVP Academic, 2016).

11. See, e.g., D. Detwiler-Zapp and W. C. Dixon, *Lay Caregiving* (Philadelphia: Fortress, 1982); R. E. Grantham, *Lay Shepherding: A Guide for Visiting the Sick, the Aged, the Troubled, and the Bereaved* (Valley Forge, PA: Judson, 1980); K. C. Haugk, *Christian Caregiving—A Way of Life* (Minneapolis: Augsburg, 1984); K. Lampe, *The Caring Congregation: How to Become One and Why It Matters* (Nashville: Abingdon Press, 2011); K. Lampe, *The Caring Congregation: Training Manual and Resource Guide* (Nashville: Abingdon Press, 2014); S. J. Menking, *Helping Laity Help Others* (Philadelphia: Westminster, 1984); A. Schmitt and D. Schmitt, *When a Congregation Cares* (Scottdale, PA: Herald, 1984); S. Southard, *Comprehensive Pastoral Care* (Valley Forge, PA: Judson, 1975); S. Southard, *Training Church Members for Pastoral Care* (Valley Forge, PA: Judson, 1982); R. P. Stevens, *Liberating the Laity* (Downers Grove, IL: InterVarsity, 1985); and H. W. Stone, *The Caring Church* (San Francisco: Harper & Row, 1983). See also K. C. Haugk and W. J. McKay, *Christian Caregiving—A Way of Life*, Leaders Guide (Minneapolis: Augsburg, 1986).

12. See L. J. Crabb Jr., *Effective Biblical Counseling* and *Basic Principles of Biblical Counseling* (Grand Rapids: Zondervan, 1975). See also L. J. Crabb Jr. and D. B. Allender, *Encouragement: The Key to Caring* (Grand Rapids: Zondervan, 1984); L. J. Crabb, *Understanding People: Deep Longings for Relationship* (Grand Rapids: Zondervan, 1987); and L. J. Crabb, *Inside Out* (Colorado Springs: NavPress, 1988).

13. G. R. Collins, *How to Be a People Helper* and *People Helper Growthbook* (Santa Ana, CA: Vision House, 1976).

14. G. R. Collins, *Christian Counseling: A Comprehensive Guide*, rev. ed. (Dallas: Word, 1988), and *Christian Counseling: A Comprehensive Guide*, 3rd ed. (Nashville: Thomas Nelson, 2007).

15. See J. E. Adams, *Competent to Counsel* (Grand Rapids: Baker, 1970), and *The Christian Counselor's Manual* (Grand Rapids: Baker, 1973).

16. See W. Backus, *Telling the Truth to Troubled People* (Minneapolis: Bethany House, 1985). See also W. Backus and M. Chapian, *Telling Yourself the Truth* (Minneapolis: Bethany House, 1980);

W. Backus and M. Chapian, *Why Do I Do What I Don't Want to Do?* (Minneapolis: Bethany House, 1984); W. Backus, *Telling Each Other the Truth* (Minneapolis: Bethany House, 1985); and W. Backus, "A Counseling Center Staffed by Trained Christian Lay Persons," *Journal of Psychology and Christianity* 6, no. 2 (1987): 39–44.

17. See C. R. Solomon, *Handbook to Happiness* (Wheaton, IL: Tyndale, 1975), and *Counseling with the Mind of Christ* (Old Tappan, NJ: Revell, 1977).

18. R. W. Kellemen, *Equipping Counselors for Your Church: The 4E Ministry Training Strategy* (Phillipsburg, NJ: P&R, 2011). See also R. W. Kellemen, *Gospel-Centered Counseling: How Christ Changes Lives* (Grand Rapids: Zondervan, 2014) and *Gospel Conversations: How to Care Like Christ* (Grand Rapids: Zondervan, 2015).

19. See chap. 4, n. 53.

20. L. M. Brammer, *The Helping Relationship* (Englewood Cliffs, NJ: Prentice Hall, 1973); R. Carkhuff, *The Art of Helping* (Amherst, MA: Human Resources Development, 1972); G. Egan, *The Skilled Helper*, 3rd ed. (Monterey, CA: Brooks/Cole, 1986); and Cormier and Cormier, *Interviewing Strategies for Helpers*.

21. Welter, "Training Retirement Center and Nursing Home Staff and Residents in Helping and Counseling Skills," *Journal of Psychology and Christianity* 6, no. 2 (1987): 45–56.

22. See P. Welter, *How to Help a Friend* (Wheaton, IL: Tyndale, 1978); P. Welter, *Connecting with a Friend* (Wheaton, IL: Tyndale, 1985); P. Welter, *The Nursing Home: A Caring Community, A Guide for Staff and Residents* (Valley Forge, PA: Judson, 1981); and P. Welter, *The Nursing Home: A Caring Community, Trainer's Manual* (Valley Forge, PA: Judson, 1981).

23. E. Osborn, "Training Paraprofessional Family Therapists in a Christian Setting," *Journal of Psychology and Christianity* 2, no. 2 (1983): 56–61.

24. See S. Minuchin, *Families and Family Therapy* (Cambridge, MA: Harvard University Press, 1974); V. Satir and M. Baldwin, *Satir Step by Step* (Palo Alto, CA: Science and Behavior Books, 1983); G. R. Patterson, *Families* (Champaign, IL: Research, 1977); V. D. Foley, "Family Therapy," in R. Corsini, ed., *Current Psychotherapies* (Itasca, IL: F. E. Peacock, 1979). See also H. A. Liddle, R. Schwartz, and D. Breunlin, eds., *Family Therapy Training* (New York: Guilford, 1985). More recently, see J. S. Ripley and E. L. Worthington Jr., *Couple Therapy: A New Hope-Focused Approach* (Downers Grove, IL: IVP Academic, 2014); and M. A. Yarhouse and J. N. Sells, *Family Therapies: A Comprehensive Christian Appraisal* (Downers Grove, IL: IVP Academic, 2008).

25. J. S. Prater, "Training Christian Lay Counselors in Techniques of Prevention and Outreach," *Journal of Psychology and Christianity* 6, no. 2 (1987): 30–34.

26. See S. Y. Tan, "Training Lay Christian Counselors: A Basic Program and Some Preliminary Data," *Journal of Psychology and Christianity* 6, no. 2 (1987): 57–61.

27. See S. Y. Tan, "Training Paraprofessional Christian Counselors," *Journal of Pastoral Care* 40, no. 4 (1986): 296–304.

28. See chap. 4, nn. 58–59.

29. R. E. Coleman, *The Master Plan of Evangelism*, 2nd ed. abr. (Grand Rapids: Revell, 2010).

CHAPTER 8

1. See C. Loganbill, E. Hardy, and U. Delworth, "Supervision: A Conceptual Model," *The Counseling Psychologist* 10, no. 1 (1982): 3–42, p. 14.

2. See M. O. Wiley, "Developmental Counseling Supervision: Person-Environment Congruency, Satisfaction, and Learning." Paper presented at the Annual Convention of the American Psychological Convention, August 1982, in Washington, DC.

3. For an example of a predoctoral internship training program in a Christian context, see S. Y. Tan, "Internship Training and Supervision in The Psychological Center at Fuller Theological

Seminary." Invited paper presented at the International Congress on Christian Counseling, Clinical Supervision Track, November 11, 1988, in Atlanta, Georgia.

4. For some helpful books on clinical supervision, see R. Ekstein and R. Wallerstein, *The Teaching and Learning of Psychotherapy*, 2nd ed. (New York: International Universities Press, 1972); G. M. Hart, *The Process of Clinical Supervision* (Baltimore: University Park Press, 1982); A. K. Hess, ed., *Psychotherapy Supervision: Theory, Research, and Practice* (New York: Wiley, 1980); F. E. Kaslow, ed., *Supervision, Consultation, and Staff Training in the Helping Professions* (San Francisco: Jossey-Bass, 1977); A. Robbins, *Between Therapists: The Processing of Transference/Countertransference Material* (New York: Human Sciences, 1988); and C. D. Stoltenberg and U. Delworth, *Supervising Counselors and Therapists: A Developmental Approach* (San Francisco: Jossey-Bass, 1987). For another book on clinical supervision written from the special perspective of pastoral counseling, see B. K. Estadt Jr., J. Compton, and M. C. Blanchette, *The Art of Clinical Supervision: A Pastoral Counseling Perspective* (New York: Paulist, 1987). For more recent books on clinical supervision, see J. M. Bernard and R. K. Goodyear, *Fundamentals of Clinical Supervision*, 5th ed. (New York: Pearson, 2013); R. I. Cohen, *Clinical Supervision: What to Do and How to Do It* (Belmont, CA: Brooks/Cole, 2004); C. A. Falender and E. P. Shafranske, *Clinical Supervision: A Competency-Based Approach* (Washington, DC: American Psychological Association, 2004); C. A. Falender and E. P. Shafranske, *Casebook for Clinical Supervision: A Competency-Based Approach* (Washington, DC: American Psychological Association, 2008); C. A. Falender and E. P. Shafranske, *Multiculturalism and Diversity in Clinical Supervision: A Competency-Based Approach* (Washington, DC: American Psychological Association, 2014); and A. K. Hess, K. D. Hess, and T. H. Hess, eds., *Psychotherapy Supervision: Theory, Research and Practice*, 2nd ed. (Hoboken, NJ: Wiley, 2008). A number of helpful journals on clinical supervision are also available, including *Counselor Education and Supervision* and *The Clinical Supervisor*, as well as a specifically Christian ministry–oriented one called the *Journal of Supervision and Training in Ministry*.

5. See Special Issues on "Supervision in Counseling I," *The Counseling Psychologist* 10, no. 1 (1982): 1–96; and "Supervision in Counseling II," *The Counseling Psychologist* 1, no. 1 (1983): 1–112; and Special Series on "Advances in Psychotherapy Supervision," *Professional Psychology: Research and Practice* 18 (1987): 187–259.

6. Series on "Training to Competency in Psychotherapy," *Journal of Consulting and Clinical Psychology* 56 (1988): 651–709.

7. See R. K. Russell, A. M. Crimmings, and R. W. Lent, "Counselor Training and Supervision: Theory and Research," in S. D. Brown and R. W. Lent, eds., *Handbook of Counseling Psychology* (New York: Wiley, 1984).

8. See E. L. Worthington Jr., "Issues in Supervision of Lay Christian Counseling," *Journal of Psychology and Christianity* 6, no. 2 (1987): 70–77. See also S. Y. Tan, "Using Spiritual Disciplines in Clinical Supervision," *Journal of Psychology and Christianity* 26 (2007): 328–35; and S. Y. Tan, "Developing Integration Skills: The Role of Clinical Supervision," *Journal of Psychology and Theology* 37 (2009): 54–61.

9. See R. A. Hogan, "Issues and Approaches to Supervision," *Psychotherapy: Theory, Research, and Practice* 1 (1964): 139–41.

10. Worthington, "Issues in Supervision of Lay Christian Counseling," 72.

11. See C. Stoltenberg, "Approaching Supervision from a Developmental Perspective: The Counselor Complexity Model," *Journal of Counseling Psychology* 28 (1981): 59–65.

12. See C. Loganbill, E. Hardy, and U. Delworth, "Supervision: A Conceptual Model," *The Counseling Psychologist* 10, no. 1 (1982): 3–42.

13. Stoltenberg and Delworth, *Supervising Counselors and Therapists*. See also C. D. Stoltenberg and B. W. McNeill, *IDM Supervision: An Integrative Developmental Model for Supervising Counselors and Therapists*, 3rd ed. (New York: Routledge, 2009); J. Gosselin, K. K. Barker, C. S. Kogan, M. Pomerleau,

and M-P. Pitre d'Ioro, "Setting the Stage for an Evidence-Based Model of Psychotherapy Supervisor Development in Clinical Psychology," *Canadian Psychology* 56 (2015): 379–93.

14. See E. L. Worthington Jr., "Changes in Supervision as Counselors and Supervisors Gain Experience: A Review," *Professional Psychology: Research and Practice* 18 (1987): 189–208.

15. See E. L. Holloway, "Developmental Models of Supervision: Is It Development?" *Professional Psychology: Research and Practice* 18 (1987): 209–16.

16. Worthington, "Issues in Supervision of Lay Christian Counseling," 72.

17. See series on "Training to Competency in Psychotherapy," 651–709.

18. See B. F. Shaw and K. S. Dobson, "Competency Judgments in the Training and Evaluation of Psychotherapists," *Journal of Consulting and Clinical Psychology* 56 (1988): 666–720.

19. See K. S. Dobson and B. F. Shaw, "The Use of Treatment Manuals in Cognitive Therapy: Experience and Issues," *Journal of Consulting and Clinical Psychology* 56 (1988): 673–80.

20. See B. J. Rounsaville, S. O'Malley, S. Foley, and M. M. Weissman, "Role of Manual-Guided Training in the Conduct and Efficacy of Interpersonal Psychotherapy for Depression," *Journal of Consulting and Clinical Psychology* 56 (1988): 681–88.

21. See H. H. Strupp, S. F. Butler, and C. L. Rosser, "Training in Psychodynamic Therapy," *Journal of Consulting and Clinical Psychology* 56 (1988): 689–95.

22. See L. S. Greenberg and R. L. Goldman, "Training in Experiential Therapy," *Journal of Consulting and Clinical Psychology* 56 (1988): 696–702.

23. See R. R. Bootzin and J. S. Ruggill, "Training Issues in Behavior Therapy," *Journal of Consulting and Clinical Psychology* 56 (1988): 703–9.

24. See Hess, *Psychotherapy Supervision*; and Hess, Hess and Hess, *Psychotherapy Supervision*, 2nd ed.

25. See chap. 4, n. 53.

26. See Stoltenberg and Delworth, *Supervising Counselors and Therapists*.

27. See P. D. Guest and L. E. Beutler, "Impact of Psychotherapy Supervision on Therapist Orientation and Values," *Journal of Consulting and Clinical Psychology* 56 (1988): 653–58.

28. See M. S. Carifio and A. K. Hess, "Who Is the Ideal Supervisor?" *Professional Psychology: Research and Practice* 18 (1987): 244–50, p. 244.

29. See D. Brannon, "Adult Learning Principles and Methods for Enhancing the Training Role of Supervisors," *The Clinical Supervisor* 3 (1985): 5–26.

30. See E. Freeman, "The Importance of Feedback in Clinical Supervision: Implications for Direct Practice," *The Clinical Supervisor* 3 (1985): 5–26.

31. See A. Rosenblatt and J. Mayer, "Objectionable Supervising Styles: Students' Views," *Social Work* 18 (1975): 184–89.

32. See S. Y. Tan, "Explicit Integration in Psychotherapy." Invited paper presented at the International Congress on Christian Counseling, Counseling and Spirituality Track, November 10, 1988, in Atlanta, Georgia. See also S. Y. Tan, "Religion in Clinical Practice: Implicit and Explicit Integration," in E. Shafranske, ed., *Religion and the Clinical Practice of Psychology* (Washington, DC: The American Psychological Association, 1996), 365–87; S. Y. Tan, "Using Spiritual Disciplines in Clinical Supervision," and "Developing Integration Skills: The Role of Clinical Supervision"; S. Y. Tan, "Use of Prayer and Scripture in Cognitive-Behavioral Therapy," *Journal of Psychology and Christianity* 26 (2007): 101–11.

33. See L. E. Lipsker, "Integration in Graduate Student-Therapist Supervision." Paper presented at the International Congress on Christian Counseling, Clinical Supervision Track, November 11, 1988, in Atlanta, Georgia. See also nn. 3 and 32.

34. Worthington, "Issues in Supervision of Lay Christian Counseling."

35. See S. Y. Tan, "Intrapersonal Integration: The Servant's Spirituality," *Journal of Psychology and Christianity* 6, no. 1 (1987): 36–37. See also R. Foster, *Celebration of Discipline* (New York: Harper & Row, 1978; rev. ed., 1988); D. Willard, *The Spirit of the Disciplines* (New York: Harper & Row,

1988); and L. O. Richards, *A Practical Theology of Spirituality* (Grand Rapids: Zondervan, 1987); as well as S. Y. Tan and D. H. Gregg, *Disciplines of the Holy Spirit* (Grand Rapids: Zondervan, 1997); S. Y. Tan, *Full Service: Moving from Self-Serve Christianity to Total Servanthood* (Grand Rapids: Baker, 2006), and S. Y. Tan, *Counseling and Psychotherapy: A Christian Perspective* (Grand Rapids: Baker Academic, 2011).

36. See H. C. Lukens Jr., "Lay Counselor Training Revisited: Reflections of a Trainer," *Journal of Psychology and Christianity* 6, no. 2 (1987): 10–13.

37. Worthington, "Issues in Supervision of Lay Christian Counseling."

38. See "Lay Counseling Survey," available from Floyd Elliott, Director of Counseling and Family Renewal, Center for Church Renewal, 200 Chisholm Place, Suite 228, Plano, TX 75075.

CHAPTER 9

1. See A. E. Bergin, "Briefly Noted—Book review of J. Roland Fleck and John D. Carter, eds., "Psychology and Christianity: Integrative Readings," *Contemporary Psychology* 27 (1982): 657. However, more empirical research on the outcome of religious and spiritual therapies, including Christian therapies, has been conducted in recent years with overall encouraging results. See J. N. Hook et al., "Empirically Supported Religious and Spiritual Therapies," *Journal of Clinical Psychology* 66 (2010): 46–72, and E. L. Worthington Jr. et al., "Religion and Spirituality," in J. C. Norcross, ed., *Psychotherapy Relationships That Work*, 2nd ed. (New York: Oxford University Press, 2011), 402–20.

2. J. R. Fleck and J. D. Carter, eds., *Psychology and Christianity: Integrative Readings* (Nashville: Abingdon, 1981), 41, 43, 53.

3. American Psychological Association. *Report of the Task Force on the Evaluation of Education, Training and Service in Psychology* (Washington, DC: American Psychological Association, 1982), 2.

4. Ibid.

5. See, e.g., B. A. Edelstein and E. S. Berler, eds., *Evaluation and Accountability in Clinical Training* (New York: Plenum, 1987); J. E. Callan, D. R. Peterson, and G. Strickler, eds., *Quality in Professional Psychology Training: A National Conference and Self-Study* (Norman, OK: Transcript Press, 1986); and E. F. Bourg, R. J. Bent, J. E. Callan, N. F. Jones, J. McHolland, and G. Stricker, eds., *Standards and Evaluation in the Education and Training of Professional Psychologists: Knowledge, Attitudes, and Skills* (Norman, OK: Transcript Press, 1987). Also see R. G. Matarazzo and D. Patterson, "Methods of Teaching Therapeutic Skills," in S. L. Garfield and A. E. Bergin, eds., *Handbook of Psychotherapy and Behavior Change*, 3rd ed. (New York: Wiley, 1986), 821–43.

6. See, e.g., P. C. Kendall, J. N. Butcher, and G. N. Holmbeck, eds., *Handbook of Research Methods in Clinical Psychology*, 2nd ed. (New York: Wiley, 1999); A. E. Kazdin, *Research Design in Clinical Psychology*, 5th ed. (New York: Pearson Education, 2016); D. H. Barlow, S. C. Hayes, and R. O. Nelson, *The Scientist-Practitioner: Research and Accountability in Clinical and Educational Settings* (New York: Pergamon, 1984); and more recently S. C. Hayes, D. H. Barlow, and R. O. Nelson-Gray, *The Scientist Practitioner: Research and Accountability in the Age of Managed Care*, 2nd ed. (New York: Pearson Education, 1999).

7. See C. E. Hill, D. Charles, and K. G. Reed, "A Longitudinal Analysis of Changes in Counseling Skills during Doctoral Training in Counseling Psychology," *Journal of Counseling Psychology* 28 (1981): 203–12; and A. P. Thompson, "Changes in Counseling Skills during Graduate and Undergraduate Study," *Journal of Counseling Psychology* 33 (1986): 65–72.

8. C. E. Hill, "Development of a Counselor Verbal Response Category System," *Journal of Counseling Psychology* 25 (1978): 461–68; C. E. Hill, C. Greenwald, K. G. Reed, and D. Charles, *Manual for the Counselor and Client Verbal Response Category Systems* (Columbus, OH: Marathon, 1981).

9. E. L. Shostrom, *Personal Orientattion Inventory* (San Diego, CA: EdITS, 1963).

10. See S. Y. Tan, "Training Lay Christian Counselors: A Basic Program and Some Preliminary Data," *Journal of Psychology and Christianity* 6, no. 2 (1987): 57–61, and other studies using the CTPQ reviewed in chap. 4.

11. E. J. Jones and J. W. Pfeiffer, "Helping Relationship Inventory," in E. J. Jones and J. W. Pfeiffer, eds., *The Annual Handbook for Group Facilitators* (San Diego, CA: University Associates Publishers, 1973).

12. See R. Carkhuff, *Helping and Human Relations: A Primer for Lay and Professional Helpers*, vols. 1, 2 (New York: Holt, Rinehart and Winston, 1969); and C. B. Truax and R. R. Carkhuff, *Toward Effective Counseling and Psychotherapy* (Chicago: Aldine, 1967).

13. See R. Jernigan, S. Y. Tan, and R. L. Gorsuch, "The Effectiveness of a Local Church Lay Christian Counselor Training Program: A Controlled Study," paper presented at the International Congress on Christian Counseling, Lay Counseling Track, November 1988, in Atlanta, Georgia.

14. See M. J. Lambert, S. S. DeJulio, and D. M. Stein, "Therapist Interpersonal Skills: Process, Outcome, Methodological Considerations, and Recommendations for Future Research," *Psychological Bulletin* 85 (1978): 467–89; and M. J. Lambert, "Implications of Psychotherapy Outcome Research for Eclectic Psychotherapy," in J. C. Norcross, ed., *Handbook of Eclectic Psychotherapy* (New York: Brunner/Mazel, 1986), 436–62, p. 445.

15. See T. M. Vallis, B. F. Shaw, and K. S. Dobson, "The Cognitive Therapy Scale: Psychometric Properties," *Journal of Consulting and Clinical Psychology* 54 (1986): 381–85. See also B. F. Shaw and K. S. Dobson, "Competence Judgments in the Training and Evaluation of Psychotherapists," *Journal of Consulting and Clinical Psychology* 56 (1988): 666–72; and K. S. Dobson and B. F. Shaw, "The Use of Treatment Manuals in Cognitive Therapy: Experience and Issues," *Journal of Consulting and Clinical Psychology* 56 (1988): 673–80.

16. See D. M. Boan and T. Owens, "Peer Ratings of Lay Counselor Skill as Related to Client Satisfaction," *Journal of Psychology and Christianity* 4, no. 1 (1985): 79–81.

17. See E. L. Shostrom, *EdITS Manual for the Personal Orientation Inventory* (San Diego, CA: EdITS, 1974), 4. See also n. 9.

18. See C. A. Schaefer, L. Dodds, and S. Y. Tan, "Changes in Attitudes Toward Peer Counseling and Personal Orientation Measured during Growth Facilitator Training for Cross-Cultural Ministry," unpublished manuscript, 1988, pp. 12–13.

19. See chap. 6, n. 16.

20. See H. N. Malony, "The Clinical Assessment of Optimal Religious Functioning," *Review of Religious Research* 30, no. 1 (1988): 3–17.

21. F. Smith, "Measuring Quality Church Growth," unpublished doctoral diss., School of World Mission, Fuller Theological Seminary, 1985.

22. R. L. Gorsuch and G. D. Venable, "Development of An 'Age Universal' I-E Scale," *Journal for the Scientific Study of Religion* 22 (1983): 181–87. For more recent updates on measures of religiosity or religiousness and spirituality, see P. C. Hill and R. W. Hood Jr., eds., *Measures of Religiosity* (Birmingham: Religious Education, 1999); P. C. Hill and E. Edwards, "Measurement in the Psychology of Religiousness and Spirituality: Existing Measures and New Frontiers," in K. Pargament, J. J. Exline, and J. W. Jones, eds., *APA Handbook of Psychology, Religion and Spirituality (Vol. 1): Context, Theory, and Research* (Washington, DC: American Psychological Association, 2013), 51–77.

23. See n. 13 and S. Y. Tan and P. Sarff, "Comprehensive Evaluation of a Lay Counselor Training Program in a Local Church," invited paper presented at the International Congress on Christian Counseling, Lay Counseling Track, November 1988, in Atlanta, Georgia.

24. See S. L. Garfield and A. E. Bergin, eds., *Handbook of Psychotherapy and Behavior Change*, 3rd ed. (New York: Wiley, 1986); M. J. Lambert, E. R. Christensen, and S. S. DeJulio, eds., *The Assessment of Psychotherapy Outcome* (New York: Wiley, 1983); J. Williams and R. Spitzer, eds., *Psychotherapy Research: Where Are We and Where Should We Go?* (New York: Guilford, 1984); J. H. Harvey

and M. M. Parks, eds., *Psychotherapy Research and Behavior Change*, Master Lecture Series, vol. 1 (Washington, DC: American Psychological Association, 1982); and I. E. Waskow and M. B. Parloff, eds., *Psychotherapy Change Measures* (Washington, DC: U.S. Department of Health, Education, and Welfare, 1975). See also the following more recent books: M. J. Lambert, ed., *Bergin and Garfield's Handbook of Psychotherapy and Behavior Change*, 6th ed. (Hoboken, NJ: Wiley, 2013); P. E. Nathan and J. M. Gorman, eds., *A Guide to Treatments That Work*, 4th ed. (New York: Oxford University Press, 2015); and K. Corcoran and J. Fischer, *Measures for Clinical Practice and Research* (2 vols.), 5th ed. (New York: Oxford University Press, 2013).

25. See *American Psychologist* 41 (1986): 111–14 (Special Issue: Psychotherapy Research), and *Journal of Consulting and Clinical Psychology* 54 (1986): 3–118 (Special Issue: Psychotherapy Research).

26. See M. J. Lambert, D. A. Shapiro, and A. E. Bergin, "The Effectiveness of Psychotherapy," in S. L. Garfield and A. E. Bergin, eds., *Handbook of Psychotherapy and Behavior Change*, 3rd ed. (New York: Wiley, 1986), 157–211.

27. See R. J. Manthei, "Evaluating Therapy Outcome at a Community Mental Health Center," *Professional Psychology* 14 (1983): 67–77.

28. See C. C. Battle, S. D. Imber, R. Hoehn-Saric, A. R. Stine, E. R. Nash, and J. D. Frank, "Target Complaints as Criteria for Improvement," *American Journal of Psychotherapy* 20 (1966): 184–92.

29. See L. R. Derogatis, R. S. Lipman, R. Rickels, E. H. Uhlenhuth, and L. Covi, "The Hopkins Symptom Checklist (HSCL): A Self-Report Symptom Inventory," *Behavioral Science* 19 (1974): 1–15. For a shorter version called the Brief Symptom Inventory, or BSI, see L. R. Derogatis and P. M. Spencer, *The Brief Symptom Inventory (BSI): Administration, Scoring and Procedures Manual 1* (Baltimore: Clinical Psychometric Research, 1982).

30. See A. F. Fazio, *A Concurrent Validational Study of the NCHS General Well-Being Schedule* (U.S. Dept. of Health, Education, and Welfare, Publication No. HRA 78–1347) (Washington, DC: U.S. Government Printing Office, 1977).

31. See D. S. Cartwright, R. J. Robinson, D. W. Fiske, and W. L. Kirtner, "Length of Therapy in Relation to Outcome and Change in Personal Integration," *Journal of Consulting Psychology* 25 (1961): 84–88.

32. See J. I. Berzins, R. L. Bednar, and L. J. Severy, "The Problem of Intersource Consensus in Measuring Therapeutic Outcomes: New Data and Multivariate Perspectives," *Journal of Abnormal Psychology* 84 (1975): 10–19

33. See J. Craig Yagel, *The Relationship of Therapist's Personality to Psychotherapy Outcome Measured Via Target Complaints Assessment and Post-Therapy Questionnaire* (doctoral diss., Graduate School of Psychology, Fuller Theological Seminary, 1984). The post-therapy questionnaires were based on previous research reported in the following publications: C. R. Rogers and R. Dymond, *Psychotherapy and Personality Change* (Chicago: University of Chicago Press, 1954); H. H. Strupp, R. E. Fox, and K. Lessler, *Patients View Their Psychotherapy* (Baltimore: Johns Hopkins University Press, 1969); H. H. Strupp, M. S. Wallach, and M. Wogan, "Psychotherapy Experience in Retrospect: Questionnaire Survey of Former Patients and Their Therapists," *Psychological Monographs* 78 (11, Whole no. 588, 1964).

34. See A. A. Lazarus, *Behavior Therapy and Beyond* (New York: McGraw-Hill, 1971).

35. The FSA questionnaire is available from Family Service Association of America, 44 E. 23rd St., New York, NY 10010. See also D. F. Beck and M. A. Jones, *How to Conduct a Client Follow-Up Study* (New York: Family Service Association of America, 1980).

36. See N. Fredman and R. Sherman, *Handbook of Measurements for Marriage and Family Therapy* (New York: Brunner/Mazel, 1987). See also n. 37.

37. See K. Corcoran and J. Fischer, *Measures for Clinical Practice: A Sourcebook* (New York: Free Press, 1987). See also the latest edition: Corcoran and Fischer, *Measures for Clinical Practice and Research* (2 vols.), 5th ed. (see n. 24).

38. Ibid.

39. Gary R. Collins, "Lay Counseling: Some Lingering Questions for Professionals," *Journal of Psychology and Christianity* 6, no. 2 (1987): 7–9, p. 7.

40. See R. B. Basham, "Scientific and Practical Advantages of Comparative Design in Psychotherapy Outcome Research," *Journal of Consulting and Clinical Psychology* 54 (1986): 88–94.

41. Alan E. Kazdin, "Methodology of Psychotherapy Outcome Research: Recent Developments and Remaining Limitations," in J. H. Harvey and M. M. Parks, eds., *Psychotherapy Research and Behavior Change*, Master Lecture Series, vol. 1 (Washington, DC: American Psychological Association, 1982), 155–93, p. 166.

42. See S. D. Imber, L. M. Glanz, I. Elkin, S. M. Sotsky, J. L. Boyer, and W. R. Leber, "Ethical Issues in Psychotherapy Research: Problems in a Collaborative Clinical Trials Study," *Journal of Consulting and Clinical Psychology* 41 (1986): 137–46.

43. See L. S. Greenberg, "Change Process Research," *Journal of Consulting and Clinical Psychology* 54 (1986): 4–9; L. S. Greenberg and W. Pinsof, eds., *The Psychotherapeutic Process: A Research Handbook* (New York: Guilford, 1986); and L. Rice and L. S. Greenberg, eds., *Patterns of Change: Intensive Analysis of Psychotherapeutic Process* (New York: Guilford, 1984).

44. See A. E. Kazdin and G. T. Wilson, "Criteria for Evaluating Psychotherapy," *Archives of General Psychiatry* 35 (1978): 407–16.

45. These four organizations can be contacted at the following addresses:

American Association of Christian
    Counselors (AACC)
129 Vista Centre Drive, Suite B
Forest, VA 24551
Christian Association for Psychological
    Studies International (CAPS
    International)
P.O. Box 365
Batavia, IL 60510–0365

(www.CAPS.net)
California Peer Counseling Association
3605 El Camino Real, Box 5
Santa Clara, CA 95051
The National Peer Helpers Association
2370 Market Street, Room 120
San Francisco, CA 94114
Tel. 415-626-1942

46. J. Durlak, "Comparative Effectiveness of Paraprofessional and Professional Helpers," *Psychological Bulletin* 86 (1979): 80–92, p. 90.

CHAPTER 10

1. See "Lay Counseling Survey," available from Floyd Elliott, Director of Counseling and Family Renewal, Center for Church Renewal, 200 Chisholm Place, Suite 228, Plano, TX 75075. I (Tan) would like to express my appreciation to Pastor Floyd Elliott for permission to summarize the findings of the survey.

2. J. Sturkie and G. Bear, *Christian Peer Counseling: Love in Action* (Waco, TX: Word, 1989).

3. For further information about the Stephen Series, contact: Stephen Ministries, 8016 Dale, St. Louis, MO 63117 (Tel. 314-645-5511).

4. See Sturkie and Bear, *Christian Peer Counseling*, 136–63.

5. See C. H. Dodd, *Dynamics of International Communication*, 5th ed. (Boston: McGraw-Hill, 1998); D. W. Sue and D. Sue, *Counseling the Culturally Diverse: Theory and Practice*, 7th ed. (Hoboken, NJ: Wiley, 2016); M. McGoldrick, J. Giordina, and N. Garcia-Preto, eds., *Ethnicity and Family Therapy*, 3rd ed. (New York: Guilford, 2005); F. A. Paniagua, and A. M. Yamada, *Handbook of Multicultural Mental Health: Assessment and Treatment of Diverse Populations*, 2nd ed. (San Diego, CA: Academic, 2013); J. V. Diller, *Cultural Diversity: A Primer for the Human Services*, 5th ed. (Stamford, CT: Cengage Learning, 2015); D. I. Smith, *Learning from the Stranger: Christian Faith and Cultural Diversity* (Grand Rapids: Eerdmans, 2009); and D. Elmer, *Cross-Cultural Connections: Stepping Out*

and Fitting In around the World (Downers Grove, IL: InterVarsity, 2002). See also chap. 3, n. 79, and P. S. Richards and A. E. Bergin, eds., *Handbook of Psychotherapy and Religious Diversity*, 2nd ed. (Washington, DC: American Psychological Association, 2014).

6. R. Edgar, "Psychological Services in the Black Church," *CAPS Bulletin* 7, no. 4 (1981): 22–24.

7. See F. Garzon and S. Y. Tan, "Counseling Hispanics: Cross-Cultural and Christian Perspectives," *Journal of Psychology and Christianity* 11 (1992): 378–90.

8. E. T. Scalise, "Counseling the Whole Person throughout the Whole World," *Christian Counseling Today* 18, no. 3 (2011): 8. See also the entire issue of *Christian Counseling Today* 18 (2011).

9. B. M. Smith and F. C. Gingrich, "The Cape Town Declaration: A Bolder Vision for Counseling as Mission Worldwide," *Christian Counseling Today* 18, no. 3 (2011): 12–16.

10. See S. Y. Tan, "Lay Counseling: The Local Church," *CAPS Bulletin* 7, no. 1 (1981): 15–20.

11. See S. Y. Tan, "Training Lay Christian Counselors: A Basic Program and Some Preliminary Data," *Journal of Psychology and Christianity* 6, no. 2 (1987): 57–61.

12. See Bruce B. Barton, ed., *The Whole Person Survival Kit for Volunteer Leadership* (Wheaton, IL: Youth For Christ International, 1976).

13. See Sturkie and Bear, *Christian Peer Counseling*, 161–63.

14. See P. Welter, "Training Retirement Center and Nursing Home Staff and Residents in Helping and Counseling Skills," *Journal of Psychology and Christianity* 6, no. 2 (1987): 45–56.

15. See P. Clement, "The Psychological Center of Fuller Theological Seminary," *CAPS Bulletin* 7, no. 4 (1981): 27–30.

16. See C. Zabriskie, "The Older Volunteer Role; A Model Program in Crime Prevention," *CAPS Bulletin* 7, no. 4 (1981): 19–22.

17. See Richard and Flakoll, "Christian Counseling Centers: Two Effective Models," *CAPS Bulletin* 7, no. 4 (1981): 12–15.

18. See C. B. Johnson and D. R. Penner, "The Current Status of the Provision of Psychological Services in Missionary Agencies in North America," *CAPS Bulletin* 7, no. 4 (1981): 25–27.

19. For some preliminary work in this area, see C. A. Schaefer, L. Dodds, and S. Y. Tan, "Changes in Attitudes toward Peer Counseling and Personal Orientation Measured during Growth Facilitator Training for Cross-Cultural Ministry," unpublished manuscript, 1988. See also two more recent books coauthored by L. Dodds on global servants as cross-cultural humanitarian workers or heroes caring for people in crisis and disaster situations: L. M. Gardner and L. A. Dodds, *Global Servants: Cross-Cultural Humanitarian Heroes, Volume 1: Formation and Development of These Heroes* (Liverpool, PA: Heartstream Resources, 2011); and L. A. Dodds and L. M. Gardner, *Global Servants: Cross-Cultural Humanitarian Heroes, Volume 2: 12 Factors in Effectiveness and Longevity* (Liverpool, PA: Heartstream Resources, 2011).

CHAPTER 11

1. L. Downs, "A Preliminary Survey of Relationships between Counselor Educators' Ethics Education and Ensuing Pedagogy and Responses to Attractions with Counseling Students," *Counseling and Values* 48 (2003): 2–10.

2. R. I. Urofsky, and D. W. Engels, "Philosophy, Moral Philosophy, and Counseling Ethics: Not an Abstraction," *Counseling and Values* 47 (2003): 118–30.

3. A. Hill, "Ethics Education: Recommendations for an Evolving Discipline," *Counseling and Values* 48 (2004): 183–204.

4. S. L. McLaurin, and R. J. Ricci, "Ethical Issues and At-Risk Behaviors in Marriage and Family Therapy: A Qualitative Study of Awareness," *Contemporary Family Therapy* 25 (2003): 453–66.

5. L. Jennings, A. Sovereign, N. Bottorff, M. Mussell, and C. Vye, "Nine Ethical Values of Master Therapists," *Journal of Mental Health Counseling* 27 (2005): 32–47.

6. See D. G. Savage, "Court Ruling That Freed Clergy from Liability for Advice to Stand," *Los Angeles Times* (April 4, 1989), pt. 1, pp. 3, 26.

7. See G. R. Collins, *Christian Counseling: A Comprehensive Guide* (Dallas: Word, 1988), 24–37.

8. See M. E. Wagner, "Hazards to Effective Pastoral Counseling," *Journal of Psychology and Theology* 1, pt. 1 (July 1973): 35–41; and 1, pt. 2 (October 1973): 40–47.

9. For a good book on the counselor's ethics written from a secular perspective, see G. Corey, M. S. Corey, and P. Callahan, *Issues and Ethics in the Helping Professions*, 8th ed. (Belmont, CA: Brooks/Cole, 2011).

10. See J. Edelwich with A. Brodsky, *Burnout: Stages of Disillusionment in the Helping Professions* (New York: Human Sciences, 1980), 14. For some good and helpful material on dealing with burnout from a Christian perspective, see R. T. Brock, "Avoiding Burnout through Spiritual Renewal," in M. G. Gilbert and R. T. Brock, eds., *The Holy Spirit and Counseling: Theology and Theory* (Peabody, MA: Hendrickson, 1985), 88–102; A. D. Hart, ed., "Special Issue on Burnout," *Theology, News and Notes* (March 1984); and C. Perry, *Why Christians Burn Out* (Nashville: Thomas Nelson, 1982).

11. See M. E. Cavanagh, "Destructive Myths about Helping Others," *International Christian Digest* 1, no. 6 (1987): 22–23. See also M. E. Cavanagh, *The Effective Minister: Psychological and Social Considerations* (San Francisco: Harper & Row, 1986).

12. See T. L. Needham, "Helping When the Risks Are Great," in H. Newton Malony, T. L. Needham, and S. Southard, *Clergy Malpractice* (Philadelphia: Westminster, 1986), 88–109.

13. Ibid., 89–90.

14. Ibid., 109.

15. See W. W. Becker, "The Paraprofessional Counselor in the Church: Legal and Ethical Considerations," *Journal of Psychology and Christianity* 6, no. 2 (1987): 78–82.

16. See "Clergy as Mandatory Reporters of Child Abuse and Neglect," Child Welfare Information Gateway (2016), www.childwelfare.gov/topics/systemwide/laws-policies/statutes/clergymandated/ for a current list of states requiring mandatory abuse report for clergy members.

17. Becker, "The Paraprofessional Counselor in the Church," 79.

18. See S. Southard, "Church Discipline: Handle with Care," in Malony, Needham, and Southard, *Clergy Malpractice*, 74–87. See also J. White and K. Blue, *Healing the Wounded: The Costly Love of Church Discipline* (Downers Grove, IL: InterVarsity, 1985).

19. The American Association of Christian Counselors' 2014 Christian Counseling Code of Ethics can be downloaded at www.aacc.net/about-us/code-of-ethics/.

20. See E. L. Worthington Jr., "Issues in Supervision of Lay Christian Counselors," *Journal of Psychology and Christianity* 6, no. 2 (1987): 70–77.

21. See A. D. Hart, *Counseling the Depressed* (Waco, TX: Word, 1987), 244–45.

22. See J. R. Beck and R. K. Mathews, "A Code of Ethics for Christian Counselors," *Journal of Psychology and Christianity* 5, no. 3 (1986): 78–84.

23. See R. R. King Jr., "Developing a Proposed Code of Ethics for the Christian Association for Psychological Studies," *Journal of Psychology and Christianity* 5, no. 3 (1986): 85–90.

24. See C. D. Stoltenberg and U. Delworth, *Supervising Counselors and Therapists: A Developmental Approach* (San Francisco: Jossey-Bass, 1987), 168–80. See also W. R. Harrar, L. VandeCreek, and S. Knapp, "Ethical and Legal Aspects of Clinical Supervision," *Professional Psychology* 21 (1990): 37–41.

25. G. Corey, M. S. Corey, and P. Callanan, *Issues and Ethics in the Helping Professions*, 8th ed. (Belmont, CA: Brooks/Cole, 2011).

26. See the American Counseling Association's Code of ethics at www.counseling.org/resources/aca-code-of-ethics.pdf.

27. See the American Psychological Association's Code of ethics at www.apa.org/ethics/code/.

28. See the American Association of Family Therapy's Code of ethics at www.aamft.org/imis15/Documents/AAMFT%20Code_11_2012_Secured.pdf.

29. See the Christian Association for Psychological Studies' Code of ethics at http://caps.net/about-us/statement-of-ethical-guidelines.

30. See the National Christian Counselor's Association's Code of ethics at www.ncca.org/Members/CodeofEthics.pdf.

31. See the Association of Certified Biblical Counselors' Code of ethics at www.biblicalcounseling.com/certification.

32. See the American Association of Christian Counselors' Code of ethics at www.aacc.net/about-us/code-of-ethics/.

33. Ibid.

34. See A. D. Hart, *Counseling the Depressed* (Waco, TX: Word, 1987), 250.

CHAPTER 12

1. This chapter is drawn from E. Scalise, *Lifeline Training Manual* (Lynchburg, VA: Blue Ridge Community Church, 2015).

2. H. Selye, *The Stress of Life* (New York: McGraw-Hill, 1956).

3. Ibid., 1.

4. A. Hart, and C. Hart Weber, *Caring for People God's Way: Stress and Anxiety* (Nashville: Thomas Nelson, 2005), 164–65.

5. See the American Heart Association at www.americanheart.org.

6. See the American Institute on Stress at www.stress.org/.

7. See the U.S. Department on Health and Human Services at http://search.hhs.gov/search?q=statistics+on+prescription+medication&HHS=Search&site=HHS&entqr=3&ud=1&sort=date%3AD%3AL%3Ad1&output=xml_no_dtd&ie=UTF-8&oe=UTF-8&lr=lang_en&client=HHS&proxystylesheet=HHS.

8. C. Figley, *Treating Compassion Fatigue* (New York: Brunner-Routledge, 2002).

9. Scalise, *Lifeline Training Manual*.

10. S. Y. Tan and M. Castillo, "Self-Care and Beyond: A Brief Literature Review from a Christian Perspective," *Journal of Psychology and Christianity* 33 (2014): 90–95, 93–94. See also: S. S. Canning, "Out of Balance: Why I Hesitate to Practice and Teach 'Self-Care,'" *Journal of Psychology and Christianity* 30 (2011): 70–74; and S. Y. Tan, *Rest: Experiencing God's Peace in a Restless World* (Vancouver, BC: Regent College Publishing, 2003).

CONCLUSION

1. See R. K. Bufford, "Christian Counseling: Issues and Trends," *CAPS Bulletin* 6, no. 4 (1980): 1–4, p. 2.

2. See J. D. Frank, "Therapeutic Components Shared by All Psychotherapies," in J. H. Harvey and M. M. Parks, eds., *Psychotherapy Research and Behavior Change*, Master Lecture Series, vol. 1 (Washington, DC: American Psychological Association, 1982), 5–37, p. 31.

3. See W. Oates, *An Introduction to Pastoral Counseling* (Nashville: Broadman, 1959), vi.

4. Dr. Tan has written a book on servanthood from a biblical perspective that can be of much help to servants of Jesus Christ, including lay Christian counselors. S. Y. Tan, *Full Service: Moving from Self-Serve Christianity to Total Servanthood* (Grand Rapids: Baker, 2006).

5. See S. Y. Tan, "Lay Christian Counseling: Present Status and Future Directions," invited paper presented at the International Congress on Christian Counseling, Lay Counseling Track, November 1988, in Atlanta, Georgia. See also S. Y. Tan, "Lay Christian Counseling: The Next Decade," *Journal of Psychology and Christianity* 9, no. 3 (1990): 59–65.

Name Index

Subject Index

305

About the Authors

SIANG-YANG TAN

Rev. Dr. Siang-Yang Tan was director of the PsyD (Doctor of Psychology) program in Clinical Psychology (1989–97) and is now professor of psychology in the Graduate School of Psychology at Fuller Theological Seminary in Pasadena, California. He is a licensed psychologist with a PhD in clinical psychology from McGill University and a fellow of the American Psychological Association.

Dr. Tan has published articles on lay counseling and lay counselor training, intrapersonal integration and spirituality, the Holy Spirit and counseling, religious psychotherapy, cognitive behavior therapy, clinical supervision and integration, epilepsy, pain, and cross-cultural counseling with Asians and Hispanics, as well as fourteen books, including *Lay Counseling: Equipping Christians for a Helping Ministry* (Zondervan, 1991), *Managing Chronic Pain* (InterVarsity, 1996), *Disciplines of the Holy Spirit* (with Doug Gregg, Zondervan, 1997), *Rest: Experiencing God's Peace in a Restless World* (Regent College Publishing, 2003), *Exercises for Effective Counseling and Psychotherapy* (second edition; with Dr. Les Parrott III; Brooks/Cole, 2003), *Coping with Depression* (revised and expanded edition; with Dr. John Ortberg; Baker, 2004), *Full Service: Moving from Self-Serve Christianity to Total Servanthood* (Baker, 2006), and a major textbook, *Counseling and Psychotherapy: A Christian Perspective* (Baker Academic, 2011).

He was the 1993 recipient of the Award for Contributions to Racial and Ethnic Diversity from the National Council of Schools and Programs of Professional Psychology (NCSPP), the 1999 recipient of the Distinguished Member Award from the Christian Association for Psychological Studies (CAPS) International, the 2001 recipient of the Gary R. Collins Award for Excellence in Christian Counseling from the American Association of Christian Counselors (AACC), the 2002 recipient of the William Bier Award for Outstanding and Sustained Contributions from Division 36 (Psychology of Religion) of APA, the 2011 recipient of the Distinguished Silver Award for Outstanding Influence and Leadership in the Development and Advancement of Christian Counseling around the

World, and the James E. Clinton Award for Excellence in Pastoral Care and Ministry from AACC.

Dr. Tan is associate editor of the *Journal of Psychology and Christianity* and serves or has served on the editorial boards of the *Journal of Consulting and Clinical Psychology, Professional Psychology: Research and Practice, Journal of Psychology and Theology,* and *Journal of Spiritual Formation and Soul Care.* He was president of Division 36 (Psychology of Religion) of the American Psychological Association (1998–99).

Dr. Tan also serves as senior pastor of First Evangelical Church Glendale in Glendale, California. He lives in Pasadena with his wife, Angela, and they have two grown children, Carolyn and Andrew. He is originally from Singapore.

ERIC SCALISE

Dr. Eric Scalise, PhD, LPC, LMFT, is the CEO of Alignment Association, LLC and president of LIV Enterprises & Consulting, LLC. He is the former vice president for professional development with the American Association of Christian Counselors (AACC), as well as the former department chair for counseling programs at Regent University. He is an adjunct professor and the senior editor for both AACC and the Congressional Prayer Caucus Foundation.

Dr. Scalise is a licensed professional counselor and a licensed marriage and family therapist with more than thirty-five years of clinical and professional experience in the mental health field. He served six years on the Virginia Board of Counseling after being appointed by Governor George Allen and reappointed by Governor Jim Gilmore. Other responsibilities have included his roles as the executive director of the International Board of Christian Care (IBCC) and member of the Board of Reference for the International Christian Coaching Association (ICCA). Specialty areas include professional/pastoral stress and burnout, combat trauma and PTSD, marriage and family issues, leadership development, addictions and recovery, and lay counselor training.

As the son of a diplomat with the US State Department, Dr. Scalise was born in Nicosia, Cyprus, and has also lived in Singapore, Bolivia, Germany, and Iceland, as well as provided consulting and missions work in Afghanistan, India, China, Hong Kong, Turkey, Sri Lanka, Italy, Greece, Israel, Australia, the Ukraine, and Malaysia. He is an author and conference speaker, and he frequently works with organizations, clinicians, ministry leaders, and churches on a variety of issues.

Dr. Scalise and his wife, Donna, have been married for thirty-five years and have twin sons, who are combat veterans serving in the US Marine Corps, and three grandchildren.

Printed in the USA
CPSIA information can be obtained
at www.ICGtesting.com
LVHW030838180124
768711LV00011B/20